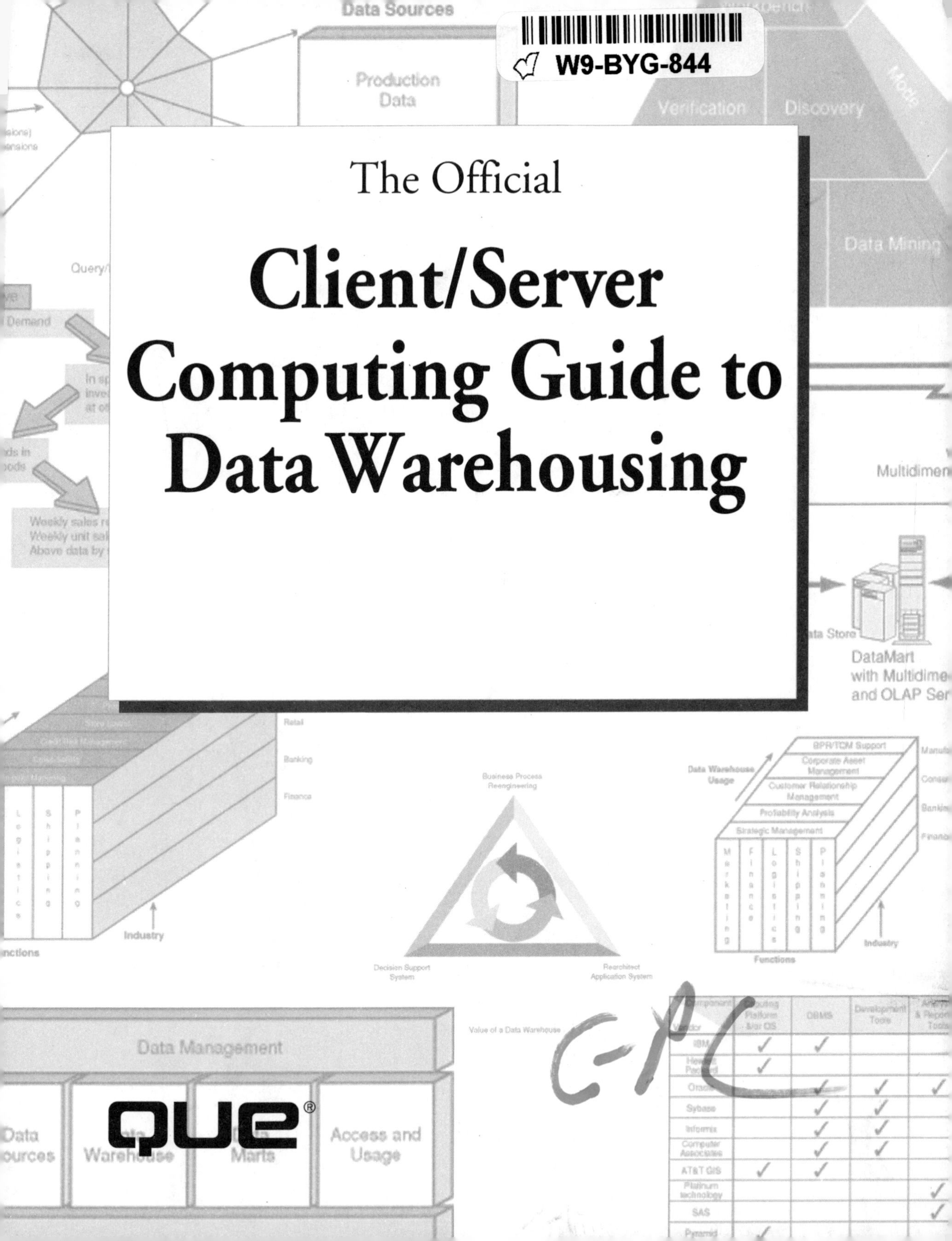

The Official

# Client/Server Computing Guide to Data Warehousing

QUE®

The Official
Client/Server Computing Guide to Data Warehousing
Written by
Harjinder S. Gill
Prakash C. Rao
QUE®
Data Sources
Production Data
Verification
Discovery
Data Mining
Multidimen
DataMart with Multidime and OLAP Se
Industry
Functions
Data Management
Data Sources
Warehouse
Marts
Access and Usage

# The Official Client/Server Computing Guide to Data Warehousing



Library of Congress Catalog No.: 95-73284

ISBN: 0-7897-0714-4



98 97 96 6 5 4 3 2 1

Interpretation of the printing code: the rightmost double-digit number is the year of the book's printing; the rightmost single-digit number, the number of the book's printing. For example, a printing code of 96-1 shows that the first printing of the book occurred in 1996.



Screen reproductions in this book were created using Collage Plus from Inner Media, Inc., Hollis, NH.

Composed in *Stone Serif* and *MCPdigital* by Que Corporation

# Credits

**President**
Roland Elgey

**Publisher**
Joseph B. Wikert

**Editorial Services Director**
Elizabeth Keaffaber

**Managing Editor**
Sandy Doell

**Director of Marketing**
Lynn E. Zingraf

**Senior Series Editor**
Chris Nelson

**Publishing Manager**
Fred Slone

**Senior Title Manager**
Bryan Gambrel

**Acquisitions Editor**
Al Valvano

**Product Director**
Nancy D. Price

**Production Editor**
Maureen A. Schneeberger

**Editors**
Don Eamon
Angela C. Kozlowski
Nanci Sears Perry

**Assistant Product Marketing Manager**
Kim Margolius

**Technical Editor**
Jan Richardson

**Acquisitions Coordinator**
Angela C. Kozlowski

**Operations Coordinator**
Patricia J. Brooks

**Editorial Assistant**
Andrea Duvall

**Book Designer**
Kim Scott

**Cover Designer**
Kim Scott

**Production Team**
Chad Dressler
Jenny Earhart
Terri Edwards
Bryan Flores
DiMonique Ford
Trey Frank
Jason Hand
Sonja Hart
Daryl Kessler
Clint Lahnen
Linda Quigley
Julie Quinn
Laura Robbins
Bobbi Satterfield
Mike Thomas
Suzanne Whitmer
Paul Wilson

**Indexer**
Carol Sheehan

# About the Authors

**Harjinder S. Gill** and **Prakash C. Rao** are founders of the Indica Group. Prior to this, they were co-founders of InfoSpan Corporation, where Harjinder was the CEO and President, and Prakash was the Vice-President of Engineering. Both have extensive experience in data warehousing, graphical user interfaces, metadata management, and software development. Their unique qualifications include development of information technology solutions that are based on client/server architectures, repositories, and metadata management—the cornerstones of data warehouse design and implementation. Harjinder holds an M.B.A. and a M.S. in Physics. Prakash holds a M.S. in Computer Science and a B.S. in Electronics Engineering.

# Acknowledgments

A book is generally produced as a result of many people pitching together. We thank Diane Anderson, David Morris, Steve Mongulla, Donna Leschisin, and David Haertzen for reviewing the manuscript for technical content and readability. We owe special thanks to Roger Wolter for the thoroughness and timeliness of his reviews. We also express our appreciation to Dr. Shashi Shekhar for his review of the data mining chapter, and to Boyd Pearce for his assistance in the data warehouse justification chapter.

We extend our thanks to the review team at Que: Nancy Price, Maureen Schneeberger, and others for patiently editing the copy for content, readability, and accuracy. We thank Damian Rinaldi at *Client/Server Computing* for initially suggesting the idea for the book. Our thanks also go out to the various people, too numerous to name, who provided background material through discussions and lively debates.

And finally we thank the most significant people in our lives. Harjinder thanks his wife Barbara for her patience and encouragement, and taking on even more responsibility for family affairs. He would like to thank his sons, Amar and Samsher, for being not only patient with his absence, but also encouraging him to get it done quickly.

Prakash thanks his wife Malathi Rao, and his children Vikram and Rajni. Their patience with late night sessions on the word processor, lights on well past midnight, and a series of canceled plans and outings to meet an ever-compressing timeline made this work possible.

Data warehouse technology is still evolving rapidly as we speak. New terms and definitions are coined by the day. New products are being announced regularly. Our effort in this book has been to give the reader a firm basis for understanding and analyzing the literature in the field, and for building and benefiting from a data warehouse. Enjoy!

## We'd Like to Hear from You!

As part of our continuing effort to produce books of the highest possible quality, Que would like to hear your comments. To stay competitive, we *really* want you, as a computer book reader and user, to let us know what you like or dislike most about this book or other Que products.

You can mail comments, ideas, or suggestions for improving future editions to the address below, or send us a fax at (317) 581-4663. For the online inclined, Macmillan Computer Publishing has a forum on CompuServe (type **GO QUEBOOKS** at any prompt) through which our staff and authors are available for questions and comments. The address of our Internet site is **http://www.mcp.com** (World Wide Web).

In addition to exploring our forum, please feel free to contact me personally to discuss your opinions of this book: I'm **75767,2543** on CompuServe, and I'm **nprice@que.mcp.com** on the Internet.

Thanks in advance—your comments will help us to continue publishing the best books available on computer topics in today's market.

Nancy Price
Product Development Specialist
Que Corporation
201 W. 103rd Street
Indianapolis, Indiana 46290
USA

# Contents at a Glance

# Contents

## 5 Understanding and Analyzing Business Needs 111



## 6 Developing and Deploying the Data Warehouse 127



## 7 The Importance of Metadata Management 147

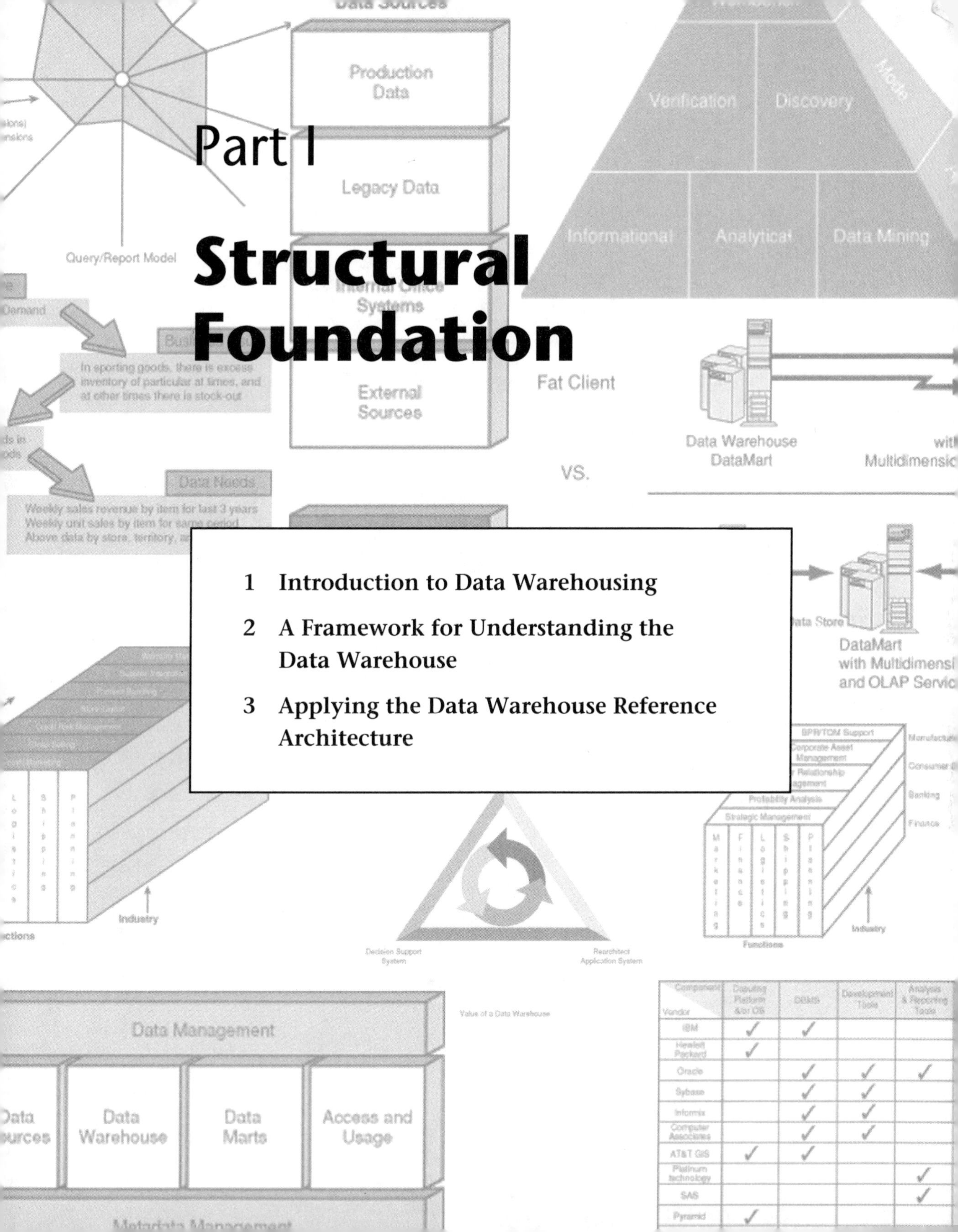


# Part I

# Structural Foundation

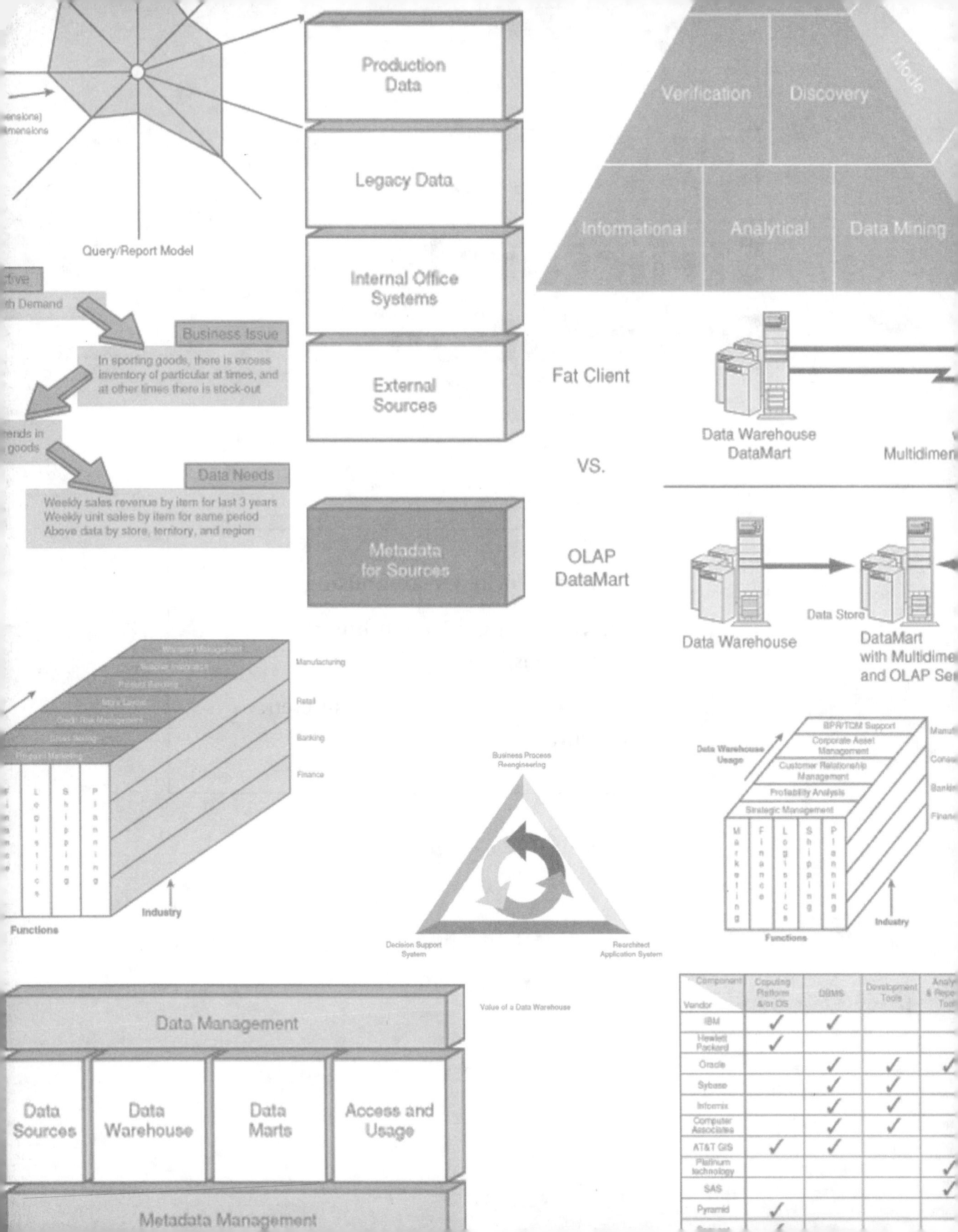

Query/Report Model
Production Data
Legacy Data
Internal Office Systems
External Sources
Metadata for Sources
Verification
Discovery
Informational
Analytical
Data Mining
Business Issue
In sporting goods, there is excess inventory of particular at times, and at other times there is stock-out
Data Needs
Weekly sales revenue by item for last 3 years
Weekly unit sales by item for same period
Above data by store, territory, and region
Fat Client
VS.
OLAP DataMart
Data Warehouse DataMart
Data Warehouse
Data Store
DataMart
Manufacturing
Retail
Banking
Finance
Logistics
Shipping
Planning
Industry
Functions
Business Process Reengineering
Decision Support System
Rearchitect Application System
Value of a Data Warehouse
BPR/TQM Support
Corporate Asset Management
Customer Relationship Management
Profitability Analysis
Strategic Management
Data Warehouse Usage
Marketing
Finance
Logistics
Shipping
Planning
Industry
Functions
Data Management
Data Sources
Data Warehouse
Data Marts
Access and Usage
Metadata Management
Component
Vendor
Computing Platform &/or OS
DBMS
Development Tools
IBM
Hewlett Packard
Oracle
Sybase
Informix
Computer Associates
AT&T GIS
Platinum technology
SAS
Pyramid

CHAPTER 1

# Introduction to Data Warehousing

Delighted customers. Enhanced profits. Increased market share. These are the basics of business in the competitive 1990s. Information technology is expected to get us there. How can an enterprise simultaneously delight customers, enhance profits, and increase market share? One of the answers is data warehouse. Data warehousing, or the process of gathering an organization's historical data into a central repository, has become a popular and key technology. In the July 31, 1995, issue of *Business Week*, the Information Management track stated "(Data warehousing is) the biggest trend in information management today. This is the technology that may finally deliver on a dream pursued by management theorists since the 1960s."

A 1994 survey of IT managers at Fortune 2000 enterprises by META Group found that more than 90 percent were planning to implement data warehouses between 1994 and 1996. In 1996, 90 percent of large corporations plan on adopting warehouse technology.

In its annual survey of Chief Information Officers to identify the top ten management issues for IS executives for 1995, CSC Partners has listed the following in priority order:

1. Aligning IS and corporate goals
2. Instituting cross-functional informational systems
3. Organizing and utilizing data
4. Implementing business re-engineering
5. Improving the IS human resource
6. Enabling change and nimbleness
7. Connecting to customers or suppliers
8. Creating an information architecture
9. Updating obsolete systems
10. Improving the systems development process

It is interesting to note that data warehouse technology squarely addresses the top three issues.

## What Is a Data Warehouse?

The definition of data warehouse today is fluid. According to W. H. Inmon, considered the father of data warehouse, "A data warehouse is a subject-oriented, integrated, time-variant, and nonvolatile collection of data in support of management's decision-making process."

According to some organizations, data warehouse is an architecture. To others, it is a semantically consistent data store (separate and not interfering with existing operational and production systems) to fulfill different data access and reporting requirements. To some others, data warehouse is an ongoing process that blends data from multiple heterogeneous sources, including historical data and syndicated data to support the continuing need for structured and/or ad hoc queries, analytical reporting, and decision support.

Much as there is divergence of views on the precise definition of data warehouse, there is clear consensus that data warehouse technology is an essential ingredient of an enterprise's decision support solution set.

As the interest in data warehouses has mounted, there are many claimers who have built a data warehouse. More often, people have built an end user access facility for browsing, reporting, and attaching Decision Support Systems (DSS). Others have exported data from their operational databases into a multi-dimensional database and attached analysis tools to the multi-dimensional databases. *Software Magazine*, in its December editorial titled "Data Warehousing deserves better," asks "What's to become of the data warehousing movement? Its goals are worthy: Get the right information to the right people at the right time so they can make decisions that could be worth millions of dollars. Simple enough. Yet applications for warehousing beyond rudimentary decision support remain few and far between. Even data warehousing champions such as Aaron Zornes of the META Group agree there's much work to do before data warehousing lives up to its potential."

A lot of the fundamental underlying problems have not been adequately tackled—for example, the challenges of the following:

- Data and metadata integration from various sources.
- Data quality: cleanup and refinement.
- Data summarization and aggregation.
- Synchronization of sources with the data warehouse to ensure ongoing refreshment of the data warehouse as new data is created inside the sources.
- Performance issues related to sharing the same computer and RDBMS platforms as the data warehouse database and tools.
- Metadata management.

So what constitutes a full data warehouse? Is there a test like the famous one for forbidden literature? How does one anticipate technology challenges and design solutions right into the architecture of the data warehouse? And how does one go about building one systematically? These are all valid questions.

## Difference Between a Data Warehouse and Operational (OLTP) Databases

A data warehouse is different from operational databases that support On-Line Transaction Processing (OLTP) applications in many ways. The data warehouse is the following:

- **Is subject oriented**—It organizes and presents data from the perspective of the end user. Most operational systems organize their data from the perspective of the application—in a manner that makes the application access the data as efficiently as possible. Often, data that is organized for easy retrieval and update by a business application is not necessarily organized so that analysts using smart and graphical query tools can ask the right business questions. This is due to the focus of the database design—application retrieval and update efficiency—at the time it was first implemented.
- **Manages large amounts of information**—Most data warehouses contain historical data that is often removed from operational systems because it is no longer needed by production and operational applications. Because of the volume of information that data warehouses must manage, they must also offer facilities for summarization and aggregation that classifies this immense volume of data. In short, data warehouses let users look for "trees in the forest." Data warehouses therefore manage information at different levels of granularity. Because of the need to manage all the historical data in addition to current data, data warehouses are much larger than operational databases.
- **Stores information on multiple storage media**—Because of the volumes of information that must be managed, data warehouses often store data on multiple media.
- **Spans multiple versions of a database schema**—Because the data warehouse must store historical information and manage it, and because the historical information was managed at different times by different versions of the database schemas, the data warehouse must deal with information that originated sometimes from different database organizations.
- **Summarizes and aggregates information**—The level of detail found in information stored by operational databases is often far too great for any informed decision making. Data warehouses summarize and aggregate information to present it in a manner that human beings can understand. Summarization and aggregation is essential to step back and understand the big picture.
- **Integrates and associates information from many data sources**—Because organizations have historically managed their operations using many software applications and many databases, data warehouses are needed to collect

and organize the data that these applications have gathered over the years in one place. Because of the diversity of storage technologies, database management techniques, and data semantics this is a challenging task.

# Who Should Read This Book?

This book is designed to provide information and convey understanding of the data warehouse technology to a broad range of readers. The following is a grouping of different types of readers based on their stake in the data warehouse:

- Executives and managers (investors) invest in the data warehouse technology and pay the commissioning of the data warehouse solution. They are responsible for approving the budget and assessing whether the payback from the data warehouse is in line with their investments. They are also interested in the longevity of their investment and its continued returns.
- Architects are responsible for laying the foundations of the data warehouse. They are charged with interpreting the investor's requirements and designing a data warehouse architecture that will meet these requirements. They are interested in the longevity, modularity, ease of implementation, and degree of fit with existing systems and technologies.
- Builders are the IT professionals who will actually build the data warehouse. They are responsible for timeliness, quality, performance, and creating satisfaction for the people who will be actually using the data warehouse on a daily basis.
- Users are the business professionals and their support staff who will be accessing and using the data warehouse as a decision support tool in their daily work. These are people whose work is information based, where the information that they acquire will help them in formulating and making business recommendations. They are specialists in analyzing the information and "slicing and dicing" it in many ways to try to unearth facts about their customers, markets, products, and use it to a competitive advantage. They are interested in "understanding what's going on in the business" and then analyzing the "what if" and "what now" for their enterprise.

The simple purpose of a data warehouse is to assist management in understanding the past and plan for the future. Even though the data warehouse has crucial strategic information in it, deriving business value from the data warehouse is a complex endeavor. To get value requires an alchemy of business skills, technical know-how, intuition, and experience. This book will assist you in understanding data warehousing technology and how to use this technology to make fact-based business decisions. And it does it with uncomplicated but effective ideas, without avoiding the hard spots.

# How the Book is Organized

This book is organized in self-contained chapters that can be read or skipped based on your focus and intent. The book consists of four sections which are discussed in the following sections.

## Part I—Structural Foundation

"Structural Foundation" begins with Chapter 1, "Introduction to Data Warehousing," which introduces the reader to the basics of data warehousing and this book. Chapter 2, "A Framework for Understanding the Data Warehouse," provides the technical architecture for building and using data warehouses. Chapter 3, "Applying the Data Warehouse Reference Architecture," shows the reader how to build his or her own enterprise's data warehouse architecture.

## Part II—Design and Construction

The "Design and Construction" section starts with Chapter 4, "Building the Data Warehouse: A Step-by-Step Guide," provides data warehouse specific guidance on building warehouses. Chapter 5, "Understanding and Analyzing Business Needs," shows how to gather and analyze the data warehouse requirements of the business user, and then design the data warehouse. Chapter 6, "Developing and Deploying the Data Warehouse," covers how to construct and roll-out the warehouse. Chapter 7, "The Importance of Metadata Management," completes the "Design and Construction" section by highlighting the special attention that needs to be paid to metadata to meet the needs of both Information Technology professionals and business users.

## Part III—Reaping the Benefits

The "Reaping the Benefits" section begins with Chapter 8, "Using the Data Warehouse," which introduces the reader to techniques and approaches on how to harvest the investment in the data warehouse. Chapter 9, "Query and Reporting: Informational Processing," focuses on access and using the warehouse with simpler query and reporting techniques. The final chapter of this section, Chapter 10, "Analytical Processing," introduces the reader to On-Line Analytical Processing (OLAP) and multidimensional analysis methods to gain additional value from the warehouse.

## Part IV—The State of the Practice

The final section, "The State of the Practice," commences with Chapter 11, "Data Mining," which describes the potential of new knowledge discovery technology and techniques to mine the data warehouse for customer understanding and other competitive advantages. Chapter 12, "What's Available: The State of the Practice," introduces the reader to the types of products and solutions available, and offers guidelines on how to analyze the range of available options. Chapter 13, "Vendor Survey: Strategies and Product Positioning," provides a broad survey of a large cadre of data warehouse vendors. The focus is on the vendor's strategy and data warehouse market positioning, which is critical to vendor selection for new initiatives like data warehousing. This section ends with Chapter 14, "Justifying the Cost of a Data Warehouse," which provides the reader ideas and techniques on developing the economic and business model for analyzing data warehouse investments.

Readers may want to read an entire section or selected chapters within a section to meet their needs and then come back for more as needs arise. A general guideline for readers is shown in Table 1.1. The keys "P" and "S" in Table 1.1 are the authors' sense of who is the prospective reader of the chapter. "P" indicates this chapter has potentially *primary interest* to this reader, while "S" indicates this chapter has *secondary interest* to that reader. Your own background, interest, and need may indicate a different selection.

**Table 1.1 Chapter Guideline for Readers**

| Chapter | Executive | Architect/ Builder | Business User |
|---|---|---|---|
| **Section I: Structural Foundation** | | | |
| 1 Introduction to Data Warehousing | P | P | P |
| 2 A Framework for Understanding the Data Warehouse | S | P | S |
| 3 Applying the Data Warehouse Reference Architecture | | P | |
| **Section II: Design and Construction** | | | |
| 4 Building the Data Warehouse: A Step-by-Step Guide | | P | |
| 5 Understanding and Analyzing Business Needs | | P | P |
| 6 Developing and Deploying the Data Warehouse | | P | S |
| 7 The Importance of Metadata Management | | P | P |
| **Section III: Reaping the Benefits** | | | |
| 8 Using the Data Warehouse | S | P | P |
| 9 Query and Reporting: Informational Processing | | P | P |
| 10 Analytical Processing | | P | P |
| **Section IV: The State of the Practice** | | | |
| 11 Data Mining | | P | P |
| 12 What's Available: The State of the Practice | P | P | P |

| | | | |
|---|---|---|---|
| 13 Vendor Survey: Strategies and Positioning | S | P | P |
| 14 Justifying the Cost of a Data Warehouse | P | P | S |
| **Appendixes** | | | |
| A Data Warehouse Planner | | P | |
| B References and Sources | | P | S |
| C Glossary | P | P | P |
| Index | P | P | P |



# Unique Value

*The Official Client/Server Computing Guide to Data Warehousing* is a must-read given the state of the data warehouse industry and the critical need to successfully plan, architect, and build data warehouses. The book offers the following:

- A reference architecture for data warehouse (which is missing from the industry) and a tool to build your data warehouse architecture
- A step-by-step guide to designing and building a data warehouse
- Techniques and tool requirements on how to extract value from the data warehouse
- Ideas on how to cost-justify a data warehouse project

## State of the Industry

The business need for data warehouse technology is well articulated. Data warehousing has the potential to provide a strategically important information technology service. Enterprise data is an asset, and business people need easy and timely access to the right data to delight customers, enhance profits, and increase market share. At this time, the following is true:

- The bleeding edge users, driven by either business pressures or opportunity, have implemented data warehouses. These users have learned that building and using a data warehouse is a daunting but rewarding endeavor.
- The leading edge vendors are selling early product and services offerings to meet the needs of leading edge users.
- Methodologies to develop data warehouses are few and hard to find.
- A framework or common viewpoint for data warehouse is missing. This makes evaluating prospective solutions and cost estimates very challenging and risky.
- Data warehouse terminology and verbiage is still jumbled and profuse. Standardization is needed.

- Many point products—products that address a data warehouse component—are available in the market. But a full and complete data warehouse solution is the responsibility of the enterprise.
- No de facto standards exist for data warehouse solutions.
- No major player is driving the data warehouse industry. There is a number of small companies with innovative products.
- Data warehouse is more at a pilot stage, and production worthiness of many data warehouse implementations is an issue.

## Focus of the Book

The focus of the book is to gently, but in a disciplined manner, teach you how to build your data warehouses on a firm foundation, and then apply data warehousing technologies to gain a sustainable competitive advantage. The book unfolds the data warehouse from two perspectives: architect and build, and cost-justify and use. After reading the book, you should be able to do the following:

- Select a doable first data warehouse project
- Cost-justify a data warehouse project
- Explain the costs and business benefits of your data warehouse project
- Develop a data warehouse strategy
- Plan a data warehouse project
- Evaluate the plan for completeness
- Architect a data warehouse and select the appropriate components of the architecture
- Construct a production-worthy data warehouse
- Develop a vendor selection plan and evaluate vendors using a common framework
- Communicate between information technology professionals and business users
- Select and utilize consultants to speed the planning, designing, and implementation activities
- Obtain maximum value from the data warehouse investment

Additionally, the attached reference architecture tool can assist you in planning, designing, and implementing the data warehouse. It also can help in data warehouse project scope selection and vendor evaluation/selection.

In summary, data warehouse is a non-trivial undertaking. It requires planning, expertise, and an integrated product set. Today's products are not totally integrated. Enterprises need to move slowly and prepare for a demanding systems integration challenge.

At the same time, data warehouses can yield the right information to business executives, managers, and analysts. Tapping the potential of a data warehouse is limited only by the capacity, capability, and creativity of the business users. Figure 1.1 shows that early experiences in data warehouse point to a broad array of usage—profitability analysis and growth, strategic management, customer relationship management, corporate asset management, and BPR and TQM support. Data warehouses are being successfully applied in the manufacturing, consumer goods and distribution, and the finance and banking sectors.

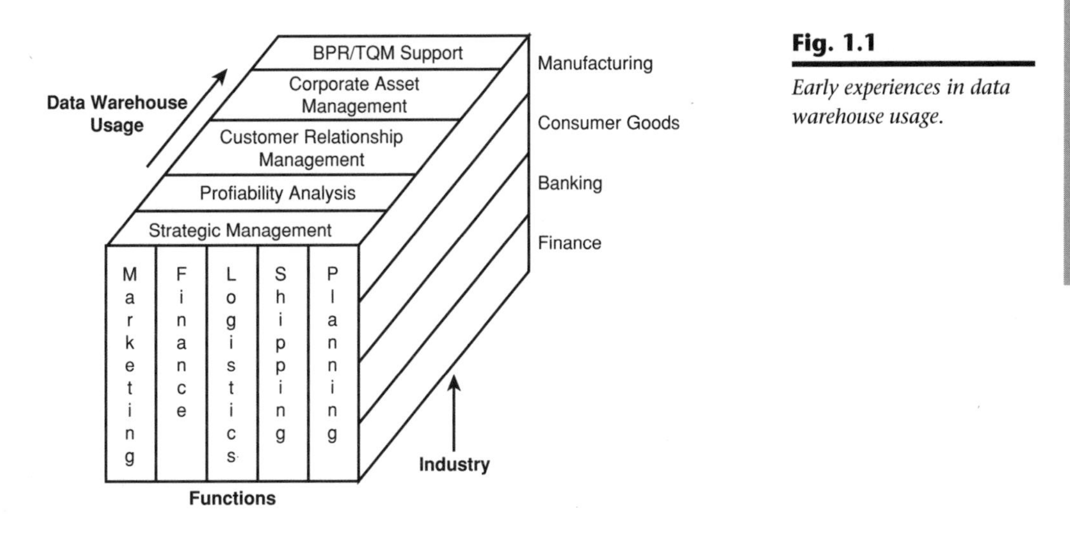


**Fig. 1.1**

*Early experiences in data warehouse usage.*

Before long, enterprises will have one or more data warehouses all focused on increasing revenue and profitability and beating the competition. Syndicated data is, as a rule, available to everyone. But the enterprise's own data in its data warehouse is a unique asset. This data is a detailed history of the enterprise's business and its relationship with its customers. Enterprises that learn to leverage their data—their data warehouse's best—are in a position to truly build plans, and execute and fine-tune them for a competitive advantage.

In the meantime, start with a business focus, build an architecture, and select a doable project. And put on your construction hard-hat as you go to work. Enjoy!

CHAPTER 2

# A Framework for Understanding the Data Warehouse

Enterprises have accumulated vast reservoirs of corporate data over the years. These reservoirs contain a gold mine of historical information related to items such as corporate performance, competitors, customers, products, warranty experience, and budgets. The hope since the 1970s was that this information could be "mined" and analyzed for strategic advantage. There were, and are, many barriers to viewing this collection of often fragmented information as one. Attempts at data integration have been made with mixed success. With the advent of data warehouses, the hope of data integration and its profitable use for business analysis may eventually be realized. However, building and using a data warehouse is complex.

## The Complexity of Building and Using a Data Warehouse

One reason for the complexity of a data warehouse is the range of skills that are required to formulate, develop, implement, deploy, and exploit the data warehouse (see fig. 2.1).

The skills required include the following:

- Business skills
- Technology skills
- Program management skills

Business skills relate to understanding the significance of the data contained in the data warehouse. At the same time, business skills relate to understanding business requirements and translating them into queries that can be satisfied by the data warehouse. The data within the data warehouse is about the enterprise's business. The value of this data is very high to people who know how to use it to formulate strategies that will improve their business and provide a competitive advantage.

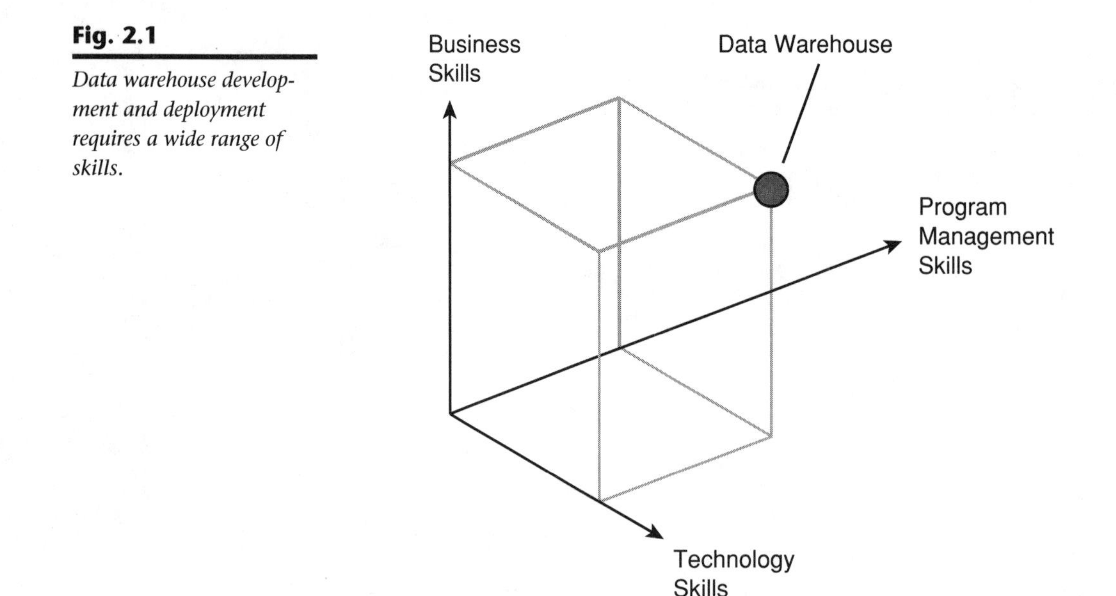


**Fig. 2.1**

*Data warehouse development and deployment requires a wide range of skills.*

Domain knowledge is specific knowledge about the business domain. This knowledge relates to items that are specific to the business and the industry in which the business operates. Often, the challenge lies in translating the enterprise's broad strategic statements into precise business inquiries and converting them into data warehouse queries and reports.

The data warehouse is often based on extracts of data from production systems. Building a data warehouse, in such cases, involves understanding how these systems store and manage their data (i.e., the definitions of their data, also commonly known as *metadata*). It also involves understanding how to build extractors, which transfer data from the production systems to the data warehouse, and synchronization software that keeps the data warehouse reasonably current with the production system's data.

Data analysis skills involve understanding how to make assessments from quantitative information and derive fact based conclusions from historical information. It includes the ability to discover patterns and trends, to extrapolate trends based on history to understand and look for anomalies or paradigm shifts, and to present coherent managerial recommendations based on analyzing data warehouse information. These skills are partly mathematical, partly statistical, and partly psychological and intuition, or experience, based.

The data warehouse stores historical (and sometimes current) business data in an organized manner, allowing specialized queries and data retrievals to be easily performed. This capability is harnessed by end user reporting, browsing, and querying tools that provide a variety of reporting functions, including the ability to progressively expose more detail (drill-down). Communication skills allow an organization to provide easy-to-use and appropriately selected end user graphical interfaces to assist the analysis tasks. An important consideration is the appropriate use of graphical techniques such as charting, tree displays, network displays, trend curves, and multi-dimensional analysis. The need is to present the numeric and discrete values stored and organized by the data warehouse using intuitive and informative displays to make trends and analysis points easily discernible.

Implementing a data warehouse is a complex task because of the need to interface with many technologies, vendors, and end users to deliver results in a timely and cost-effective manner. A poorly managed data warehouse implementation can easily overrun its budget. Coupled with the complexities of implementing the warehouse itself, is the need to pace the data warehouse implementation with the learning curve of users and an organization's appetite to absorb technology. The implication of this is that scope selection, requirements analysis, and choice of pilot project implementation play a big part in successful delivery of data warehouse technology in a business setting. Good project management is essential to make this happen.

The data warehouse, in essence, is a database application that uses its own database management system. This database management system derives its data from other database systems which support a business' daily operations. The operational databases may be implemented in a variety of technologies, such as DB2, IMS, VSAM, Oracle, Sybase, Informix, DL/I, and Flat Files. Most contemporary database managers who support the actual data warehouse itself are relational. Examples of these are the DB2/X family, Oracle, Sybase, and Informix. Various transportation mechanisms bring the data from the production sources to the data warehouse. Various propagation and replication methods are used to keep the data consistent across all of these databases. Extractors are used to extract and load information from one database to another.

The extracted data must be made uniform so that data from different sources can be combined inside the data warehouse. This process is called transformation. Transformation involves decoding data that was encoded inconsistently in different sources—for example state abbreviations, product codes, and business locations. Transformation software transforms the data on its way to ensure that the data is compatible with the receiving database. Developing, or selecting and integrating, these pieces of software requires data management and database management skills. Skills are also needed in the area of tuning database query execution to obtain acceptable performance out of the data warehouse solution.

# The Importance of a Framework

A framework is a way of looking at something complex and making it understandable by using a set of simplifying analogies to help break a complex solution into smaller components.

Why is the framework important? A framework breaks complexity down into manageable components and therefore provides a foundation for analysis. Analysis allows the implementor to anticipate problems and costs long before they are physically manifested. Understanding the framework allows human beings to manage complexity. The framework allows various people to conceive, build, and deploy a data warehouse to classify investments, effort, risk, and technologies into well understood compartments. The framework assists these people in moving from concepts to execution.

The framework also supports the idea of multiple viewpoints. This allows people with different viewpoints and objectives to view the same thing in a way they understand.

# An Information Systems Framework

One of the original frameworks for understanding how Information Systems are built is the Zachman framework.

In his landmark paper of 1987, John Zachman viewed the building of a large and complex Information System as similar to building a large and complex building. Trying to figure out where to start the building task is a daunting challenge! There are a variety of people involved in the construction of a building. The owners or investors are interested in a building that meets their residence needs and lifestyles. The architect is interested in designing a building that incorporates the needs of the owners as effectively, efficiently, and aesthetically as possible. The builder is interested in receiving precise directions to perform his task. Each of these people views the building differently. The owner views it as a financial investment and measures its worth against its cost. The architect views it as a floor plan and specifications for building materials. The builder may view the building as a set of electrical and plumbing plans to construct the building.

Zachman also showed how each of these people had an interest in various dimensions of the building. The builder's plumber was interested in the plumbing view while the electrician was interested in the electrical wiring and fixtures.

Zachman then showed how the views and dimensions could be combined to form a matrix that is called the *Zachman framework* (see fig. 2.2). The Zachman framework represents the top-down, business driven, or owner's perspective, as well as the bottom-up, builder driven, or implementor's view of an information system.

Each cell in the Zachman framework (row/column intersection) represents an architectural representation (model) as seen by a class of stakeholders of the system. Formally, the rows represent viewpoints, or perspectives, and each column represents an aspect or view of the system.

In much the same way as the Zachman framework, the data warehouse must be viewed from many perspectives by the various people interested in its construction and usage. Reduced to its essence, a data warehouse can be viewed as a mission critical business software application that uses one or more databases for storing and retrieving information. What makes the data warehouse different from an operational business application is the way its data is organized and the amount of data stored. The transactional data that supports an operational application is organized for fast storage and retrieval in well known and predictable ways. The data inside a warehouse is organized to support a rich variety of analysis tasks; the access paths taken to retrieve data for decision making and decision support cannot be predicted or controlled in advance.

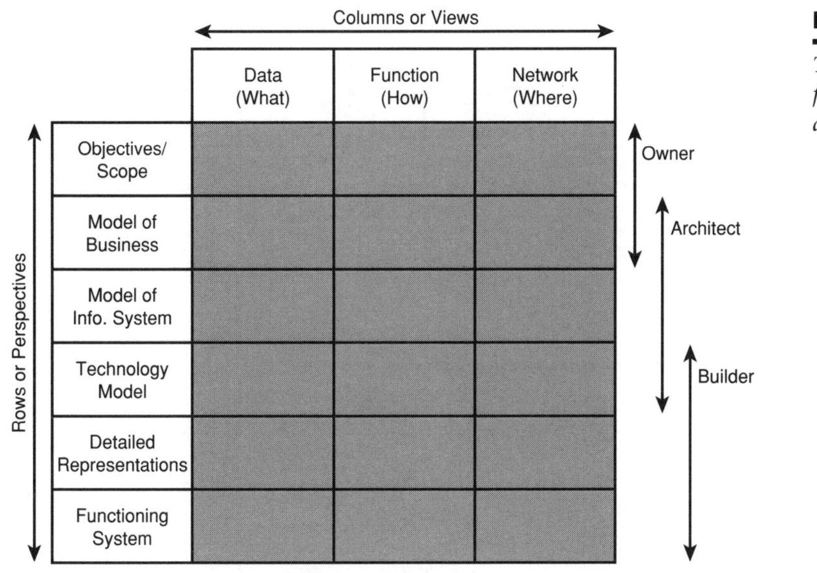


**Fig. 2.2**

*The Zachman framework for information systems architectures.*

Other differences between operational data and warehouse data include update optimization versus query optimization, recent history versus long history, and programmer access versus business user access. After deployment, a data warehouse acquires a life of its own, evolving in directions that are as diverse as its users (see fig. 2.3).

The data warehouse industry and its underlying information processing technology has evolved over the years. In the information management industry, there has been a change in thinking about the role of a data warehouse. In the initial stages, there was a belief in the industry that a robust production database system, along with the ability to support a wide variety of queries and reports, would provide the entire range of decision making support that an organization needed.

Over the years, organizations kept collecting information and generating reports, some of marginal value. During the late 1980s, it became evident that data was available in plenty but information was not. Due to the volume and granularity of data available, it became impossible to use the production information systems for anything other than to support operational decision making. Two key concepts became increasingly important: aggregation—combining multiple concepts together such as product sales by customer by market—and summarization—combining large amounts of detailed data to derive summaries that had less data but more information. Aggregated and summarized data had greater perceived value to the executive and the operational staff in understanding the complexities and peculiarities of their business. Aggregated and summarized data provided a concise capture of business trends and customer trends. It was this promise that drove early implementations of data warehouse technology. Another key issue preventing the implementation of data warehouses was the proliferation of isolated application systems and databases and the lack of data integration across applications.

**Fig. 2.3**

*Evolution of information processing technology and its shifts in focus.*

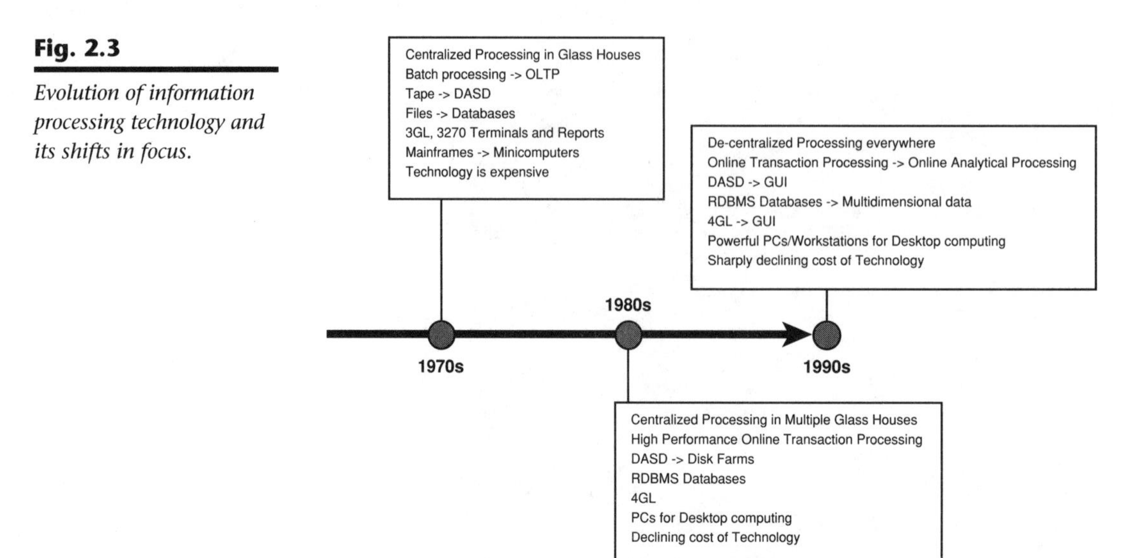


While the early implementors wrestled with the complexity of manually implementing database extractions, data aggregations, data summarizations and, multidimensional data analysis, others tried to use Executive Information Systems (EIS) to provide summarized and aggregated reports. Their conclusion was, for performance reasons, that it was good to separate the production databases from the warehouse databases. The availability of low cost client/server processing hastened this transition. This brought up the problems of replicated data and the need to keep the warehouse synchronized with the production databases. Vendors have, in the meantime, stepped in with products and technology solutions to meet these challenges.

As organizations start implementing a data warehouse, they are finding new ways to use the information from the data warehouse to support many activities, such as the following:

- **Increasing customer focus**—Markets don't buy, customers do! The data warehouse contains historical information which can be analyzed by a customer, for example. Such an analysis yields a customer's buying preferences, buying timing, budget cycles, and appetites for spending. This information can be used by the Sales and Marketing departments to tune a sales campaign directed towards the customer.

- **Repositioning products and managing product portfolios**—As products age in the marketplace, it becomes increasingly important for companies to analyze their product portfolios to determine products they must continue, products they must withdraw, and products they must try to reposition. The historical information inside the data warehouse allows companies to compare the performances of products by quarters, by years, and by geography to tune their product strategies.
- **Making environmental corrections to marketing plans**—By linking the data warehouse to external sources of information, such as Dow Jones and information subscription services (syndicated services), companies can analyze environmental impacts on their market plans. For example, if the syndicated services indicate that the largest market for a company's products and services is in the 20–30 year old range, the company can analyze its customer penetration for this range and gear up to change its marketing plans based on its analysis.
- **Analyzing operations and looking at sources of profit**—Often, it is very useful for a business to know the factors that contribute to its profitability. These are factors such as customers, products, services, business units, locations, and markets. The company has accumulated a wealth of data over the years. Being able to analyze this wealth of data to determine sources of profitability is a very useful benefit of the data warehouse.
- **Managing the customer relationship**—Data warehouses provide a wealth of historical data useful for identifying sources of customer frustration, as well as opportunities for closer relationships. For example, multiple contacts between the company's sales representatives and the same customer may confuse a customer. The data warehouse integrates multiple application systems and can help guide the various points of contact.
- **Managing the cost of corporate assets**—Data warehouses integrate the bills of materials for a variety of products and services offered by the company. Using this integrated view allows a business to identify items commonly used across multiple products. This can form the basis for striking volume supply arrangements at reduced prices from the supplier. It can also form a basis for consolidating suppliers. Looking at the history of purchases also allows a company to manage its procurement and inventory in tune with its consumption patterns.

# Data Warehouse as a Mission Critical System

As organizations start relying more and more on the availability of information and access to a data warehouse, it takes on the role of a *Mission Critical system.*

When does a system become Mission Critical? A software application becomes a Mission Critical system when trust has been established in its operations and it starts being used on a daily and ongoing basis (see fig. 2.4). It also becomes critical to the mission of the business that it supports. Its failure can result in the failure of the business itself.

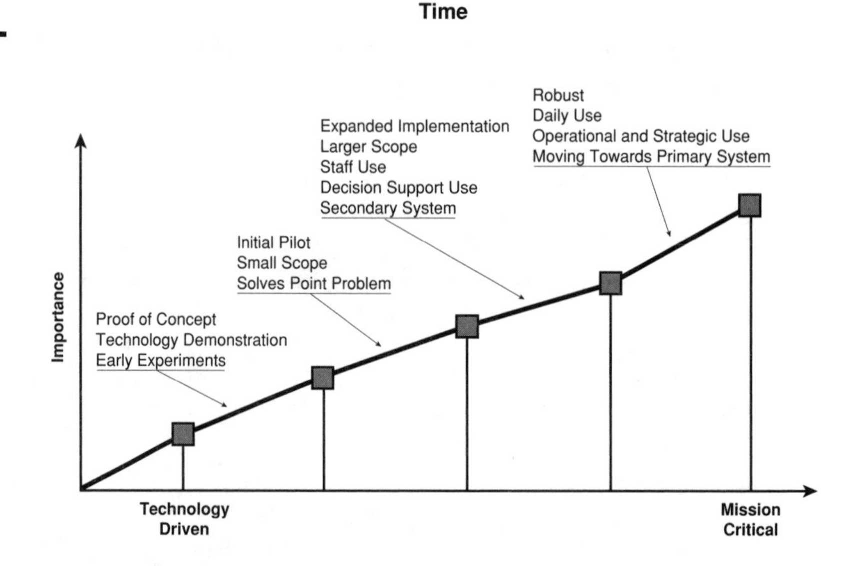


**Fig. 2.4**

*How a new technology is incorporated into an important Mission Critical system (Technology Maturity Cycle).*

As the company starts to increasingly use data warehouse information for day-to-day activities, its availability becomes more and more important. Empirical patterns of information use indicate that as more and more information becomes easily and quickly available, more and more people postpone requesting the information till the very last minute! When this occurs, it becomes extremely important that the data warehouse system, and all the applications that provide access to it, be available 100 percent of the time.

The requirements of a Mission Critical system include the following:

- Availability
- Consistency and accuracy
- Robustness
- Standards
- Business requirement-based
- Compatibility with existing technology and infrastructure base
- Used on a daily basis
- User-friendly

- Performance
- Auditability
- Security

Understanding the requirements of a Mission Critical system allows you to define the requirements of a data warehouse.

# Data Warehouse Requirements

How does one start formulating requirements for a data warehouse? There are many ways to view a data warehouse. They are as follows:

- A data warehouse is simply a business application system with its own database. This database is populated from other operational databases, not from raw data that is entered. The data warehouse provides a set of features and functions to implement business processes and dovetail with other business processes outside the scope of the data warehouse. In much the same way as other business application systems, the data warehouse is required to provide these prescribed sets of features and functions as efficiently and effectively as possible to the end user.
- A data warehouse is a latent capability. It stores summarized information that is organized along business subjects, such as customers and product, to make the information more amenable to analysis. The burden of displaying, organizing, and reporting the information stored inside the data warehouse falls on the tools that must attach to the data warehouse. In this view, the data warehouse is a latent capability which becomes useful only when reporting and analysis tools are intelligently applied against the data stored inside the warehouse. The requirement is for the warehouse to support a broad range of access tools, operated by a broad range of end users. The warehouse must also store and manage a broad scope of information to serve a broad clientele.
- The data warehouse is a historical database, which is like an aggregation of many years of online transactional information, organized to make storage efficient and retrieval easy. In this view, the requirements of the warehouse are to organize large volumes of data efficiently and compactly. The requirements are also to provide summarization techniques to make it easy for end users to comprehend the lessons of history.
- The data warehouse is sometimes an operational data store. It delivers operational data to a wide range of users by making copies of the data from the operational database systems. In such a view, the data warehouse is required to effectively and efficiently distribute operational data to a broad range of users. The warehouse is also required to make technological changes needed to move the operational data from its operational database to the storage technology used inside the data warehouse.

It is clear that the requirements of the data warehouse can be as varied and diverse as the classes of users who wish to use the data warehouse for business benefits. It therefore becomes necessary to classify the requirements of data warehouses using classical techniques.

The Zachman framework that was referred to earlier is one of the most effective ways of viewing a system from many perspectives. The requirements that are visible from each of these perspectives are the requirements that are posed by the people who have those perspectives. Though the exact requirements for the data warehouse are discussed in the following sections, you will now lay the groundwork needed to understand the various perspectives of the data warehouse.

In his paper, Zachman referred to the following people who have an interest in an Information System:

- The owner or investor in the Information System who is trying to solve a business problem using Information Technology.

  The owner's view is generally measured in dollars and cents and the perspective he/she has is of business terms and processes. The owner's interest in technology is generally restricted to analysis of investments and payback, and assessments of risk and schedules. The executive investor or sponsor sees the data warehouse as a component of DSS (Decision Support System) in the overall business perspective (see fig. 2.5).

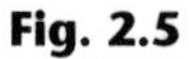

**Fig. 2.5**

*Scope of business challenges addressed by data warehouse technology.*

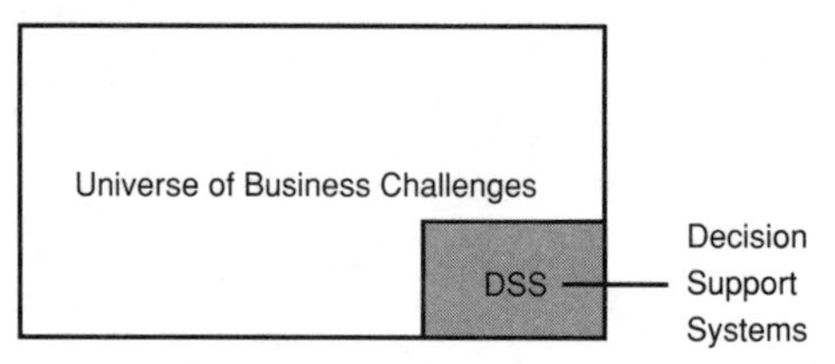


  In DSS, the owner is looking at the data warehouse to provide analysis and rationale to make business decisions. Most of the analysis capabilities provided by the data warehouse is based on historical data and the extrapolation of trends. The areas where the investor needs Decision Support are the areas of interest to the business as a whole—Sales, Marketing, Finance, Strategic Management, Product Planning and Development, Customer Support, Human Resources, etc.

- The business user who must use the data warehouse on a regular basis to perform business functions. This user's perspective of a data warehouse is a clearly defined and prescribed set of processes and steps that he/she must follow to perform the business analysis and function. The business user is often not interested in how the data warehouse is set up or how it is architected. They simply require the data warehouse to perform advertised functions correctly and efficiently.

- The architect who must understand both the business needs of the data warehouse as well as the implementation technology that is needed to fulfill those needs. The architect must:
  - Know short term and long term business needs
  - Understand current and planned technology investments in computing platforms, and database management systems
  - Understand the availability of data from operational systems
  - Understand data security issues

  The architect is the broker between the investor who has commissioned the system based on a high-level view of business needs and the builder who needs detailed specifications to build the data warehouse.

  From the business end, the architect sees the business entities and processes captured as information in the data warehouse. He/she also sees the various ways in which the information must be organized inside the data warehouse to support the end user's needs. From the technology end, the architect sees how the data warehouse will interact with existing operational systems and applications to load the data warehouse with information and keep it current and consistent. Often, the architect is also responsible for matching the data warehouse implementation to current investments in technology.

- The builder who is responsible for physically installing and integrating the various components of the data warehouse. The builder places operational and deployment requirements on the warehouse, such as availability, recoverability, and security. One example of the builder's perspective of the data warehouse is that of a Mission Critical client/server system that is based on relational technology, local area networks, and is implemented in C and C++.

The Zachman framework also describes various dimensions that these perspectives may take. Zachman describes the Data perspective as the What, the Process perspective as the How, the Geographical or Network perspective as the Where, the business rationale as the Why, and then goes on to add the When dimension as well.

If you recall the Zachman framework as representing two dimensions of a system, the rows represent the various perspectives of the stakeholders (such as owner, architect, and builder), and the columns represent the view of a system (such as data, process, and network). Figure 2.6 is an example of three types of stakeholder perspectives with six different views.

**Fig. 2.6**

*Perspectives of the data warehouse as viewed through the Zachman framework.*

| | WHAT | HOW | WHERE | WHO | WHEN | WHY |
|---|---|---|---|---|---|---|
| Owner | • DSS for Customer Revenue Analysis | • Analyze Historical Data | • Marketing Dept. Office | • Marketing Dept. | • Monthly<br>• Quarterly<br>• Annually | • Business<br>• Objectives<br>• Making Promo Decisions |
| Business User | • Subject Areas<br>• Dimensions<br>• Granularity | • Drill Down<br>• Report<br>• Query | • Desktop<br>• Dept. Conference Room | • Managers<br>• Analysts | • Currency of Information | • Operational Objectives<br>• Decision Support |
| IT Implementor | • Subject Areas<br>• WH Metamodel | • Data Warehouse and DataMart Functions | • LAN<br>• Corporate Network | • DA/DBA<br>• Domain Analyst<br>• Appl. Programmer | • Data Warehouse & Load Refresh Cycle | • Technical Objectives |

# Requirements Perspectives

One way to look at benefits is to look at business needs met by the architecture. The needs for a reference architecture are different for each of the stakeholders: the investor/owner, the architect, the end user, and the builder.

## Investor/Owner

The investor/owner of a data warehouse is involved at the inception of the data warehouse concept in an approval and review capacity. He/she approves the initial acquisition and, sometimes, the ongoing operational costs and upgrades needed to keep the system useful. During the inception, the primary support the architecture must provide for this stakeholder is to provide a framework for performing planning and coordination activities, forecast of costs and benefits, and risk management.

Planning comprises the assessment of the following:

- The full range of products and services
- The personnel and skills needed
- The impact on the existing business environment and people
- The impact on technology investments

Cost and Benefit analysis estimates the cost of a data warehouse solution for initial deployment and for ongoing maintenance and upgrade. Factored into this analysis is the estimated payoff obtained by delivering data warehouse information to the user's workstations. A rough Return on Investment (ROI) and Return on Assets (ROA) calculation framework is also required.

A risk management framework is required to allow the investor/owner to identify alternative implementation paths and evaluate the tradeoffs for the various implementation options. The risk management framework must also offer alternatives for phased implementation of data warehouse technology and support for make or buy decisions.

The architecture must provide the common vocabulary and language to communicate the investor/owner's needs to the designers and builders.

## Business User

The day-to-day user of the data warehouse is the business user. He/she is primarily interested in *using* the information from the data warehouse to meet business objectives and to improve personal and organizational productivity, efficiency, and effectiveness. The objective of this user is to use the additional knowledge of customers, products, services, and the enterprise's internal organization to provide a superior grade of service, build higher quality products, and create new innovations that "delight" the customer, while operating with higher margins and lower costs.

Business users want access to extracted operational data that is "clean and credible" and is available in a manner that makes it simpler to analyze. The historical data must be time stamped so users can study and analyze trends. They need to cut the data in a variety of ways and from different perspectives, and use a range of desktop analysis tools to understand and assimilate the data. These business users need to convert data into facts, convert facts into knowledge, and use the knowledge to arrive at decisions and recommendations. They want to present the results of this analysis in a manner that is coherent, logical, and succinct to other team members and managers.

The architecture must map the components deployed by the business user for analysis, as well as the mechanisms needed to transport and deliver the data to the business user.

## Designers and System Builders

The Information Technology (IT) organization is generally responsible for developing, installing, and deploying the data warehouse. It is also responsible for the maintenance and upgrade of the data warehouse. IT's initial focus is to achieve a rapid, cost-effective, error-free initial installation followed by a series of modular upgrades, and automatically synchronized and scheduled database updates with minimal human intervention. The IT organization is measured by the following:

- The quality (accuracy and timeliness) of the data in the data warehouse
- The responsiveness with which data is made available to business users
- The ease of use that is offered to business users
- The appropriateness of data formats and content from the perspective of the business user
- The range and volume of data that is made available within the data warehouse
- The timely implementation within the project budget

During the implementation phase, the architects and designers need an architectural framework to show the major components of the data warehouse application and how the components fit together. This architecture must do the following:

- Enable IT to analyze systems and products from vendors and evaluate how vendor offerings fit into their architecture.
- Show IT where to start and obtain the minimal core set of components necessary to start an economical data warehouse.
- Indicate the potential components of the implementation phases and support future implementation decisions such as, "which components can be extended? replaced? dropped?" as the solution is expanded in later phases.
- Provide for components to perform ongoing refresh and update of the data warehouse data, and for components to provide major systems administration and management activities.
- Provide a security framework. Data warehouses, because of the summarized and aggregated information offer a tempting target for competitors.

From the system builders' perspective, the data warehouse architecture must clearly separate the data sources (what data is available) from the form and format in which the data is presented and structured for the end user. The architecture must show the components that do the following:

- Perform the extraction of data from operational systems
- "Clean and refine" this data
- Add time stamps and origin of the extracted data
- Structure and store the data to support a range of analysis tools and information analysis requirements

The data warehouse architecture must map the components into the various implementation blocks to enable the system builder to accurately proceed with an implementation. The system builder also has to make difficult decisions regarding the scope of data that must go into the warehouse. This data selection scope is easier when end users know exactly what they want. Sometimes the scope of data has to evolve as users start using the system. The architecture must support analysis to understand how the warehouse can be tailored with exactly the right information.

The system maintenance staff is responsible for ongoing operations of the data warehouse. Their responsibilities are to provide periodic refresh of information as operational data changes over time. They are also responsible for expanding the scope of information delivered to the end user over time, as users state or define new information needs. The architecture must reflect the need for maintenance staff to reorganize the information as well as their need to perform data warehouse remodeling extensions.

# Need for Common Architecture

Just as the Zachman framework serves to separate the various perspectives of a data warehouse, there is a need for a framework that separates the various components of a data warehouse solution. This common framework, called the reference architecture, will allow you to reduce the variety of information needed to build a data warehouse to a common classification. This classification will allow you to make comparisons between competing vendor choices, evaluate tradeoffs, and discover gaps that you must fill with internal software development. The word *reference* is used to signify that the architecture is vendor independent and characterizes the "generic" nature of all data warehouses.

Why is the reference architecture important? The reference architecture does the following:

- Provides a common "blueprint" framework. It is necessary for the investor, the architect, and the builder to have a common terminology and frame of reference when discussing costs, estimates, risks, and progress in implementation schedule.
- Creates a lasting foundation for implementing the enterprise vision. The framework is a durable method of capturing a vision. Often, the vision is grand and far reaching, but the appetite for resources and spending is limited. The reference architecture allows the vision's fulfillment in phases while still preserving the vision itself.
- Provides for alternatives in implementation. For example, many organizations have contemplated data marts and data warehouses as separate facilities. The data mart serves a narrower clientele on targeted departmental needs, while the data warehouse serves the enterprise. A framework that clearly separates these two, allows an organization to build a series of data marts, and later, a data warehouse, is very powerful.
- Provides mapping of vendor offerings within the reference architecture framework. Because data warehouse technology is early in the technology maturity cycle, solutions are vendor driven rather than customer driven. Each vendor uses a different terminology for their solution components. A common reference framework allows the customer to make evaluations and selections with an apples-to-apples comparison.
- Highlights production-worthy solution components. As the data warehouse solution is deployed, issues related to daily and production use of the solution will come up. These must be resolved by adding components to the initial solution. Having a reference architecture as part of the implementation and deployment allows the builder or deployment staff to identify the components and add them to the solution framework.

Using a reference architecture as the foundation for building a data warehouse yields the following benefits:

- **Architectural trade-offs**—The reference architecture breaks up the solution into well understood components. Each of these components can be built entirely, bought entirely or bought in components and integrated into the solution. For example, one could buy a complete data warehouse manager from

Prism Solutions, could build a home grown data warehouse using a Sybase relational database management system, or could integrate a Red Brick Warehouse as a component with an existing application for metadata management. The reference architecture therefore provides a basis for tradeoff analysis.

- **Cost/benefits estimates for investment analysis**—The reference architecture also divides the solution into identifiable cost or payback components. For example, populating the information into the warehouse is a cost offset by the payback of decision support tools which use that information. Investors have to balance the cost of the loading and synchronizing components of the warehouse against the potential payback of query and analysis.
- **Determination of level of reusability of existing investments**—The reference architecture contains components related to technology infrastructure. Many organizations would like to preserve current investments in technology. With the reference architecture, it is possible for these organizations to map their current investments into the architecture components and integrate and purchase only the components that are not available.
- **Assessment of technology risks**—Each of the components in the reference architecture is on a different technology maturity curve. This is because of the complexity and sophistication of each of the components and the state of industry practice in building those components. With the reference architecture, it is possible to isolate high risk components from low risk ones based on their positions on the technology maturity curve.
- **Assessment of "production issues"**—The reference architecture exposes components used on a daily basis. These components must therefore be engineered to meet a production use rather than a casual and occasional use. Production strength qualities must be listed and the components that require them must be evaluated and strengthened. The list of production qualities can also be used for vendor evaluation of the components.
- **Selection of compatible architectural components to ease integration**—The complex nature of the data warehouse solution, and the fact that no single vendor offers a satisfactory solution to meet every customer's need, dictates the combination of compatible components and timely delivery of an integrated solution.
- **Compatibility assessment of existing investments and vendor offerings**—Existing investments are a business reality. Any vendor proposal to do away with current investments must be compared with proposals that complement and extend current and planned investments.
- **Scope selection of implementation**—One way to manage the budget of a data warehouse project is to manage the scope of its implementation. Scope can be managed in many ways, such as the following:
    - Selection of metadata
    - Selection of sources of data

- Implementing a data mart only
- Selection of technologies that the warehouse will manage (e.g., Relational Database Systems only)

- **Staffing and Skills enhancement planning**—As mentioned earlier, data warehouse planning, implementation, deployment, and usage require a wide range of skills. The reference architecture maps each of these skills to the appropriate architectural component. This allows for a planned ramp-up of project personnel based on identification of skills and when they are needed.
- **Build versus buy decision-making**—The reference architecture progressively breaks down the data warehouse solution into increasing levels of detail. At any level, build versus buy decisions can be made for each component. This allows an organization to integrate the components it needs and build only the components that are not commercially available.
- **Creation of a comprehensive program and project plan**—The reference architecture provides a basis for building program and project plans that are driven by the components that must be bought, developed, or integrated. This separation of components will also allow sequencing of vendor supplies and support in a manner that is dovetailed into the overall program and project plan.



# Reference Architecture

The reference architecture is first described from a high-level abstract and simplified view of the data warehouse as the following:

- A collection of data extracted from operational databases
- Software to condition the data for access by users
- A set of applications and tools that perform a complex set of queries and analysis

Subsequently, we will systematically decompose the reference architecture into further detail. This will assist the understanding of a simple conceptual framework, while at the same time expose the details that are necessary for an orderly and proper implementation. Wherever possible, popularly used and understood terminology is used. The industry is still in its infancy and terms and definitions have not been standardized. Currently, different terms are being promoted by various vendors in their marketing literature.

Figure 2.7 shows the top level components of the reference architecture. The data warehouse reference architecture divides the components of the data warehouse into blocks such as Data Source, Data Mart, Data Warehouse, and Access and Usage, and layers such as Data Management, Metadata Management, Transport, and Infrastructure. Blocks relate to specific data warehouse functionality. Layers represent the environment needed to implement the blocks.

**Fig. 2.7**

*An overview of the data warehouse reference architecture.*

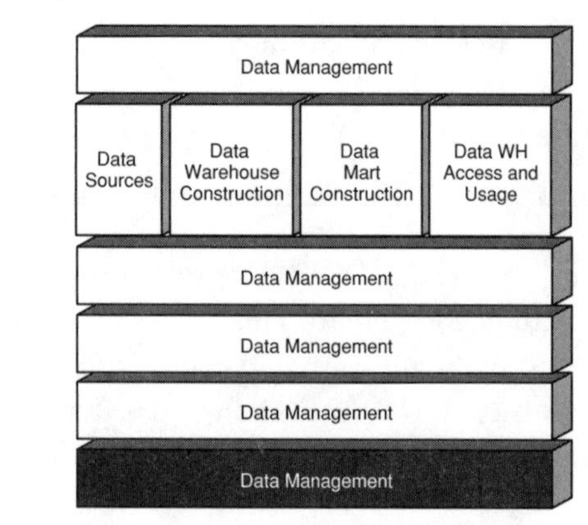


The blending of the Data Warehouse and Data Mart approaches is reflected in the reference architecture. The reference architecture therefore offers the widest canvas of implementation options for an architect. The horizontal Data Management and Metadata Management layers correspond to the activities that relate to extraction, loading, update and refresh that are needed to keep the data warehouse and Data Mart supplied with information.

The other horizontal layers correspond to common services that are essential to the Data Warehouse and Data Mart blocks. These common services are Infrastructure and Transport. An additional layer is also depicted in the reference architecture called Tools, Technologies, and Roles. This layer is used to support a data warehouse methodology that allows the construction and deployment to be process, tools, and methodology driven.

The Data Warehouse construction, the Data Mart construction, and the Data Warehouse Access and Usage blocks, along with the layers of Data Management and Metadata Management, are the areas of new investment in a data warehouse project. The Data Sources block, along with the Transport and Infrastructure layers, are the existing investments of the enterprise.

The reference architecture offers a rich set of implementation choices. It is likely that implementors will choose the implementation that matches their specific needs and ignore the components of the architecture they deem unnecessary. The reference architecture provides many implementation options for the architect. You can do the following:

- Proceed to build an enterprise-wide data warehouse, a set of data marts, or both while reserving the right to postpone the data warehouse/data mart decision.
- Select a few data sources to build the data warehouse, while reserving the right to add more in the future.

- Define a multi-platform, multi-level architecture based on the use of different kinds of platforms for the various architecture components (mainframe-based Data Sources, mainframe-based Data Warehouses, server-based Data Marts, and workstation-based End User Access and Usage).
- Select technology components for Transport (Middleware) and Infrastructure (RDBMS and IMS database technology) to match the selections of multi-platform, multi-level architectures for the Data Sources, Data Warehouse, Data Marts, and end user Access and Usage.

The next set of figures (figures 2.8 through 2.15) show the components associated with each of the major architecture blocks in the earlier figure. The components shown here correspond to currently known and available technology. The architecture framework allows additional components to be added as and when they become available and are used universally. In these figures, the shaded blocks represent activities that deal with Metadata Management. Metadata results from almost every activity that operates upon and changes the data inside a data warehouse in its journey from the Data Sources into the Data Warehouse or Data Mart.

## Data Sources Block

The Data Sources block can be divided into the following categories, as shown in figure 2.8.

**Production Data.** Production data refers to operational databases that hold the information collected from operational applications. These operational databases can come in a variety of technologies, such as relational, non-relational, or file-based.

**Legacy Data.** Legacy data is off-line, or archived, data stored away because it is not needed to support currently operational applications. This data, however, has significant historical value for trend analysis and must be brought into the data warehouse with the application of the right time stamps. This data is also useful for data mining purposes.

**Internal Office Systems.** These are sources of data not currently stored in an operational database or used by an operational business application. In general, this data is the following:

- **Unstructured**—such as in non-electronic forms
- **Structured**—as in reports, charts, spreadsheets, and word processing documents
- **Semi-structured**—as in annual reports or SEC filings

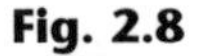

**Fig. 2.8**

*The components of the Data Sources architecture block.*

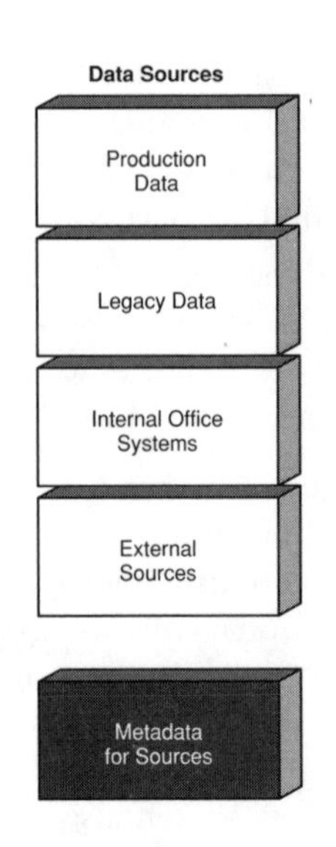


This data is useful for supporting analysis across departments.

**External Systems.** These data sources are not controlled, owned, or operated by the enterprise. These can be in electronic form—such as Dow Jones or Dun & Bradstreet—or competitive analysis briefings from market research firms; or they can be non-electronic form, such as competitive reports from consultants or articles in magazines or newspapers—like the *Wall Street Journal*, *Fortune*, and *Business Week*. External sources include syndicated data.

**Metadata for Sources.** Metadata is the definitional information about the data from the sources. The metadata includes the name of the data captured and extracted from the data sources, the definition of the data contents (fields), the date of creation, and the source or origination point of the data.

In the case of Internal Office and External Systems, metadata could also include a summary description, the storage location, and the access and control parameters of the document which contains the data.

## Data Warehouse Construction Block

This major block of the architecture consists of the following components (see fig. 2.9):

- The Refinement component is responsible for standardizing, cleaning and scrubbing, filtering and matching, and time stamping origin information to data extracted from the selected data sources.

In the Refinement component, the metadata is mapped to the standard data names and definitions. Additional metadata is created and captured for time-stamping the extracted data, the source of the extracted data, and missing fields that have been added.

- The Re-engineering component is responsible for conditioning the data to meet the analysis needs of the business user. Re-engineering in the data warehouse context is different from re-engineering of applications or business processes. Re-engineering involves the following activities:
    - The integration of different types of data from multiple systems to create new data
    - The partitioning data into time-phased series for analysis
    - The pre-calculation of summary information and derivation of other information required by the business user
    - The translation and formatting of data from different sources so it can be combined uniformly and consistently
    - The transformation and re-mapping the stored data to the original data sources to enable ongoing refreshing for the newly derived, created, or transformed data

    Metadata is created and captured in the re-engineering component for the following:

        - The integrated data, summary data, pre-calculated, and derived data
        - The data granularity and partitioning
        - The translation and transformation rules that were applied to the data
        - The mapping rules and the maps between the data sources and the warehouse data are also captured
        - The data warehouse component is responsible for the data modeling of the data warehouse, the reduction of large volumes of data into manageable chunks, and the metadata of the logical and physical data warehouse

The data modeling activity derives the data warehouse data model from the enterprise data model, if one exists, or creates the new data model. The database design issues addressed in this component include data partitions, subject areas, and granularity where granularity is "the single most important aspect of design of a data warehouse." Also included is the actual database design model and the subsequent casting of the physical database schema of the data warehouse.

**Fig. 2.9**

*The components of the Data Warehouse construction architecture block.*

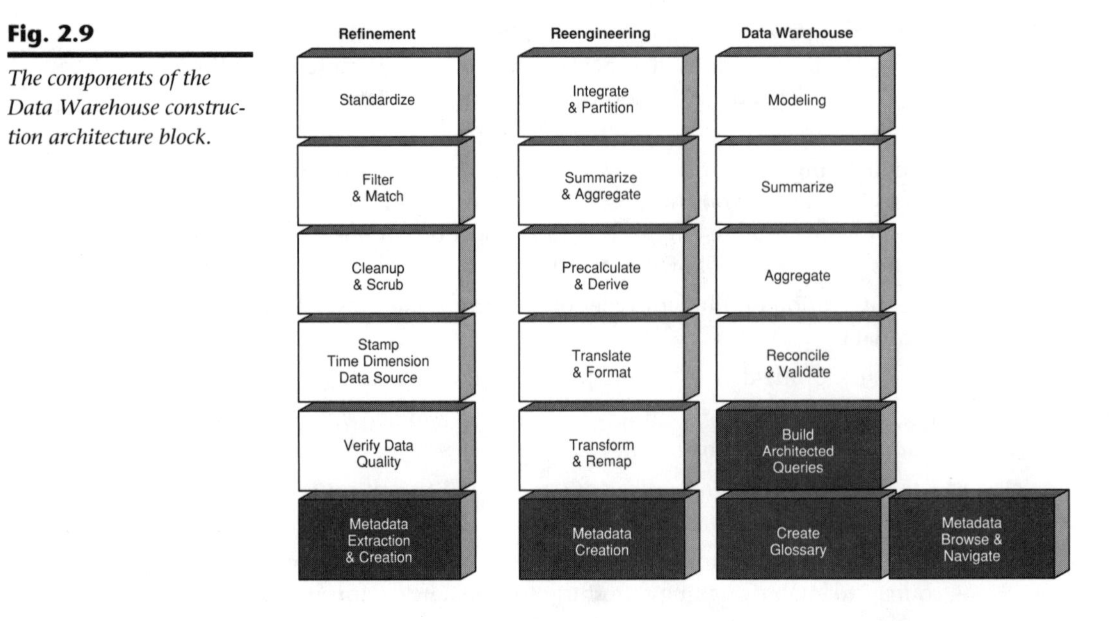


Data handling reduces the large volumes of incoming data and previously stored data using techniques of aggregation and summarization. It is a part of this component and is responsible for creating highly summarized data from lightly summarized data. The degree of summarization refers to the level of aggregation of the data. For example, weekly summaries are less summarized than quarterly summaries.

Metadata that captures the following is an essential part of the data warehouse:

- The structure of the data warehouse itself
- The description of the database
- The navigation paths and rules for browsing the data warehouse
- The business glossary
- The list of architected and pre-defined queries and reports

Metadata guides the user in appropriate context-enhanced browsing and navigation of the metadata and hence the data warehouse. As older detailed information and the light summaries in the warehouse are reduced/condensed to new highly summarized information, the metadata of these actions is captured. The data warehouse rules of filtering and matching, reconciliation and validation, and aggregation and summarization are captured as part of the total metadata.

## Data Mart Construction Block

The Data Mart construction block is the second major block of the architecture. This block is used to create a Data Mart from the contents of a data warehouse. The following components are required to construct the Data Mart (see fig. 2.10).

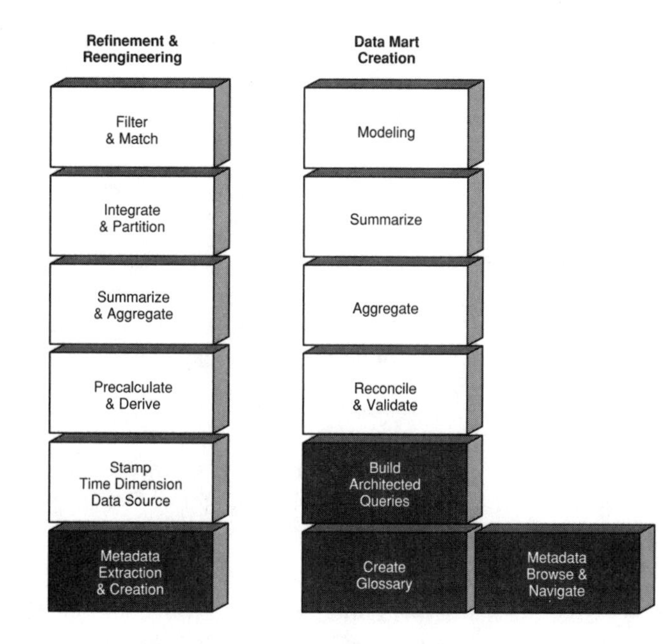


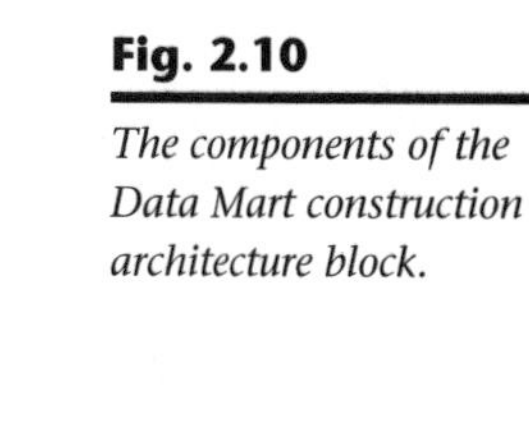

**Fig. 2.10**

*The components of the Data Mart construction architecture block.*



The data mart has components similar to the data warehouse. The primary difference between the two is the focus of the end user. The data mart components apply a different set of re-engineering and refinement steps to the business objectives of their end users. Because of the reduced complexity and scope of refinement and re-engineering tasks in the data mart, these activities have been combined into a single Refinement and Re-engineering block. The Data Warehouse block is replaced by the Data Mart creation block.

The data mart is optional for most organizations who already have a data warehouse. On the other hand, some organizations may simply implement a number of data marts and no corporate wide data warehouse at all! In such cases, the scope and complexity of the refinement and reengineering activities is on the same scale as that required for the data warehouse. In cases where an organization feeds its data marts from the corporate data warehouse, a number of refinement and reengineering activities have already been performed.

The refinement and re-engineering component is responsible for the following:

- The filtering and matching the data to be extracted from the data warehouse
- The integration of the data warehouse into newer or redefined subject areas
- The creation of new summaries or aggregations

- The creation of highly summarized data from lightly summarized data in the data warehouse
- The pre-calculation and derivation of new data, all with appropriate time and source stamping

The Data Mart creation block has the same components as those for the Data Warehouse creation block described earlier. The difference lies in the focus of each of the components. The modeling block in the data mart, for example, is focused on the needs of the individual department that owns the data mart, while the corporate modeling block serves a much broader need. The summarizations performed in the data mart are based on the timeframes and granularities of the department rather than all the departments of the corporation.

The shaded components in figure 2.9 represent activities related to metadata management. A detailed description of metadata management and types of metadata that must be maintained in the data warehouse is described in Chapter 7, "The Importance of Metadata Management." The appropriate metadata for all the above activities is also extracted and stored in the data mart.

When no data warehouse exists, the Refinement and Re-engineering components described in the Data Warehouse construction block would apply in the construction of the data mart. In the context of this architecture, the Data Mart component is essentially identical to the Data Warehouse component described earlier in the Data Warehouse construction block.

## Data Warehouse Access and Usage Block

The third major block of the data warehouse architecture consists of two components: Access and Retrieval, and Analysis and Reporting. This is the block that provides the payoff and the value to the entire data warehouse implementation. As Mr. W. H. Inmon, widely regarded as the "father of the data warehouse," states, "The Holy Grail for the end user is insight as to why business has been conducted the way it has been in the past and how the business can be conducted more effectively in the future." Figure 2.11 shows the components in detail.

The Access and Retrieval component provides access directly to the data warehouse, bypassing the data mart, and to the data mart. This component is also responsible for transforming the retrieved data into multidimensional views or for storing into a multidimensional database for subsequent analysis. The data from the data warehouse and data mart can be "downloaded" into local store, with or without translations and transformations, for local analysis, data mining, and reporting. An important consideration is the range of queries from pre-defined to ad hoc to iterative to drill-down, and these queries may access small to very large amounts of data. Such issues are addressed in this component. Metadata access and browsing is also included in this component.

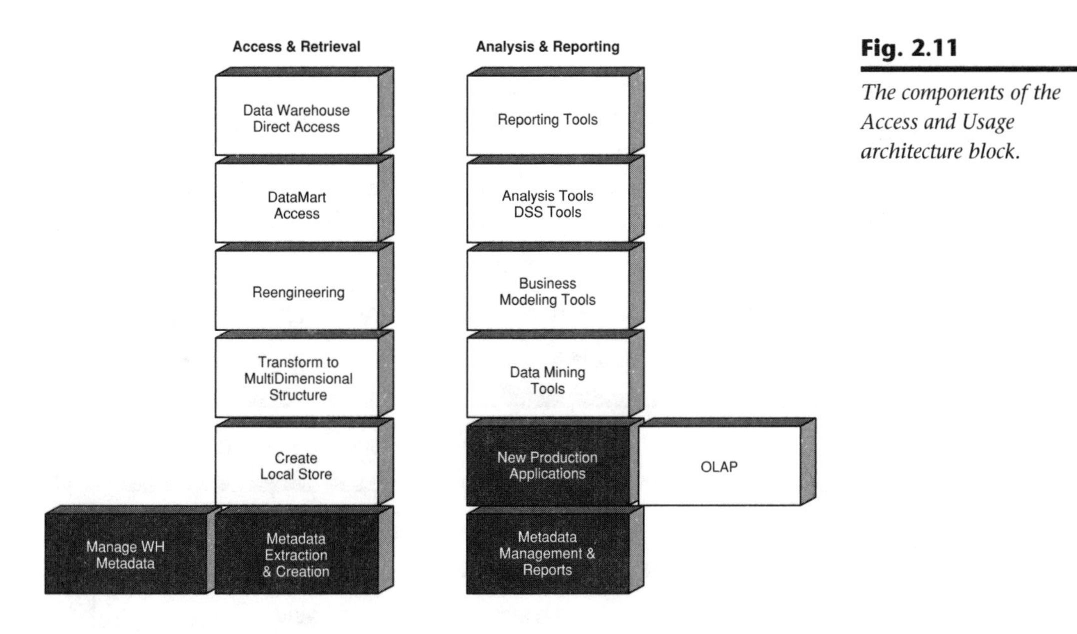


**Fig. 2.11**

*The components of the Access and Usage architecture block.*



Metadata browsing and navigation aids the business user in the following:

- Understanding what is in the data warehouse/data mart (name, description, content, value, version, source, and so on)
- Understanding the context of the data and the transformations that occurred from the time the data was extracted until it was stored in the data warehouse/ data mart
- Determining the location of the data
- Verifying the reliability of the data
- Figuring out how to access and use the actual data

The Analysis and Reporting component is responsible for the family of tools and applications needed to get value from the data warehouse and data mart. These tools can be classified into reporting tools, analysis and decision-support tools, business modeling and analytical processing tools, and data mining tools. Tools for navigating the metadata to understand and report on the contents of the data warehouse/data mart are also the responsibility of this component.

Metadata tools provide assistance to the systems builder and maintenance staff in understanding, monitoring, and managing the data in the data warehouse/data mart. Other metadata tools, especially with user-friendly navigation and browse capability, provide the road map of the data to the business user. This road map guides the business user in understanding the data in the right context, with information on level of granularity, level of summarization, derivation rules applied, and source and date of origin of the data.

As a profitable byproduct, new production applications that leverage and use the data (and the metadata) can also be a part of this component.

## Data Management Layer

The tasks for extracting, loading, refreshing, enforcing security, archiving, and restoring the data warehouse from archives is supported by the Data Management layer (see fig. 2.12).

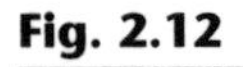

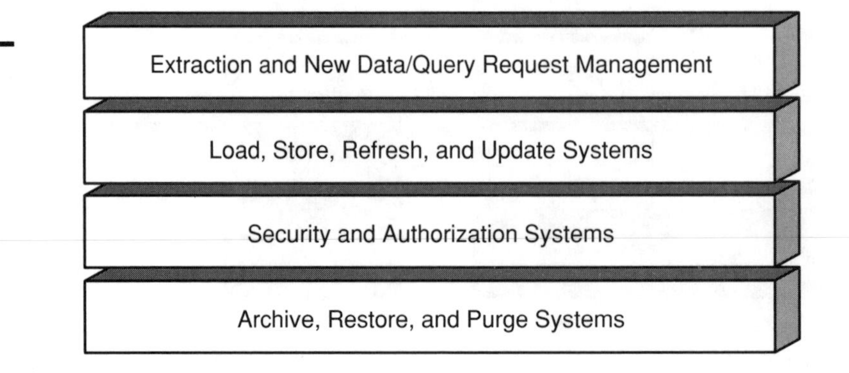


**Fig. 2.12**

*The components of the Data Management architecture layer.*

From the data warehouse perspective, the items of particular interest in the data management layer are the following:

- Extracting the appropriate data from the selected data sources for further refinement and re-engineering and storage in the data warehouse
- Tracking and fulfilling requests for new data from either new or current data sources
- Capturing the appropriate changed data in the operational data sources, and then refreshing or updating the data warehouse

This data management layer incorporates the standard data management policies, procedures, schedules and operations for security, access authorizations, archive and restore, and purge of the data. A particular challenge is presented by the potentially very large size of the data warehouse. The size of the data warehouse impacts data compaction management of multiple indexes, the physical placement of data and indexes, and the rapid background restore from multiple media. Issues of parallel processing of queries, and the use of parallel processors for data access and retrieval are also managed in this layer. Managing the metadata controlling these activities is the responsibility of the metadata management layer.

## Metadata Management Layer

The data warehouse architecture is built on the concept of data definitions, or *metadata.* Metadata pervades every activity of the data warehouse. Data sources are characterized by the definition of the incoming data. Adding time stamps requires the definition of additional timestamp related metadata. Adding source stamps also creates new metadata. The activity of summarization requires the creation of new columns to hold the summarized information. The *Metadata Management* layer of the reference architecture is responsible for managing the metadata that is used by the data warehouse, such as the full and complete description of the data stored in the data warehouse (see fig. 2.13). A detailed discussion of metadata management is available in Chapter 7, "The Importance of Metadata Management." Metadata also provides guides and pointers to the data located inside the data warehouse.

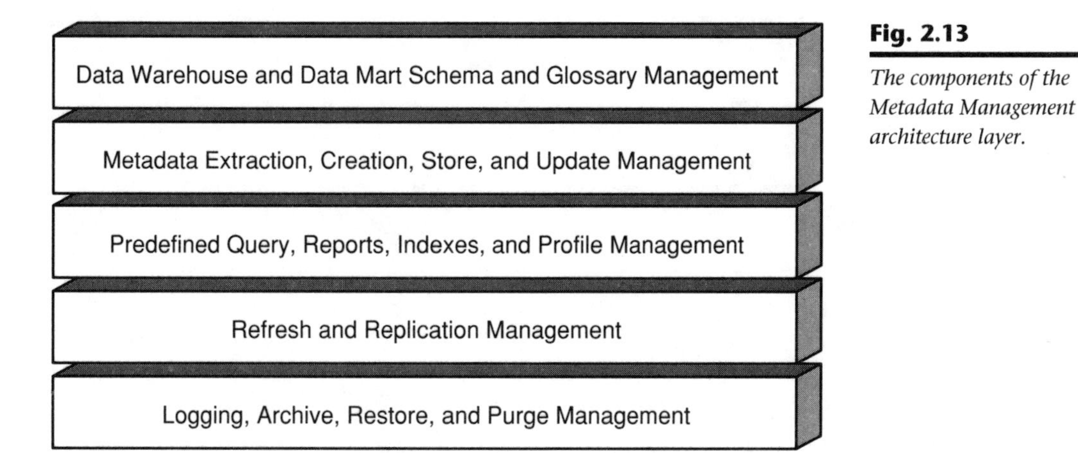


**Fig. 2.13**

*The components of the Metadata Management architecture layer.*

The data warehouse and the data mart logical and physical data models and schemas, along with the technical and business glossary, are also stored and managed in this layer. The enormous challenge of managing very large databases with their attendant complexity in the areas of multiple indexes, data compaction, compound keys, and versions of data is addressed and managed in this layer.

The Metadata Management layer is responsible for controlling the following:

- The standard data definitions (including the technical definitions and business descriptions) of the data stored in the warehouse
- The metadata captured and created in the Refinement and Re-engineering blocks
- The metadata on granularity, partitions, subject areas, aggregation, and summarization
- The metadata describing the pre-defined and architected queries and reports
- The metadata describing indexes and profiles that improve data access and retrieval performance
- The metadata describing the rules for the timing and scheduling of the refresh, update, and replication cycle

## Transport Layer

The task of transporting the data between the various blocks of the architecture is provided by the Transport layer of the architecture. This layer uses refresh and replication technology, data transfer and delivery networks, and middleware components. It also provides security and authentication for transport requests (see fig. 2.14).

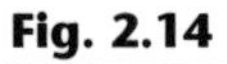

**Fig. 2.14**

*The components of the Transport architecture layer.*

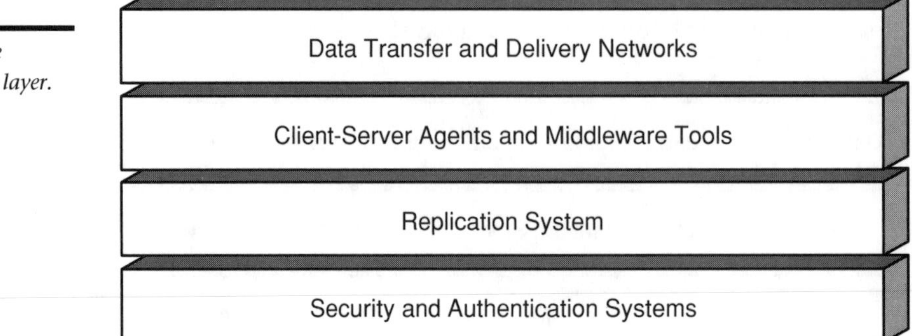


The Transport layer also addresses the necessary communications bridges between the hardware/software platforms that are separated as a result of platform partitioning of the various blocks of the reference architecture.

The Data Transfer and Delivery Networks component of the Transport layer contains the following types of systems:

- Network protocols, such as TCP/IP, SNA/APPN, and IPX
- Network management frameworks, such as Hewlett Packard's OpenView, IBM's NetView, and SunSoft's SunNet Manager
- Network operating systems
- Network types, such as Ethernet, Token Ring, and FDDI

The client/server agents and middleware component contains the following types of systems:

- Database gateways, such as Information Builders' EDA/SQL, Sybase Enterprise Connect, and IBM's DRDA/DDCS
- Message oriented middleware, such as IBM's MQSeries
- Object Request Brokers (ORBs), such as IBM SOM, DSOM, Hewlett Packard's ORB Plus, and DEC's Object Broker

The replication systems component of the transport layer contains the following types of systems:

- Propagation and replication systems, such as IBM's Data Propagator Relational (DPropR) and Non-Relational (DPropNR), Sybase Replication Server, and Oracle's Symmetric Replication

- Built-in replication facilities within database gateways such as Information Builders' EDA/SQL
- Data warehouse-specific products, such as Prism Solutions' Warehouse and Change Manager

The requirements for the security and authentication systems are slowly evolving as organizations try to understand the nature of the data that is managed inside the data warehouse. Commercial solutions must be supplemented with system integration services to tie together security and authentication across the various components of the data warehouse. This is especially true in client/server implementations of the data warehouse.

## Infrastructure Layer

The components of the Infrastructure architecture layer are shown in figure 2.15.

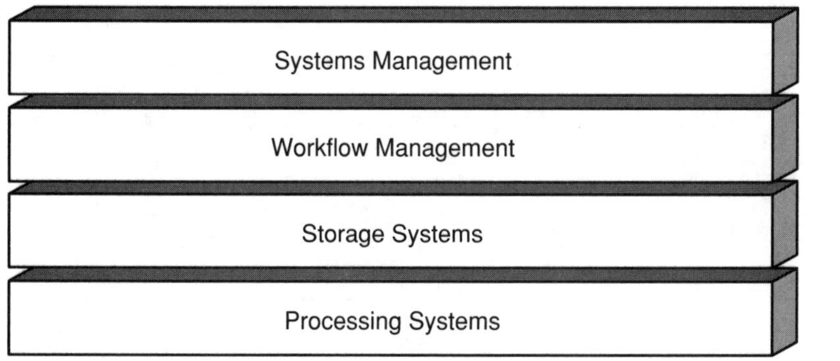


**Fig. 2.15**

*The components of the Infrastructure architecture layer.*

The systems management component provides capabilities for the systems builder and the business user to invoke, manage, and terminate tools and applications.

The Workflow Management component supports the process integration and management to coordinate the orderly and specified execution of tools, applications, and activities to correctly complete the data warehouse and data mart extraction, refresh, replication, update, aggregation and summarization, and other maintenance and systems administration tasks. It is the automation of the many tasks required to maintain and refresh the data warehouse and data mart, as well as to provide pre-defined reports and query results, that increases the efficiency and the productivity of both system builders and business users.

The storage systems component provides the database and file management services for the data sources, the data warehouse, and data mart database catalogs, and the multidimensional and local store for the Access and Usage block.

The processing systems component is the underlying operating environments of the major blocks: Data Sources, the Data Warehouse and Data Mart, the Access and Usage Tools, the Middleware, and the other infrastructure components discussed previously.

Other important systems of the Infrastructure layer that must be considered are the following:

- Configuration managers
- Storage managers
- Security managers
- Software distribution managers
- License managers
- Performance monitors
- Capacity analyzers

## Detailed Reference Architecture

The overall detailed architecture is shown in figure 2.16. It is an expansion of all the architecture components described earlier.

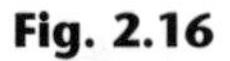

**Fig. 2.16**

*An overview of the detailed reference architecture based on combining the detailed block and layer components.*



# Benefits of the Reference Architecture

The reference architecture brings value to all the essential activities required to design, implement, and deploy a data warehouse. Different activities benefit different people who are involved in building and using the data warehouse.

Figure 2.17 shows the benefits to people who are not directly involved with the mechanics of implementing the data warehouse, primarily investors/owners, business users, and business/IT planners. The columns of the matrix display various categories of people who have a stake in the data warehouse but are not directly involved in its implementation. The rows of the matrix in figure 2.17 represent various dimensions of benefit/value derived by each of these categories of stakeholders.

| Value and Benefits vs Roles | Investors/Owners | Business Users | Business & IT Planners |
|---|---|---|---|
| Risk Analysis and Management<br>Costs and Benefits Analysis<br>Evaluation of Current Investments | P | P | S |
| Strategy and Planning<br>Technology and Obsolescence Management<br>Skills Analysis and Management<br>Project Simulation | S | P | P |
| Team Communications<br>Requirements Communications and Analysis | P | P | P |
| Architecture & Design | | | |
| Construction and Operations<br>Vendor Evaluation<br>Tool and Product Evaluation<br>Maintenance and Enhancement Management<br>Systems Administration<br>Project Management | | | |

**Fig. 2.17**

*Values and benefits for business related stakeholders.*

Figure 2.18 shows the benefits/values derived by people who are directly responsible for planning and implementing the data warehouse: architects, designers, systems builders, and operations and maintenance staff. The rows of figure 2.18 display various dimensions of benefit. The columns represent the categories of people involved in the development of the data warehouse.

| Value and Benefits vs Roles | Architects | Designers | Systems Builders | Operations and Maintenance Staff |
|---|---|---|---|---|
| Strategy and Planning<br>Technology and Obsolescence Management<br>Skills Analysis and Management<br>Project Simulation | S | | | |
| Team Communications<br>Requirements Communications and Analysis | P | P | P | P |
| Architecture & Design | P | P | S | S |
| Construction and Operations<br>Vendor Evaluation<br>Tool and Product Evaluation<br>Maintenance and Enhancement Management<br>Systems Administration<br>Project Management | S | S | P | P |

**Fig. 2.18**

*Values and benefits of reference architecture for builders and implementors.*

The reference architecture provides the commonly understood and defined framework of communication, a common vocabulary and language, that allows all the stakeholders—owners/investors, planners, architects, designers, builders, implementors, and the users of data warehouse technology—to talk to each other and understand what each is saying. It is also a simulation vehicle that allows for a variety of estimation and planning activities to proceed before a data warehouse implementation occurs on a large scale. It offers a path and a guide for vendors to identify their contributions in a manner that complement an organization's current investments. It is a framework that communicates the skills needed to evaluate, buy, build, and maintain various data warehouse components. It also provides a basis for selecting service assistance from consultants and service providers.

The existence of a common framework of understanding benefits all stakeholders. Benefits include a clarity of understanding of the technology, and how to use the technology and the data warehouse-based solution to run their business. Architectures make things clear because they extract the details into manageable chunks that allow people to evaluate tradeoffs and make decisions. They also identify the borders between components to reflect real world boundaries between vendor products and vendor skills. This allows buyers to understand what vendors have to offer, how these offerings fit into the "big picture," and how they fit with each other. It also allows them to understand vendors' specialty skills, so as to bring in the right vendor to do the right job.

## Summary

- Building and deploying a data warehouse is a complex task requiring a broad range of skills and an understanding of a broad range of technologies.
- Frameworks help us to understand and break down complexity. The Zachman framework for information systems architecture can be applied to data warehouses as well.
- In a world of multiple technologies, multiple vendors, multiple definitions and terms, a common architecture is required to make comparisons, choose options, estimate risks, and establish benchmarks. This architecture is called the reference architecture.
- The reference architecture is designed to meet the common requirements of all stakeholders of the data warehouse. We presented the reference architecture for data warehouse and its major architectural blocks.
- The reference architecture provides benefits to all stakeholders. It provides a firm foundation for planning, analysis, estimation, risk assessment, and a blueprint for implementation.

CHAPTER 3

# Applying the Data Warehouse Reference Architecture

The previous chapter introduced the concept of a data warehouse reference architecture. The reference architecture is a unified and common way of looking at the components of a data warehouse solution. Figure 3.1 shows the reference architecture components.

The data warehouse reference architecture is an important planning aid. It provides a conceptual framework for analyzing various implementation choices. For example, the reference architecture can be used for the following tasks:

- Evaluation of current investments
- Costs and benefit analysis
- Risk analysis and management
- Vendor evaluation
- Tool and product evaluation
- Maintenance and enhancement
- Project planning and management
- Technology and obsolescence
- Skills analysis and management
- Project simulation
- Architecture and design

**Note**

The exact process that describes how the architecture is used to perform selected tasks above will be described in later parts of this section.

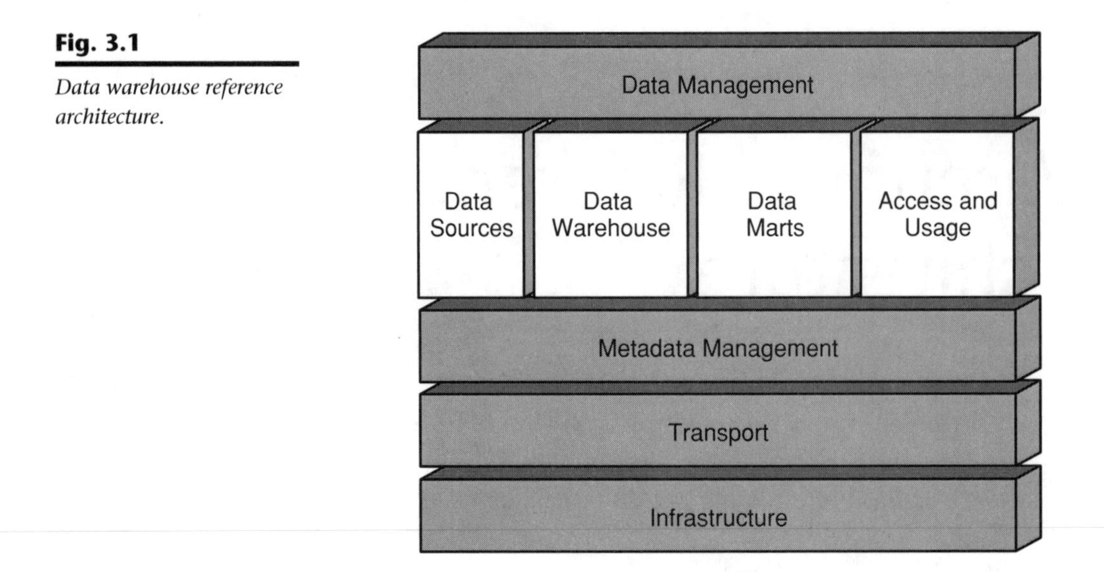


**Fig. 3.1**

*Data warehouse reference architecture.*

The data warehouse reference architecture divides the components of the data warehouse into *blocks* such as Data Sources, Data Mart, Data Warehouse, and Access and Usage, and *layers* such as Data Management, Metadata Management, Transport, and Infrastructure. Blocks relate to specific data warehouse functionality. Layers represent the environment needed to implement the blocks.

# Using the Reference Architecture for Analysis

There are two ways in which the data warehouse reference architecture can be used for analysis—vertical cuts and horizontal cuts. These are the two ways in which the reference architecture may be "cut" or partitioned.

## Vertical Cuts

Vertical cuts represent slices of the architecture that correspond to block boundaries. Each of the cuts separate the blocks and segment the layers. All blocks that lie within the same cut therefore share the same layers (environment). In other words, if the Data Sources block and the Data Warehouse construction block are in the same cut, they must reside on the same platforms and share the same mechanisms for transport and infrastructure. If the sources run on DB2 on an MVS mainframe, the data warehouse will also run on DB2 on the same MVS mainframe. Vertical cuts therefore create hardware/software platform boundaries.

Why are vertical cuts useful? Vertical cuts are a way to make sweeping scope-related decisions. Examples of such sweeping scope-related decisions are:

- Should the data source and data warehouse run on the same platforms?

- Should there be data marts at all?
- Should there be a data warehouse at all? Will data marts be more appropriate?
- Should the data warehouse access and usage tools be directly connected to the data sources?

Figure 3.2 shows an example of an organization's decision to locate its data warehouse on the same platform as its data sources.

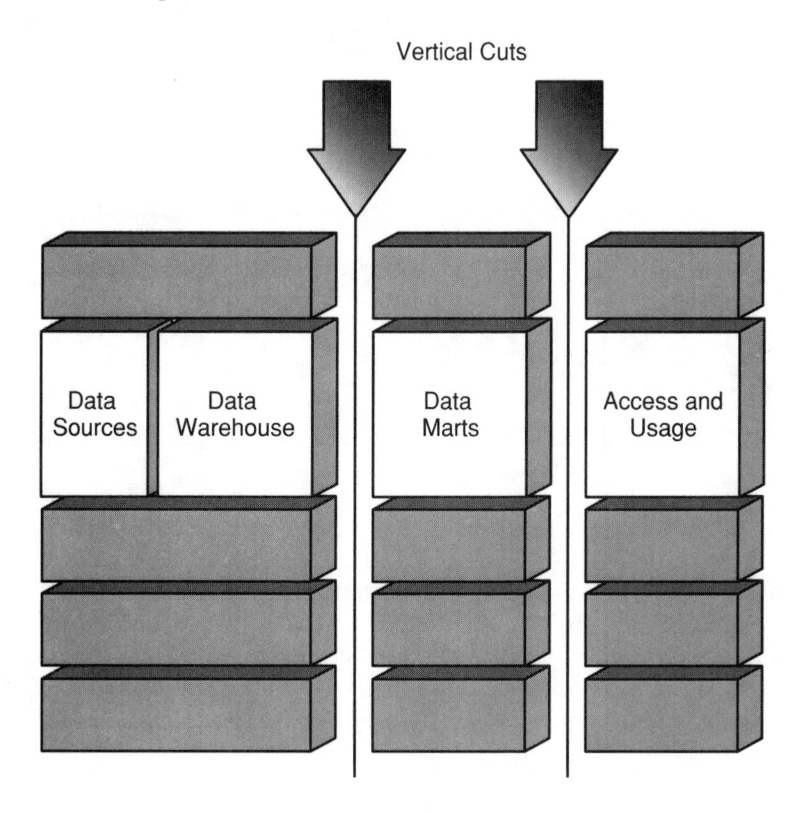


**Fig. 3.2**

*Vertical cut of the reference architecture to locate the data warehouse on the same platforms as the data sources.*

The organization decided to incorporate the data sources and data warehouse in one partition, the data mart in another, and the data access and usage into a third. This partitioning effectively imposes a three-level implementation where the first partition may run on a mainframe such as an IBM 3090 using DB2 on MVS. The warehouse will then also reside on the same platform. For the second partition, one can then use a superserver such as RS6000 using Sybase System 10 on AIX that runs the data mart components. For the transport, replication technology can be used to copy the DB2 information into the data mart servers.

Figure 3.3 shows another example of an architecture cut that reflects an organization's decision to separate the platforms that contain data sources from the ones that run the data warehouse, the ones that run data marts, and the workstations that are used by end users.

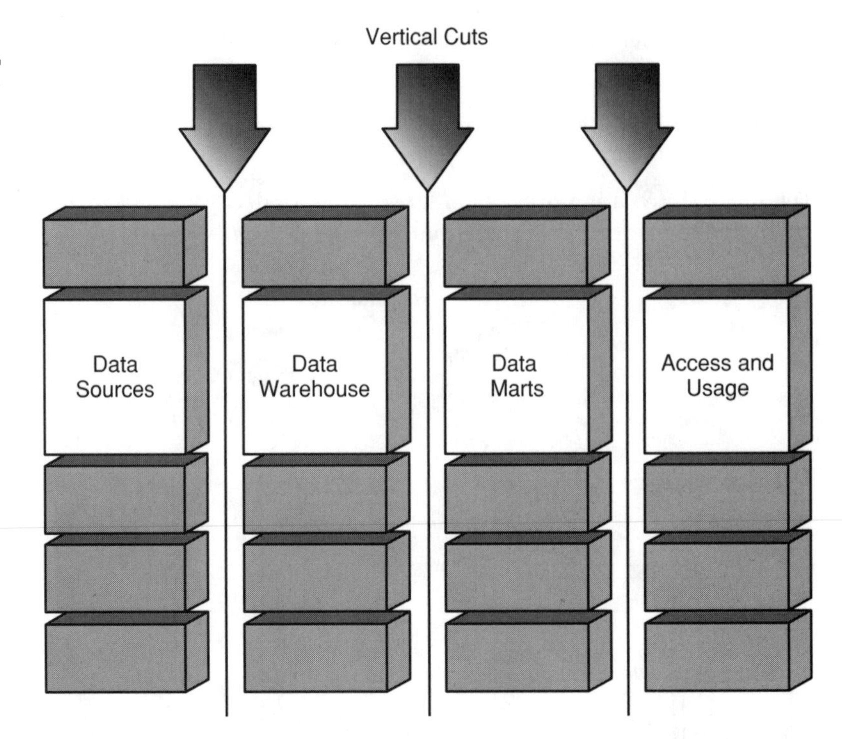


**Fig. 3.3**

*Vertical cut of the reference architecture to separate warehouse components based on mainframe and client/server considerations.*

In this example, a series of cuts are made that correspond to the data sources on a host mainframe, the data warehouse on a server, the data mart on the same or another server, and the access and usage platform located on client workstations. This corresponds to a situation where the host is not required to provide the storage and processing capabilities for storing the data warehouse information or for the cleaning, scrubbing, and re-engineering activities that are required by the warehouse. The data warehouse server can be a multi-processor based superserver that provides adequate processing support.

Figure 3.4 shows an example of an organization's decision to completely do away with a corporate data warehouse.

The organization in the example was interested in simply providing data marts on superservers located at various departments in the enterprise, without having a data warehouse. This solution will then directly connect the data mart to the data sources and locate the cleaning, scrubbing, and re-engineering activities on the data mart superserver. This offers a very focused start for an initial data warehouse implementation.

## Horizontal Cuts

As mentioned earlier, the process of making vertical cuts is the process of making sweeping scope-related decisions. Vertical cuts therefore establish the scope of data warehouse implementation. Once the vertical cuts have been established, the implementation must consider a number of implementation-related dimensions. These dimensions range from what personnel and skills are needed to implement the data warehouse, to making vendor and product selections for various data warehouse components, to making build versus buy decisions. These dimensions are called horizontal cuts of the architecture.

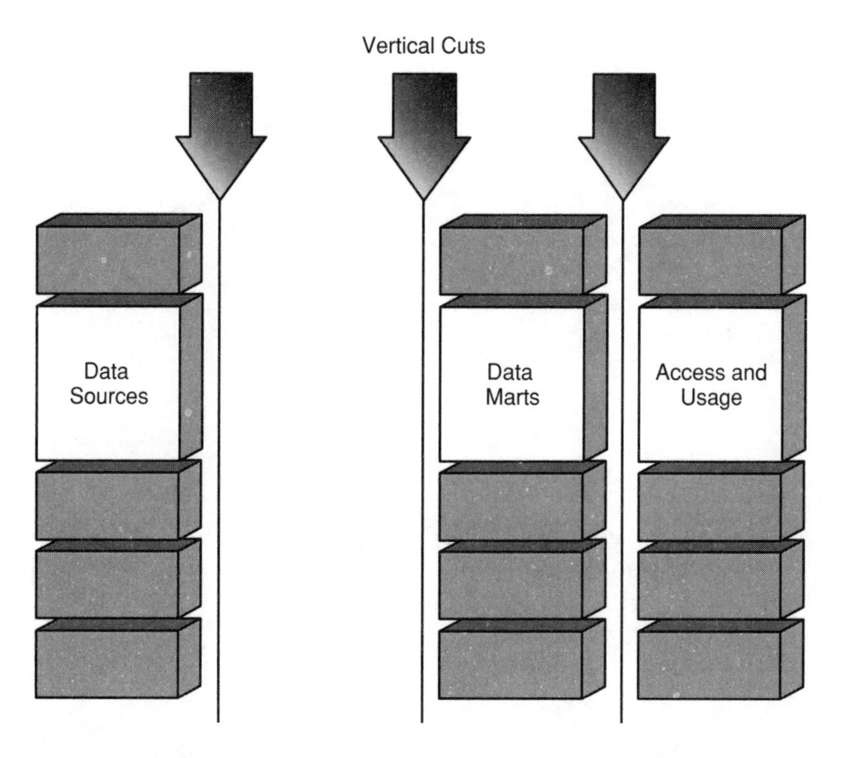


**Fig. 3.4**

*Vertical cut of the reference architecture to quickly start a warehouse implementation using only data marts.*

Horizontal cuts are useful because they break down the complexity of the planning task. Detailed implementation is exactly what the word "detail" implies: a large number of items from a wide range of disciplines. Horizontal cuts are useful in separating this range of disciplines and planning for them one at a time using the same reference architecture as a common classification scheme.

Figure 3.5 shows a horizontal cut through the reference architecture that helped an organization understand the roles of the people involved in the data warehouse implementation. Identification of these roles helped the organization set up the project team, as well as identify the right kinds of skills needed to make the project successful.

Figure 3.6 shows another horizontal cut as the organization prepared to put a program plan together for a data warehouse implementation.

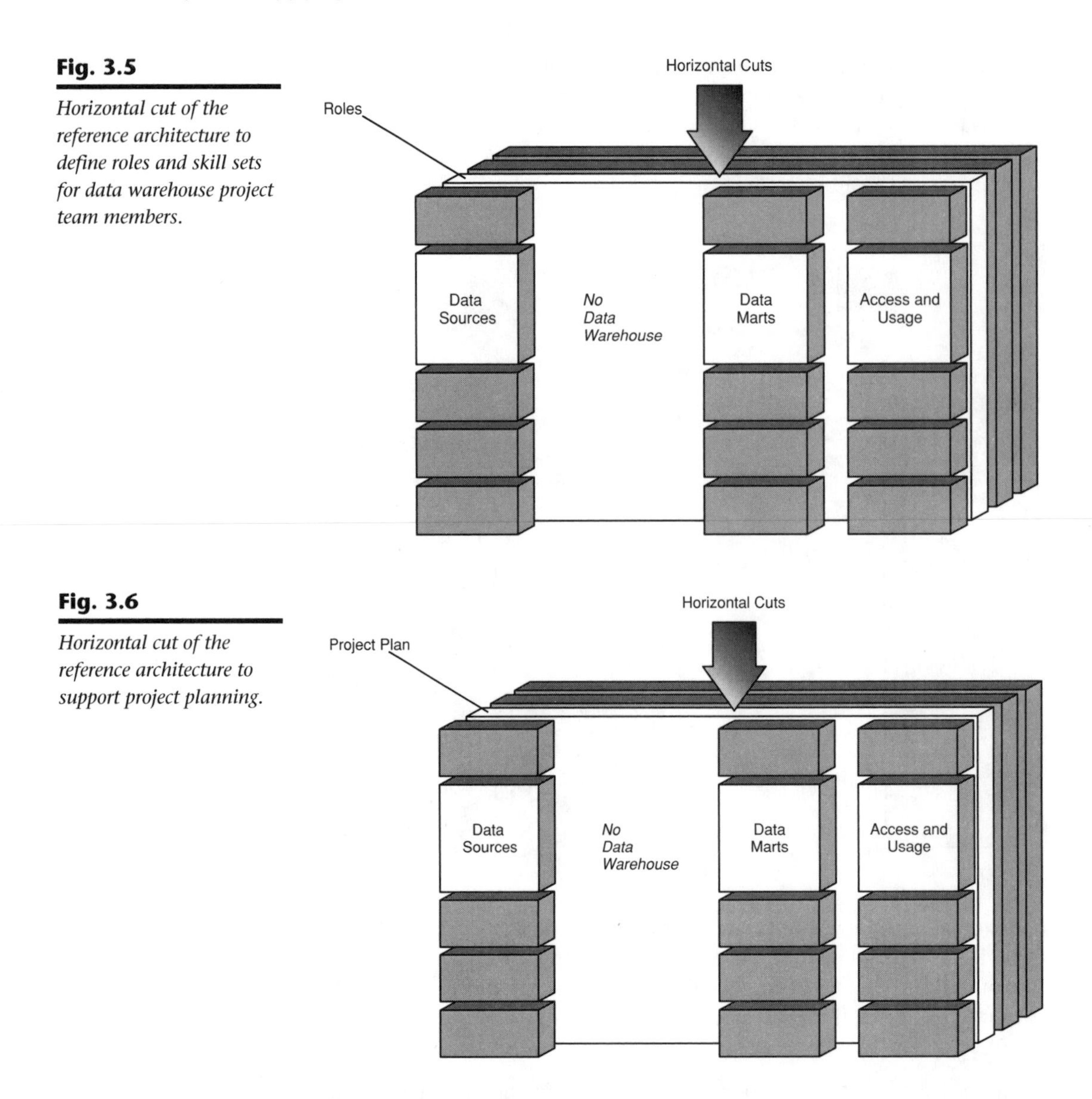


**Fig. 3.5**

*Horizontal cut of the reference architecture to define roles and skill sets for data warehouse project team members.*

**Fig. 3.6**

*Horizontal cut of the reference architecture to support project planning.*

In this example, the organization was able to quickly build an initial plan for implementation. The major tasks fell into the various architectural blocks. The minor tasks were determined by decomposing the reference architecture into more detail. Notice that the organization, during the vertical cut phase, had decided to do away with a centralized data warehouse. Instead, they decided to implement a set of departmental data marts to service the end users.

# An Abstract View of the Data Warehouse Reference Architecture

The following section builds on the concept of vertical and horizontal cuts and describes an abstract view of a data warehouse design that goes far beyond the reference architecture. In this view, the architecture of a data warehouse is elevated to the generalized architecture of any system. The process of design (in this case, the process of selecting a data warehouse implementation architecture) is the process of selecting a point in design space. The following section is primarily of interest to data warehouse architects.

## Design Spaces

Architecture planning has been studied in detail, as has been the activity of design representation. One of the most powerful views that has been proposed in design representation is that a specific design is a point in a design space. All design activity is therefore focused in reaching that point optimally.

To help us understand this concept a little better, think of a design space as being defined by many axes that we will call dimensions. Each one of these axes represents an aspect of the design. Examples of such aspects are target computer platforms, user groups, relational database systems, query and reporting tools, and scope of information that must be addressed by the data warehouse. Figure 3.7 illustrates a graphical view of a design space for these aspects.

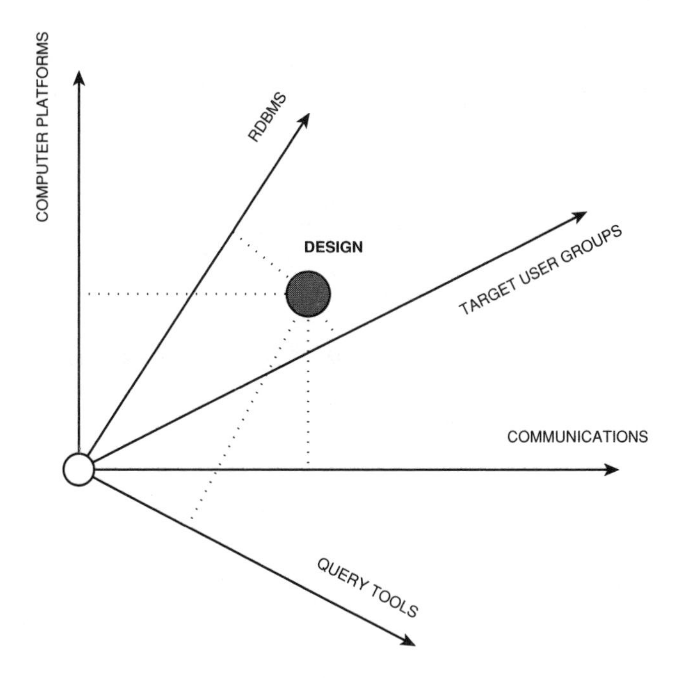


**Fig. 3.7**

*A design space consists of many axes of candidate choices. Design is a point inside design space.*

The process to arrive at an architecture for a specific implementation include the following steps:

1. Define the various architectural dimensions. The reference architecture is an excellent start. The blocks of the reference architecture all represent various dimensions of the design space. Since each of the blocks of the reference architecture is further subdivided into smaller blocks, these smaller blocks represent sub-dimensions of the main dimension.

   At this time, major simplifications can be obtained by deciding the overall strategies, such as client/server data warehouse, mainframe and terminal access, data marts only, or data warehouse only. The data warehouse and the operational store are the same or the data warehouse contains data that is copied from the operational store.

   Each of these strategies has implications on whether a dimension of the design space exists and the available set of viable choices for a dimension.

2. Specify the choices available along these dimensions. Choices can be drawn from the current set of investments and strategic directions or they can be candidates for purchase.

3. Select a specific choice for items along each dimension. Keep in mind that choices previously made will have to be consistent with succeeding choices. For example, if the choice of MVS/3090 has already been made for the computer platform, the choices of Informix and Sybase as RDBMS selections may not be available along the RDBMS dimension. In other words, earlier choices may impose restrictions on other choices down the road. It is therefore important to select those dimensions that are strategic (for example, computer platforms, database platforms, workstations, departments, and workgroups) earlier and leave some of the data warehouse information scope selections for later examination.

4. After all the choices have been made, the collection of choices made represents a candidate architecture for data warehouse implementation. This must be examined in detail to ensure that the choices are consistent with organizational directions and objectives and are also technologically compatible with each other.

## How the Reference Architecture Partitions Design Space

The reference architecture presented in Chapter 2, "A Framework for Understanding the Data Warehouse," is a method for partitioning the design space. The reference architecture is again shown in figure 3.8 for recapitulation.

Figure 3.9 shows how the reference architecture partitions the data warehouse design space.

Figure 3.9 is simply a different representation of the reference architecture. Each of the blocks and layers in the architecture represent a dimension of design for the data warehouse. As mentioned earlier, strategic decisions at this stage must be made to simplify the architecture building process. For example, if an organization has decided to only implement data marts, the data warehouse construction dimension does not need to be considered. At this level of the reference architecture, the design space partitioning is very "coarse grain." For each of the dimensions at this stage, we can draw a subspace that is defined by the dimension. The sub-dimensions that define the subspace are represented by the smaller blocks that are contained within the major blocks of the reference architecture. For example, the data warehouse construction dimension is further divided into sub-dimensions as shown in figure 3.10.

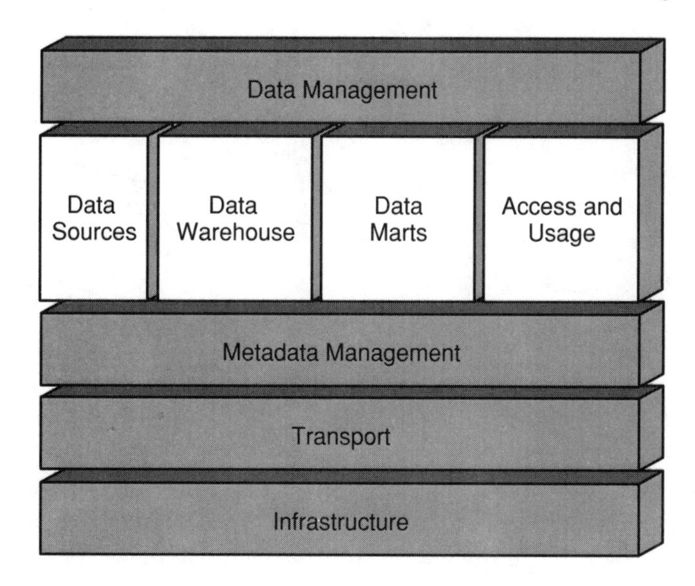


**Fig. 3.8**

*Data warehouse reference architecture.*

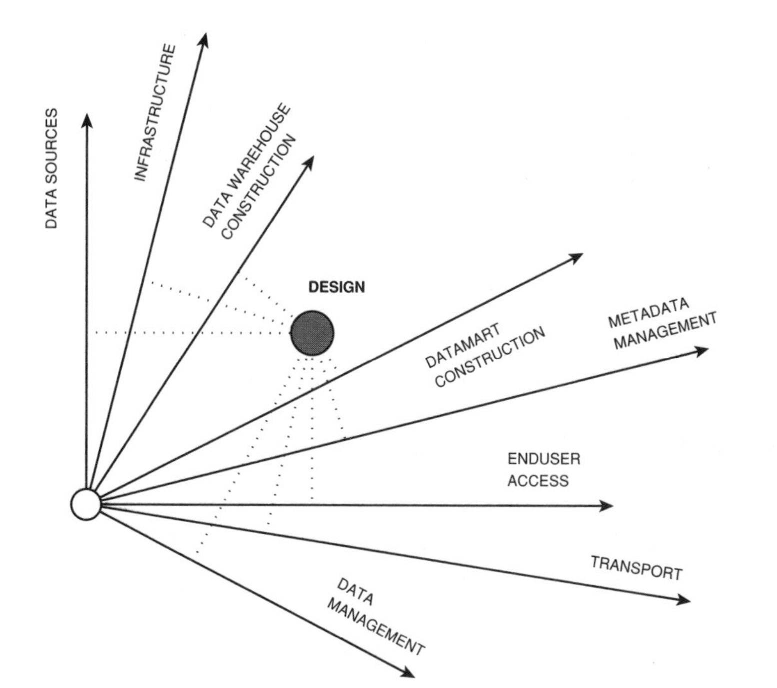


**Fig. 3.9**

*How the reference architecture partitions DW design space.*

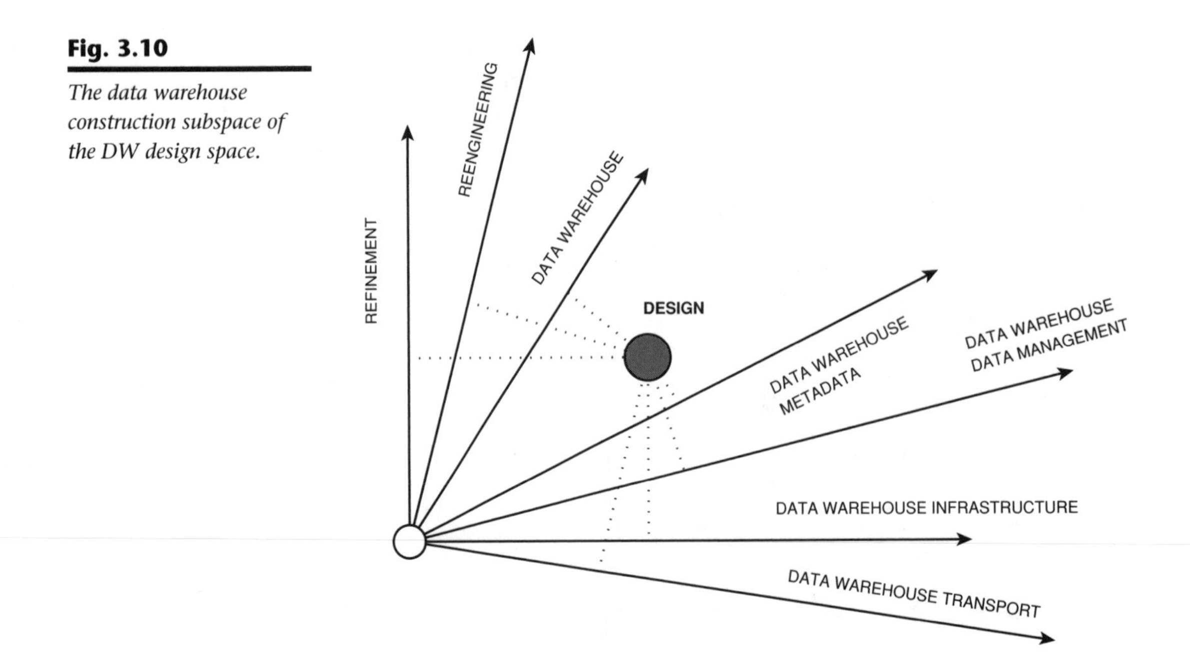


**Fig. 3.10**

*The data warehouse construction subspace of the DW design space.*

Figure 3.10 is simply a new way of representing a vertical slice through the reference architecture that isolates the Data Warehouse block of the architecture and its related Data Management, Metadata Management, Infrastructure, and Transport segments of the layers. Each of these items represents a decision point for design and are therefore represented as dimensions in figure 3.10.

Partitioning at this level allows for "finer grain" specifications of dimensions. Notice that the layers of the reference architecture (Metadata Management, Data Management, Infrastructure, and Transport) contribute dimensions to all the blocks (Data Sources, Data Warehouse, Data Mart, and End User Access).

We can carry out this decomposition process of dimensions into sub-dimensions further for each of the dimensions in figure 3.10. Figure 3.11 shows the sub-dimensions of the refinement dimension in figure 3.10. Figure 3.11 displays the various design choices that must be made for the refinement component of the Data Warehouse block.

# Using the Indica Data Warehouse Planner Tool

The Indica Data Warehouse Planner is a software tool supplied with this book that allows the user to graphically navigate through the various blocks of the data warehouse reference architecture and "drill" down hierarchically to expose finer levels of architectural detail. At the same time, the user can use the reference architecture as a classification schema and enter elements of his/her real world to map them against the reference architecture. The Data Warehouse Planner is a graphical tool that provides a list of categories under which users can collect information about their specific implementation of the data warehouse. The Planner can therefore be used as a data collection and data organization tool that allows data warehouse implementors and other stakeholders to perform various forms of analysis (see fig. 3.12).

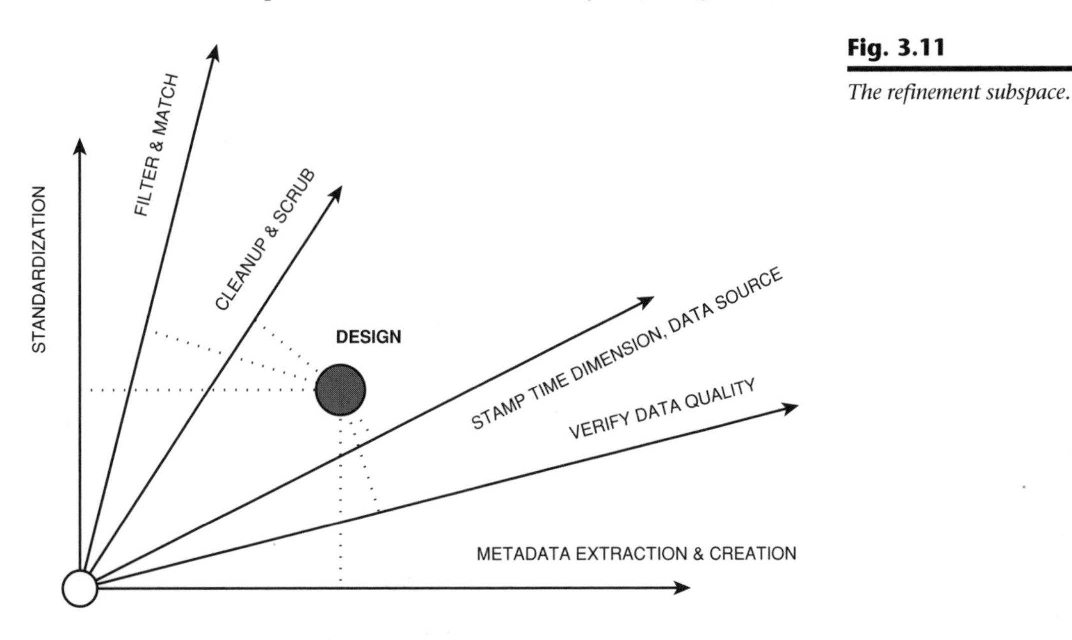


**Fig. 3.11**

*The refinement subspace.*

The Reference Knowledge Base, part of the Indica Data Warehouse Planner, is a base of information that contains architectural options available to the architect (see fig. 3.13). These options can either represent a base of existing hardware, software, and business systems or they can be built up as an industry reference of available vendor offerings. The Knowledge Base is organized in the same classification as the data warehouse reference architecture. The Knowledge Base contains the same blocks and layers as the data architecture. It also has two well-defined horizontal layers for storing and managing data warehouse software components and data warehouse functions. At the same time, the blocks and layers of the data warehouse reference architecture are broken down into one more level of decomposition.

## How is the Knowledge Base of the Planner Built?

There are many ways to do this. Examples of Knowledge Bases are provided with the software to provide a "quick start." Another way is to start with the Planner and use the entry screens to enter knowledge about the organization's data warehouse related environment and build up an evolving Knowledge Base. A variation of this method is to have multiple teams start the knowledge-gathering activity and bring it together by merging these knowledge bases to build a single corporate Knowledge Base.

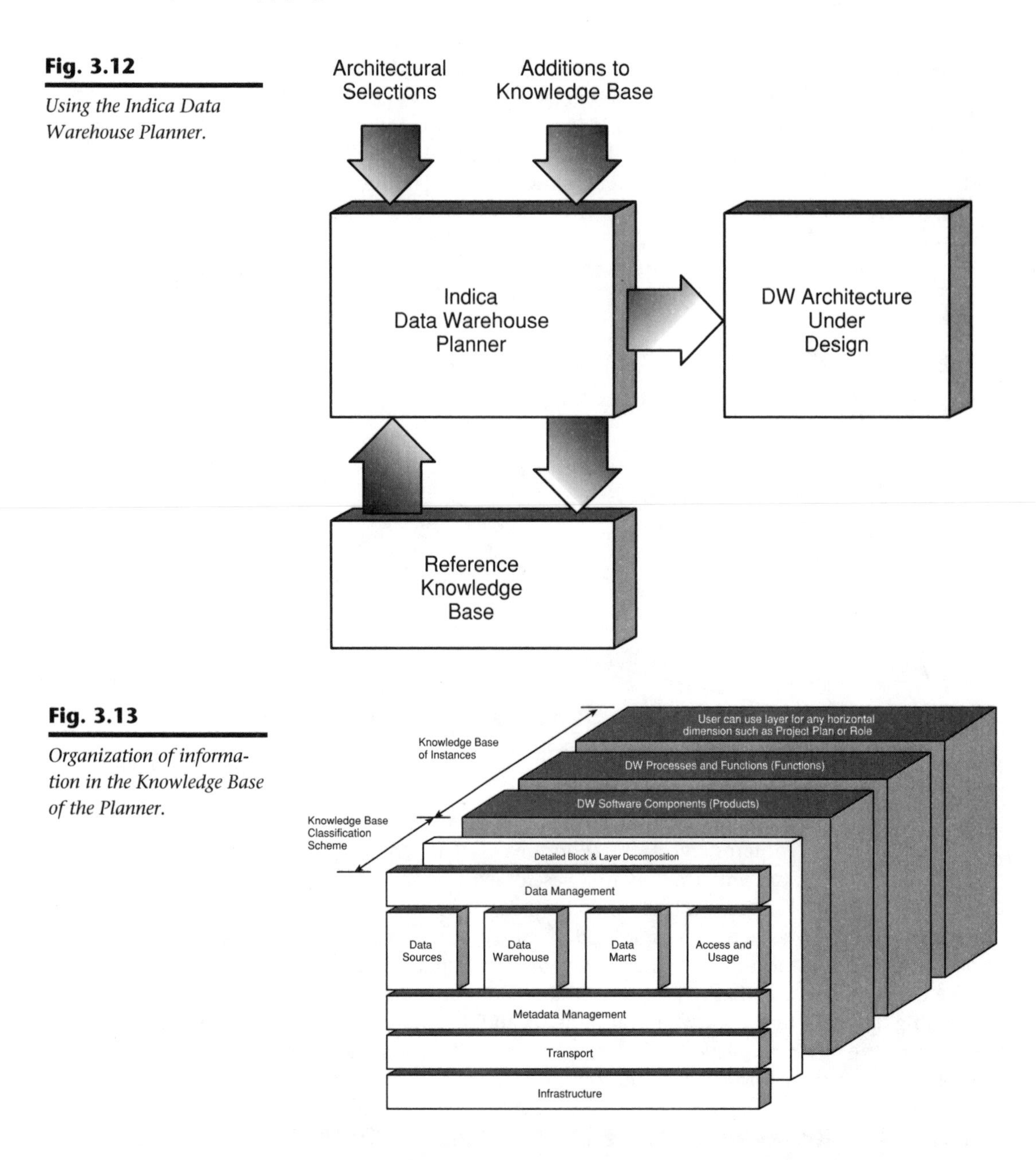


**Fig. 3.12**

*Using the Indica Data Warehouse Planner.*

**Fig. 3.13**

*Organization of information in the Knowledge Base of the Planner.*

## What Level of Architectural Detail Must be Used?

The Indica Data Warehouse Planner can be operated at the highest level of abstraction of the reference architecture. This level contains the major blocks and layers of the data warehouse reference architecture. This level is used when the information that is available is approximate and empirical, such as at the planning, project scope definition, and project cost estimation phases of a data warehouse project. Operating the Planner at this level is ideal for the following kinds of tasks:

- People and skills planning and baselining
- Vendor comparisons
- Risk assessments
- Platform and existing investment compatibility assessments

The next, more detailed, level of abstraction of the data warehouse is used when more precise information is available and must be used. This is typically used during the implementation phase of a data warehouse project. The Data Warehouse Planner must be operated at this level of detail for the following kinds of tasks:

- Project planning
- Detailed vendor evaluations
- Detailed risk assessments at the task level
- Development of a data warehouse implementation methodology

Figure 3.14 shows how different kinds of tasks can benefit from different levels of detail of the reference architecture.

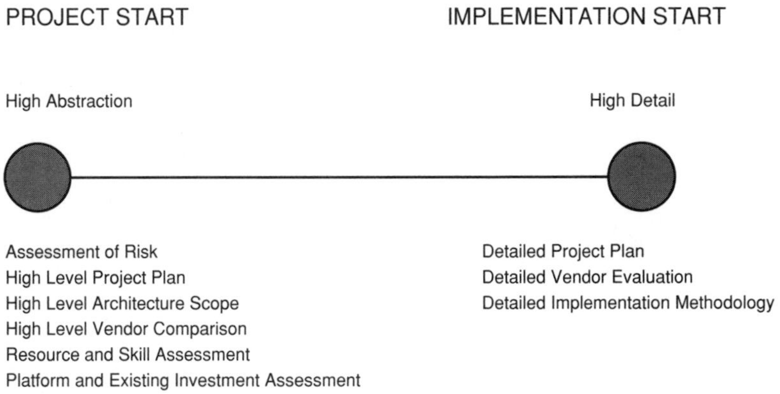

**Fig. 3.14**

*Using the two levels of abstraction for the right type of task.*

The following sections will describe how the capabilities of the Data Warehouse Planner can be harnessed to perform various tasks. Each of the examples use the following format:

- Business challenge.
- Issues.
- How to use the reference architecture (and Planner) to address the challenge. The examples used are provided in the CD-ROM accompanying this book. They are stored as architecture plan documents with the `.PLN` file extension.

# BUSINESS CHALLENGE: Data Warehouse Program/Project Planning and Scope Selection

High-level project planning is used at program inception when an organization is trying to understand broad scope and implementation issues and is trying to make decisions on architectural scope. Once the organization is committed to a data warehouse implementation program, more detailed planning is necessary to ensure that the project is successful (see fig 3.15).

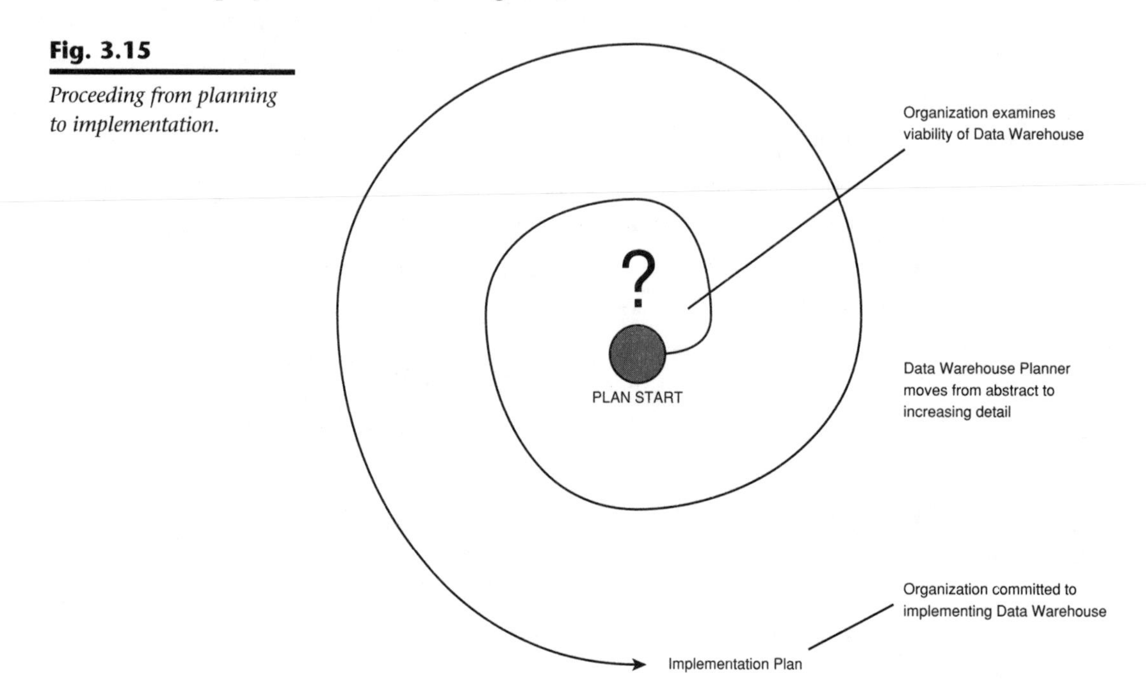


**Fig. 3.15**

*Proceeding from planning to implementation.*

## Issues

At the enterprise level, an organization may want to use the Planner to examine the following issues:

- Identifying all relevant data sources from inside and outside the organization that must service the data warehouse. The organization also wishes to leverage the data sources across multiple departments and business units. It also wishes to standardize the process of extraction, the platforms that perform the task, and the business rules that are used for transformations, summarizations, and aggregations.

- Defining a central corporate data warehouse that contains the master data warehouse and definitions of metadata and receives the data extracted from the data sources.
- Identifying multiple data marts that must support various business departments. The organization wants to reuse data warehouse components that perform identical operations on identical data as far as data warehouse management is concerned.
- Providing individual business units and departments the freedom to access the data marts using the access, query, and reporting tools they are already familiar with.
- Sharing a common infrastructure of communications, middleware, computing, and RDBMS processing platforms wherever possible.

**High Level Issues.** From the perspective of high-level project planning, the organization has the following needs:

- Decentralization of data mart development efforts. Resources and tasks must be coordinated to avoid replication and redundancy and the explosion of diverse platforms and processing.
- Centralized extraction and metadata management to ensure consistency, accuracy, availability, and control.
- Gathering requirements for query and analysis from various departments and business units.
- Centralized requirements analysis to understand commonality and reuse potential.
- Centralized dimension analysis for determining the structuring of multidimensional databases and summarization objectives.
- Centralized development of logical models for the data warehouse. Decentralized development of data mart logical models after the centralized logical model is complete. The centralized logical model is developed in an evolutionary manner based on analysis of hierarchy of information needs.

**Detailed Issues.** The following are detailed issues:

- How to develop a work breakdown structure for data warehouse implementation that has the major tasks and detailed breakdowns of these tasks into subtasks.
- How to partition tasks based on common skills and group them together.
- How to build a reasonable schedule for the project.
- How to identify the various kinds of resources that are required for successful implementation and deployment.

## Planner Reference Knowledge Base

An example Reference Knowledge Base that was built is shown in Table 3.1.

**Note**

Codes such as FDTA and FDSR are used internally by the Indica Data Warehouse Planner to organize information. A Prefix of *F* indicates a function; *P* indicates a product. The codes DTA, DSR, DWH, DMR, SCC, INF, MDM, and TRN represent the reference architecture blocks and layers. Any prefix used before an architectural item such as "Role" or "Plan" indicates the use of the Planner to model dimensions other than products and functions. The digits that appear after the code reflect the level of abstraction in the architecture.

**Table 3.1 Knowledge Base Example—Roles and Skills Needed**

| Architecture Name | High Level Plan |
|---|---|
| **Data Sources** | |
| FDSR00 | Plan–Financial System Data Extraction |
| FDSR00 | Role–Financial System Database Administrator |
| FDSR00 | Role–Corporate Data Administrator |
| **Data Mart** | |
| FDMR00 | Plan–Data Mart Design, Implementation, and Launch |
| FDMR00 | Role–MarketData Data Administrator |
| FDMR00 | Role–MarketData Database Administrator |
| FDMR00 | Plan–Marketing and Sales Data Mart |
| FDMR00 | Departmental Data Mart for Marketing |
| FDMR00 | Condition Data for Data Mart |
| **Access and Usage** | |
| FACC00 | Plan–Marketing Department User Training |
| FACC00 | Plan–Sales Department User Training |
| FACC00 | Data Mining Capability |
| FACC00 | Decision Support Systems |
| **Metadata Management** | |
| FMDM00 | Plan–Data Mart Data Administration |
| FMDM00 | Plan–Data Mart Log, Archive, Refresh |
| FMDM00 | Role–Data Mart Database Administrator |
| FMDM00 | Manage Data Mart Metadata |

| Architecture Name | High Level Plan |
|---|---|
| **Transport** | |
| FTRN00 | Role–Corporate Telecommunications Operations Network Facilities Administrator |
| **Infrastructure** | |
| FINF00 | Role–Data Operations Computer Administration Personnel |
| FINF00 | Role–Data Operations Facilities Management Personnel |
| FINF00 | Role–Data Mart Facilities Manager |
| FINF00 | MarketData Database |
| **Transport** | |
| FTRN0101 | Transfer data to Data Mart |
| FTRN0104 | Need Network Security Mechanism |



The Planner can also be used to explore more detail as shown in Table 3.2.

**Table 3.2 Knowledge Base Example—Functions**

| Architecture Name | Major Functions |
|---|---|
| **Access and Usage** | |
| FACC00 | Deliver Data to Workstations for Analysis |
| FACC00 | Query and Reports of Sales by Geography |
| FACC00 | Summary Reports by Territory and Organization |
| **Data Management** | |
| FDTA00 | Data Refreshment and Synchronization (Data Mart) |
| FDTA00 | Data Security and Authorization (Data Mart) |
| FDTA00 | Data Archive Restore and Purge Systems (Data Mart) |
| **Transport** | |
| FTRN00 | Data Mart LAN System |
| **Infrastructure** | |
| FINF00 | Configuration Managers |
| FINF00 | Storage Managers |
| FINF00 | Security Managers |

(continues)

**Table 3.2 Continued**

| Architecture Name | Major Functions |
|---|---|
| **Infrastructure** | |
| FINF00 | Software Distribution Managers |
| FINF00 | License Managers |
| FINF00 | Print Managers |
| FINF00 | Performance Monitors |
| FINF00 | Problem Managers |
| FINF00 | Administrative Managers |
| FINF00 | Capacity Analyzers and Managers |
| **Data Mart** | |
| FDMR00 | Role–End User Training Curriculum Development |
| FDMR00 | Role–Data Conditioning Manager |
| FDMR0101 | Filter and Match |
| FDMR0102 | Integrate and Partition |
| FDMR0103 | Summarize and aggregate |
| FDMR0104 | Precalculate and derive |
| FDMR0105 | Stamp: Time Dimension and Data Source |
| FDMR0106 | Metadata Extraction and Creation |
| FDMR0107 | Other Re-engineering and Refinement Tasks |
| FDMR0201 | Modeling–Building Data Mart Models |
| FDMR0201 | Data Modeling for the Data Mart |
| FDMR0201 | Data Flow Modeling for Data Mart Workflow |
| FDMR0202 | Summarization by Quarter |
| FDMR0202 | Summarization by Month |
| FDMR0202 | Summarization by Week |
| FDMR0202 | Summarization by Product Line |
| FDMR0202 | Summarization by Business Unit |
| FDMR0202 | Summarization by Geographic Region |
| FDMR0202 | Summarization by Sales Region |
| FDMR0203 | Aggregation by Product Family |
| FDMR0203 | Aggregation by Department |
| FDMR0204 | Reconcile and Validate |

| Architecture Name | Major Functions |
|---|---|
| **Data Mart** | |
| FDMR0205 | Build Architected Queries |
| FDMR0205 | Aggregation by ZIP Code for Volume of Sales |
| FDMR0206 | Create Glossary |
| FDMR0207 | Select Metadata Browse and Navigation Tools |
| FDMR0208 | Other Data Mart Tasks |
| **Access and Usage** | |
| FACC00 | Direct Data Mart Access |
| FACC00 | Select and Transform Data Mart Data to Multidimensional Structure |
| **Data Management** | |
| FDTA00 | Weekly Update of Data Mart from Field Sales BAS |
| FDTA00 | Monthly Update of Data Mart from A/R System |
| **Metadata Management** | |
| FMDM00 | Role–Data Mart Metadata Manager |
| FMDM00 | Extract and Manage Summary Reports List |
| FMDM00 | Capture Multidimensional DBMS Information and Reports |

# BUSINESS CHALLENGE: Building a Data Warehouse that Incorporates Existing Investments

Most organizations have undergone the evolution of Information Technology by the time they decide to implement the data warehouse. They will, in general, have already automated their business processes and collected large volumes of operational data. Most will generally be using mainframe-based and client/server software applications to collect, organize, and administer this data. They already have, in place, communications systems that transfer data between databases and applications, applications and applications, and databases and databases.

Most organizations would also have developed standards for procuring technology to ensure that incoming technology is compatible and works well with existing mission critical systems.

The investments in this infrastructure run into several millions of dollars, as is the investment in human resources for running and managing them. At the same time, the prospect of adding new data warehouse functions to existing processing and storage capacity is a daunting task. This is because of the potential for new data warehouse applications causing processing and storage bottlenecks with current mission critical applications that are supporting the daily existence of the enterprise.

## Issues

The following are detailed issues:

- How to accommodate platforms and equipment that are currently in operation into the data warehouse solution. Examples of such items include the following:
    - Database management systems that provide the data needed by the warehouse. These are operational systems that are currently managing operational (OLTP) data and will not change in the near future.
    - Selections of RDBMS platform vendors that the organization has already standardized.
    - Selections of server computer platforms that the organization has already standardized.
    - Selections of workstations that will support end users people are currently using or are planned for the near future.
    - Network and communications systems that are already connecting user workstations, servers and host mainframes.
    - Selections of host mainframes that the organization has standardized and will continue to use into the near future.
- How to assess the degree of incompatibility (and therefore the additional expense and impact) of proposed data warehouse component acquisitions with existing platforms and equipment.
- How to resolve conflicting requirements of proposed data warehouse acquisitions with existing platforms and equipment.

## Planner Reference Knowledge Base

Table 3.3 shows how a hypothetical organization baselined (listed) existing investments that were potentially reusable in the proposed data warehouse architecture.

**Table 3.3 Knowledge Base Example—Existing Investments**

| Architecture Name | Corporate Financial Systems |
|---|---|
| **Data Source Functions** | |
| FDSR0101 | Corporate Order Entry System |
| FDSR0101 | Corporate Accounts Receivable |

| Architecture Name | Corporate Financial Systems |
|---|---|
| **Data Source Functions** | |
| FDSR0104 | External–D&B Credit Ratings Database |
| FDSR0105 | Corporate Data Dictionary on DB2/MVS |
| FDSR0105 | Access Database–D&B Credit Ratings Database Metadata |
| **Data Management Functions** | |
| FDTA00 | A/R–Extraction from DB2/MVS RDBMS |
| FDTA00 | Order Entry System–Extraction from IMS Database |
| FDTA00 | DB2/MVS–Utilities for Log, Backup, Restore |
| FDTA00 | DB2/MVS–Performance Monitor |
| FDTA00 | DB2/MVS–Security and Access Control |
| FDTA00 | DB2/MVS–Archive and Restore |
| FDTA00 | DB2/MVS–Change Management |
| **Metadata Management Functions** | |
| FMDM00 | A/R–DB2/MVS Catalog for Metadata |
| FMDM00 | Order Entry System–IMS Metadata from DB/DC System |
| **Metadata Management Products** | |
| PMDM00 | DB2/MVS Catalog Manager–Corporate Data Dictionary |
| PMDM00 | DB2/MVS Catalog Manager–DB2/MVS metadata |
| PMDM00 | DB/DC System–IMS metadata |
| **Transport Functions** | |
| FTRN00 | Private WAN (SNA) |
| FTRN00 | Local Area Networks for Departments |
| **Transport Products** | |
| PTRN00 | IBM DRDA over SNA (APPC/LU6.2) |
| PTRN00 | OS/2 LAN Server |
| PTRN00 | OS/2 Warp–Server OS |
| PTRN00 | Token Ring for Local Area Networks in Departments |
| PTRN00 | SNA (Private WAN) |

(continues)

**Table 3.3 Continued**

| Architecture Name | Corporate Financial Systems |
|---|---|
| **Infrastructure Functions** | |
| FINF00 | A/R–Relational Database |
| FINF00 | DCE security of DB2/MVS |
| FINF00 | Order Entry System–Hierarchical Database |
| FINF00 | Data Center Processing (System/390 with MVS) |
| FINF00 | Enterprise-wide Query Capability |
| FINF00 | PC Workstations for A/R System Access |
| FINF00 | IBM 3270-type terminals for A/R and Order Entry System |
| **Infrastructure Products** | |
| PINF00 | IBM DB2/MVS |
| PINF00 | IBM IMS |
| PINF00 | IBM System/390 with MVS |
| PINF00 | ESCON channels |
| PINF00 | IBM OS/2 LAN Server with OS/2 Warp |
| PINF00 | Workstations–IBM PCs with OS/2 Warp |
| PINF00 | Workstations–IBM PCs with OS/2 2.1 |
| PINF00 | Workstations–IBM PCs with Windows 3.1 |
| PINF00 | Workstations–IBM 3270-type terminals |
| PINF00 | Access Database (D&B Credit Ratings Database Metadata) |

## BUSINESS CHALLENGE: Data Warehouse Project Team Selection and Roles of Team Members

Chapter 2 discussed the complexity of building a data warehouse. The complexity is due to the demand for a broad range of specialized skills. An organization that is planning to implement and deploy data warehouse technology must be equipped with the right people. Often, identifying which of these skills is needed, and when, is a business challenge. Because of the specialized skills and the expense of procuring them, it often becomes necessary to use a few specialized people for a brief interval on contract. On the other hand, certain specialized skills are needed during the deployment phase of the data warehouse on a continual basis.

## Issues

The following are detailed issues:

- What types of skills are required for data warehouse implementation?
- What existing people resources can we use on the project?
- What are the durations for which various skills are required during the course of the project?
- Which skills are required only during the development phase and are not required during the deployment phase of the warehouse?

## Planner Reference Knowledge Base

Table 3.4 provides an example of a special skills and human resource assessment that was performed by a hypothetical organization.

**Table 3.4 Knowledge Base Example—Development and Deployment Roles**

| Architecture Name | Data Warehouse Roles |
|---|---|
| **Data Management** | |
| FDTA00 | Role–Data Operations Application Programmers |
| FDTA00 | Role–Data Operations Systems and Facility Managers |
| **Data Sources** | |
| FDSR00 | Role–Financial System Database Administrator |
| **Data Warehouse** | |
| FDWH00 | Role–Corporate Database Administrator |
| FDWH00 | Role–Corporate Warehouse Administrator |
| FDWH00 | Role–Contractor's Application Programmers |
| **Data Mart** | |
| FDMR00 | Role–MarketData Data Administrator |
| FDMR00 | Role–MarketData Database Administrator |
| FDMR00 | Role–Marketing Department IS Support Person |
| **Access and Usage** | |
| FACC00 | Role–Marketing Department IS User |
| FACC00 | Role–Sales Department IS User |

(continues)

**Table 3.4 Continued**

| Architecture Name | Data Warehouse Roles |
|---|---|
| **Metadata Management** | |
| FMDM00 | Role–Marketing Department Data Administrator |
| FMDM00 | Role–Corporate Data Administrator as Liaison |
| FMDM00 | Role–Marketing Department Database Administrator |
| **Transport** | |
| FTRN00 | Role–Corporate Telecommunications Operations Network Specialist |
| FTRN00 | Role–Corporate Telecommunications Operations Network Facilities Administrator |
| **Infrastructure** | |
| FINF00 | Role–Data Operations Computer Administration Personnel |
| FINF00 | Role–Data Operations Facilities Management Personnel |
| FINF00 | Role–Data Operations Processor and Storage Administration and Management |
| FINF00 | Role–Data Operations Facilities Management |

# BUSINESS CHALLENGE: Merging Departmental and Corporate Data Warehouse Architectures

In very large organizations, often there are many IT teams in different business units engaged in the same data warehouse development activity. These teams are building distinctly different data marts, or there is duplicated effort towards a corporate data warehouse. Often these teams support different business objectives for different business units. Often, the systems that are built by these teams are similar in architecture because of a single set of common corporate guidelines and standards.

Over time, it becomes desirable to integrate these diverse efforts. The integration has many business benefits that are obvious:

- Consolidation of customer information
- Consolidation of product information
- Consolidation of suppliers
- Consistency of business processes
- Uniformity of customer interfaces

- Portfolio analysis of products and services
- Cost analysis, revenue analysis, and margin analysis

The business challenge: How can the organization merge these parallel efforts?

## Issues

The following are detailed issues:

- What are the issues with merging architectures?
- What are the issues of merging data and information?
- What are metadata management issues?
- What are data management issues?
- What are transport related issues?
- What are infrastructure related issues?
- What are extraction related issues?

## Planner Reference Knowledge Base

An example of a data mart architecture that was planned by a departmental team is shown in Table 3.5.

**Table 3.5 Knowledge Base Example—Components**

| Architecture Name | Data Mart |
|---|---|
| **Data Source Functions** | |
| FDSR00 | Order Entry System |
| FDSR00 | A/R |
| **Data Source Products** | |
| PDSR00 | Extractor–IBM DataRefresher |
| PDSR00 | Extractor for DB2–IBM DpropR |
| PDSR00 | Extractor for IMS–IBM DpropNR |
| **Data Mart Functions** | |
| FDMR00 | Marketing and Sales Data Mart |
| **Data Mart Products** | |
| PDMR00 | IBM Visual Warehouse |

(continues)

**Table 3.5 Continued**

| Architecture Name | Data Mart |
|---|---|
| **Access and Usage Functions** | |
| FACC00 | Direct Data Mart Access |
| FACC00 | Transform to Multidimensional Structure |
| FACC00 | Create Local Store |
| FACC00 | Data Analysis and DSS |
| **Access and Usage Products** | |
| PACC00 | IBM Visualizer |
| PACC00 | IBM QMF |
| **Data Management Functions** | |
| FDTA00 | A/R–Extraction from DB2 |
| FDTA00 | Order Entry System–Extraction from IMS |
| FDTA00 | DB2's Utilities for Log, Backup, Restore |
| FDTA00 | DB2's Performance Monitor |
| FDTA00 | DB2's access control |
| **Data Management Products** | |
| PDTA00 | Data Refresher–IBM DataRefresher |
| PDTA00 | Data Update for DB2–IBM DpropR |
| PDTA00 | Data Update for IMS- IBM DpropNR |
| **Metadata Management Products** | |
| FMDM00 | Need to extract and manage metadata |
| **Metadata Management Functions** | |
| PMDM00 | IBM DataGuide/2 |
| **Transport Functions** | |
| FTRN00 | Transfer data to data mart |
| FTRN00 | Need network security mechanism |
| FTRN00 | SNA |
| **Transport Products** | |
| PTRN00 | IBM DataHub |
| PTRN00 | IBM DRDA over SNA (APPC/LU6.2) |

| Architecture Name | Data Mart |
|---|---|
| **Transport Products** | |
| PTRN00 | Data Replication for DB2–DpropR |
| PTRN00 | Data Replication for IMS–DpropNR |
| PTRN00 | OS/2 LAN Server |
| PTRN00 | Token Ring |
| PTRN00 | SNA on private WAN |
| **Infrastructure Functions** | |
| FINF00 | DB2 (A/R) |
| FINF00 | DCE security of DB2 |
| FINF00 | IMS (Order Entry System) |
| FINF00 | System/390 with MVS |
| FINF00 | ESCON channels |
| **Infrastructure Products** | |
| PINF00 | IBM DB2 |
| PINF00 | IBM IMS |
| PINF00 | IBM System/390 with MVS |
| PINF00 | Workstations–IBM PCs with OS/2 |
| PINF00 | Workstations–IBM 3270-type terminals |

An additional business challenge arose when the group planning the data mart architecture above merged with the Field Sales organization—another corporation's business unit that had its own data warehouse with the architecture described in Table 3.6.

**Table 3.6 Components of the Data Warehouse of a Candidate Merger Organization**

| Architecture Name | Field Sales BAS |
|---|---|
| **Data Management Functions** | |
| FDTA00 | Field Sales BAS–Extraction from Oracle RDBMS |
| FDTA00 | OpenVision–Utilities for RDBMS Log, Backup, Restore |
| FDTA00 | Platinum Technology–Oracle RDBMS Performance Monitor |
| FDTA00 | Oracle–RDBMS Access Control |

(continues)

**Table 3.6 Continued**

| Architecture Name | Field Sales BAS |
|---|---|
| **Data Source Functions** | |
| FDSR0101 | Field Sales Branch Automation System |
| FDSR0102 | Archived Files–Sales History |
| **Data Source Products** | |
| PDTA00 | Oracle RDBMS Utilities |
| **Transport Functions** | |
| FTRN00 | Field Sales BAS LAN |
| **Transport Products** | |
| PTRN00 | Solaris with SunNet |
| PTRN00 | TCP/IP of Field Sales BAS |
| PTRN00 | Oracle SQL*NET |
| **Infrastructure Functions** | |
| FINF00 | Field Sales BAS RDBMS (Oracle) |
| FINF00 | Field Sales BAS Processor (SUN SPARC and Solaris) |
| FINF00 | BAS PC based Workstations for Administration |
| FINF00 | BAS UNIX Workstations for Sales Analysis |
| **Infrastructure Products** | |
| PINF00 | Oracle RDBMS (Solaris Version) |
| PINF00 | SUN SPARC Server with Solaris |
| PINF00 | BAS Workstations–Compaq PCs with Windows 3.1 |
| PINF00 | BAS Workstations–SUN SPARC |
| PINF00 | BAS Workstations with Oracle SQL*NET |
| **Metadata Management** | |
| PMDM00 | Oracle Data Administration System |

As one can clearly see, by contrasting the data warehouse architecture of the proposed merger against the corporate architecture presented in the first example, the acquisition and merger of an organization with a different architectural strategy can have severe impact on the overall organization. The Planner allows IT architects to plan and manage architectural mismatches.

# Summary

This chapter has concentrated on using the data warehouse reference architecture presented in Chapter 2 to analyze and resolve various issues of data warehouse planning and implementation (the Indica Data Warehouse Planner supplied with this book was used as a software tool to support planning activities):

- The two major methods of partitioning the reference architecture were described. The vertical cut partitions the architecture into blocks and segments of layers. The horizontal cut partitions the entire reference architecture (blocks and layers) into the many dimensions (project plan, people, skills) required to implement the data warehouse.
- The Indica Data Warehouse Planner uses a Reference Knowledge Base of information. This information is used to characterize the environment in which the data warehouse will be implemented. The Knowledge Base has two levels of classification: high level and detail level. Knowledge Bases can either be built up from existing environmental information or from proposals for procurement.
- The process of creating a data warehouse architecture is the process of selecting compatible items from the Planner's Knowledge Base.
- Various business challenges were discussed along with issues they bring out. Methods for using the reference architecture to address these challenges were also discussed.

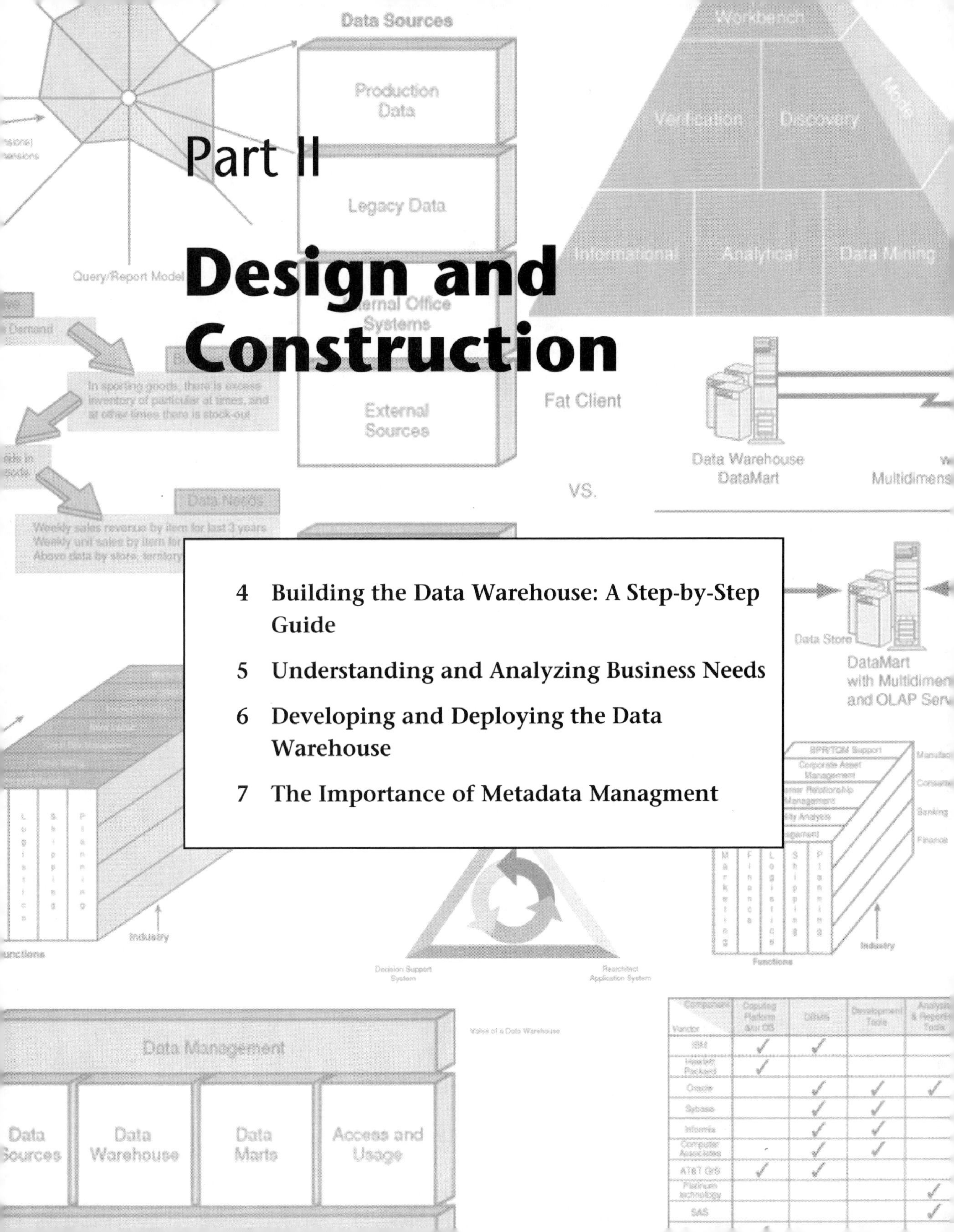


# Part II

# Design and Construction

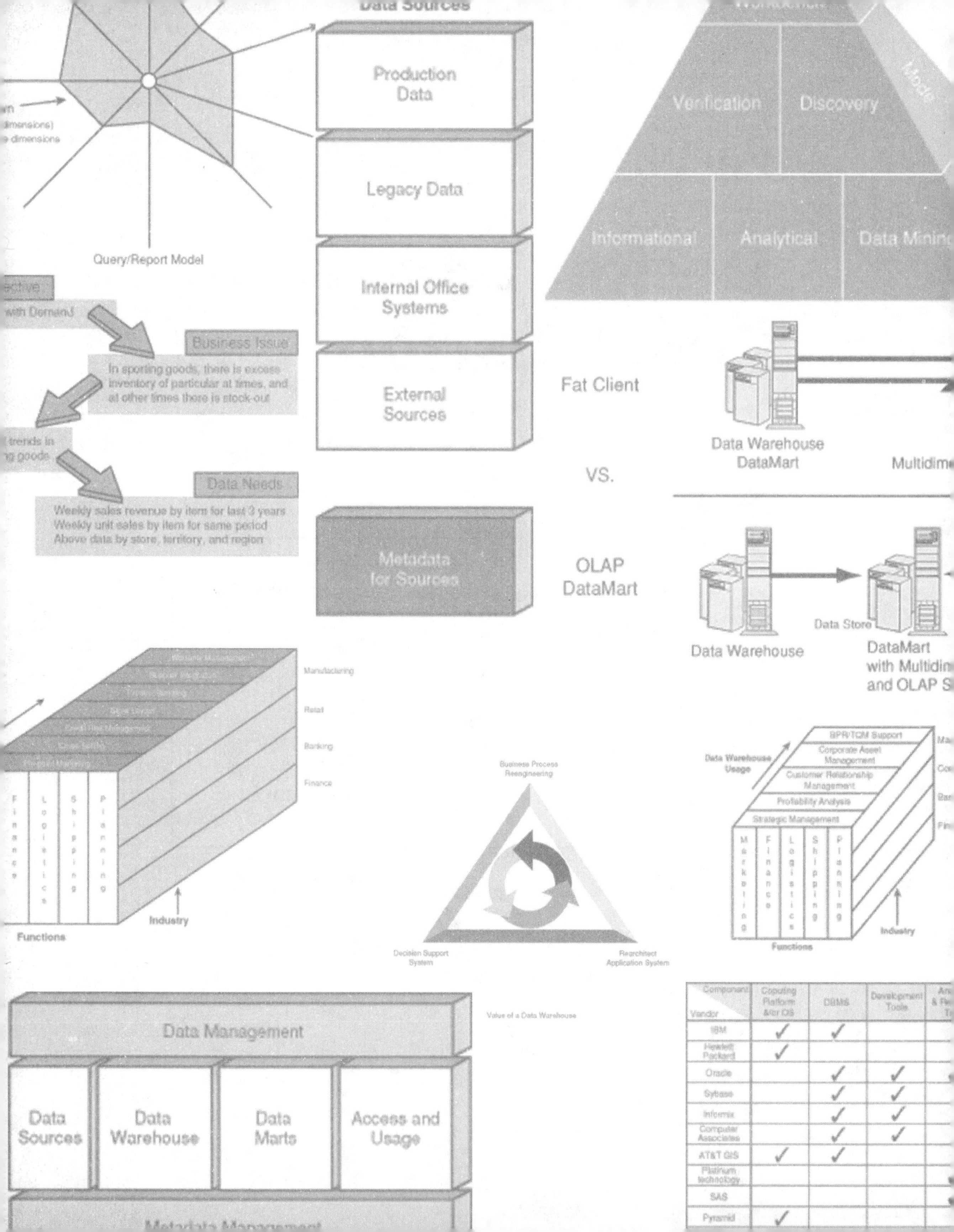

Query/Report Model
Business Issue
In sporting goods, there is excess inventory of particular at times, and at other times there is stock-out
Data Needs
Weekly sales revenue by item for last 3 years
Weekly unit sales by item for same period
Above data by store, territory, and region
Production Data
Legacy Data
Internal Office Systems
External Sources
Metadata for Sources
Verification
Discovery
Informational
Analytical
Fat Client
VS.
OLAP DataMart
Data Warehouse DataMart
Data Warehouse
Data Store
Manufacturing
Retail
Banking
Finance
Industry
Functions
Business Process Reengineering
Decision Support System
Rearchitect Application System
Value of a Data Warehouse
Data Warehouse Usage
BPR/TQM Support
Corporate Asset Management
Customer Relationship Management
Profitability Analysis
Strategic Management
Data Management
Data Sources
Data Warehouse
Data Marts
Access and Usage
Component
Vendor
Computing Platform &/or OS
DBMS
Development Tools
IBM
Hewlett Packard
Oracle
Sybase
Informix
Computer Associates
AT&T GIS
Platinum technology
SAS
Pyramid

CHAPTER 4

# Building the Data Warehouse: A Step-by-Step Guide

Chapter 2 introduced you to the concept of a reference architecture. The reference architecture was used to break down the complexity of the data warehouse into simpler, more understandable elements. In Chapter 3, you learned how the reference architecture could aid a variety of data warehouse planning tasks. This chapter presents a step-by-step approach to building the data warehouse. This chapter also addresses the up-front issues before you get to the technical implementation.

## The Development Lifecycle

The data warehouse follows the same development lifecycle as all software development. The lifecycle phases are the same, as is the sequence of lifecycle phases. Figure 4.1 shows the classic software development lifecycle.

### Planning

Figure 4.2 shows the steps that must be followed for implementing the planning phase of the data warehouse system. Some of the steps in figure 4.2 can be followed simultaneously (in parallel), which shortens the duration of this phase.

Each step defined is discussed in further detail in the following sections.

**Select the Implementation Strategy.** One of the most important first steps is to decide on the overall implementation strategy. This decision has a great deal to do with the culture of the organization and is based on how tasks are accomplished within the organization. The following implementation strategies have been popular:

- The top down approach
- The bottom up approach
- A combination of top down and bottom up

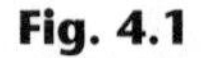
**Fig. 4.1**

*The software development lifecycle used for data warehouse.*

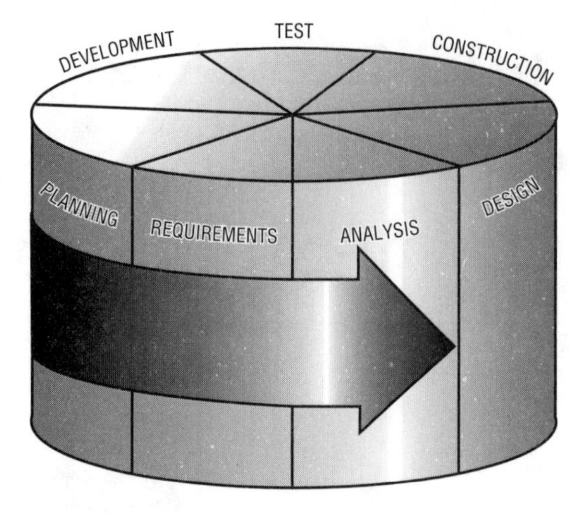

**Fig. 4.2**

*These steps show the planning needed for the data warehouse system.*

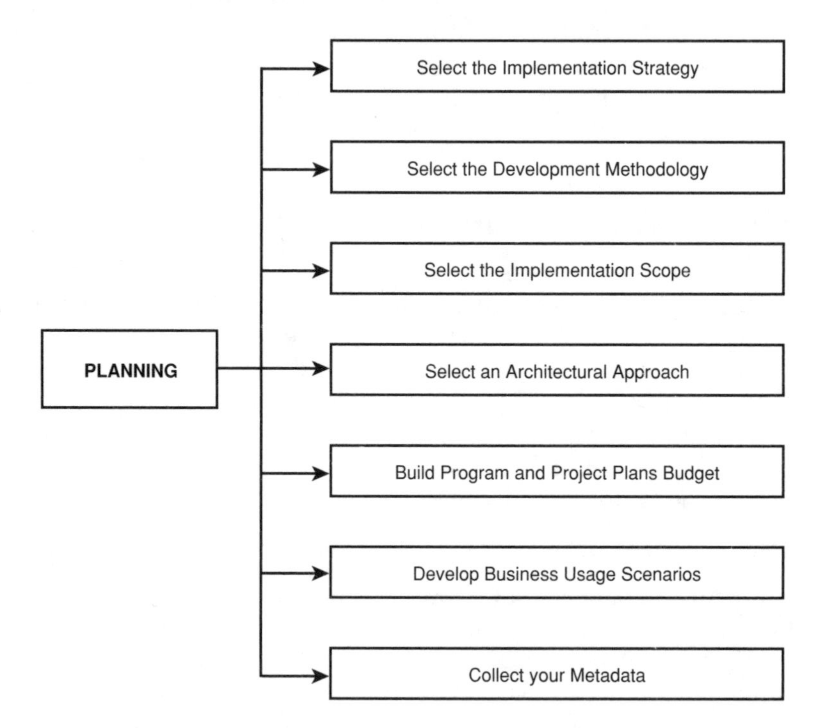


You should evaluate each approach and determine which approach is appropriate at which phase of the technology maturity cycle (see fig. 4.3).

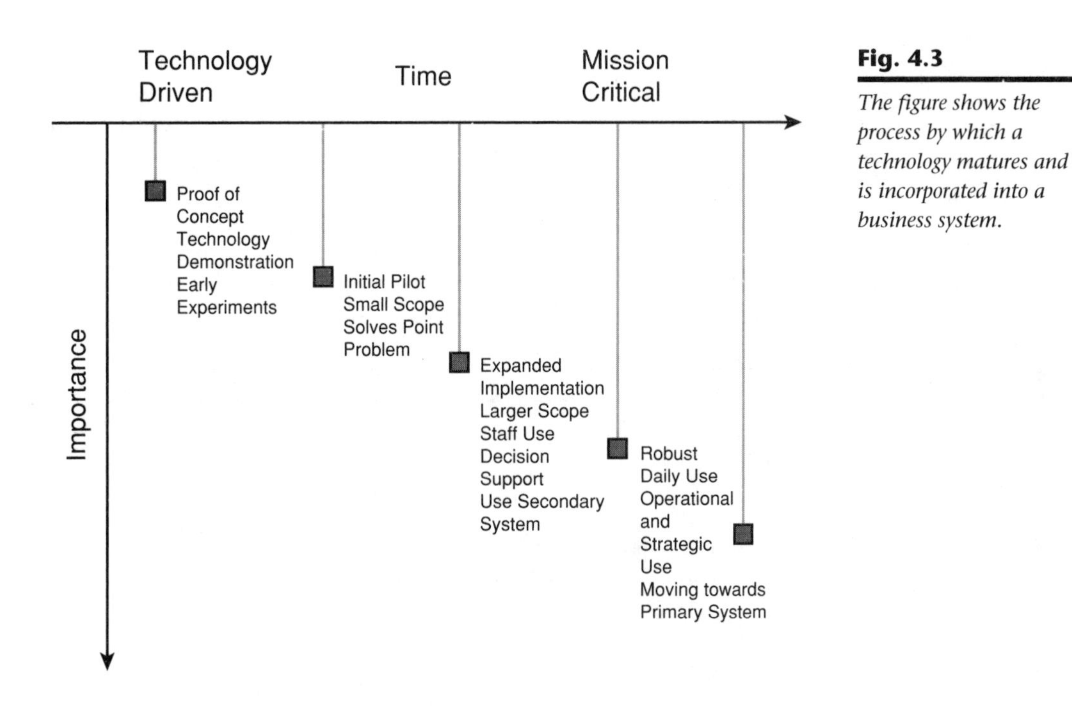


**Fig. 4.3**

*The figure shows the process by which a technology matures and is incorporated into a business system.*

Figure 4.4 shows how each of the three implementation approaches fit against the various drivers.

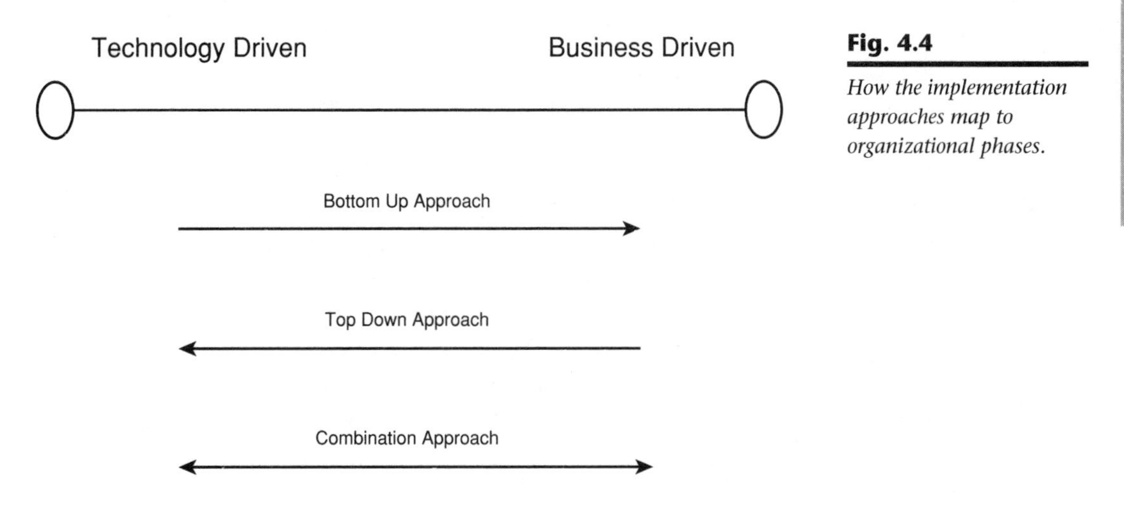


**Fig. 4.4**

*How the implementation approaches map to organizational phases.*



***Top Down Approach.*** In this approach, the business requirements to be met by the proposed data warehouse solution are identified first. These are the primary drivers for the implementation of the data warehouse. Often, this is a difficult task because, as mentioned previously, a data warehouse is often a capability rather than a feature (the data warehouse holds information and organizes this information in a manner suitable for external tools to display and manipulate the information). Therefore, the end user cannot exploit the capability built into the data warehouse without external tools that harness this capability. As a result, it is difficult to formulate the scope of the capability, except in broad business terms such as "The data warehouse will contain information on customers, suppliers, markets, and products." The scope formulation (and, therefore, the requirements formulation) is specified as data boundaries that define the territory of the data warehouse. Figure 4.5 shows the pros and cons of using the top-down approach to data warehouse implementation.

**Fig. 4.5**

*This example shows the pros and cons of the top down approach.*

| Pros | Cons |
|---|---|
| Business Requirements clearly delineate the boundaries of the Warehouse implementation and can therefore be a very cost effective and focused way of implementing the Data Warehouse solution. | Opportunities sometimes lie outside the current Business horizon. Missed opportunities can result from too much focus. |
| The technology is driven by the business rather than vice versa. | Technology can provide a push to the business and competitive advantage that is not very obvious initially to the business. |
| It is easy to communicate the benefits of the Data Warehouse to decision makers and investors. | The initial expectations may restrict pursuing potentially higher payoff objectives, once the Data Warehouse has been implemented. |

The top down approach to planning and implementing a data warehouse is recommended under the following scenarios:

- When the implementing organization is familiar with the technology and has extensive experience in the development of applications based on identifying business requirements in a top down manner.
- When executives, decision makers, and investors have a clear set of objectives that they envision for the data warehouse.
- When executives, decision makers, and investors have a clear idea of where the data warehouse fits within their organizational structure as a decision support tool.
- When executives, decision makers, and investors have a clear idea of how using the data warehouse is a subprocess of a business process already in place.

A top down approach is useful in cases where the technology is mature and well-understood, and where the business problems that must be solved are clear and well-understood. Applying the top down approach provides an excellent fit between the technology and the business objectives and, when done properly, yields maximum effect for every dollar spent. Top down approaches can be architected. A clear, long-term architecture can be defined.

***Bottom Up Approach.*** The bottom up approach generally starts with experiments and prototypes that are technology-based. A specific, well-understood subset of the business problem is selected and a solution is formulated for this subset. Implementing the bottom up solution is generally quicker because it involves fewer people making fewer decisions to solve a smaller business problem. The bottom up approach is useful in the early blocks of technology maturity. This approach allows an organization to move forward at considerably less expense and to evaluate the benefits of technology before making significant commitments. In the data warehouse area, a bottom up approach usually is taken to implement a data mart, a small executive information system, or a departmental warehouse that is clearly oriented to answering a few well-chosen queries in a focused domain, such as accounting, market analysis, and product management. Figure 4.6 shows the pros and cons of using the bottom up approach in implementing a data warehouse.

| Pros | Cons |
|---|---|
| The need for implementation and to get started sometimes far outweighs top down analysis and long term considerations. | After the initial implementation, it is good to step back and see how the solution can scale up to serve the whole enterprise. |
| In the earlier Blocks of technology maturity, this approach allows an organization to evaluate technology benefits without huge commitments. | The failure of a single bottom up project can delay the implementation of potentially beneficial technology. |
| Involvement of a few people working on a narrow scope can speed up implementation and decision making. | The initial team has to step back and get the buy in of a larger team to expand the scope of the initial solution. |

**Fig. 4.6**

*An example of the pros and cons of using a bottom up approach for building a data warehouse.*

The bottom up approach to planning and implementing a data warehouse is recommended under the following scenarios:

- When the implementing technology is at the left end of the technology maturity curve. There is a large and conservative opposition to new technology without due consideration.
- When the organization is not yet committed to data warehouse technology but is looking for a technology evaluation to determine how, where, and when to deploy the technology.
- When the organization is trying to get a feel for the costs and overheads of implementing and deploying data warehouse technology.

- When the business objectives that are to be met by the proposed data warehouse implementation are not clear, nor is it clear which current or proposed business processes will be affected by use of the data warehouse.
- When the organization is making an opportunistic, rather than a strategic, investment in data warehouse technology.

A bottom up approach is useful in making technology assessments and is a good technique for organizations that are not leading-edge technology implementors. This approach also is a good way for a business to take advantage of technologies that are early in the maturity cycle without committing itself to large risks.

***Combination approach.*** In the combined top down/bottom up approach, an organization can exploit the planned and strategic nature of the top down approach while retaining the rapid implementation and opportunistic application of the bottom up approach. This approach relies on two components:

- A top down architecture, standards, and design team that will carry the know-how from project to project and that can step back and convert tactical decisions into strategic ones.
- A bottom up project team that is directed towards implementing a very focused, narrow, but far-reaching, business solution in a short period.

The combination approach has the advantages of the other two approaches but is trickier to manage as a project. This approach is recommended under the following circumstances:

- When the implementing organization has experienced architects on board. The organization has had a base of building, documenting, applying, and maintaining data architectures, technology architectures, and enterprise models and can easily move from the concrete (as in the metadata inside operational systems) to the abstract (logical models or abstractions that are based on the nature of the business rather than on the technology used to implement systems).
- When the organization has a committed project team that has a clear focus on where they want to apply data warehouse technology. Often, this team is a departmental one, comprised of end users and Information Systems staff that has a clear vision for solving a clear and currently felt business need.

The combination top down/bottom up approach is best suited for opportunistic and rapid deployment of data warehouse technology while reserving the right to build a strategic solution that has long-term value.

**Select the Development Methodology.** The software industry has evolved many types of development methodologies. Each methodology has its own merits and shortcomings. Theoretically, the development of a data warehouse can be done using any of these methodologies. In reality, the requirements of a data warehouse implementation rule out the use of any methodology that requires a long requirements gathering and analysis phase, a monolithic development phase that takes several months, and a deployment phase that also takes several months. Two popular techniques in software development are described in the following two sections.

***Structured Analysis and Design (Waterfall) Method.*** In this method, a set of requirements is initially collected. These requirements are analyzed and progressively broken down. A design then is built, using the results of analysis. The design starts as an abstract level and is progressively broken down into more concrete levels until the system's code emerges. Structured Analysis and Design lends itself to building systems that satisfy clearly known and specified requirements. An analogy used for the Waterfall method is the way in which General Motors used to build automobiles in the 1970s. Figure 4.7 shows the classic Waterfall development method.

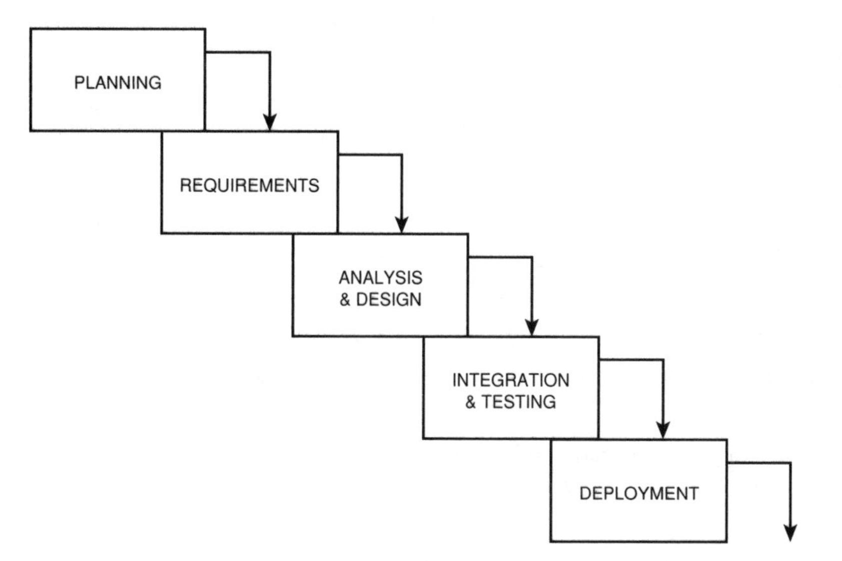


**Fig. 4.7**

*In the Waterfall method, water always flows downhill.*

***Spiral Development Method.*** In this method, the emphasis is on speed and delivery with a recognition that requirements cannot be clearly identified or initially specified. The approach is based on the observation that it is easier to redirect a deployed system based on new requirements than to build a complete solution based on inadequate or unavailable requirements.

The spiral method, therefore, advocates the rapid generation of increasingly functional systems with short intervals between successive releases (see fig. 4.8). The interval between releases is used to identify and implement added functionality, improvements and fixes. An analogy for the spiral method was the way in which the Honda Motor Company rapidly evolved the Honda Accord from a functional, plain-looking, economy car at its inception into a luxurious, high-priced automobile that quickly outsold all other brands for many years.

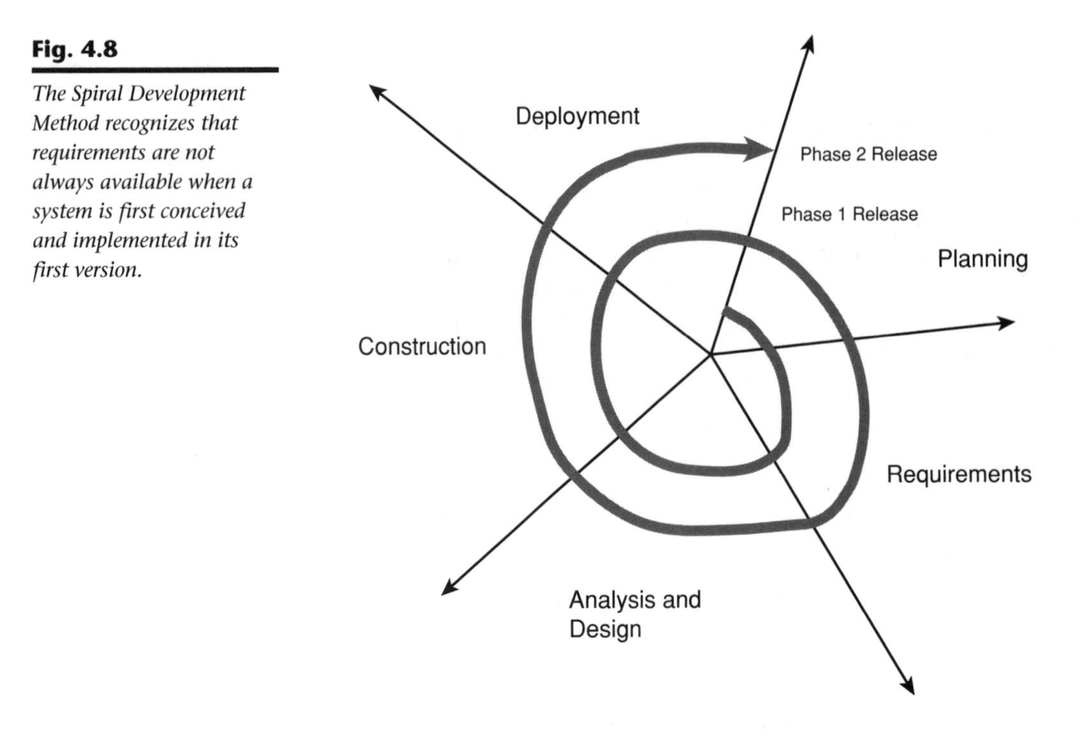


**Fig. 4.8**

*The Spiral Development Method recognizes that requirements are not always available when a system is first conceived and implemented in its first version.*

The spiral method lends itself eminently to database applications development, data warehouse development, and the development of Object Oriented (OO) systems.

In the product development domain, the spiral development method is used when the following situations arise:

- The direction of a market and its requirements cannot be clearly predicted in advance.
- Time to market is an important ingredient in the implementation of a product.
- Iterative improvement is necessary for making market corrections.
- Sustained competitive advantage comes from a rapid onslaught of improvements rolled out continuously.
- It takes an organization at least six months to absorb successive software releases.

The development of data warehouses exhibits all the preceding characteristics. The spiral method is therefore an excellent choice for development methodology for data warehouses.

**Develop the Business Objectives.** The first step in undertaking any major and complex task is to develop a list of business objectives that the system must fulfill. There are those who claim that you can simply start building a data warehouse based on understanding the various data sources that must feed the warehouse with no initial analysis of the end uses of the warehouse. This is a case of fitting the objectives around one's reality and claiming success, rather than starting with a list of objectives and building a system that meets these objectives.

The setting of objectives for the data warehouse is a complex task. This is because the data warehouse, in much the same way as the databases that feed it with information, is a long term capability. It must provide a broad range of information for a broad range of analysts and end users. It is sometimes difficult to even start documenting the needs of these customers. Another source of difficulty arises from the difference in perspectives, terminology, and definitions of information from the viewpoint of the IT staff who manage the data sources and the end users/analysts who want to derive decision support from the data warehouse.

One simplification results from the view of the data warehouse as an internal "product" for an enterprise—it is a software system whose objectives are to provide decision support to a purely internal audience. With this view, it is possible to apply the body of currently available product planning expertise to plan the objectives of the data warehouse, which is commonly done by asking the following questions:

- **What is the target market (the potential audience) for the data warehouse?**

  The answer is based on degree of perceived need and value. Persons with a higher perceived need will place a higher perceived value on data warehouse services. The selection of a target audience is complicated by needs for workstations, network connectivity, and a degree of familiarity of the audience with computer technology.

- **What are currently used or planned platforms?**

  This relates to the "ease of buying and deploying" the data warehouse solution. The answers must address a wide range of platform dimensions such as servers, client workstations, graphical user interfaces (GUI), and database engines (in particular, relational database management systems, communications).

- **What are the planned capabilities in terms of features and functions?**

  The answer relates to the value perceived for each feature by end users. The investment needed to develop capabilities of dubious value is a waste of resources. Also, consider whether a minimum set of features (critical mass) must be delivered for the data warehouse solution to be useful. Features and functions fall into the following two categories:

  - Features and functions that are visible and can be used by external end users of the data warehouse.

  - Features and functions that are not visible externally but must be implemented inside the data warehouse in order to deliver its capabilities.

- **What are the various data sources that can and/or must be integrated into the data warehouse?**

  The answer has technology implications based on the difficulty of extracting data from legacy databases. Also, consider external sources of data that provide market, customer, and competitive information. Examples of these sources are Dow Jones, Standard & Poor, and Dun & Bradstreet. These are commonly termed *syndicated data.*

- **When should the data warehouse become operational?**

  The answer is complex and is based on many factors. Competitors are already using data warehouse technology to target key customers and roll out improved services. A department within the organization is already incapable of performing its functions due to unavailability of key information about customers and historical data.

**Select an initial implementation Scope.** In most organizations, the primary motivation of the data warehouse project is an early first implementation that brings immediate benefits to a group of users. After defining an overall direction and an overall set of objectives for the data warehouse, it becomes necessary to quickly derive a limited scope for the first implementation. The scope of a data warehouse project can be restricted along many dimensions (see fig. 4.9).

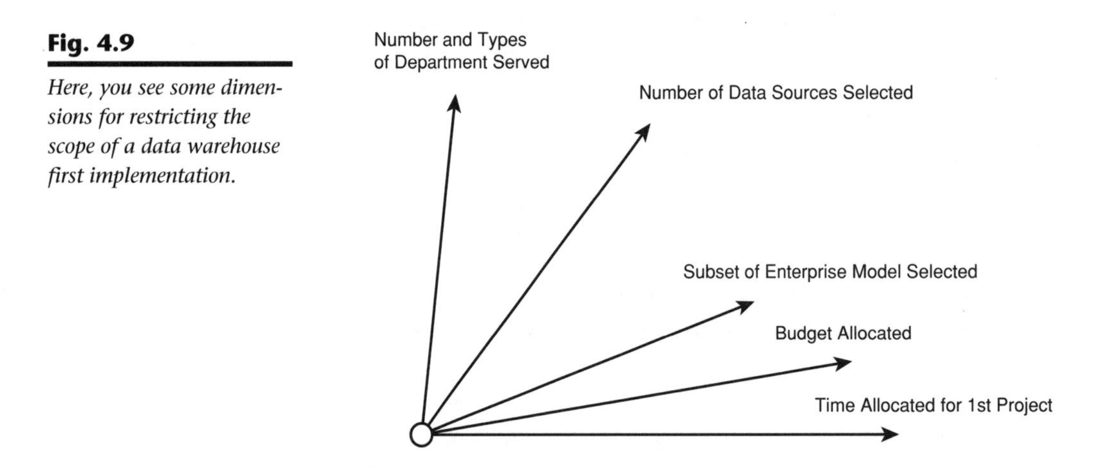


**Fig. 4.9**

*Here, you see some dimensions for restricting the scope of a data warehouse first implementation.*

The dimensions can be broadly divided into two major categories:

- Scope determined from the perspective of the business user of the data warehouse
- Scope determination based on technology considerations

To determine scope from the perspective of the business user, you should ask the following questions:

- **Who are the departments that need to use the data warehouse initially?**

  Within these departments who will be using the data warehouse, and for what purpose? The selection of a limited number of departments can significantly reduce the data and metadata requirements of the data warehouse.

- **What are the range of business queries that must be initially answered by the data warehouse?**

  The business queries directly determine the aggregations, summarizations, integration, and re-engineering that needs to be performed on the data coming from data sources. The scope of business queries also will restrict the number of data dimensions, the variety of reports, and the amount of desktop downloads that place demands on the data warehouse implementation.

The more specific the query formats (such as "Give me the sales by quarter for the last three years of customers buying pepperoni pizza in the Minneapolis area"), the easier it is to come up with dimensions and aggregation and summarization specifications, as well as the range of business entities that must be tracked within the data warehouse.

To determine scope from the technology perspective, you should ask the following questions:

- **What is the size of the data warehouse metamodel?**

  The data warehouse metamodel is the model that stores the definition of warehouse data. The definition is stored inside the warehouse manager's catalog and is used by all query and reporting tools as a blueprint for the construction and execution of queries against the warehouse. The size of the metamodel is a direct indicator of the size of the data that must be managed within the warehouse. Restricting the initial metamodel, therefore, restricts the amount of data that must be managed by the first implementation of a data warehouse.

- **What is the size of data inside the data warehouse?**

  The data warehouse contains not only current data but also historical data that was collected over many years. The degree of summarization determines how much of this data is compressed and summarized. If the data warehouse were to provide the ability for business queries to "drill down" to the actual historical record, the data warehouse is required to support data management for huge volumes of data. The size of this data has a direct bearing on the execution time of business queries. Making sensible choices about providing support for drill-down only where required and managing summarized records rather than detail are techniques for restricting the scope of the initial implementation.

- **What are the input sources of data and how many are they?**

  The data warehouse is populated with information that comes from production databases that are supporting daily operations. After the data from these databases is loaded into the data warehouse, they must be kept synchronized with the original sources. This is a significant overhead on the data warehouse, especially when the sources are not amenable to new relational database features, such as replication services that make the synchronization tasks easier. Therefore, the initial selection of data sources (their database types) and numbers of sources has a strong influence on the ability to deliver an early implementation.

- **How usable is the data from the data sources?**

  Legacy databases have presented significant challenges in the way they organize data, the lack of cleanup and scrubbing facilities, and the quality of the data they contain (in the absence of data filtering and cleanup at capture time). The selection of such sources can cause significant implementation delays while these challenges are being addressed.

- **How well are the data sources documented?**

  The availability of documentation that describes the organization of data in legacy databases is a strong need. The quality of this documentation largely determines the success of being able to extract data from these sources. Related to this question is the availability of people who are familiar with these legacy data sources and can fill any gaps in the available documentation.

- **What is the level of Integrated Management Facilities?**

  The implementation of a data warehouse is quicker in an environment of data dictionaries, repositories, and database catalogs that are up-to-date and contain accurate data definitions. The bulk of the extraction and loading from data sources hinges on the understanding and structure of the source data.

- **What is the availability of logical models and CASE tools? Is there an Enterprise Data Model available?**

  A number of organizations have adopted Computer Aided Software Engineering (CASE) tools for modeling their data and processes. With the culture of CASE, it is far quicker and easier for an organization to define/design the metamodel for its data warehouse. Furthermore, this metamodel can be quickly assembled from parts of the Enterprise Model and then augmented with metadata that results from summarization, integration, and aggregation activities.

- **Can existing skills and human resources be used? Will the data warehouse be implemented on existing platforms or on platforms similar to existing ones?**

  The data warehouse is, in many ways, an extension of an organization's data architecture. The availability of database administrators, data administrators, and programmers who already understand the data architecture and have worked with it on a daily basis can accelerate the implementation of a data warehouse. The implementation of the data warehouse on existing platforms or those similar to them also can reduce the technology challenge posed by development on new platforms.

Some scope guidelines for data sources that can assist the implementor include the following:

- Try to stay with 1-2 sources initially. Try to select RDBMS based sources (Relational).
- Expand the initial scope by adding OLTP data sources incrementally.
- Add syndicated data sources after the data warehouse has become operational.
- Add non-electronic sources last.

**Select an Architectural Approach.** Chapter 3 discussed at length the architectural flexibility for implementing a data warehouse. The following architectural choices are available to the data warehouse implementor:

- **Operational storage versus using copies of operational data**—The traditional view is that data warehouses make copies of operational and historical information and store them privately for use. It may be desirable architecturally to do away with the need for copying (and subsequent needs for synchronization) and use the operational stored data in read-only applications that do not alter the data. The data warehouse metamodel, in such an architecture, is a virtual schema that points to the metadata of operational databases. Queries against the warehouse then will simply fetch data from the operational database, directly under the guidance of the data warehouse metamodel.
- **Data warehouse only**—This architecture recognizes that a number of operations that are applied against data sources such as cleanup, integration, summarization, and aggregation are commonly needed by all data warehouse applications. It makes sense, therefore, to apply these operations one time and bring in data from data sources into a centralized data warehouse. (The concept of centralization is "logical"—the data itself may be stored in distributed databases.) In such an architecture, a single logical data warehouse feeds all end users with information for decision support.
- **Data marts only**—This architecture recognizes that every functional department in an organization has its own specific needs and a single corporate data warehouse cannot meet all these needs. The concept of a data mart is that of a strip mall, serving a neighborhood rather than a large department store that serves an entire suburb or city.
- **Data warehouse and data marts**—This architecture is a recognition that a department's specific data warehouse needs must be addressed along with the need for a corporate data warehouse. The corporate data warehouse acts as a collector and distributor of information from data sources throughout the organization.
- **Platform and infrastructure partitioning**—Chapter 3 covered architectural cuts. Architectural cuts are used to partition the platforms for the data warehouse, the data marts, data sources, and end user tools. The architectural flexibility available here is to share platforms between data sources and the data

warehouse or to use separate platforms for data sources, data warehouse, data marts, and end user workstations. Sharing common platforms reduces the complexities of data extraction and data transformation. At the same time, this sharing may be unfeasible because of lack of available processing capacity and trained personnel. The cost of upgrading mainframe resources is also a significant challenge in co-locating mainframe-based data sources and the data warehouse on the same host.

- **Two-tier client/server architecture**—One architectural option is using two layers of platforms. In the Two tier client/server architecture, one layer contains the clients and the other layer contains the server. The server may be either a workstation or a mainframe host. In this option, the end user access tools execute on the client, and the data sources, data warehouse, and data mart reside on servers—either the same or different servers. *Clients* are graphical applications that rely on the client workstation's processing capabilities.
- **Three-tier client/server architecture**—In this architectural option, there are three layers: a workstation-based client layer, a server-based intermediate layer, and a mainframe-based third layer. The mainframe-based (host) layer is responsible for running the data sources and optional source data transformations. The servers run the data warehouse and data mart software and also store the warehouse data. The client workstations run the query and reporting applications, and also may store local data that is unloaded from the data warehouse or data mart server.

**Build a Program and Project Plans Budget.** One of the most important aspects of planning is to be able to perform the following:

- **Articulate both a program plan and a set of project plans**—A *program plan* is an overall vision for the data warehouse activity and its role in the organization's daily and weekly life. The data warehouse is an important decision support system that can be used by all departments of the enterprise. The data warehouse can be used as a planning aid for continuous improvements to operations as well as to provide competitive leaps forward, based on analysis of data. The program plan, therefore, maps the various departments and business units that will use the data warehouse. The program plan also will set priorities on implementation to meet critical business needs first. Project plans, however, are plans for specific implementations of the data warehouse. If the program plan provides strategy, project plans provide tactics. Project plans also incorporate the priorities of the program plan.
- **Reserve an adequate budget for the program while committing the expense for specific projects**—Planning for this budget can be based on two approaches:
    - **Cost estimation, based on the organization's history with software development**—The software lifecycle phases can be allocated percentages based on past history.

- **Cost estimation, based on the reference architecture**—The reference architecture can be used as a breakdown of data warehouse components. It can, therefore, be used as a bill of materials for a data warehouse. Each component of the reference architecture (Data Sources, Data Warehouse, Data Marts, End User Access, Data Management, Metadata Management, Transport, and Infrastructure) can be broken down into sub-components and costed out separately.

- **Provide measures for estimating the payback of the data warehouse**—Estimating payback from the data warehouse is a task complicated by the long delay between analysis and resulting actions. Some of the measures that can be used are as follows:
    - Measures of cost recovery or cost savings
    - Measures of opportunity creation
    - Measures of revenue creation
    - Measures of market growth
    - Measures of competitive advantage
    - Measures of customer satisfaction

**Develop Business Usage Scenarios.** The data warehouse, like other software developments, is used by people other than the developers and managers. One key success factor in ensuring that the warehouse is usable is to have the end users involved in setting the expectations of what the data warehouse can deliver. Business scenarios are an important requirements prototyping tool. A business usage scenario consists of the following ingredients:

- A clearly identified business user, such as an automobile accessories product manager, with a clearly identified business role.
- A functional area that is sponsoring the data warehouse or data mart and will use it when it is delivered, such as product planning and market analysis.
- One or more business queries of crucial interest to the functional area that is not currently satisfied by existing information systems (e.g., "What are the sales by quarter of automobile air-conditioning equipment for the last two years in the European market? What is the correlation between average summer temperatures per country and the sales of air-conditioning equipment?"). Business queries must be stated in precise English employing commonly used business language that is understood by the end users of the functional area.

A question typically asked is, "Why are business usage scenarios useful?"

Business scenarios help to clarify end user expectations of the data warehouse. Some of these expectations are ultimately met by using appropriate data sources. Others (as in the preceding example, requiring the correlation between weather conditions and sales of air-conditioning equipment) need external data from syndicated sources. Building business usage scenarios helps to articulate these expectations.

Business usage scenarios are useful in the following instances:

- **Building acceptance criteria for the data warehouse**—End users have a hard time articulating technology-related expectations. They have a clear(er) understanding of business related expectations. In practice, clearly stated requirements provide effective scope controls for a software development project.
- **Identifying the data warehouse metamodel**—This helps to build a boundary on the scope of the data warehouse metamodel. If an organization has already built an enterprise model, this is simply the exercise of selecting the proper subset of the Enterprise Model.
- **Identifying the amount of historical information needed**—This also has a clear bearing on project scope and the complexities of data extraction, scrubbing, integration, transformation, summarization, and aggregation. All economies made here translate into large operational economies. It is, therefore, better to plan with specific user directives than to overplan, "just in case."
- **Identifying the dimensions of interest to end users**—Dimensions such as time, location, business unit, and product line have a clear bearing on summarization activities needed. By selecting only the dimensions that are useful to end users such as "by quarter," "by year," or "by month," the data warehouse is built around "natural" business cycles rather than around assumptions of IT staff.
- **Identifying the need for data marts/data warehouse**—Analyzing the business usage scenarios will enable the IT staff to determine whether a data warehouse only, a data mart only, or a combination architecture is most appropriate.

**Collect Your Metadata.** Part of the planning phase for a data warehouse is the need to collect various items of design relating to metadata. *Metadata* is the term used for definitions of data. Metadata is the blueprint ingredient used for constructing the warehouse. Many organizations currently have a data administration function responsible for collecting and organizing metadata. Others have a database administration function responsible for defining and administering databases, and by implication, the metadata of the databases. The metadata collected during the planning phase of the data warehouse is from many sources such as the following:

- Enterprise models built by the organization are abstract data models used to characterize the types of information that an organization needs, collects, and uses. Enterprise models should be based on the nature of the business, not on the current information systems that are producing and consuming information. Many organizations, however, built enterprise data models from a bottom up perspective, starting with the organizations of their current databases. Enterprise models are built by using Data Modeling CASE tools. Generally, they are based on the Entity-Relationship (E-R) Modeling methodology.
- Repositories and data dictionaries that are managed by data administrators contain definitions of operational data located in various relational and

nonrelational databases. These are kept up-to-date and provide a valuable source of definitions to start building data extractors for extracting operational data.

- External sources of data that are required to answer business queries are either structured or unstructured for access and retrieval. Structured data is provided from third party information sources, such as Dow Jones and syndicated data sources. The metadata that defined data from these sources is to be incorporated into the data warehouse metamodel.

## Requirements

The Requirements phase of the data warehouse implementation is a precise specification for the functions that will be delivered by the warehouse. In addition to the features and functions needed, the requirements will clearly describe the operating environment in which the data warehouse will be delivered. The requirements phase is, in summary, a transition from the Owner's view of the Zachman Framework to the architect's view.

The amount of requirements gathering that you must do is dependent on the implementation approach that you take. If you take the top down approach, the requirements gathering activity is significantly large. But, because the needs are driven from the business, they are well-understood and can, therefore, be easily cataloged. If you take the bottom up approach, most of the requirements are built opportunistically based on hope and expectations. The primary driver here is rapid and low-cost implementation—any implementation.

**Requirements Analysis Framework.** One straightforward way of looking at requirements is through the various perspectives of the Zachman framework as described in Chapter 2. The Zachman framework is a way to look at an information system from various stakeholder perspectives. Each stakeholder has a different dimension of expectations of the system—the requirements of the system. Figure 4.10 shows the steps in requirements analysis.

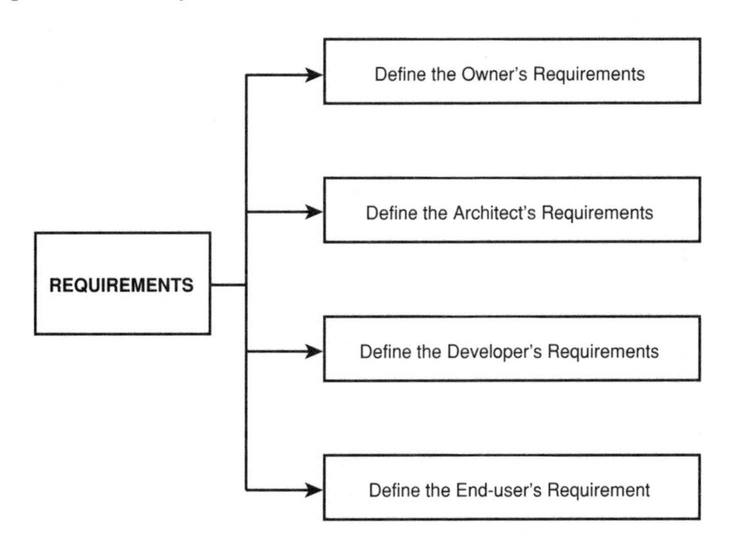


**Fig. 4.10**

*This shows the requirements for the data warehouse solution from the various perspectives of the people involved in its planning and implementation.*

**Owner's Requirements.** Some questions that the owners (or investors) of the data warehouse pose are the following:

- Why are we building a data warehouse or a data mart? What business problem will it address?
- What are the business objectives?
- Who are the stakeholders? Who is the customer? Sponsor?
- How much will it cost?
- When will it be ready?
- What is the impact on people? Skills? Organization?
- What does it do to our current computer investments?
- Do we have the skills to do it?
- What are the risks?

The requirements gathering must provide answers to these questions. These requirements then will form an acceptance criteria from the owner's perspective. Potential requirements gathering areas include the following:

- Business objectives
- Data warehouse/data mart scope and objectives, customers, and stakeholders
- Customer requirements
- Sources of data
- Plan, such as budget, schedule, resources
- Impact on current investments, such as people, technology, and training

Part of the business requirements are also scope specifications for the data warehouse in terms of the following:

- **Subject Areas**—These are topics of interest to various business functions. Careful selection of subject areas can contain the scope of the data warehouse implementation while maximizing its usefulness. For example, the marketing department may have an interest in one or more of the following topics:
    - Market research
    - Competitive analysis
    - Buyer behavior
    - Market segmentation product (market matching)
    - Pricing and budgeting decisions
    - Product decisions
    - Promotion decisions
    - Channel decisions
    - Forecasting trends
    - Benchmarking

Analysis of the selected topics yields specific subject areas for the marketing department (see fig. 4.11).

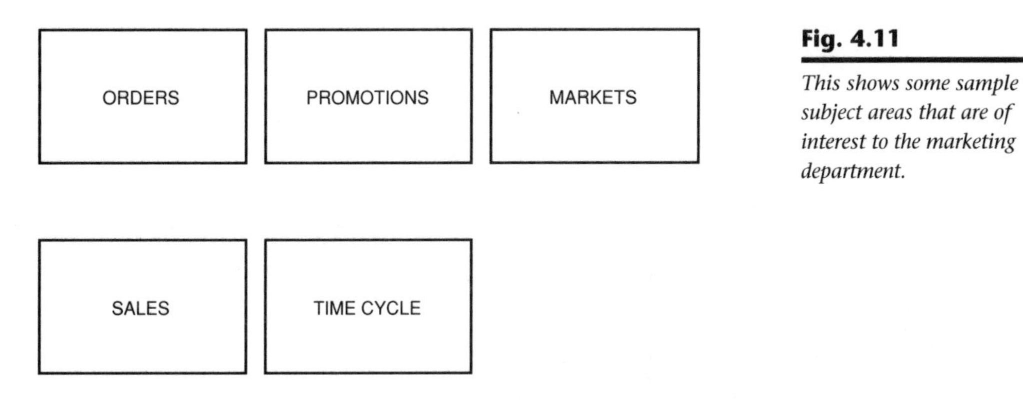


**Fig. 4.11**

*This shows some sample subject areas that are of interest to the marketing department.*

- **Granularity**—This refers to the level of detail of information required. Granularity has a direct bearing on the aggregation and summarization activities that must be performed on the source data. The lower the granularity, the higher the amount of detail. Operational data is generally deemed to be at the lowest level of granularity. To increase its granularity (and its usefulness to decision makers), operational data must be summarized and aggregated further. Generally, the more the granularity, the greater is the amount of processing needed to convert and summarize operational data. At the same time, large granularity data needs less storage volume and also can be queried rapidly and conveniently. The cost of summarization and aggregation is a continual one for every refresh of the data warehouse when the operational data sources gather new information.

  Figure 4.12 shows the data pyramid that describes the relationship between the following:

  - Increased granularity
  - Increased usefulness to higher levels of decision makers
  - Decreased volume of data
  - Increased computation

  Examples of granularity in business queries are shown in the following list:

  - What is the fewest number of customers/sales representatives (not the name of specific customers for that sales rep)? This can help to determine if customers are well-serviced or salespeople are overloaded.
  - Who is the highest revenue bookings/sales rep (not the individual revenue bookings for that sales rep)?

- What is the revenue per region in the last six quarters (not daily revenue per region)?
- What are the names of the top ten products per region for sales volume (not the actual sales volume)?

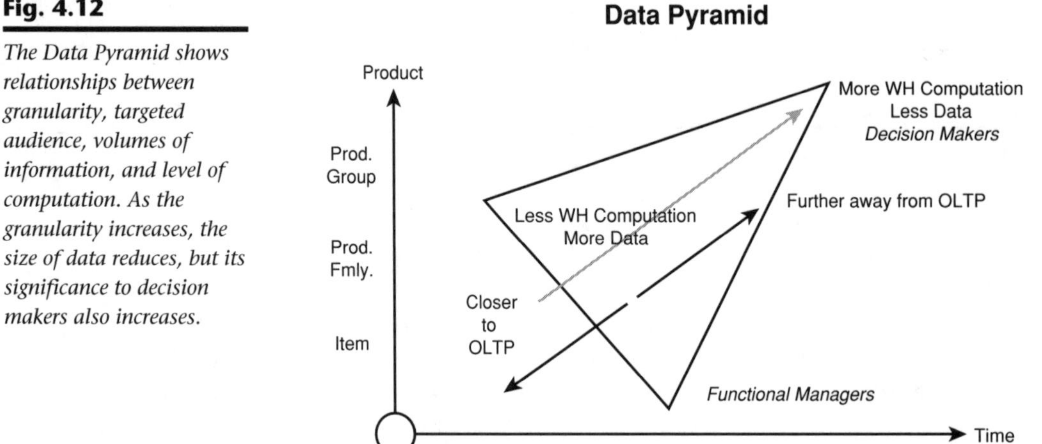


**Fig. 4.12**

*The Data Pyramid shows relationships between granularity, targeted audience, volumes of information, and level of computation. As the granularity increases, the size of data reduces, but its significance to decision makers also increases.*

- **Dimensions**—Data warehouses organize a large store of operational and historical data using multiple dimensions of categorization. An important one is *time*. Operational data is time stamped at the source to establish a time reference to the data. Subsequently, the data warehouse is capable of grouping all data that occurred within the same time range in response to a business query requesting, for example, sale of a specific product within the last quarter. The following dimensions are commonly used within business queries:
  - Time
  - Customer groups
  - Product families
  - Geography and location
  - Organization structure
  - Organization specifics
  - Industry specifics

  Figure 4.13 shows the expansion of some of these dimensions to indicate how they are used for data classification within the data warehouse.

**Architect's Requirements.** The architect is the person responsible for laying out the various components of the data warehouse to support current and future needs. The quality of the architecture effort will determine the following:

- Range of functions and features offered
- Range of platforms needed for implementation

- Use of standards and open interfaces
- Flexibility for adding enhancements

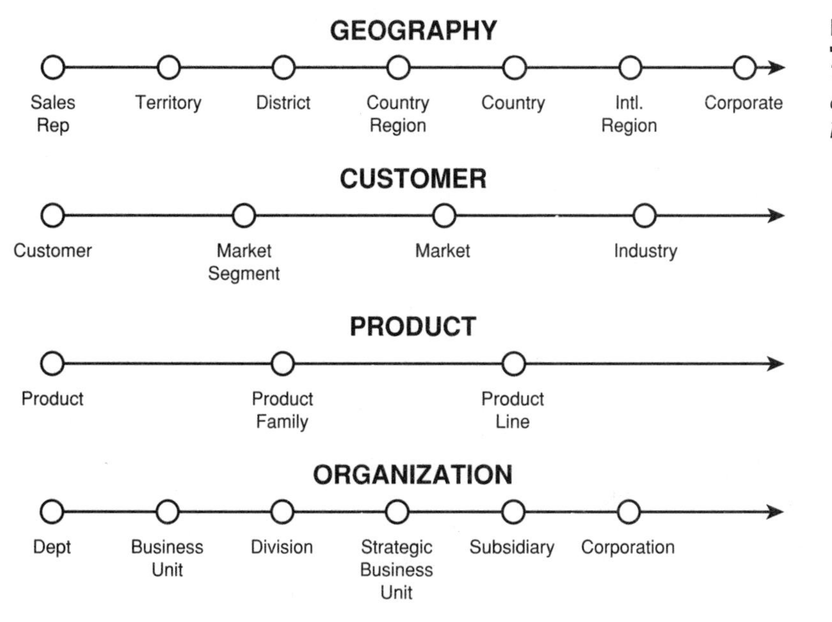


**Fig. 4.13**

*This shows what is of common interest to most business organizations.*



Architects must compile a set of requirements that match the owner's view as well as a set of requirements that reflect the technology implementation. One of the most well-structured approaches for architecture design is known as Enterprise Architecture Planning (EAP). In this methodology, the following three types of architectures are developed:

- **A Data Architecture**—This describes the items of data and their relationships. Data characterization is viewed as a fundamental activity. The reason is that applications cannot be developed without defining the data that they must create or modify. Data architectures generally are depicted as Entity-Relationship Models.
- **An Application Architecture**—A system is a combination of a number of applications. Together, these applications deliver the functionality of a system. The application architecture is defined after the data architecture is characterized. The application architecture is a catalog of applications along with the functions that they deliver and interfaces between applications. The application architecture is also mapped against the data architecture using a "CRUD" matrix—each application is cross referenced with one or more data items that it creates (C), reads (R), updates (U), or deletes (D).
- **A Technology Architecture**—The technology architecture is a depiction of all technology components. A technology architecture is built by breaking down

a system into component technology items such as server computer, user workstation, graphical user interface, RDBMS, and data dictionary/repository, and then selecting candidates based on evaluation criteria such as compliance to ANSI and industry standards, cost, and compliance with internal standards.

Each of these architectures can be developed by using the data warehouse reference architecture as a categorizing mechanism. The data architecture can be developed by identifying the various data and metadata elements of the various blocks of the reference architecture. The applications architecture can be developed by listing the various applications (and their features and functions) for the various blocks of the reference architecture. The technology architecture also is developed by listing the various selections for the blocks and layers of the reference architecture.

**Developer Requirements.** If the architect views the data warehouse in the abstract, the developer must view it in the concrete. The developer's requirements are much closer to the implementation architecture. The developer requires that the data, application, and technology architectures that the architect has developed are further broken down into specific applications, interfaces, computers, databases, communications, and user-interface screens. The developer's requirements are therefore a refinement of the architect's requirements with decisions made regarding platform selections and partitioning of the data architecture and applications architecture on the selected platforms. The developer's requirements also are related to detailed depictions of the technology architecture down to specification of items such as programming languages, RDBMS access, and communications protocols. Additionally, the following requirements are also needed by developers:

- **Technology requirements**—The technology requirements for the various blocks of the reference architecture are the following:
    - For the Data Sources block, you need data and metadata sources, data and metadata extraction, data storage, data administration and management, networks and communications, OLTP processors and operating environment, workflow management, and standards.
    - For the Data Warehouse block, you need refinement and reengineering data staging, networks and communications, data warehouse processors and operating environment, data warehouse data and metadata store, metadata catalog, workflow management, and standards.
    - For the Data Mart block, you need refinement and reengineering data staging, networks and communications, datamart processors and operating environment, data mart data and metadata store, metadata catalog, workflow management, and standards.
    - For the End User Access and Tools block, you need access and retrieval middleware; local store; multidimensional data environment; metadata navigation and reporting tools; standards; business user tools such as analysis and reporting, business modeling, data mining, data surfing, and On-Line Analytical Processing (OLAP); and new production applications.

- **Deployment requirements**—Deployment requirements relate to the capability of the data warehouse to provide access and to distribute information in a timely and convenient manner. The data warehouse must provide a range of access methods for end user tools and specialized data warehouse applications. It also must provide a range of connectivity paths from dialups using a laptop, to workstations connected to a Local Area Network (LAN). The following requirements topics must, therefore, be considered for effective deployment of the data warehouse:
  - Access methods
  - Delivery methods
  - Access tools
  - Connectivity requirements
  - Client platform requirements
- **Data warehouse production readiness requirements**—In addition to the deployment-related issues, several requirements are related to the production worthiness of a data warehouse solution. A data warehouse system becomes a production system when it becomes Mission Critical and is used on a frequent basis for operational and strategic decision support.

  Production readiness requirements relate primarily to managing robustness and availability, maintaining consistency and accuracy of information, managing performance as data storage grows, definition of policies and procedures for update and maintenance of both the data warehouse metamodel and the data, providing access control, and security procedures. Some of the production readiness requirements include the following:
  - Maintaining the consistency, reliability, and currency of information.
  - Managing metadata and the data warehouse metamodel.
  - Ensuring that the transport mechanisms, databases, computers, and communication mechanisms are up and available all the time.
  - Providing immediate technical support and Help Desk capabilities for assisting users when the system is down or when they have operational questions.
  - Provide access security and authentication polices and procedures.
  - Managing the size of databases used by the data warehouse, including the selection of *Very Large Database technology* (*VLDB*), which includes selection of multiple levels of storage on multiple types of media (optical disks, jukeboxes, hard drives). Typically, in a data warehouse project, data storage costs are about 50 percent of the hardware budget.
  - Improving the access response time. Performance improvements can be achieved by making retrieval efficient as well as managing the size of data that the data warehouse must maintain. Improvements can be achieved through the use of arrays, multiple indexes, selective turnoff of locking mechanisms, purging unused data, and archiving low-usage data.

- **Requirements for development and deployment personnel and their skills**—Development of the data warehouse needs a broad range of skills as described in Chapter 2. Different phases of development need different sets of skills. Some of these skills are very expensive and needed only for short periods. A useful requirements gathering activity is to identify what skills are needed for which phase of the data warehouse development lifecycle. Another method for identifying skills is to use the data warehouse reference architecture to categorize skills, based on the architectural blocks and layers.

The data warehouse implementation is a team effort. After identifying the different team members, it's also important to define their roles in the project. This can be done using the reference architecture by mapping various team-member roles within the architectural blocks and layers.

**End User Requirements.** The end user views the data warehouse as a large black box whose primary access is through query and reporting applications and tools, along with some kind of map for the information stored within the data warehouse. The end user requirements may fall into one or more of the following categories:

- **Workflow**—How does the functionality offered by the data warehouse fit into the end user's daily workflow?

  Figure 4.14 below shows a sample process for market research in the absence of decision support capabilities offered by the data warehouse.

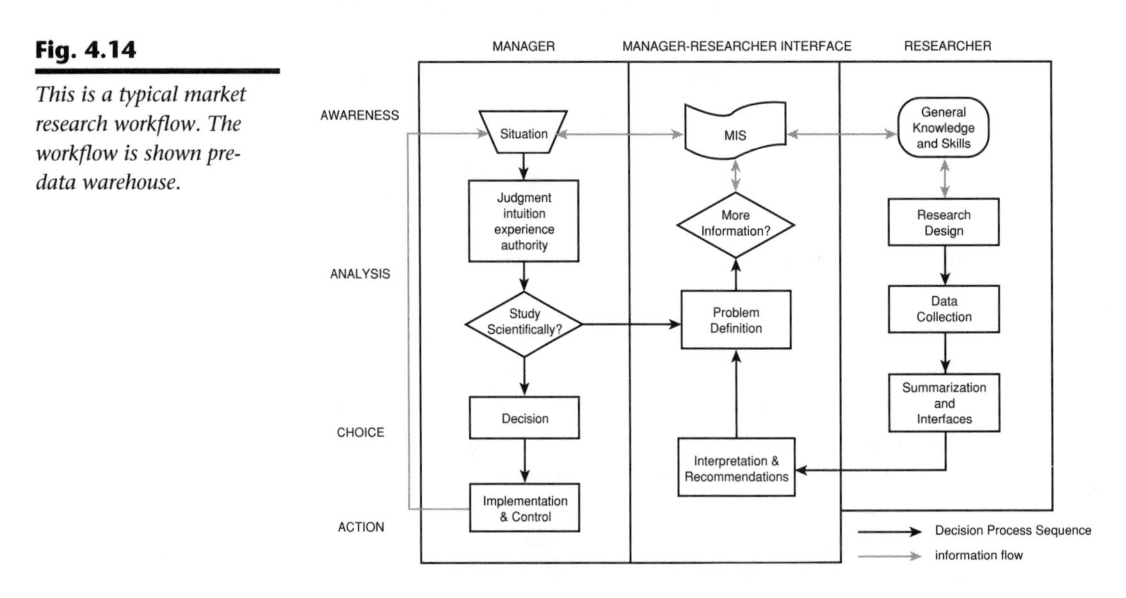


**Fig. 4.14**

*This is a typical market research workflow. The workflow is shown pre-data warehouse.*

Figure 4.15 shows how the data warehouse capabilities are incorporated into a modified workflow. In this scenario, the end user is the market research specialist armed with access to the data warehouse.

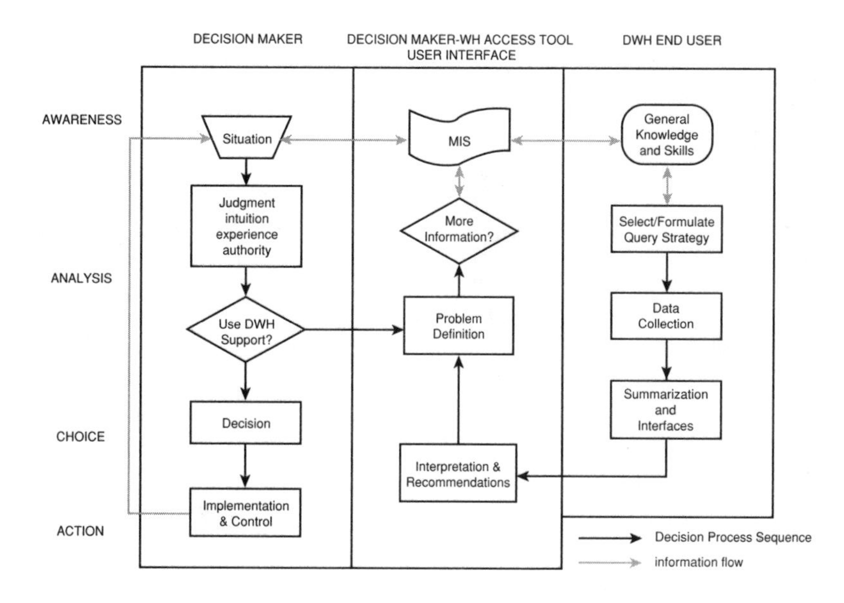


**Fig. 4.15**

*This shows how the data warehouse is incorporated into the sample market research workflow.*

- **Query Requirements**—In the planning phase, I mentioned the use of business usage scenarios as a valuable tool for prototyping the capabilities of the data warehouse and also for setting end user expectations. Query requirements capture sample business queries stated in end user terminology (see fig. 4.16).

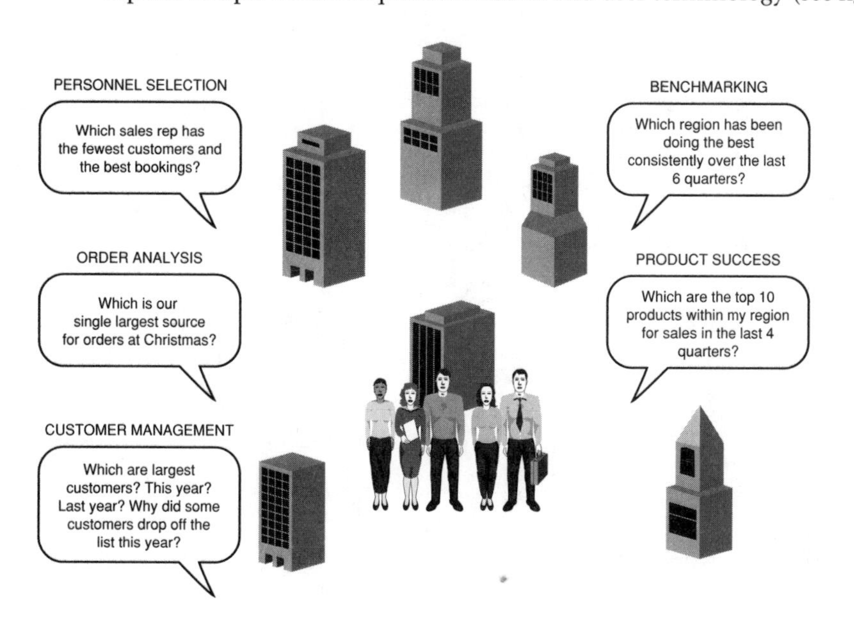


**Fig. 4.16**

*These are some sample business queries from the sales department that the proposed data warehouse must address.*

The queries posed by the marketing department may differ somewhat from queries posed by the sales department (see fig. 4.17).

**Fig. 4.17**

*The marketing department is interested in using the data warehouse to answer some of the sample business queries shown in this figure.*

A third department, such as shipping, may be focused internally on cost management and, therefore, have queries that are completely operational in nature (see fig. 4.18).

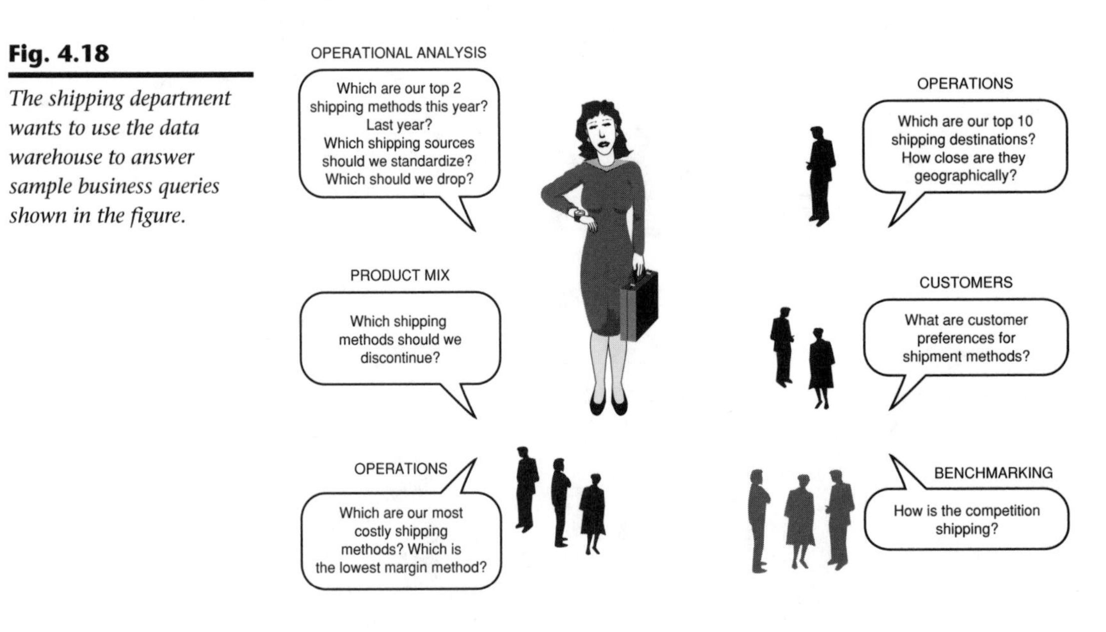


**Fig. 4.18**

*The shipping department wants to use the data warehouse to answer sample business queries shown in the figure.*

- **Reporting Requirements**—Each end user previously described has diverse reporting requirements. Examples of reporting requirements for each of these departments include the following:
  - What are the bookings by sales representative for each of the last 12 months?
  - What were the quarterly sales for each district and region for the last eight quarters?
  - What were the sales by product line for each district for the last 24 months—seasonal months only?
  - What is the monthly promotion expenditure by media for the last two years?
  - What was the quarterly budget for each ad agency for the last four quarters?
  - What are the monthly product sales by product line for each district for the last 24 months?
  - Where is the report for monthly product ships by shipping method and destination for the last 12 months?
  - For each major customer, what were the shipments for each week in the last quarter?

Figure 4.19 is a matrix that shows the various data access needs for various types of end users.

| Access Type | Executive Information System | Structured | Ad-hoc |
|---|---|---|---|
| User | Executive Managers | Managers Analysis | Analysts |
| Characteristics | Business user pre-defined | Business user or IT pre-defined | Business user defined Business user knows data |
| | No to low flexibility | Low to moderate flexibility | Flexible |
| | Sophisticated graphics Drill down | Graphical point/click Drill down | Graphical point/click Data Mining |
| | Development Intensive Predominately IT-developed and maintained | Business user and/or IT-developed and maintained | Developed and maintained by Business user; IT assists |

**Fig. 4.19**

*The Data Access Matrix shows how the various types of data warehouse users have different access characteristics.*



End users also can specify data query requirements. Examples of data query requirements are the following:

- Fast access, good manipulation, and great presentation
- Meet needs of a variety of users

- Allow users to create own query using business terms they already know and offer consistent data structures
- Drill-down without re-access
- Require minimal training and support
- Supports current hardware, software, and warehouse DBMS

End users can also specify the types of data analysis they want to perform on the data after it is retrieved from the data warehouse. Examples of data analysis requirements include the following:

- **Types of Activities:**
  - Slice and dice—Separate data items in various ways
  - Drill-down—Expose progressively more detail
  - Data mining—Look for hidden data patterns
  - Datasurfing—Browse in an undirected manner
  - Download and make local modifications
  - Build business models, for example, using spreadsheets
- **Data Viewing:**
  - Two-dimensional—spreadsheets, relational
  - Multi-dimensional
  - Reports and charts
  - Living sample database

## Analysis

The analysis phase of the data warehouse development lifecycle involves the conversion of requirements gathered in the earlier requirements phase into a set of specifications that can support the design. In the abstract, there are three major input specifications for the data warehouse. These are the following:

- Business focus requirements that delineate the boundaries of information that the data warehouse must encompass. The business focus will also determine the audience and its information requirements.
- Data source requirement specifications that delineate the boundaries of information available from current data sources.
- End use and access requirement specifications that define how the information from the data warehouse will be used. Along with this is a specification of the kinds of tools and display techniques that they use.

The process of analysis then is to derive logical and physical data models for the data warehouse and data marts and define the processes needed to connect the data sources, the data warehouse, the data marts, and the end user access tools together.

A detailed discussion of selected analysis techniques is available in Chapter 5, "Understanding and Analyzing Business Needs."

Because of the complexity of the analysis task and the need for special skills that are technology and domain-related, certain vendors are offering "standard industry models" for specific industries such as banking, insurance, and the airline industry. The hypothesis here is that organizations in the same industry share similar business challenges, business definitions, and terminology, and similar business cycles and business linkages. By providing a standard data warehouse logical and physical model, it is possible to "jump-start" a data warehouse implementation. These vendors also offer customization services to make small modifications to the models they supply. This approach still requires the characterization of data sources and mapping the data sources to the industry specific model supplied by the vendor.

## Design

In the design phase, the logical models developed in the analysis phase are converted to physical models. The processes identified in the analysis phase to connect data sources to the data warehouse, the data warehouse to the data marts, and the data warehouse/data marts to end user workstation-based tools are converted into designs for programs that will perform the tasks required by the processes. Processes needed internally by each block in the data warehouse reference architecture also are identified and detailed.

You can find the following two primary activities under the design phase:

- Detailed design of the data architecture
- Detailed design of the application architecture

The data architecture design activities comprise the following:

- Developing physical data models for the data warehouse and data mart storage databases. Additionally, physical models also may need to be developed for local storage needed by end user tools.
- Mapping the physical data models of the data sources into the physical models of the data warehouse/data marts. This mapping assists the extractors and refinement and re-engineering processes inside the data warehouse/data mart in performing their functions.

The application architecture design is comprised broadly of the following families of applications:

- Processes that are internal to data sources and relate to cleanups or partial extractions of information and processes that connect the data sources to the data warehouse (or data marts if no data warehouses are needed)
- Processes that are internal to the data warehouse and are used for housekeeping purposes
- Processes that connect the data warehouse to the data marts (if used)
- Processes that are internal to the data marts (if used) and are used for housekeeping purposes

- Processes that connect the data warehouse (or data marts) to end user tools
- Processes that are internal to the end user workstations and are used for establishing connectivity to the data warehouse and data marts and for launching analysis tools
- Processes that support management and administration and housekeeping tasks for the data warehouse as a system

The data warehouse reference architecture section (discussed in Chapter 2) contains a detailed list of all these processes. It is an invaluable tool for the design effort. Again, because of the complexity of the design effort, vendors are trying to offer standard products that have already-implemented parts of the data and process architectures described previously in this chapter. The data architectures that they have implemented are based on the "standard industry models" already described. Vendors have also formed alliances with RDBMS vendors in an attempt to deliver "packaged" solutions.

## Construction

The construction phase is responsible for physically implementing the designs developed during the design phase. By judicious "make versus buy" decisions, it is possible to integrate a data warehouse solution fairly rapidly. Also, by judiciously incorporating existing investments, it is possible to speed the development task.

Construction of the data warehouse is similar to construction of a large relational database system. The majority of the applications that need to be constructed is the following:

- Programs that create and modify the databases for the data warehouse and data marts. Vendors offer automatic generation capabilities for such programs.
- Programs that extract data from relational and nonrelational data sources. Some vendors offer facilities for automatic generation of such programs.
- Programs that perform data transformations such as integration, summarization, and aggregation. Vendors also offer facilities for automated generation of these programs.
- Programs that perform updates of relational databases.
- Programs that search very large databases. A number of end user tools have optimized search facilities for the queries they generate. A number of relational vendors also offer query speedup facilities and capabilities for parallel retrieval.

As you can see, the primary challenges during the construction phase are the following:

- Understanding how to incorporate existing investments in platforms, technology, and know-how
- Making smart "make versus buy" decisions
- Proper selection and evaluation of vendor supplied components

- Systems integration capabilities to tie vendor systems together with existing data sources and existing and proposed data access tools
- Metadata management

## Deployment

The deployment phase deals primarily with the challenges of installation, commissioning, and use of the data warehouse solution. Several organizations have already had experience in deploying and commissioning business information systems. They have had experience in the various activities required such as the following:

- Providing initial installation including facilities for initial data connections to sources and for data update and synchronization
- Planning and delivering a staged implementation (rollout)
- Providing training and orientation for all classes of users
- Planning and implementing platform upgrades and maintenance needed by the data warehouse solution when necessary
- Providing user and systems administration
- Providing archive and backup capabilities
- Providing recovery capabilities
- Ensuring integration into the existing infrastructure
- Providing access controls and security
- Ensuring full availability and processes for handling breakdowns of the systems and its infrastructure components

In addition to the normal requirements of deployment for any business information system, the data warehouse system has the following additional requirements:

- Most information systems are built and managed by a technical staff (IT). The level of documentation of the metadata in those systems is often only suitable to a technical audience. Most end users of the data warehouse are non-technical. They need to see definitions of the information contained in the data warehouse in terms and language they understand.
- At inception, the data warehouse is perceived primarily as a decision support capability, not a mission critical capability. Most business information systems that provide operational support are embraced, sometimes unwillingly, as mission critical systems on delivery. Because of these differences in perceptions, a need exists to actively market the information that the data warehouse provides to end users. Only after end users enthusiastically use data warehouse information on a daily basis does the data warehouse become a Mission Critical system.

Based on the preceding considerations, deployment of the data warehouse requires the following additional capabilities not normally associated with business information systems:

- **Information Merchandising**—Information merchandising is the process of treating information itself as a commodity product. A commodity product has clearly exhibited aspects of creating consumer demand, appeal, and perceived usefulness. It also has an aspect of packaging and delivery. To the salesperson who is analyzing sales trends and history on his or her laptop, the sales information from the warehouse is simply a commodity that is needed for the moment. It needs to be delivered in a format compatible with a spreadsheet that is running on this workstation. Merchandising also is showing end users how to usefully deploy data warehouse information to their advantage, by showing example usage scenarios.
- **Information Directory/Catalog**—The information catalog for the data warehouse contains listings of information elements, standard business queries, and standard reports available from the data warehouse. The listings are in language (and possibly in multimedia) that is familiar and obvious to the user. Information catalogs are updated and delivered to users as regularly as subscriptions.
- **Information Browsers**—With the widespread interest and popularity of browsers, data warehouse information can also be delivered and distributed to users in a manner that allows them to browse and selectively download information.

Some of these capabilities are already available. The important lesson to remember is that the data warehouse is a method for delivering the information that was historically managed and controlled by an IT department to a group of users who understand the business but not necessarily the technology. The concept of viewing information as a commodity forces the purveyor of information to consider the merchandising aspects of commodity products and draw upon the body of knowledge that was developed in this area over the years.

## Expansion

The spiral development method was described as a key ingredient for rapid initial deployment of a data warehouse. The spiral method also calls for a rapid evolution of features and functions based on the lessons learned from every deployment. As the data warehouse starts seeing use on a regular basis, some of the following areas of enhancement may be foreseen:

- Business queries could not be formulated or satisfied because of the limitations imposed by the data warehouse metamodel. These limitations can arise due to lack of certain summarizations or aggregations not being performed in the initial implementation.
- Business queries that involved external data sources that were not part of the initial implementation. Certain business queries needed information from syndicated data sources that relate to environmental factors.
- Performance of key components of the data warehouse was not satisfactory. The data warehouse was not refreshed frequently enough. End user access tools took a long time for the initial load of information from the warehouse.

- Other departments now want to set up their own data marts. It now becomes necessary to increase the scope of the data warehouse metamodel.

To exploit the advantages offered by the Spiral model, it is important to start gathering requirements for the next iteration of the development cycle as soon as one iteration is delivered. Most major software releases need to be delivered at a minimum of six-month intervals for effective use. Most application development projects must be delivered within approximately the same time frame for management attention and approval.

# Summary

- You can divide development of the data warehouse into the classic software-development lifecycle phases. Although the phases are the same, unique variations exist that relate specifically to data warehouse for tasks within the phases.
- Planning is an important phase of data warehouse implementation. Decisions made during the planning phase have significant impact on the implementation scope and size of effort. Key planning decisions include selection of top down, bottom up, or combination approach; selection of an appropriate data warehouse architecture; selection of appropriate scope of information, data sources, and metamodel size; and estimation of program and project plans and budget justifications.
- During the requirements phase, a variety of requirements must be considered. These requirements are business-driven and technology-driven. Careful selection and specification of requirements at this stage can provide a bounded project that delivers results quickly.
- The analysis phase is important as it determines how the requirements will be met. The analysis phase focuses primarily on the conversion of requirements specifications into metamodel specifications for the data warehouse. The metamodel specifications are then used to generate the data warehouse extractors and transformation, integration, summarization, and aggregation software.
- The construction phase highlights the various "build versus buy" tradeoffs. By appropriate selection of vendor-supplied components, it is possible to build a quick and effective data warehouse first implementation. The reference architecture described in Chapter 2 is an important tool for analyzing and evaluating vendor offerings.
- The deployment phase in the data warehouse development lifecycle has a unique component called *information merchandising*. This recognizes that the commodity supplied by the data warehouse to its end users (customers) is information itself. As a commodity product, information also must be merchandised as consumer goods. Merchandising involves stressing availability, benefits, and packaging for end user appeal.

CHAPTER 5

# Understanding and Analyzing Business Needs

Chapter 4 discussed the full development lifecycle for a data warehouse. In this chapter, we focus on business needs and methods of analyzing business needs in order to model them and represent them adequately within the data warehouse. Business needs are the primary motivation for building the data warehouse.

## Analysis Framework

In order to analyze business needs from the perspective of the kinds of information that is managed by operational systems, it is important to step back and look at the various categories under which information can be classified.

The most important analysis is that of the nature of business itself, its relationships to information, and the responsibilities of the various end users in the perspective of the business. In this view, the information is classified into categories that allow broad prioritization. An example is a classification of information into cost categories and revenue categories. Information elements that describe the production of products or the administrative functions of an enterprise fall into this category. Information elements that relate to customers, sales, and orders relate to the revenue category. This view is known as the *top-down view*.

We must also look at the information that is available and can be potentially used by the data warehouse. This information is currently being captured, stored, and managed by operational systems and may be documented at various levels of detail and accuracy. This is known as the *data sources view*.

The information that is stored inside the data warehouse must be organized differently from the way it is organized in the data sources. Often, pre-calculated totals and counts (summaries and aggregates) are stored inside the data warehouse. Frequently, additional information such as source, date, and time of origin has been added to the incoming data to provide historical context—known as the *data warehouse view*.

Figure 5.1 shows how these views relate to the various components of the data warehouse.

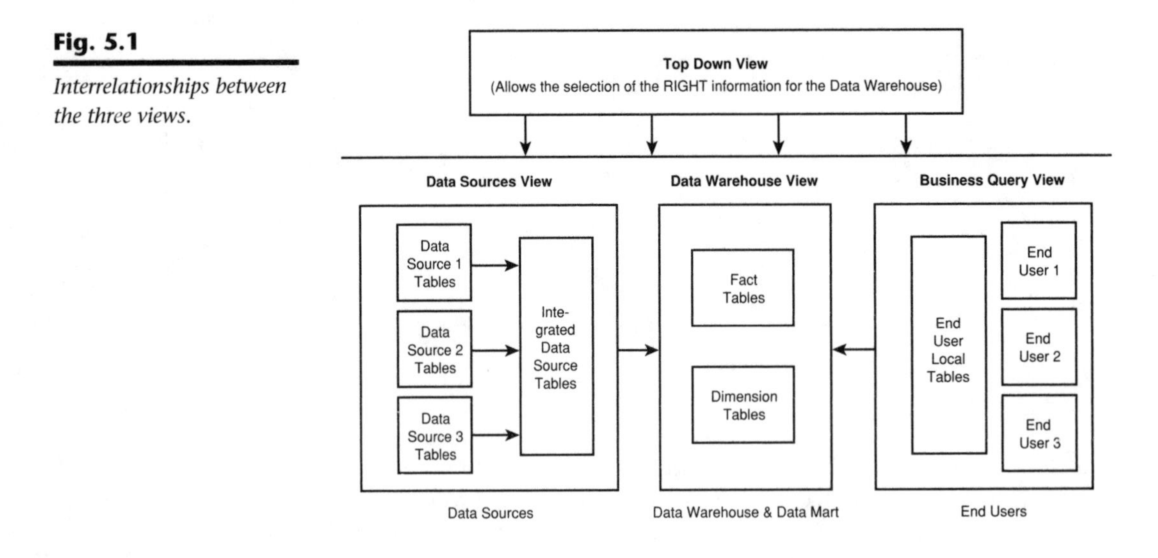


**Fig. 5.1**

*Interrelationships between the three views.*

## Top-Down View

A business's primary purpose is to make profit for its investors. Figure 5.2 shows how the primary profit objective is broken down into its two components: revenue and cost.

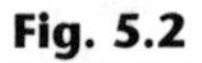

**Fig. 5.2**

*Business Objectives Analysis.*

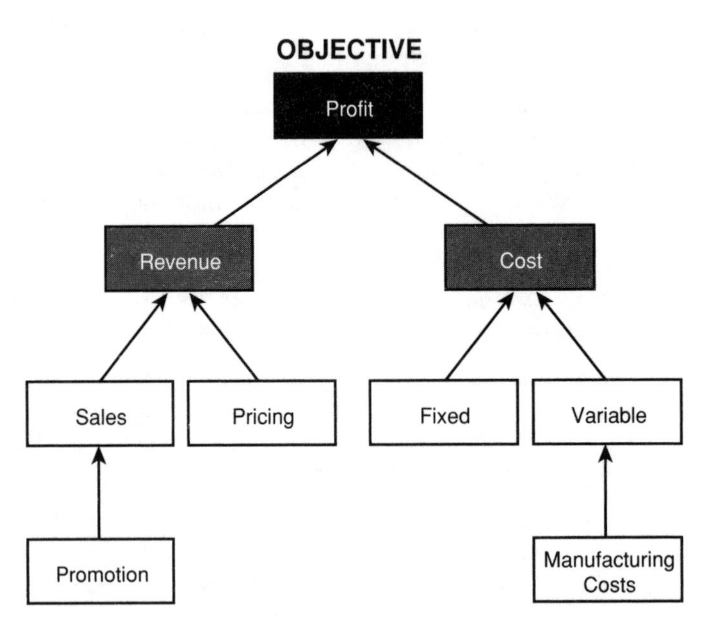


The business collects information on revenue producing activities, as well as cost producing activities. Figure 5.3 shows the roles of various people in managing these activities and items.

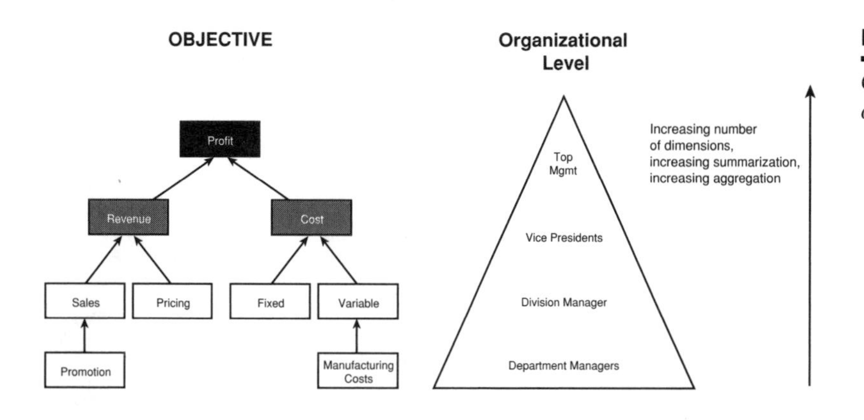


**Fig. 5.3**

*Organization roles versus organizational objectives.*

As can be seen in this figure, top management's role is to ensure that profit and margins are preserved or grown over time. Vice Presidents are responsible for managing the revenue and cost components, and division managers are responsible for component activities that produce revenue or consume cost.

How does all this fit into the role of the data warehouse? A data warehouse is primarily a Decision Support System. The business objectives from the top-down view focus the area where the data warehouse may be applied: *revenue management* or *cost management*. Each of these focuses calls for a different set of information that must be managed by the data warehouse and a different set of analysis techniques that must be used by end users. Revenue management has much to do with forecasting future sales based on past sales, environmental patterns, and buying trends. Cost management, on the other hand, has to do with tight operational control and monitoring various business cost measures. Benchmarking is an important tool for cost management. Revenue management may need external data sources that predict environmental trends.

The top-down view is amenable to classical business analysis techniques such as the Value-Added Chain analysis (see fig. 5.4).

## Data Source View

The data warehouse loads and stores data from many data sources. These data sources are characterized by one or more of the following:

- **Multiple storage technologies**—Data sources may have been implemented in IMS, DB2, Oracle, Informix, VSAM, or a host of relational and non-relational database systems. This is a result of maintaining and deploying legacy systems while also bringing in new technology in newer systems. In addition to the database organization method (relational versus non-relational), further complications that arise are multiple data encoding, transmission standards (EBCDIC and ASCII) for data, and connectivity challenges (SNA, TCP/IP).
- **Multiple data definitions**—Examples include *synonyms* (two data elements that contain the same data but have different names) and *homonyms* (two data

elements that have the same name but contain different types of data). The absence of a robust data administration function increases the likelihood of such events significantly.

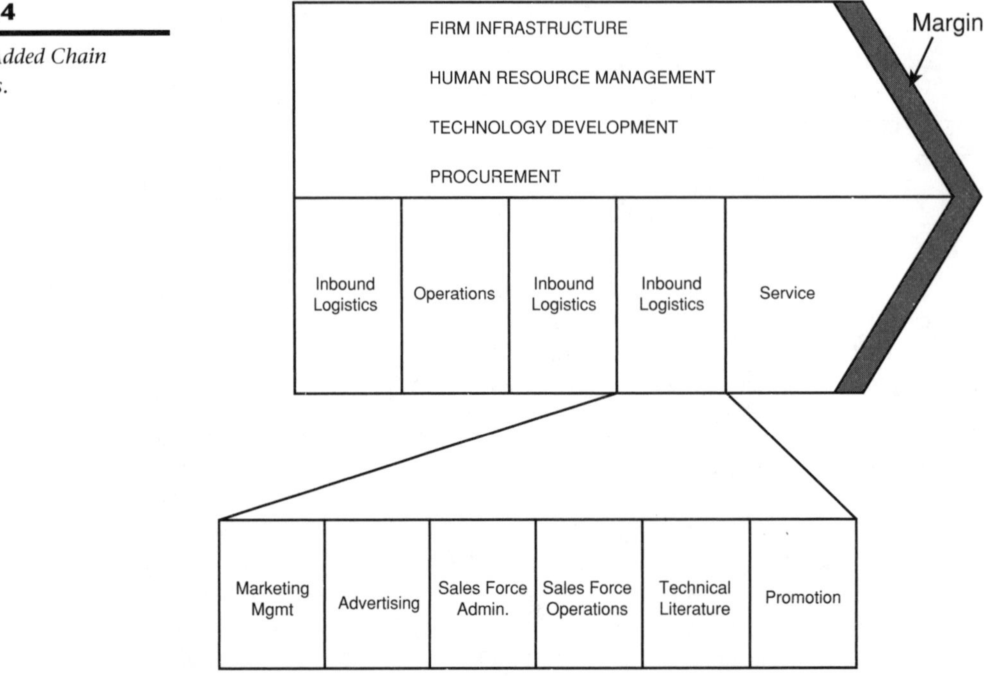


**Fig. 5.4**

*Value-Added Chain analysis.*

- **Null fields**—This is for certain data sources because the applications that were initially built did not require the definition of those fields. The lack of a robust database administration function increases the likelihood of application developers also defining the database constraints.
- **Format differences (datatype and length) between similar fields in two different databases**—Format differences occur because the databases that defined data differently did it from the narrow perspectives of the applications that they supported, rather than from the need to apply organizational standards to data definitions.
- **Encoding differences**—Different data sources can use different encoding schemes for data. Encoding differences also occur when the organization moves from one encoding standard (internal or external) to another.
- **Duplicates**—Duplicates result when two isolated data sources capture identical information without realizing that another system is also capturing the same information. Duplicates also result when information was not part of a key field and was not edited for uniqueness. Inadvertent duplicates are created when long data elements are truncated to match shorter data elements from another data source.

Each data source can be viewed as a pipe supplying data into the data warehouse. The challenge that the data warehouse analyst faces is the task of mixing the contents of these many pipes judiciously, while keeping the contents organized. The task ahead, therefore, is to:

- Model or represent the legacy data sources using the data element terms and definitions that they currently use (as-is representation). This is the "inventory" of data sources.
- Transform these models into one common form of representation. Data sources that are non-relational (e.g., hierarchical) are modeled in the same way as relational sources.
- Clean up the names of the data elements to achieve a degree of commonality. This includes identifying homonyms and synonyms.
- Select the subsets of data elements that are required by the data warehouse. Not all data elements need to populate the data warehouse. Work with business executives and business analysts to determine what portion of this information is valuable in the data warehouse.
- Integrate similar data sources into subject data models.
- Integrate similar data sources into a consolidated source model.
- Transform the consolidated source model into a warehouse model by adding time stamps, identification of origin (origin stamps), partitioning, derived elements, and providing model extensions to store precalculated aggregates, summary values, and decoding. Work with business analysts who provide management reports to business executives to determine the level of aggregation required, the frequency of data loads, and the number of cycles (monthly, quarterly, or yearly) to be maintained within the data warehouse.

It is important to remember that the steps above are used by the analyst to determine which data sources and which data elements in those data sources must supply the data warehouse with data. Once the data warehouse model is in place and the data extractors have been built, ongoing refreshment can be performed without the intermediate analysis. The analysis is still necessary for building extensions to the data warehouse or expanding the scope of data that the data warehouse must manage. Another important use of the analysis is to help in traceability when the quality of the data in the data warehouse is in question. For traceability, a complete routing of the data, right from the data source to the data warehouse, is as important as the way it was presented to the user as a query.

## Data Warehouse View

The data warehouse is organized differently from operational databases. The data warehouse model (and data management) differs from those of the operational databases in the following ways:

- The data model in the operational databases is geared towards elimination of redundancy, coordination of updates, and support of transactions that repeatedly perform the same types of operations many times a day on the same data.

In the data warehouse, the data model is geared towards supporting a wide range of queries and retrieving information on a timely basis. There is little, if any, updating of the data warehouse by the end user.

- The data model in operational databases is highly normalized to support consistent updates and maintenance of referential integrity. In the data warehouse, it is highly de-normalized to provide instant access without having to perform a large number of joins.
- The data model in operational databases is only of consequence to the database and application developers. It is often very complex and large. The data model in the data warehouse, however, must be comprehensible to end users, as the primary purpose of the data warehouse is to provide visibility and access to the data in a easy and convenient manner.
- The data inside operational databases is only that needed for current operations. Data that is not needed is very quickly archived to prevent degraded performance of operational systems. Data in the data warehouse is both operational and historical. The volumes of data that are contained in the warehouse are in the hundreds of megabytes to the hundreds of gigabytes. Data management for databases of these sizes requires a completely different approach.
- Operational databases store very little derived data. Most applications that operate against operational databases derive data as they go, whenever they need it. Data warehouses, on the other hand, store large amounts of derived data to save the effort and time of computing the derivations again. This is because these derivations are made not only against operational data, but also against historical data. There is no possibility of computing these derivations "on-the-fly."
- Operational databases contain *all* the data that is needed by an enterprise for supporting its operations. Data warehouses, on the other hand, contain only data that has value over time.
- Operational data is lightly summarized, often only for reporting purposes. Data warehouses precompute and store highly summarized data.

Because of these differences between operational databases and the data warehouse, different modeling techniques have been proposed for data warehouses. These techniques differ from the approach used for traditional operational database design, i.e., logical modeling, normalization, and then selective denormalization to achieve performance improvements. One of the most popular techniques is called the *multi-dimensional star model*. This model represents data as an array in which each dimension is a subject around which analysis is performed. Time is always one of these dimensions. The other dimensions are dependent on the business problem being analyzed. This model will be described in more detail later in this chapter.

The fundamental reasons for normalization in operational database design was to restrict the issues of data replication and redundancy and the loss of database integrity. Even though the screens of the application provided a view to the user that was non-normalized, the application logic "under the covers" implemented the integrity constraints and protected the database from losing its integrity. This was how the underlying structure of the database was insulated from the end user. In the data warehouse, the primary goal is to "expose" the database to the user. Since the user will not be making any changes, the consequence of having a denormalized system to database integrity is minimal. The focus in the data warehouse then, is to provide database tables that are wide and contain all the dimensions of interest to the user. The goal of the data warehouse data model design is ease of use and ease of comprehensibility to (sometimes fairly uninitiated) end users.

Developing a normalized data model was an essential step in designing an efficient data warehouse. The star model is the basis for online analytical analysis. The star model represents a specific business perspective on data warehouse information. However, denormalization reduces the flexibility necessary for supporting multiple perspectives. One of the implementors also mentions the difficulty of adding additional dimensions to the fact table and the resulting exponential impact on the data warehouse's size.



## Business Query View

The *business query view* is the perspective of data in the data warehouse from the viewpoint of the end user. One of the reasons for the popularity of the star multidimensional data model is that it closely mirrors the way a business analyst views a query. In fact, a multidimensional table is an exact rendering of a multidimensional query. To the analyst, posing the query is therefore an activity synonymous with querying the multidimensional table directly. The business query, therefore, is a request for facts, sometimes called measures, along various dimensions. (e.g., dollar sales of automobile air conditioners in Europe for the last six months). The fact table contains the sales information. The dimensions are time (past six months), product (air conditioners), and location (Europe). By organizing the data warehouse along these dimensions and fact tables, the business query can be easily formulated and satisfied.

Business queries also contain *subqueries*, or *break points*, for example, by month, by city, or by country. These break points must also be incorporated as dimensions and linked to the fact tables.

Business queries are important starting points to define the data warehouse schema. The analyst can derive information on the subject areas by making a master list of business queries and inferring a common list of subject areas. Figure 5.5 shows an example of the subject area for the marketing department based on queries that it created.

An important point to note is that subject areas are defined based on the perspective of the end user. They are not based on the way that the source data of the warehouse is organized. This is in keeping with the design philosophy that the data warehouse is trying to provide open and transparent access to its data, as compared to the actual organization of an operational database which must be shielded from end users and protected through internal mechanisms. Figure 5.6 shows an example from the sales department.

**Fig. 5.5**

*Synthesis of subject areas from business queries for marketing.*

- **What are the monthly promotion expenditures by media for the last 2 years?**
- **What was the quarterly budget for each ad agency for the last 4 quarters?**
- **What are the monthly product sales by product line for each district for the last 24 months?**

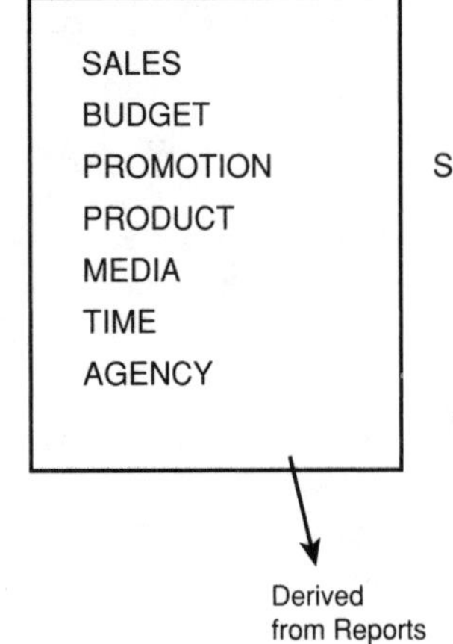


**Fig. 5.6**

*Synthesis of subject areas from business queries for sales.*

- **What were the bookings by sales representative for each of the last 12 months?**
- **What were the quarterly sales for each district and region for the last 8 quarters?**
- **What were the sales by product line for each district for the last 24 months – seasonal months only?**

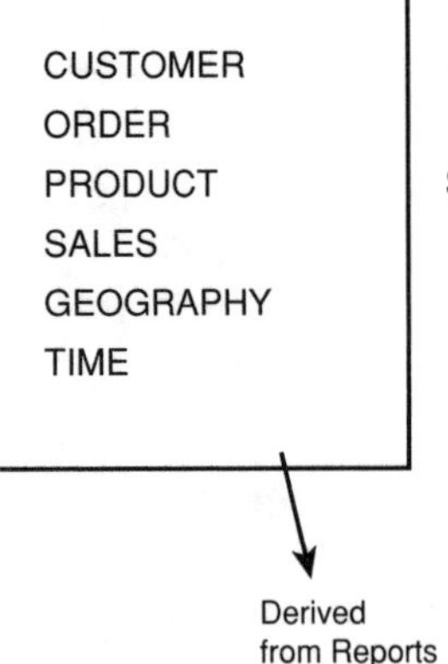

When the subject areas from multiple departments are combined, one sees potential for overlap and reuse of information. Business queries can therefore be viewed as a bottom-up source of specifications for the data warehouse model. Each business query can be thought of as a single perspective. Combining the subject areas from multiple queries provides a combination of multiple perspectives and the potential for more flexible star models.

# Modeling Data Sources

Data sources are modeled using traditional data modeling techniques. The Entity-Relationship Model is a popular modeling technique. CASE tools are commonly employed to build Entity-Relationship Models. CASE tools also offer extraction facilities for extracting models from existing databases. The models extracted represent the exact physical organization of the database as it currently exists. These are very appropriate starting points to determine what data elements are necessary for the data warehouse.

After all the data sources are modeled and after the subject areas have been defined based on the business queries that must be answered by the data warehouse, a tabulation must be made of data elements and the subject areas under which they can be classified (see fig. 5.7).

| Subject Area/Topic | Source | Technology | Object |
|---|---|---|---|
| CONTRACT | OLTP | Contract | Table |
| CUSTOMER | OLTP | Customer | Table |
| MARKET | Marketing | .... | .... |
| ORDER | OLTP | .... | .... |
| PRODUCT | Marketing, OLTP | .... | .... |
| PROMOTION | Marketing | .... | .... |
| SALES | Marketing, OLTP | .... | .... |
| SHIPPING | OLTP | .... | .... |
| TIME | Marketing | .... | .... |

**Fig. 5.7**

*Tabulation of data source technology objects by subject area.*

# Modeling the Data Warehouse

Many techniques for data warehouse modeling have evolved and are still evolving. Some of the popular techniques used are explained in the following sections.

## Star Schema

As the name suggests, the star schema is a modeling paradigm that has a single object in the middle connected to a number of objects radially (see fig. 5.8). The star schema mirrors the end user's view of a business query: a fact such as sales, compensation, payment, and invoices are qualified by one or more dimensions (by month, by product, by geographical region). The object in the center of the star is called the *fact table* and the objects connected to it are called the *dimension tables.*

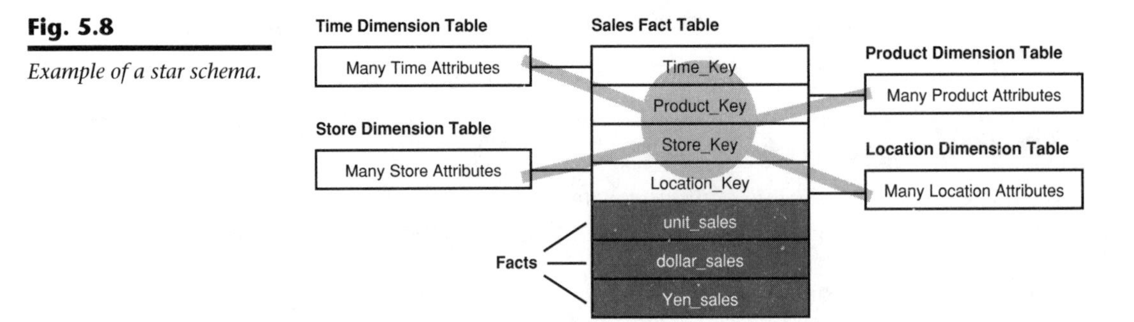


**Fig. 5.8**

*Example of a star schema.*

The figure displays only the private columns of the fact table and the foreign keys to the dimension tables. The dimension tables contain non-key attributes that describe the values of the dimension. For example, the Store dimension table may have non-key attributes—Square Feet Area, Lease Type, Company owned/Franchised—and key attributes—Store ID. Queries against the fact table simply fetch lists of pointers to dimension tables. When the queries against the fact table are joined with queries against the dimension table, a rich range of information can be retrieved. The dimension tables allow drill-down and aggregation of search criteria via joins.

A simple logical star schema consists of one fact table and several dimension tables. Complex star schemas have hundreds of fact and dimension tables. A fact table contains the basic business measurements and can consist of millions of rows. Dimension tables contain business attributes that can be used as SQL search criteria, and are relatively small. Some of the techniques that improve the performance of queries in a star schema (due to the joins with large tables) include the following:

- Define aggregations in existing fact tables or new aggregation tables. For example, both detail sales and regional sales can exist in the same fact table with an aggregate indicator column to differentiate rows. Alternately, you can create a regional sales aggregation table.
- Partition the fact table so that most queries access one partition only.
- Create separate fact tables.
- Create unique numeric indexes or other techniques to improve join performance.

## Snowflake Schema

The snowflake schema is an extension of the star schema where each of the points of the star radiates into more points (see fig. 5.9). In this form of schema, the star schema dimension tables are more normalized. The advantages provided by the snowflake schema are improvements in query performance due to minimized disk storage for the data and improved performance by joining smaller normalized tables, rather than large denormalized ones. The snowflake schema also increases flexibility of applications because of the normalization and, therefore, lowers the granularity of the dimensions.

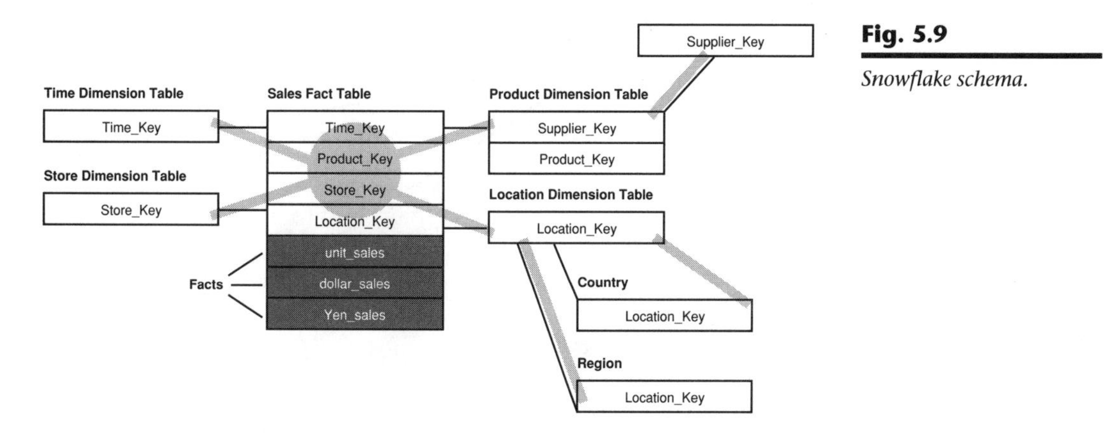


**Fig. 5.9**

*Snowflake schema.*

The snowflake schema increases the number of tables that the user must deal with and increases the complexities of some of the queries that must be mapped. Some new tools shield users from the physical database schema and allow him/her to work at a conceptual level. The tools map user queries into the physical schema. They need a DBA to make the mappings one time when the tools are installed.

### Mixed Schema

The mixed schema is a compromise between the star schema based on fact tables and unnormalized dimension tables, and the snowflake schema where all the dimension tables are normalized. In the mixed schema, only the largest dimension tables are normalized. These tables generally contain volumes of columns of highly denormalized (duplicated) data.

## Modeling Business Queries

The modeling technique used to understand, model, and analyze business queries is to build query footprints. Figure 5.10 shows a typical query footprint model.

In this figure, the Subject area of the query is isolated from its dimensions. This allows you to look for potential fact table and dimensional candidates for the data warehouse model. Figure 5.11 shows the query footprint obtained by applying this technique to the query "Annual Sales by product line by territory."

Figure 5.12 illustrates another query footprint for a product-based business query.

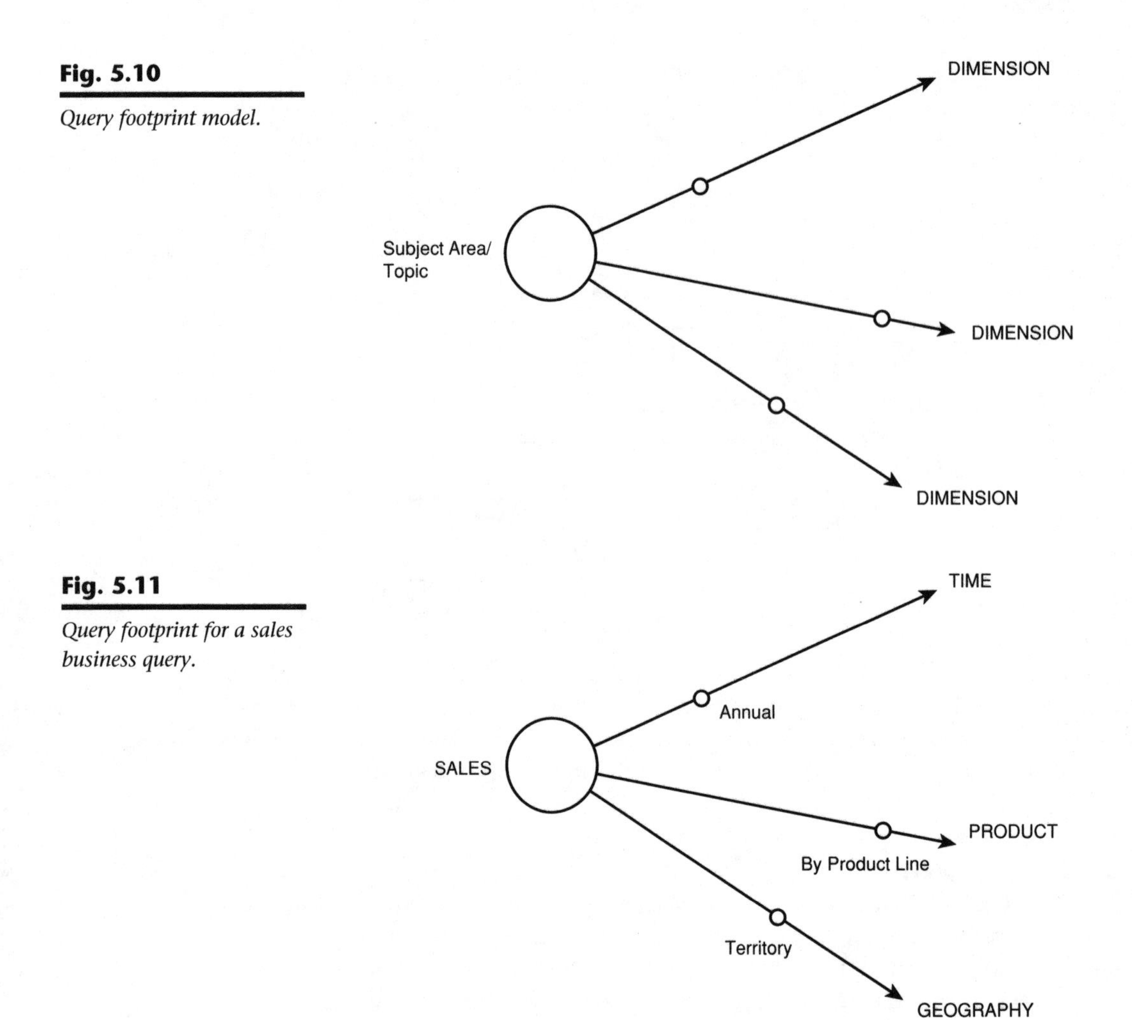


**Fig. 5.10**

*Query footprint model.*

**Fig. 5.11**

*Query footprint for a sales business query.*

Once the query footprints are identified for each business query, the queries and their footprints are consolidated (see fig. 5.13).

The resulting consolidated diagram for each subject area is called a Starnet model (see fig. 5.14). This is the combined representation of all the business queries.

Each of the subject areas are associated with various dimensions. The Starnet model can form the basis for the data warehouse model development using any of the modeling techniques described in the previous section.

The Starnet model is very versatile. A number of analytical techniques can be applied against the model. One example is to explore aggregation—combining one or more dimensions to come up with fewer dimensions. Figure 5.15 shows how aggregation works for the Starnet model.

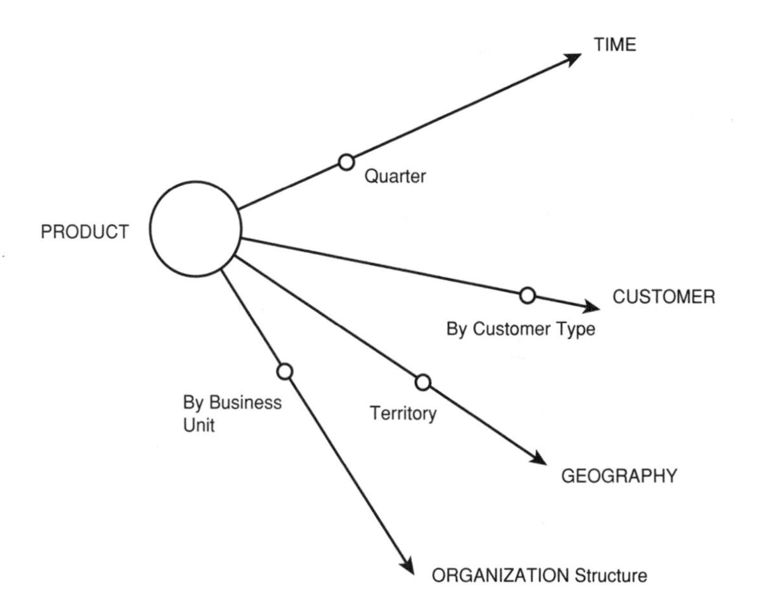


**Fig. 5.12**

*Query footprint for a product-based business query.*

- **Sales Reps. by Customer by Bookings**
- **Orders or Contracts or Spot Sales by Size by Geography**
- **Customer Revenue Size by Year**
- **Regional Sales by Quarter**
- **Product Orders by Product Line by Year**
- **Product Sales by Promotion Event**
- **Percentage of Shipping by Type of Shipment Method by Year**
- **Product Sales by Region by Quarter**
- **Competition Sales by Region by Year**
- **Demographics by Region and District**
- **Shipping Costs by Shipping Method**
- **Volume of Shipments by Destination**
- **Shipments by Shipping Method by Day**

**Fig. 5.13**

*Consolidation of business queries.*



The Starnet model can also be used for identifying drill-down requirements (see fig. 5.16). The business query footprint is a polygon that joins the appropriate Starnet model points. *Drill-down* is the polygon defined by moving one point closer to the center along the axes of the Starnet.

Experience has shown that most dimensions fall into a few categories. One example of a universal dimension is time. Figure 5.17 shows example dimensions.

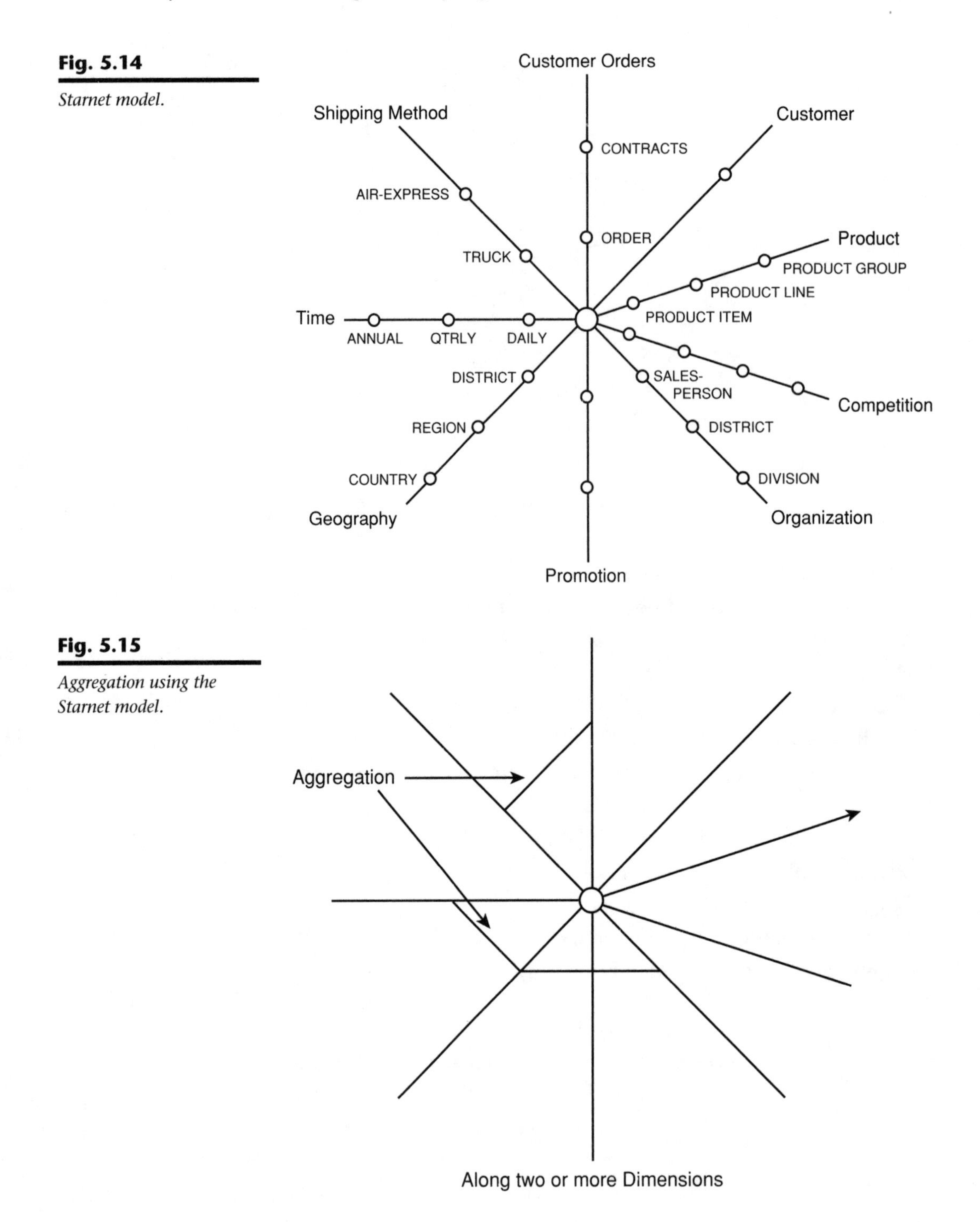


**Fig. 5.14**

*Starnet model.*

**Fig. 5.15**

*Aggregation using the Starnet model.*

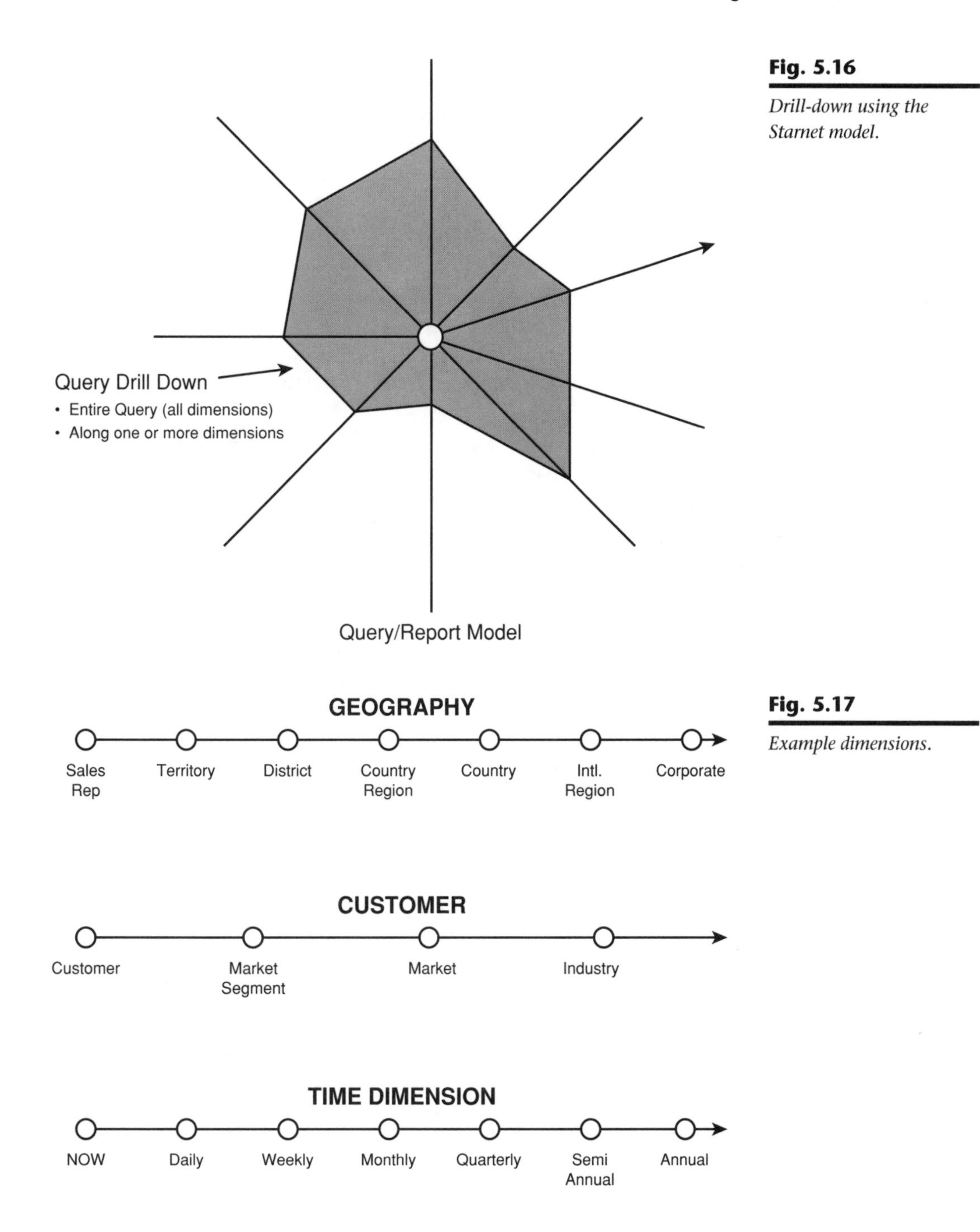


**Fig. 5.16**

*Drill-down using the Starnet model.*

**Fig. 5.17**

*Example dimensions.*

## Summary

- Understanding and analyzing business needs involves understanding four different types of views—a top-down view of the business focus, a data sources view, a data warehouse view, and a business query view. Each of these views requires a different modeling approach for representation and analysis.
- The top-down view of the business can be modeled using standard business techniques. Analysis can also proceed based on standard business techniques.
- The data source view can be modeled using standard data modeling techniques, such as Entity-Relationship Modeling. Because of the challenges of multiple technologies, formats, and naming conventions, it is important to reduce models of multiple data sources into a single model representing the source information.
- The data warehouse view is modeled using techniques such as the multidimensional star model, the snowflake model, and the mixed model. Each of these models deviate from classical normalization techniques and mirror more closely the end user's view of the data warehouse.
- The business query view is modeled using a Starnet model. The Starnet model allows the capture of a query's "footprints" and mapping of activities such as drill down and drill up. The Starnet model provides a bottom-up start for the data warehouse modeling based on analysis of business queries.

CHAPTER 6

# Developing and Deploying the Data Warehouse

This section deals with various aspects of deployment of the data warehouse from its initial deployment to the need for administration—from dealing with platform upgrades and maintenance to the challenges of deriving performance and managing the tremendous volumes of data that must be stored.

## Initial Deployment

A successful initial deployment is essential to the success of a data warehouse project. The major steps that are involved in the initial deployment are the following:

- Initial installation
- Rollout planning
- Training and orientation

### Initial Installation

In the majority of cases, organizations plan an initial pilot deployment of a smaller scale data warehouse to support a small group of highly motivated and proficient users. The deployment of any new technology is fraught with risks, regardless of the merits and ultimate benefits of the technology. Managing the initial deployment is critical for achieving early success. Initial deployment of data warehouse technology can present a steep learning curve to the user in many ways.

The mechanics of installing the user components of the data warehouse can be difficult for users. Because of the need to connect graphical tools with network, middleware, and communications software and the idiosyncrasies of personal workstation configurations, the installation process can be fraught with risk and potential for disappointment. Support from Information Systems (IS) and systems administration personnel is critical for a smooth installation.

The On-Line Analytical Processing (OLAP), query, and data access tools can present a significant learning challenge. The training for users must include how to solve problems using the tools in addition to operating the tools themselves. This "applications training" must be provided using real data to solve real or simulated business problems on warehouse data rather than using standard training databases. Solving sample business challenges as examples can illustrate the use of these tools far more vividly and clearly than a number of contrived examples generally used in vendor provided training.

Users can run into security barriers as they begin to start using data warehouse access and usage tools. The security and access control plan must be clearly defined and implemented before the initial deployment process starts. When users are brought in, they have clear security access and their security profiles are well understood by them as well as by the administrator of the data warehouse.

## Rollout Planning

After the initial small group of users are using the data warehouse and the process related issues are ironed out, the IS solution must be scaled up for a larger audience. The rollout phase is the phase where a standard solution is stamped out and distributed to large audiences of users. The goal for the preparations before the rollout is to build a "cookie cutter" distribution. All the components of the distribution are clearly identified and processes for handling, installing, and integrating these components are clearly established, verified, and tested. Rollout preparation must therefore include the following steps:

- **Standardizing the components of the data warehouse solution that must be distributed (rolled out)**—Standardizing components is the process of selecting the same type of component from the same vendor, adopting the same installation processes, using the same configuration parameters, and selecting the same operating platforms.
- **Standardizing installation and deployment processes for rollout**—Standardizing a process involves documenting the process in a clear, step-by-step manner, describing the list of prerequisites (including the skills of the operator) and applying the steps in the process to verify that they do work.
- **Planning the method of rollout distribution**—Different organizations use a variety of rollout methods. The most expensive, and probably the most effective, is to send out trained personnel to install the solution at the various rollout sites. The least expensive method is to distribute the solution over a network with a list of prerequisites and a set of process manuals. Often this is coupled with Help Desk assistance and emergency travel.

## Training and Orientation

The role of training and orientation in the insertion of any new technology can never be overstated! Training provided by component vendors is not sufficient for end users and data administration staff. The data warehouse is a systems solution that is comprised of a number of technology components. The systems solution has a life that is larger than the sum of its components. Data warehouse-specific training programs must be constructed. Separate programs are necessary for training end users and data warehouse administrative personnel. In addition, intense training in physical database design, database systems administration, and database performance improvement and tuning may be necessary and must be purchased from the vendors of those systems.

# Platform Upgrades and Maintenance

The data warehouse is constructed using many purchased components and several developed ones. As a complex systems integration solution, the effect of changes in any of these components can be far-reaching and have tremendous negative impact if not managed properly.

Typically, a data warehouse is a complex cross-platform solution where components of the solution run on different platforms. The data sources typically run on a mainframe or superserver, the data warehouse itself runs on a mainframe or more often on a superserver, the data marts run on other servers, and the end user access, query, and OLAP tools run on workstations. Linking these is a web of communication networks. The storage for the data sources is often in non-relational technology such as IMS or relational technology such as DB2. The storage for the data warehouse is usually a mainframe or server based relational database manager such as DB2, Oracle, Sybase, or Informix. The storage for access tools is often desktop-based such as Microsoft Access or a multidimensional database such as RedBrick. The mainframe operating systems are typically MVS or other proprietary non-IBM host operating systems, while the server operating systems are generally UNIX, OS/2, or NT. The client workstations generally run OS/2, NT, or Microsoft Windows. With such a large variety of components from a range of vendors, the task of tying it all together is challenging. Once these are all tied together, changes in any of these must be managed. Figure 6.1 shows the deployment complexity of a client/server systems solution.

Some of the challenges relate to vendor support for specific platforms. Vendors are driven by business needs to support popular platforms and, thereby, sell large volumes of identical products. Support for platforms that are not popular is limited at best, unavailable at worst. Another factor is the change of popularity of platforms over time. It is difficult to predict which platforms will remain popular for large intervals of time.

Platform upgrades follow a familiar path of dependency. At the bottom (or the top, depending on the perspective) is the computer hardware, followed in order by operating systems, communications, graphical user interfaces, databases, and application support libraries. With each new computer model, an operating system frequently announces to take advantage of improvements in processing. Escorting announcements of new operating systems is the announcement of communications drivers that connect the operating system to the outside world. With the operating system is also the announcement of graphical user interfaces that provide users with a newer (easier) paradigm for interfacing with the new computer and operating system. The announcements of database management system upgrades follow these announcements. Each of these announcements creates a need for upgrading the data warehouse environment, but not all of the upgraded products are available at the same time because of the development dependencies between them.

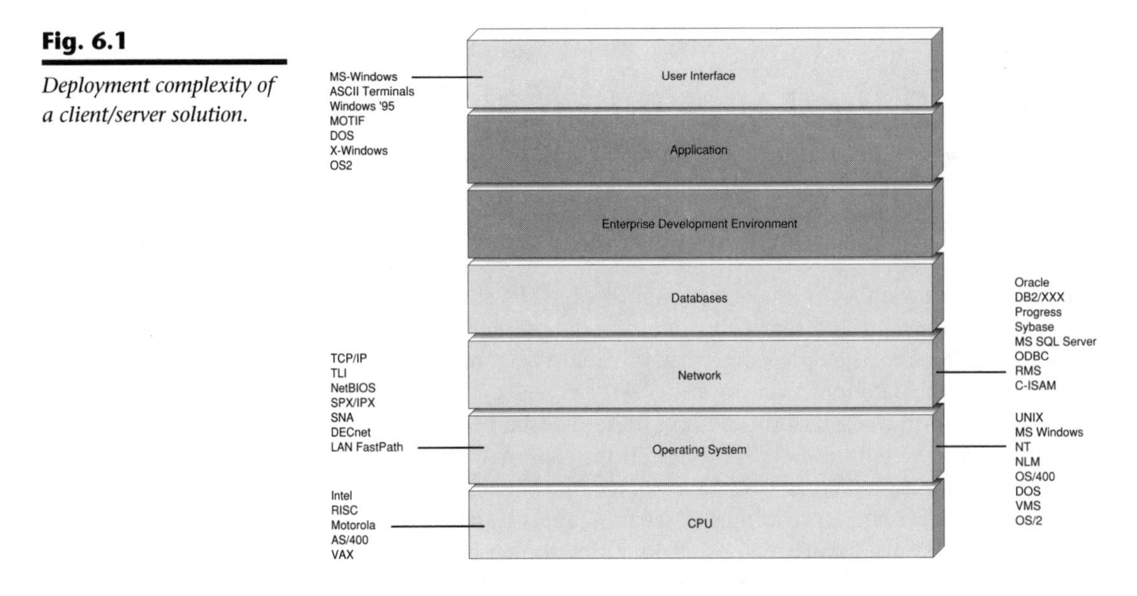


**Fig. 6.1**

*Deployment complexity of a client/server solution.*

Once the data warehouse has been built and deployed, a platform upgrade and maintenance plan must be built to manage announcements of new releases from component vendors. Without such a plan, the data warehouse platforms are frozen in time on the day the system is delivered and installed. The plan must be driven by the organization's needs for an upgrade—not the vendor's need to force an upgrade. Any upgrade plan must restrict major upgrades to, at most, twice a year based on the tumult that is caused when the upgrade is performed. A list (bill of materials) of data warehouse components and a clear assessment of impact for each of the components of the data warehouse must be available as part of the upgrade plan.

The reference architecture for the data warehouse is an important catalog for the components that are likely to change over the life of the data warehouse. The primary blocks of the reference architecture that catalog physical components of the data warehouse are the Infrastructure and Transport blocks.

## Infrastructure Block

The Infrastructure block of the reference architecture is shown in figure 6.2.

## Transport Block

The components of the Transport block of the reference architecture are shown in figure 6.3.

## End User Access and Usage

The components for End User Access and Usage are shown in figure 6.4.

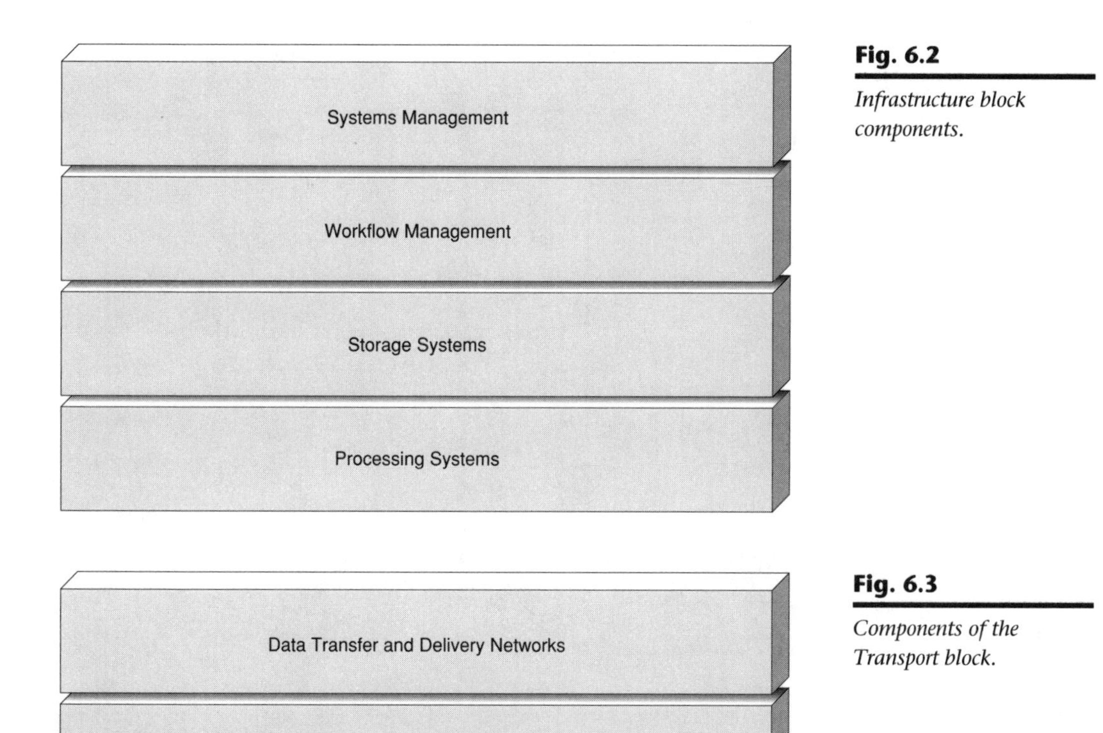


**Fig. 6.2**

*Infrastructure block components.*

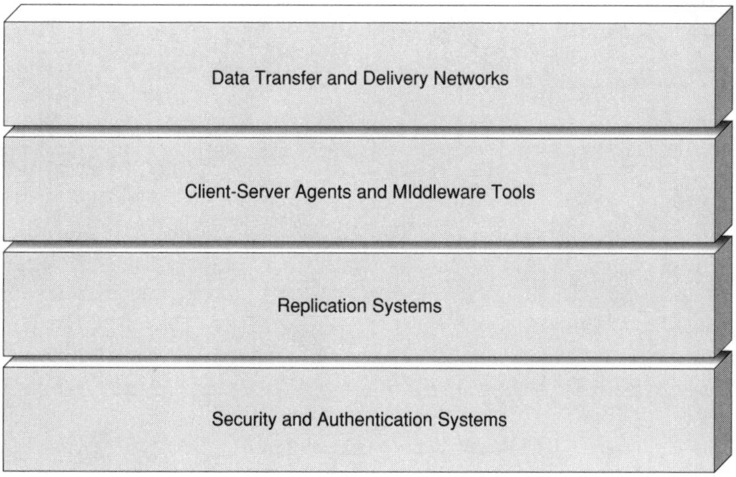

**Fig. 6.3**

*Components of the Transport block.*



## Data Management

The Data Management layer encompasses the Data Sources, Data Warehouse, Data Mart, and Access and Usage blocks of the reference architecture (see fig. 6.5). These represent vertical cuts, i.e., the components of the Data Management layer must be defined separately and exist separately for each of these blocks.

## Metadata Management

The Metadata Management layer is also similar to the data layer—it encompasses the Data Sources, Data Warehouse, Data Mart, and Access and Usage blocks of the reference architecture (see fig. 6.6). Separate components of Metadata Management must therefore be defined for each of these blocks.

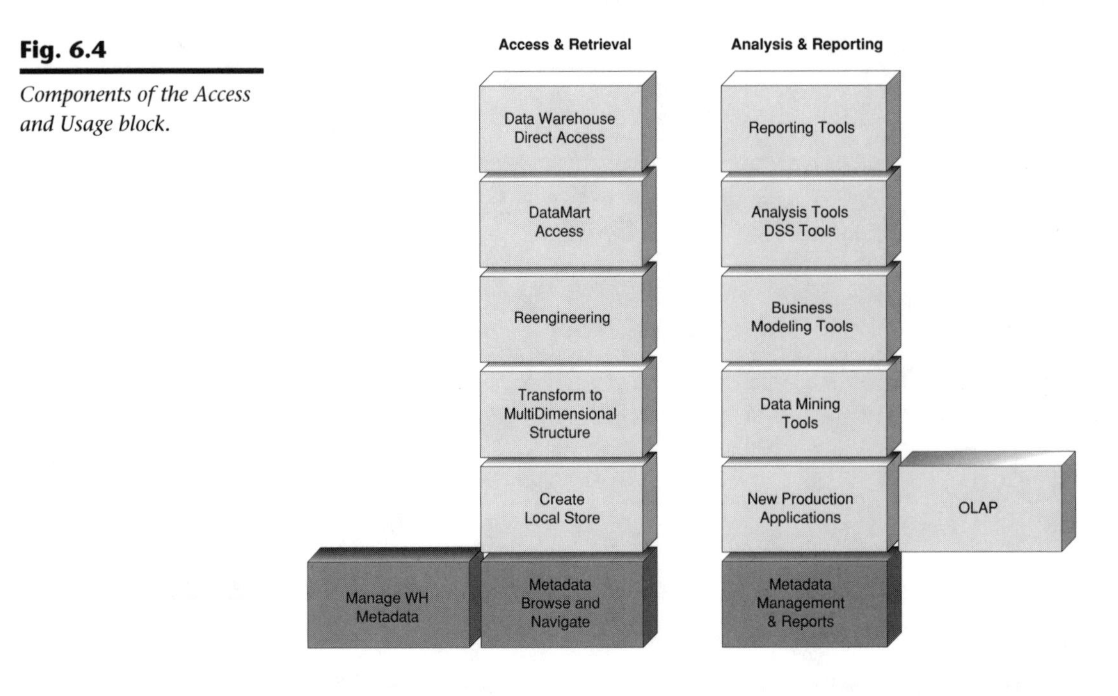


**Fig. 6.4**

*Components of the Access and Usage block.*

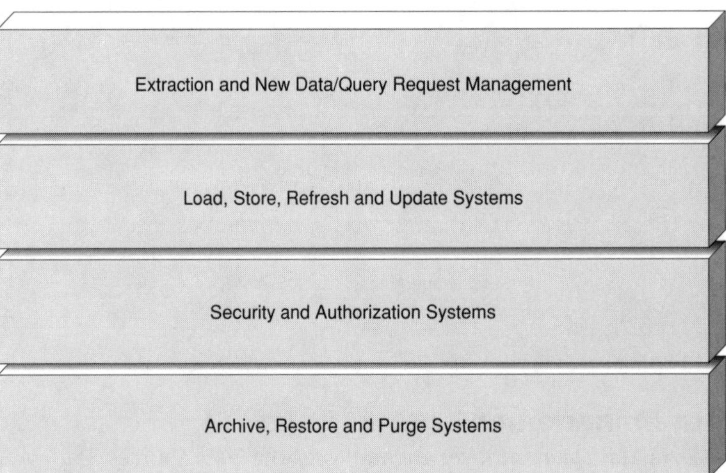


**Fig. 6.5**

*Components of the Data Management layer of the reference architecture.*

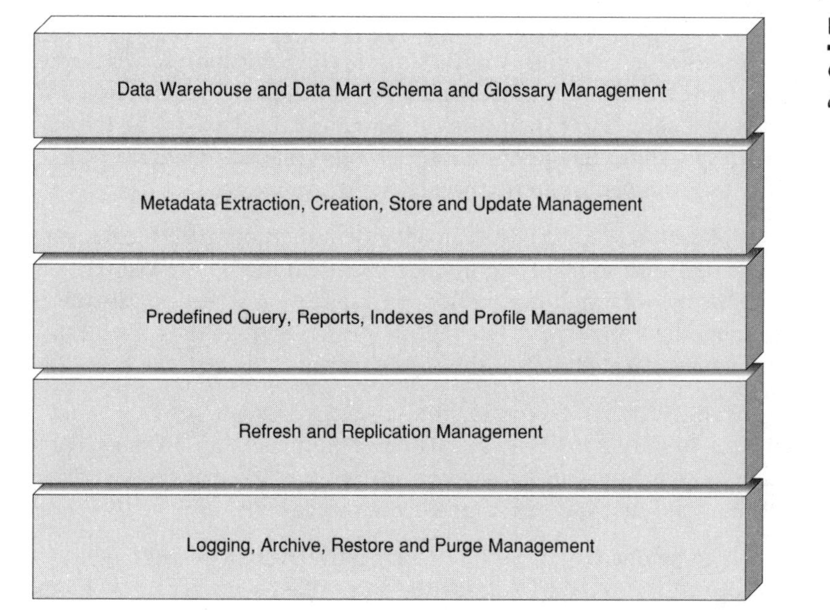


**Fig. 6.6**

*Components of the Metadata Management layer.*



# Data Warehouse Administration

The next section describes the various aspects of data warehouse administration. Data warehouse administration starts from the moment the data warehouse is deployed. The following aspects of data warehouse administration are discussed:

- Data refreshment, update, and replication
- Data source synchronization
- Disaster recovery
- Access controls and security
- Managing data growth
- Managing database performance
- Data warehouse enhancement and extension

Each of the items above will be discussed further in the following sections of this chapter.

## Data Refreshment, Update/Replication

There has been considerable interest in replication technology in recent times. Simply put, *replication technology* is the persistent ability to make copies of data inside one database (the *data source,* also sometimes called the *primary site*) on another database that is connected to it on the same machine or on a different machine (the *data target,* or *secondary site* or *data repository*). Replication services also allow change management of the copied data and allow only changes to be propagated from the source to the target. Replication is a very useful way to deliver data from one system to another on an ongoing basis while keeping changes under control. The replication server is often a third machine running a database that manages the replication process between the source and the targets. Changes to data inside the source are detected by the replication server. The corresponding changes for all information that was replicated are then sent on to the target server for application to the replicated data.

**The Promise of Replication.** Replication is a convenient method to keep data warehouse data synchronized with sources. It is also a convenient method to keep data marts synchronized with data warehouses. The same replication server can distribute replicated data to more than one target. The replication server therefore serves as a distribution channel for replicated data to multiple data marts.

Replication is a convenient method to build "hot standby" database systems. A *hot standby* is a database system that is identical to the system it backs up. In the event of failure of the source system, applications can be switched to the target system because it contains exactly the data that was stored inside the source system.

Replication systems can be one way or bi-directional between sources and targets. They can be event-driven (triggered by administrator specified events such as changes in data values) or time-dependent (performed at specified time intervals).

**Challenges with Replication Systems.** Replication servers are limited by the number of processes used to detect changes in data inside the source. If there are a number of applications updating the source simultaneously and there is only a single process monitoring the change log, the replication server can fall behind in applying the changes to the targets.

Replication systems can be non-invasive (they do not affect the performance of the source or target systems that they manage), or they can be invasive (they affect the access of applications or users using the database by locking them out as they work). If improperly planned, replication systems can cause numerous complications, from causing data to be out of sync, to eroding performance, to hogging multi-million dollar communication networks.

**Managing Replication.** Replication systems can present a potential drain on computing and communications resources. They can also have an impact on existing operational systems. They must be managed with an overall strategy that recognizes the potential for these issues. The strategy must include the following:

- **Definition of a replication architecture**—Replication architecture consists of a diagram that represents sources and targets. Popular choices are hub and spoke structures for mainframe oriented organizations where data from the mainframe is replicated to multiple servers. Servers which are spokes in one structure can themselves become hubs in another structure for further distribution of data. A parallel replication architecture consists of a set of peers that are connected to each other for replication purposes. Definition of replication architecture involves knowledge of data flows, organizational hierarchy, and business process flows.

- **Planning network traffic**—This involves planning network bandwidth, assessing existing capacities, and estimating data flow between replication servers, sources, and targets. Based on the periodicity of replication—as events occur or on a fixed periodicity—networks have to manage data flow. This also places a tremendous burden for network availability 100 percent or the need to put recovery procedures in place for incomplete replication processes.
- **Assessing information processing requirements**—It is important to assess the exact level of data currency needed by replication targets. By meeting exact requirements for replication currency, the tendency to overdesign replication frequency can be avoided. Every need for data currency must be examined on a case-by-case basis. Any requirement for immediate replication of data must be examined in detail to see if it is really necessary. By replicating less frequently and by propagating changes less frequently, the use of communications and systems resources is made more efficient.
- **Scheduling replication processes efficiently**—Scheduling is an important way to manage resource conflicts. Scheduling efficiently involves minimizing need for network bandwidth, use of off-peak times for effecting replication transfers, transferring data over multiple time zones, and the use of time and event triggers to control when replication occurs.

## Source Synchronization

One of the challenges that must be addressed, once a data warehouse has been deployed and is operational, is the challenge of data synchronization. *Data synchronization* is the coordination of simultaneous updates by multiple users to the same data. Almost all databases prevent two users from changing the same data at the same time at the same place by placing concurrency controls. The problem occurs when the same data is replicated at multiple places and each of those users believes that the data they see on their screens is wrong and needs changing. Some of these issues are aggravated when the replication system takes large amounts of time to propagate changes or when there are variable update times for different replication targets, thus causing unpredictable propagation of updates. In the purest sense, a data warehouse should not be allowing updates in the first place. In reality, once it is operational and the data it contains is freely accessible and available, people have a tendency to correct what they perceive are errors in data values.

## Disaster Recovery

After the data warehouse has been deployed, one of the administrative challenges is to come up with a disaster recovery plan. Given the demographics of computers and the widespread use of mainframe systems for fielding operational applications, the data warehouse is often one of the first forays of a business into client/server architectures for a Mission Critical system. The likelihood is very high that the personnel responsible for deploying and administering the data warehouse are coping with steep learning curves related to client/server communications, server based relational database management systems, graphical user interfaces, workstation operating systems, and server operating systems. The key players in the task of data warehouse administration are often themselves just beginning to learn the ropes of client/server system management. Often, the system management tasks are outsourced and a disaster recovery plan also has to address this reality.

Once the data warehouse is operational, the pressures from management and users to have continued access will increase. Without a disaster recovery plan in place, the repercussions to the deployment personnel are significant. Rehearsing the disaster recovery drill should be part of the development and pre-deployment activities. Once the warehouse is up and running, it is difficult to shutdown, bring up the server, and re-install the database management system.

Follow these recommended rehearsal steps:

1. Take down the server including the operating system (OS).
2. Re-install and reconfigure the OS.
3. Re-stripe the drives.
4. Re-install and reconfigure the RDBMS, monitors, and middleware.
5. Reload and re-index the data.

Performing drills such as these will expose gaps in knowledge, documentation, and vendor support. Hopefully, this will happen in time to prepare for the real disaster.

## Access Controls and Security

Security and managing access to data inside the data warehouse is very important. As the degree of summarization increases, the value of the data becomes increasingly higher. Summarized information that can assist an enterprise in making decisions is just as valuable to the competition! Controlling access to the data warehouse is still an evolving area of technology. The task is complicated by a number of factors:

- The data warehouse is built primarily as an open collection of enterprise data. It can assist in decision making and can be used by analysts and operational staff in improving their operations and deriving strategic and sustained competitive advantage. The addition of security controls flys against the need to be open.
- Users access data inside the data warehouse at different levels of summarization. The same user can start with highly summarized data and "drill-down" progressively into increasingly detailed data. Other users can operate at a single level of summarization. It is difficult to manage access at the table and row level for data for each of these users.
- The nature of OLAP and data access tools in the data warehouse arena has been exploratory. Most users use the data warehouse by employing a "discovery process." The addition of cumbersome security controls can make this very frustrating as users are prevented from proceeding further in their explorations.

  Since the data warehouse does not manage Mission Critical operational data, the nature of the security threat is not that of causing damage to data but of disclosing corporate secrets and strategies. Countering this threat involves containing access on a "need to know" basis. The security policy must also provide restrictions on drill-down capabilities and access control of specific summarized data tables and operational detail. Permissions must also be managed for restrictions of resource usage such as ability to create temporary tables and ad hoc queries.

Other threat scenarios are nuisance scenarios where hostile users tie up large amounts of resources—essentially making the data warehouse unavailable. Managing runaway queries, creation of temporary tables, and applying resource limits to user profiles can begin to address these challenges. The design of an access control and security plan is therefore an essential activity in the deployment process. Because of the nature of client/server applications, managing security from a single point of control is difficult. Users have user IDs and passwords which are often different for their workstation, network access, remote login into the server, and remote login into one or more databases. When a user departs, a clean up crew has to remove access controls in a number of systems. Planning applications that manage the cleanup and removal of these multiple access controls can assist the task of managing security within the data warehouse.



## Managing Data Growth

The data warehouse can potentially store data volumes that are several orders of magnitude larger than operational databases. This is because the warehouse manages historical information in addition to current or almost current operational data. As time marches on, today's current data becomes tomorrow's historical data and must be stored and managed exactly like the historical data from a year ago.

Bill Inmon states four major reasons why data warehouses contain significantly larger amounts of information than operational databases. They are as follows:

- The data warehouse contains historical data as well as current detail. A data warehouse typically contains five to ten years of data in its final mature state.
- Data is stored at the detail level in the data warehouse. The detail is required for reconciliation of various data from various departments whenever there are conflicts in interpretation of the data.
- The end user always wants more data than is available. End users' appetite for historical data is insatiable. Whatever the warehouse stores is always less than the end user's need. As a result, there is an increasing spiral of demand for data as the use of the data warehouse becomes common place.
- The growth of data in the data warehouse due to spontaneous creation of summary data is seldom planned. End users create additional amounts of data that they want to leave behind "for a future purpose at a later date if it becomes necessary." The capacity planner, who is responsible for planning the storage capacity of the data warehouse, can do a fairly good job of anticipating detail data requirements as well as pre-defined and pre-calculated summaries. What he/she cannot do is to anticipate the volumes of data that are generated and stored by analysts as they go through the "discovery" process through the warehouse.

Several common-sense business and management practices can be employed to contain and manage data growth:

- Increased use of summarization techniques significantly reduces the amount of data. As we proceed from highly detailed information to highly summarized information, there is a reduction in several order of magnitudes for the amount of storage required. On the other hand, to provide drill down capabilities for the detail, all the data must be stored and available for access regardless of degree of summarization.
- Containing the degree of drill-down capability significantly reduces the amount of data. Although the immediate response is "I want all the data," end users can generally manage their tasks with less detailed data than they demand. Alternative access paths to detailed drill down data may be provided which would satisfy the occasional need for detail at the lowest level of granularity.
- Limiting the length of historical data that must be stored inside the data warehouse. Business characteristics change significantly over the years. Business characteristics may also be cyclical and repeat themselves over intervals of time. Limiting the storage of historical information to the last business cycle may be more productive than deriving analysis on data of marginal value.
- Limiting the scope of data that must be managed using knowledge of business events which have altered the circumstances in which the data was gathered. When two corporations merge, for instance, the benefit of their individual historical data may not be the same when combined.
- Removing unused detail based on reference history. An interesting pattern of data warehouse is that over time, as the data inside the data warehouse grew, the actual percentage of data that was used for query processing shrank. As a result, even though the warehouse contained more and more data, less and less of it was being used by queries, i.e., less and less of it was useful to the corporation. One solution to this issue was to find out and remove data that was not being referenced by queries at all. Removing this unused data resulted in economies of storage and also overall improvements in query processing efficiency.

After all these techniques are used, the problems of data growth still remain for the information that is left behind and must be managed by the data warehouse. Data warehouses can range from a few gigabytes to several terabytes. The investment in storage costs at the server are a significant component of the overall cost of implementing the data warehouse. Managing this storage also represents a significant challenge. There are two broad strategies for storage:

- Distributing the data across many storage devices attached to many servers. This strategy intensifies the data integrity, management, and storage challenges because of the distributed nature of the storage. On the other hand, this strategy increases the reliability and availability as storage devices can be reused in the event of a damaged server or when a server is changed.

- Storing and managing the data in a central pool of storage devices that can be accessed intelligently by many servers. This strategy optimizes storage utilization and optimizes the storage investment.

The nature of demands placed by the data warehouse on the underlying databases are different from those placed by operational applications on operational databases:

- Data warehouses typically load and move data in large chunks. Operational systems tend to update small chunks of information through focused transactions.
- Historical data expands the data warehouse with each update. This expansion is significantly larger than the manner in which operational systems grow. Operational systems also jettison their history by archiving the data at periodic intervals. They always manage restricted amounts of data and use archiving to ensure that the data does not grow beyond specified limits. Data warehouses, on the other hand, always grow.
- Users need all possible access to all possible data. Sizable amounts of temporary tables are created and need to be stored and available. Large amounts of temporary storage space are also required to perform large merges that are required for data warehouse queries.
- Similar to operational transactions, data warehouse transactions tend to look up data, not update it.

In summary, the overall requirements placed by the data warehouse on the storage and retrieval systems are to retrieve and move large pieces of data efficiently and store lots of it. Database management systems that provide parallel operations through large data channels are required. The use of intelligently cached disk arrays, closely coupled to a backup and archival system, allows for multiple user access without waiting on disk seek and access times. The backup window for warehouse data is significantly shortened due to the large data warehouse database sizes.

## Managing Database Performance

The data warehouse is a demanding database application. The performance of queries is therefore closely determined by the physical database organization. In addition to the regular "good practices" list for database physical design, a number of performance enhancement activities must be undertaken. Some of these are described in the following sections.

**Parallel Query Execution.** In this method for improving database performance, a database query is split up into components and all components that can be simultaneously executed will be executed in parallel through concurrent processes. The performance of the query is therefore at the highest speed given the natural data dependencies within the query. Several vendors offer transparent parallel execution of queries. The designer of the query does not need to have a knowledge of how the query must be broken down into parallel components.

**Intelligent Partitioning of Tables.** In this method, the system administrator is responsible for efficient partitioning of tables across multiple disks and skipping unavailable data and uninvolved table partitions. Partitioning should also provide the ability to execute backups and restores at the partition level. This allows the backup/restore of portions of a table, thereby increasing the availability and reliability of other parts that are not being backed up or restored. This is particularly important in the data warehouse environment where table sizes can reach several hundred gigabytes for fact tables.

**Advanced Indexing Methods.** Database vendors are offering advanced indexing schemes that they claim are more efficient and provide tremendous performance improvements for data warehouse related applications. One of the schemes, called *bitmap indexing technology*, significantly improves response time over traditional indexing methods by greatly reducing the number of read operations to the data. Besides allowing more users to access the warehouse simultaneously, bitmap indexing also facilitates the ability for users to pose a series of queries to analyze data.

Traditional methods of indexing are both sequential and indexed. In sequential access, a file or table is read from start to end until the value that is being searched is encountered. This is inefficient for large tables where the penalty for searching is highest for values that do not exist and where the location of a value determines the time taken to access it. On the other hand, sequential indexing is useful for applications that update records in succession.

Non-sequential indexed methods, on the other hand, maintain an arrangement of records to reduce the amount of searching for a record value. Traditionally, the Binary Tree (b-tree) index has been used to store the values as a tree. An incoming search value is compared against the value of a tree node. The search branches to the left if the value is less than the value at the root of the tree, or right, if it is greater. The search is repeated until either the value is found or the search falls off the tree. Because of the binary nature of the search and the organization of values in a tree, the b-tree search is several orders of magnitude faster than the indexed search for large volumes of data.

Another popular form of indexing is the hash indexing. A mathematical formula based on the values of a record is calculated and stored. The same formula is applied to an incoming value and all records that match the hash value are returned. Hashed indices are useful when the key values and searched values are distributed over multiple columns. The b-tree and the hash method work well with high cardinality data—data with many different values. The b-tree method breaks down for low cardinality data—where several data items have the same column value.

Hashed and b-tree indexes work well in transaction oriented systems where the number of rows being accessed by a transaction is typically low. They also perform reasonably well on updates. After a number of changes are made, the b-tree has to be rebuilt. Both hashing and b-tree begin to break down with complex queries that have combinations of `AND`s and `OR`s in the SQL `WHERE` clause. The query optimizer is confused by conflicting optimization needs and the performance of the resulting query execution is often poor. Data warehouse queries are almost always complex and therefore almost always poorly executed by such systems.

Bitmap indexing has been designed to address the issue of poor response time for complex queries. The fundamental principle in bitmap indexing is that almost all of the operations on database records can be performed on the indices without resorting to looking at the actual data underneath. By performing operations primarily on indices, the number of database reads is reduced significantly. Bitmap indices take up significant storage but speed up complex query execution. As with all indexing schemes, building a bit map index slows down data entry. In a data warehouse, this penalty is often paid infrequently as during loading of the data warehouse, and during refresh operations. Updating a bitmap index can take substantially longer than updating a b-tree index.

To get the best of all worlds, database vendors are offering a combination of the various indexing methods. These combinations are based on the use of b-trees, bitmaps, and record ID lists. Getting the most out of database indexes requires using the appropriate form of indexing for the appropriate type of table. Skilled database designers who understand what is in the database and how it is used to get the good database performance are also required. Physical design of the warehouse database, therefore, is a key item for deriving performance.

**Use of Clustering.** In the warehouse, sequential access of large data quantities is the norm. This form of processing benefits most from clustering. *Clustering* is the term used by database designers to physically locate tables that are related close to each other. Declaring a cluster of tables results in tables sharing neighboring areas of disk storage. Clustering is a technique that is very useful for the kind of sequential access of large amounts of data that the data warehouse demands. Sequential pre-fetch can produce dramatic performance gains when accessing a large number of rows.

**Eliminating Referential Integrity Checks.** Referential integrity is an important feature for operational database applications. Referential integrity is a requirement for the database manager to verify additions and deletions against relationships specified between two or more tables. This adds a necessary but severe performance penalty for operational databases. In the data warehouse, however, referential integrity may be redundant because only data that is already checked is loaded or refreshed. Turning off referential integrity can yield significant performance gains in such an environment. The need for referential integrity for the data warehouse becomes questionable when the range of domain values for data changes over time. In fact, changing domain values are characteristic of historical information.

**Protecting against runaway Queries.** A *runaway query* is a query that absorbs increasing system resources as it executes. Queries use temporary tables for storing internally generated data during the process of execution. If a query is badly formed, this requirement for temporary tables can exceed the space available. Most database systems, including DB2, provide the ability to specify resource limits for a query. This prevents runaway queries from affecting not only the individual user's performance but performance all around for everyone using the data warehouse.

## Data Warehouse Enhancement and Extension

Success breeds an appetite for more. As the initial warehouse deployment is enthusiastically embraced by the initial set of users, requests will invariably stream in for more—more information from existing data sources, more data sources that are not being currently tapped, and more external sources such as documents, spreadsheets, and syndicated data sources such as Dun & Bradstreet, Standard & Poor's, Moody's, and A.C. Nielsen.

**More Data from Existing Sources.** Adding more data from existing sources involves extending the data model of the data warehouse and linking incoming data to existing fact tables and dimension tables inside the warehouse. Adding more data also involves extending data refinement and re-engineering activities to the new data. If the new data is completely defined by the existing warehouse metadata, only the data refinement and re-engineering activities need to be applied, since the data can be accommodated by existing warehouse tables.

**New Data Sources from Inside the Organization.** Adding new data sources that involve extending the data model of the data warehouse is a more complex addition. Dimensional analysis of the source data model must be performed and new fact tables or extensions to existing fact tables need to be defined. New dimension tables may also have to be defined for the data. In addition, an analysis must be performed to determine the overlap of the new data with existing data warehouse data. The analysis will yield requirements for refinement and re-engineering to fit the new data into the data warehouse.

**New or More Syndicated Data Sources.** Syndicated data sources are commercial sources of information that can be purchased. A classic example is a database from a major consumer survey company that describes the profiles of prospective customers, their habits, buying patterns, and income profiles. Syndicated data sources provide much needed environmental information for marketing activities. They can also provide information on regulatory activities, competitive comparisons, product surveys, consumer surveys, and a rich range of mailing lists.

Incorporating a syndicated data source is considerably more difficult that accommodating operational applications that are homegrown. This is because the syndicated sources provide data in a fixed format and place the burden of processing the data on the consumer of the data. The data extraction techniques that were discussed earlier are more applicable to database resident data. Syndicated sources generally provide large files with fixed structures. These must be loaded into a database locally before they can be processed for extraction and for loading the data warehouse.

**Incorporating Non Electronic Information.** There is no magic restriction that the data warehouse must manage only information that is available in the operational databases. Many organizations have tried to use paper documents for retrieving historical information. Extracting and loading non-electronic information is a complex task that involves the following:

- **Conversion of non-electronic information to electronic**—This involves rendering paper documents into magnetic media. The information is typically converted using a scanner that produces an electronic image of the paper document.
- **Conversion of an electronic image to text based information**—The electronic image is not suitable for data processing and must be converted into text. Software that performs optical character recognition (OCR) is generally used for this purpose. Recognition accuracy can vary from very poor to excellent depending on factors such as the quality of the image, the choice of fonts in the initial document, and the degree of contrast of the paper and text.
- **Creation of metadata that describes and organizes the information within the document**—Once the metadata is loaded into the warehouse, it is used to organize the information inside the data warehouse.
- **Extraction software that extracts data from the text information that was recognized by the OCR software**—The extraction software must understand the metadata of the warehouse in order to generate load streams that match the metadata.



# Scope Management

The key to a successful data warehouse, as in any large and complex project, is selecting the right scope and solving the right amount of the right problem for the right user. Scope selection will determine whether a data warehouse implementation team is overreaching with the consequent risk of losing credibility, or is building a reputation one successful project at a time.

## Business User Needs Addressed

In an earlier section on requirements gathering and analysis, you were introduced to the process of acquiring a list of sample business queries that users would like to see the data warehouse address. This is a good starting point for determining and restricting scope. The business queries automatically define the boundaries of the various entities that must be stored in the data warehouse, the dimensions, and the degree of summarization required. Scope restriction can therefore be applied to the following:

- Queries
- Dimensions
- Reports

## Technology Considerations

Technology imposes a significant demand in data warehouse investment. Complexity imposes a significant risk in both schedule and delivery potential. The following can be used to restrict the scope of the first implementation of a data warehouse:

- Size of warehouse metamodel
- Size of data stored in the data warehouse
- Size of data from input sources
- Variety of input source technologies (relational and non-relational)
- Number of input sources
- Level of usability of input source data (degree of documentation of metadata, data quality, data relevance)
- Quality of input sources
- Documentation level
- Availability of people familiar with data sources
- Degree of integrated data management
- Availability of well-organized metadata in repositories/data dictionaries
- Availability of well-designed and documented enterprise/logical data models and CASE tools

## Implementation Timeframe

One usual technique for accelerating an implementation project is to set a limit on the implementation schedule. The goal is to achieve whatever is possible within the time frame of the proposed limit. An accelerated data warehouse implementation can benefit from such an approach. This approach is recommended whenever there is a tremendous call for action. Comparatively, this is certainly not a recommended approach for building and deploying an architected data warehouse that will serve the organization for many years.

## Budget Allocation

Similar to the schedule-driven project is the budget-driven project. The scope control for this project is primarily financial. The challenge in such a project is to manage resources and deliver results when the only control used is the amount of money available. This approach is not recommended as often, mainly because there is no recognition that a data warehouse requires a minimum investment to get off the ground.

## Resource Allocation

Resource allocation is another popular method of controlling a project's size. One key requirement for a data warehouse project is a critical mass of skills and personnel. Critical mass consists of a variety of skill families and experience with integrating client/server applications and deploying them in the past. Limiting the resource allocation for a data warehouse project often starves the project of people with the right skills and experience and significantly increases the risk of failure.

## Summary

- Initial deployment success is critical for an organization to embrace data warehouse technology. Careful planning of the initial deployment as well as the rollout is absolutely necessary for success. Training and orientation are essential components of initial deployment. Training must be geared towards real world usage of the system, not toy examples from data warehouse component vendors' training programs.
- Platform upgrades and maintenance in a client/server environment is complex and often frustrating. There are a number of platform dependencies and upgrade announcements that are rarely coordinated and available at the same time. A wait-and-see approach to implementing upgrades can pay off. Consolidating component upgrades and restricting the number of upgrades in a year can help manage the complexity.
- Data warehouse administration is a complex task that involves data refreshment of the warehouse, data source synchronization, planning for disaster recovery, managing access control and security, managing data growth, managing database performance, and data warehouse enhancement and extension.
- Scope management is also a key to achieving success in the first data warehouse implementation. Scope management can be implemented in a number of ways such as controlling the number and range of queries, dimensions, reports; limiting the size of the data warehouse; or limiting the schedule, budget, or resources. Some of these are not recommended as being conducive to a long term data warehouse implementation.

CHAPTER 7

# The Importance of Metadata Management

*Metadata* is popularly defined as *data about data*. In a database, metadata is the representation of the various definitional objects of a database. In a relational database, this representation would be the definitions of table, column, database, view, and other objects. In a broader sense (and for the purposes of this section), we use the term metadata to signify anything that defines a data warehouse object—whether it is a table, a column, a query, a report, a business rule, or a transformation within the data warehouse. This broad definition of metadata allows us to encompass the definition of all significant objects within the data warehouse.

Understanding these definitions is essential for all aspects of data warehouse development—from developing extract programs from the source databases that feed the data warehouse with data, to transforming data from multiple databases so that this data can be stored in a common format within the warehouse.

## What is Metadata?

Metadata pervades all aspects of the data warehouse. This is attested in the reference architecture shown in figure 7.1, where the shaded blocks correspond to the metadata needed to support the blocks above it.

Metadata consists of the following types of items:

- Location and description of data warehouse servers, databases, tables, names, and summarizations
- Rules for automatic drill-up/down and across business dimension hierarchies such as products, markets, and charts of accounts
- End user defined custom names or aliases for the more technically named data headings and facts
- Rules for end user defined custom calculations
- Personal, workgroup, and enterprise security for viewing, changing, and distributing custom summarizations, calculations, and other end user analysis
- Descriptions of original sources and transformations

- Logical definitions of tables and attributes of the data warehouse
- Physical definitions of tables and columns, as well as their characteristics
- Mapping of data warehouse tables to each other
- Extract history
- Alias information
- Summarization algorithms
- Subject area location
- Relationship history
- Ownership/stewardship
- Access patterns
- Reference tables and encoded data
- Aging and purging criteria
- Data quality indicator
- Security
- Units of measure

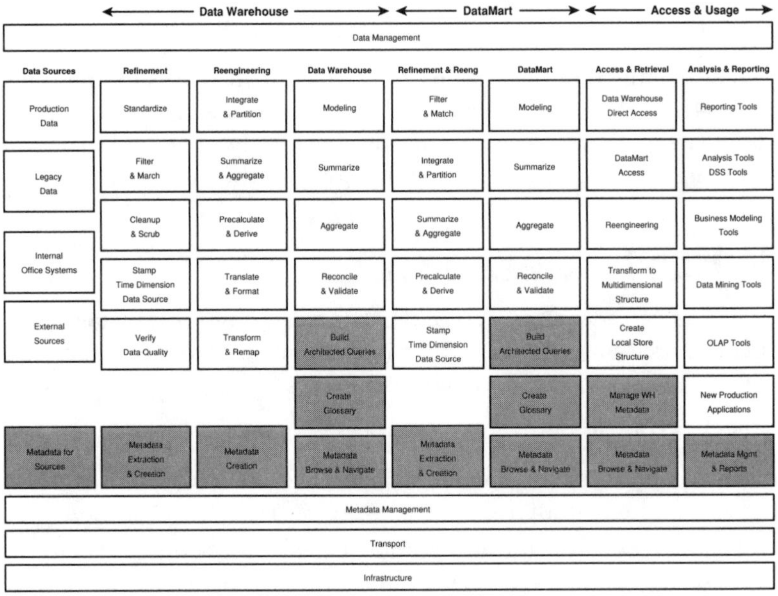

**Fig. 7.1**

*Every block of the data warehouse has a metadata component that is shown shaded in the figure. These components contain the definitions needed by the block to perform its functions.*

Additionally, metadata also may contain mapping components that assist in the following tasks:

- Identification of operational sources
- Simple attribute to attribute mapping
- Attribute conversions
- Physical characteristic conversions
- Encoding and reference table conversions
- Naming changes
- Key changes
- Defaults used
- Default reason
- Logic to choose from multiple operational sources
- Algorithmic formulae used

Figure 7.2 shows an example of a metadata element.

| | |
|---|---|
| Entity Name: | Customer |
| Alternate Names: | Client, Account |
| Definition: | A customer is a person or enterprise that has purchased goods or services at least once from the corporation. |
| Create Date: | January 15, 1992 |
| Last Refresh Date: | April 5, 1995 |
| Keys(s): | Customer ID, Customer Location |
| Refresh Cycle: | Extracted every month |
| Archive Cycle: | Archived after 6 months |
| Data Steward: | Jane Doe |
| Data Owner: | Bill Doe |
| Access Patterns: | Last Access Date May 30, 1995 |

**Fig. 7.2**

*The metadata for an entity (or file record or table) usually contains an authoritative business definition of the entity and information such as point of contact and commonly used synonyms.*

Figure 7.3 shows an example of attribute metadata. Attributes also carry information on physical characteristics needed for conversions.

**Fig. 7.3**

*The metadata for an attribute (or column or field) also contains a business definition, a list of synonyms, historical information about its creation, and data warehouse related parameters such as transformation and conversion information.*

| | |
|---|---|
| Attribute Name: | Customer Name |
| Alternate Names: | Account Name, Client Name |
| Definition: | Customer Name is the official name used by the person or enterprise that is the customer. |
| Create Date: | March 30, 1992 |
| Last Refresh Date: | April 5, 1995 |
| Key Indicator: | N (NonKey) |
| Source of Data: | Order Entry System, Customer File Attribute is Acct_Name |
| Transformation/ Conversion information: | From 20 characters to 35 characters |
| Summarization/ Derivation Algorithm: | None |
| Default Used: | None |
| Multiple operational sources: | No |

# Why is Metadata Important?

Metadata is like the roadmap to data. In much the same way as a library card catalog points to both the contents and the location of books within a library, metadata points to the location and meaning of various information within the warehouse.

Consider a physical warehouse that stores the items sold by a catalog merchandiser. The customer who wants to place an order must know what merchandise is available, make a selection, and present a catalog number for the item that she or he wants to buy. Often, a catalog is provided that indicates the available items and how much these items cost. The people who staff the warehouse receive the order that contains the catalog numbers of the items to fulfill the order. They then walk through various aisles of the warehouse, picking the items, and then they consolidate the order at the front for customer pickup. In a separate activity, goods coming in to stock the warehouse are sorted by catalog numbers and stored in appropriate places within the warehouse. Throughout this process, the catalog numbers and definitions of the items ordered are key for all the people who staffed the warehouse and service the customer.

In a similar way, the data warehouse also must maintain a catalog of items that it manages. End users are like customers—they originate requests for information based on a selection that they make from a catalog. The process that fulfills the request must know where the information is located within the warehouse.

The data warehouse must therefore contain a component that fulfills the catalog functions (like the card catalog or the warehouse catalog) for the information that it manages. This catalog must be organized to supply the following capabilities:

- It must serve as a map to locations where information is stored in the warehouse. This map is important to those who want to know what is stored in the warehouse. It also is important for business applications that use the data warehouse itself as storage for their information. The map is important for people who administer the data in the warehouse. It also is important for development staff, who must write either software that queries the warehouse or software that integrates query and reporting tools with the warehouse. Often, the catalog is the schema of the data warehouse's database. Because most data warehouses use a Relational Database Management System (RDBMS), the schema contains items such as the definitions of tables, columns, views, indices, constraints, queries, stored procedures, triggers, policies, and databases.
- Optimally, the catalog of the data warehouse must have two definitional components for every item—the definition needed by the database technology (such as the table name, table owner, table type, column names, datatypes, and defaults) and the definition needed by a business user. This business definition is slanted towards common business terms and definitions and is not subject to the limits imposed by technology (such as limit on the length, inability to use the space, non-alphanumeric characters, and so on).
- It must provide a blueprint for the way in which one kind of information is derived from another. Summarization is an example of such a derivation. Historical data over the last ten years may be presented as summarized by year, month, and quarter to support the needs for analysis. The addition of a time dimension to operational and historical data also must be captured by the catalog as metadata definitions with time domains. Other dimensions that are added to incoming data also must be represented by appropriate metadata.
- It must provide a blueprint for extractors that extract data from operational business applications and deposit them into the warehouse. Extractors are responsible for understanding the organization of the incoming data and the organization of the target database in which the data will be stored. They are responsible for making format conversions, providing defaults, or truncating and rounding information.
- It must store the business rules that are built into the warehouse. Business rules are the formal guidelines that organizations establish to resolve data inconsistencies and to implement business policies. Business rules are used when inconsistent and incompatible data must be "cleaned up" from the operational sources before being stored within the data warehouse.
- It must store the access control and security rules to enable administering security. Access controls and security rely on permissions being attached to metadata.
- Metadata must track changes over time. Often, the organization of data that a corporation collects over the years has also changed. The customer metadata collected from 1985 to 1990 may differ in organization than the data collected from 1991 to 1995 because of changes made in the databases and application

systems that support order processing. For another example, when the corporation merged with another, the information systems from the two organizations were integrated over a period of three years, resulting in a different organization of data.

- Metadata must be versioned to capture its change history.
- The structure and content of the data warehouse needs to be stored.
- The system of record (or source, usually the legacy applications) for the data warehouse must be clearly and formally identified.
- The integration and transformation logic that moves the data from the operational environment to the data warehouse environment must be made available as a regular part of the data warehouse metadata.
- The history of refreshment needs to be stored as a part of the metadata to enable users to determine its timeliness and accuracy.
- Metrics need to be stored so the end user can determine whether a request will be a large or small one before the request is submitted.

## Importance of Metadata During Warehouse Development

As observed in the reference architecture, during the development of the data warehouse, metadata is used in the following components:

- Data source extraction
- Data refreshment
- Data source transformation
- Data source scrubbing
- Data source summarization and aggregation
- Data warehouse database design
- Query and report design

If the process of capturing the metadata is carefully performed during these activities, the metadata is automatically available to end users during the deployment stage of the data warehouse.

The development process is an engineering process. It must, therefore, be explicitly documented to provide reproducibility and for evolutionary quality improvement. Metadata that is created as a result of this process must, therefore, be versioned for change management purposes. For example, every operational schema of the data warehouse catalog must be versioned. The business rules and process rules that were used for conversions, scrubbing, transformation, summarization, and aggregation must be captured.

The design of metadata for a data warehouse is a dramatic shift in paradigm for information analysts who have been analyzing and designing databases to support operational systems. The focus during the design of an operational database is to create normalized data models attributed with atomic data. Until now, the primary concern was to eliminate data redundancy by using normalization. The objective of eliminating data redundancy is to prevent problems of update and for maintaining data consistency.

The design of metadata for the data warehouse needs a complete change in mindset. The focus of the design of metadata for the data warehouse is to represent a rich range of relationships to the analyst, often with a large amount of redundancy. Because updates are not a primary issue within the data warehouse, no price is associated with the data redundancy other than the storage overheads. Often, economies of processing are obtained by performing and storing joins as tables. The change in mindset for the analyst is adapting from a famine of data redundancy to enjoy a feast!

Another shift in paradigm for the information analyst is the emphasis of operational systems on current metadata. Most operational applications operate only with the current organization of the database and the data. Old data is archived (hopefully!) along with older versions of the database organization. Within the data warehouse, the organization of previous versions of the operational database are important because the metadata must be used to extract historical data. Metadata versioning within the data warehouse is an important consideration.

An important aspect of metadata is the need to maintain mappings all the way from the sources to the data warehouse through the process of extraction, refinement, and re-engineering. These mappings need to be maintained for the following purposes:

- **Verification of data quality**—The mappings contain information on the various changes that the data underwent before it was stored inside the data warehouse. This "audit trail" is very important if the decisions that are made based on the analysis and interpretation of warehouse data are to be accurate.
- **Synchronization and refresh**—As new operational information is generated and must update the warehouse, the new data must undergo transformations that are identical to previously loaded warehouse data. Maintaining the mappings and algorithms for transformation is therefore essential to repeat the process of transformation on refreshed data.
- **Integration**—The mappings establish relationships between data that reflect business rules of interest to end users. Without the mappings, the end user is presented with isolated pieces of data that are not conducive to decision support.

Figure 7.4 shows the mappings that are maintained by the metadata for the data during its journey through the data warehouse.

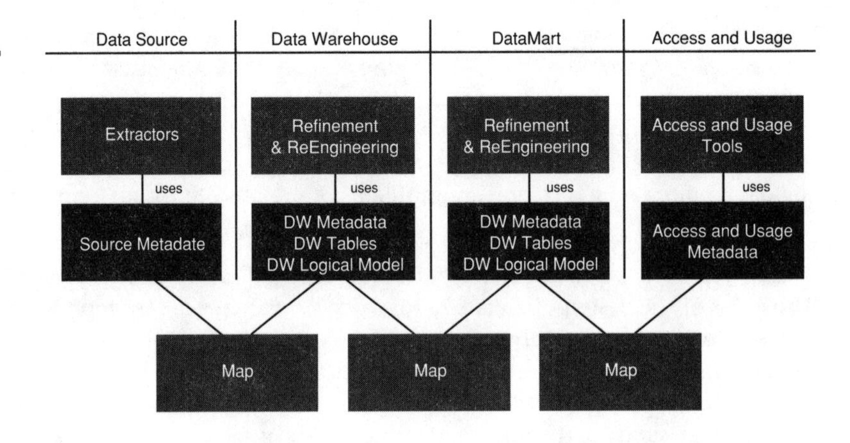


**Fig. 7.4**

*The figure shows different kinds of metadata that are created and stored and must be maintained for each of the blocks of the data warehouse.*

The following section shows how metadata is used for sample data warehouse development activities:

## Data Source Extraction

Figure 7.5 shows the role of metadata in the data warehouse reference architecture for the Data Sources block.

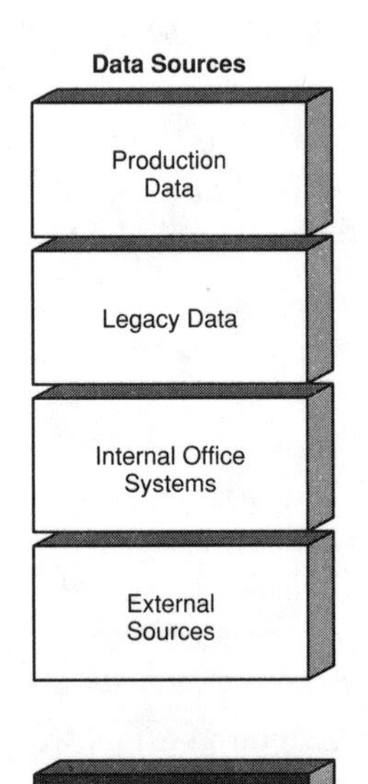

**Fig. 7.5**

*Metadata for the Data Sources block deals with the definition of the databases that feed the data warehouse as well as the data definition of warehouse items extracted from office systems and external sources.*

The role of metadata is key to the task of integrating data from multiple sources. Some of the challenges encountered during integration are described in the following list:

- **Identification of source fields**—Source data is contained in a variety of technologies, from file-based systems to relational databases. The names of the fields of information are often cryptic and challenging to understand. The use of a dictionary or an authoritative source of definitions of the fields is invaluable in identifying which fields must be loaded into the data warehouse.
- **Tracking changes in data organization over the history of the data**—Changes in application systems, database organization, or mergers and reorganizations are usually responsible for these challenges. It is necessary then, to develop one consistent organization of data inside the data warehouse (target), and then perform the data conversions from the various source formats to this target. Examples of changes in organization include changes in lengths of attributes, changes in datatypes, changes in coding schemes, and changes in key fields.
- **Applying defaults intelligently for data fields that were purposely or inadvertently not entered**—Applying defaults must be done consistently so that the data warehouse does not contain inconsistent information. Applying defaults in a consistent manner involves supplying the same sets of default values repeatedly, under the same circumstances.
- **Resolving inconsistencies in encoding schemes**—Often, different application systems use different encoding schemes to represent data. One application may use an M/F syntax to represent gender, and another application may use 0/1 for the same representation. It doesn't matter what encoding is actually used within the data warehouse, provided that it is consistent and unique. The process of data extraction must consider the conversion of codes to this single, consistent encoding scheme.
- **Attribute-to-attribute mapping**—Similar fields from multiple sources must be mapped together, so that data from these fields is loaded into the same target field within the data warehouse. To enable this, metadata information on the attributes is necessary to tell us which fields must be mapped together.
- **Attribute conversions**—Often, incoming fields of information from multiple data fields exist in different formats (length and datatype). Metadata is needed to indicate the format of each of the incoming fields. Based on observing the formats of incoming fields and the format of the target field that they must populate within the data warehouse, conversions can be defined. These conversions modify the data to make it compatible for loading into the data warehouse. Typical conversions are truncation, padding, or rounding.

As a by-product of collecting, transforming, or moving data from source databases into the data warehouse, the following kinds of metadata can be captured and stored:

- Full descriptions of source and target schemas
- Itemized source to target mappings

- Conversion variables defined during the transformations
- Data transformation rules
- Data retrieval options
- Exception handling options
- Conversion steps
- Conversion reports

## Data Refinement and Re-Engineering

The Data Refinement and Re-Engineering block is responsible for cleaning up the data from the sources, adding source stamps and time stamps, transforming data to match the data organization of the data warehouse, and precalculating the values of summaries and derived data.

Figure 7.6 recapitulates the various steps in data warehouse refinement and re-engineering.

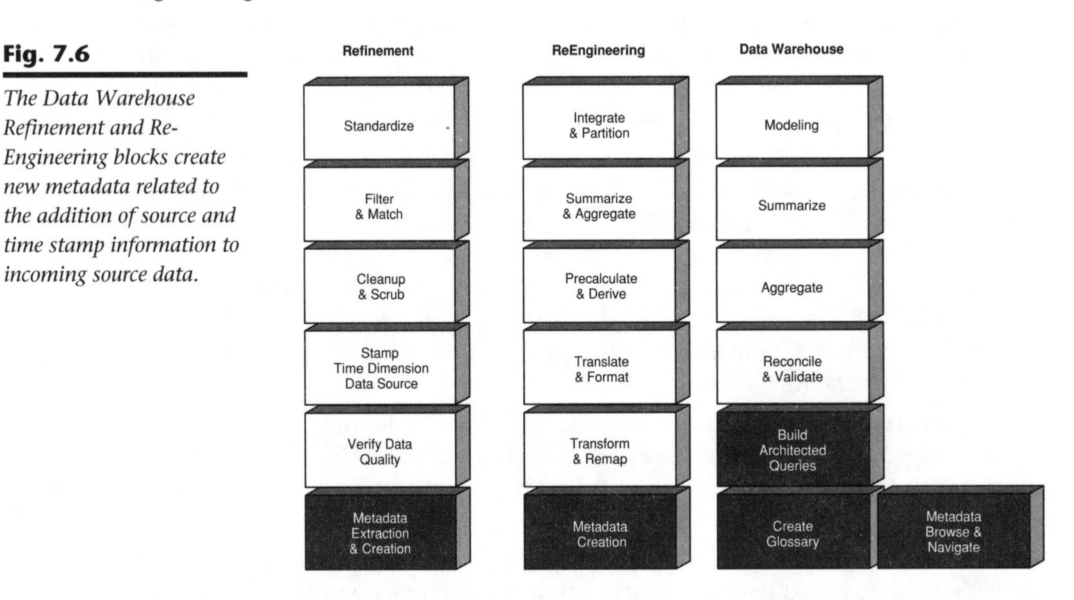


**Fig. 7.6**

*The Data Warehouse Refinement and Re-Engineering blocks create new metadata related to the addition of source and time stamp information to incoming source data.*

**Integration and Partitioning.** During the *partitioning* step, a single piece of incoming data is divided into two or more pieces of data within the data warehouse. The need for partitioning arises when operational systems store data in one table that would be best separated into separate tables in the data warehouse—often for performance reasons. It is desirable that the concepts contained within the data object be separated.

Metadata for the incoming data must be used to derive two or more pieces of metadata for the target data warehouse. Programs are then developed to divert incoming data into the multiple target locations. Another reason to partition is to flexibly divide a set of data into many compartments, which then allows different forms of analysis. Examples of partitioning from this perspective are partitioning data by date, by line of business, by geography, or by organizational unit. The metadata indicates the attributes that are associated with a given set of data.

**Summarization and Aggregation.** The simplest form of summarization is the formation of cumulative structures. This is done by simply summing up counts for various attributes. For example, order by customer per day is the total of all orders placed by a specific customer in a specific day. This information is obtained by searching all orders for a specific customer for a specific day, and then accumulating the total amount inside a new field. The process of summarization, therefore, adds new fields to the data that need to hold summarized totals. At the same time, the indication of which fields to total, how the total may be formed, and where the total must be stored is a specification of a summarization process. This also must be stored within the data warehouse as metadata to enable this process to be applied repeatedly.

More complex summarizations include rolling summaries—such as accumulation of orders per week, or orders per month per customer that are derived from the orders per day per customer. Each summarization step results in addition of new fields as well as the need to store the rules for the summarization step.

**Precalculation and Derivations.** Precalculations and derivations are computations that are applied to the data warehouse with no user intervention or request. These computations are computed, stored, and made available as fields of data within the data warehouse. Precalculations and derivations create additional data fields.

The algorithms used to precalculate and derive new fields from existing data warehouse fields also must be stored and managed as metadata inside the data warehouse. For example, from the weekly pay, FICA, and other taxes, the annual pay and deductions may be precalculated. Precalculated annual salaries may be used for analysis purposes by end users without performing the calculation every time the analysis is required.

**Transformation and Remapping.** The operational data sources that provide the data warehouse with data usually are organized as normalized or somewhat normalized relational tables. The schema needed for analysis generally is a star schema, where a central fact table is joined to a number of auxiliary tables. Transformation and remapping is the process of converting the data source information into rows that are suitable for populating the fact tables of the data warehouse. The remapping process involves assembling the rows of the fact table from multiple tables. The belief is that the price that is paid one time during the assembly of these rows is paid back many times over during analysis.

The process of transformation and remapping therefore uses two database organizations or schemas—the organization of the incoming data and the organization of the star schema of the data warehouse. Automatic transformation programs are generated based on the maps between these schemas.

## Access and Usage

Figure 7.7 shows the role of metadata in the Access and Usage block of the data warehouse.

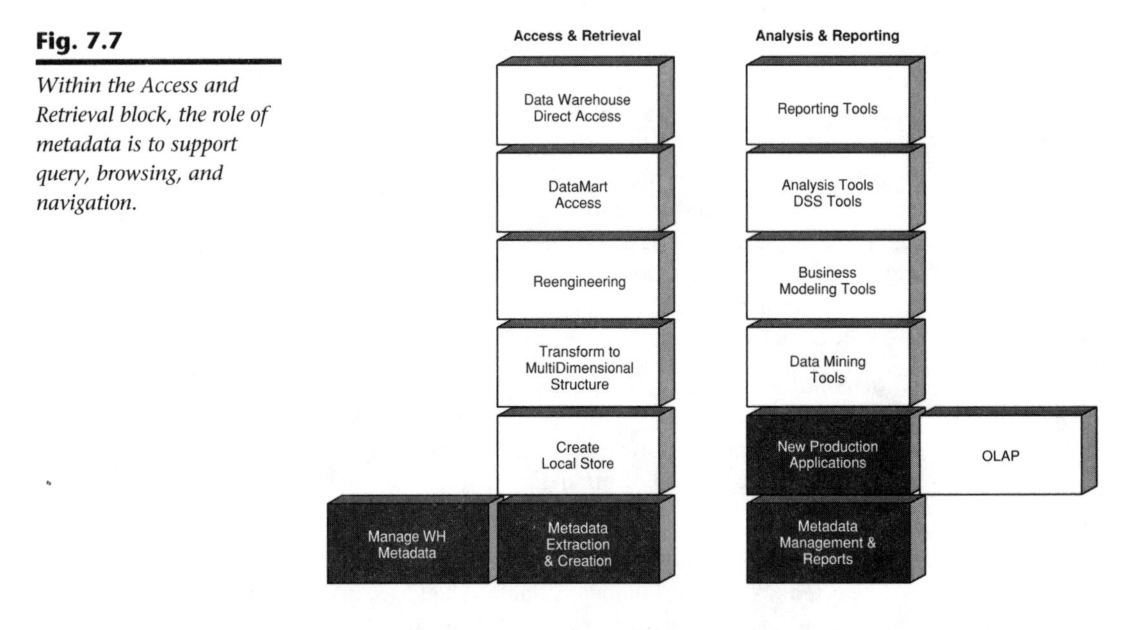


**Fig. 7.7**

*Within the Access and Retrieval block, the role of metadata is to support query, browsing, and navigation.*

The primary role of metadata within the Access and Retrieval blocks is to provide a navigational path for query and drill-down tools. Metadata also is created as a result of applying queries and creating temporary data storage. Access tools can use the metadata that is created to navigate through the data.

The primary role of metadata inside the Analysis and Reporting _blocks is to store predefined reports and queries and to point to them. The user then can efficiently retrieve predefined reports and queries by navigating the metadata that organizes them.

# Storing and Managing the Metadata Persistently

After the warehouse is deployed, the metadata is the roadmap for the end user. Not all the metadata generated during the development process of the data warehouse is usable or of interest to the user of the warehouse. Among the metadata that is of interest is the metadata that defines which information is available and accessible by the user. Also, definitions of reports and queries that are available to the user are of interest to the business user of the warehouse. Users also are interested in receiving estimates of query execution times. Metadata generated during the development phase of the data warehouse must be stored and organized properly. Multiple approaches have been proposed for storing and managing metadata:

- **Use of a dedicated commercial or homegrown data warehouse information directory**—This information directory stores and manages the metadata and is dedicated to the data warehouse application. This directory is accessible to all internal data warehouse programs, such as extractors, refinement and re-engineering programs, and transformation programs. Simultaneously, the directory is also accessible to end users for browsing, navigation, data fetches, and queries. The requirements for this kind of directory is discussed further at the end of this chapter.
- **Use of a commercial or homegrown repository/data dictionary**—A repository or data dictionary is a general-purpose cataloging device, usually used to store, classify, and manage metadata. Repositories are classified by using a classification scheme known as the *information model*. The information model contains a list of various categories of metadata and associations between these categories. The repository is a very flexible, general-purpose metadata management device that can be used for more than simply managing data warehouse metadata. For example, the definition of the data sources also may be persistently managed within the repository or data dictionary.

## Data Warehouse Information Directories

As the importance of metadata management assumes a primary role in the development and deployment of data warehouses, vendors are offering integrated information directory services that tackle the various aspects of metadata management. The information directory is built on the following assumptions:

- Data warehouse administrators and designers have a separate need to manage technological metadata in the form that it exists. Often, this exists as detailed technical specifications with cryptic names and definitions that are imposed by the limitations of the systems in which they were implemented.
- Business end users, however, want to see and understand metadata at a business level. A translation must be provided from the technological definitions and terms so that the business users can understand and fully appreciate what they can do with the information stored inside the data warehouse.
- Business users need some form of a navigation facility that enables them to "travel the roads" of their data warehouse. Often, this navigation facility must be intuitive, graphical, and must progressively guide the user to a chosen destination. Often, as part of the navigation facility business users also need to pull up information at will and make local copies of it for further analysis.

Figure 7.8 shows the anatomy of a typical information directory.

The technical directory primarily supports technical staff that must implement and deploy the data warehouse. The information contained within the technical directory is compatible with this kind of audience and contains the terms and definition of metadata, exactly as they appear in operational databases. The following information is contained in the technical directory:

- **Metadata for Data Sources**—Information on the databases that are sources of data for the data warehouse. Operational or external source system location, filenames, file types, field names and characteristics, aliases, version information, relationships, volume metrics, volatility, data owner, and authorized users.
- **Data Cleanup Rules**—Rules for restructuring records and fields, field value decoding, and translation; rules for supplying missing field values; and rules for data integrity and consistency checking.
- **Rules for Data Transformation**—Transforming data to add the element of time, definition of algorithms for deriving values and rules for derivation of summaries.
- **Rules for mapping Source Data to Target**—Rules for filtering and merging data from different files and sources to target fields within the data warehouse.
- **Metadata for Data Targets**—Data warehouse target system location, file name and type, field names and aliases, version information, date last updated, frequency of update or refresh, indexed fields, relationships, data owner, authorized users, volume metrics, and end user access patterns.

**Fig. 7.8**

*The information directory provides separate information directories for technical and non-technical audiences in addition to navigation facilities.*

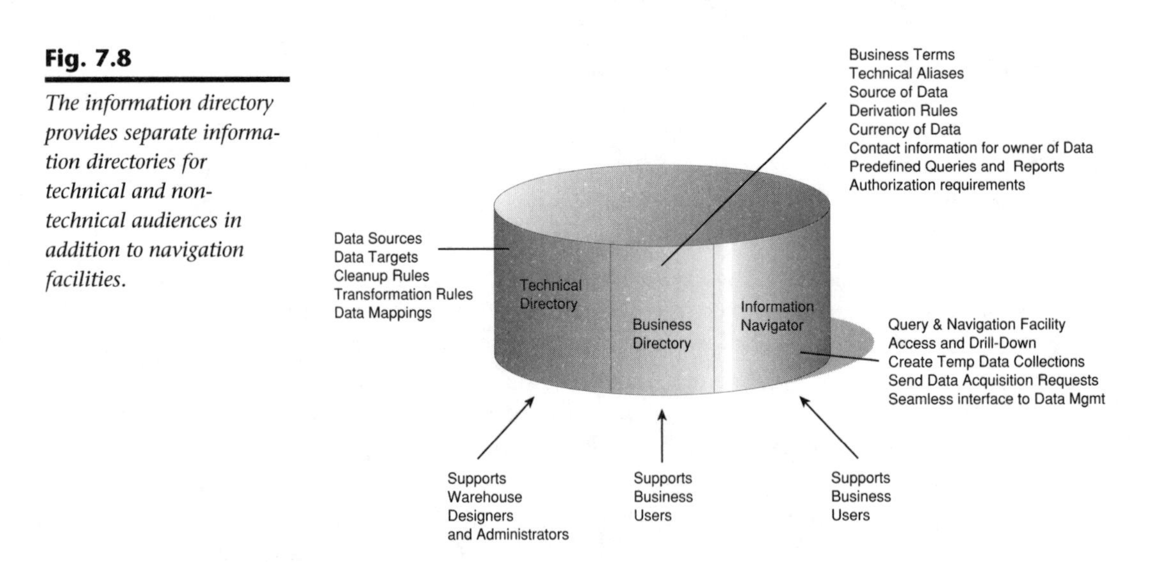


The business directory primarily supports business end users who do not have a technical background and, therefore, cannot use the technical directory to determine what information is stored inside the data warehouse. The business directory contains the following kinds of information:

- Business terms are used to describe data. These terms are the business equivalents of metadata names.
- Associations between technical names/aliases (metadata names) and the business term that describes them to the business user.

- Description of data warehouse data sources in business terms, derivation rules in English terms, and currency of data in common terms that end users can understand.
- Descriptions of predefined reports and queries that are available inside the data warehouse. These queries and reports are described in terms that can be understood by business users.
- Contact information for the owners of data items.
- Authorization requirements for access to data items.

The information navigator is a facility that allows users to browse through both the business directory and the data inside the data warehouse. The information navigator primarily supports business users who are not proficient in formulating complex database queries, but are instead served with a graphical point-and-click tool that allows them to navigate through the data warehouse.

The information navigator generally supports the following types of capabilities:

- **Query and access**—This capability is used to inquire and to perform *drill-down* into the information contained within the business directory. Drill-down is the ability to progressively unfold more detailed information as directed by the user.
- **Launch previously created (canned) queries and reports**—This capability also can create temporary or permanent data to use for analysis.
- **Send requests for data distribution**—This capability enables the user to make distribution requests to the data warehouse administration staff.
- **Attach data warehouse access and query tools**—This capability enables the user to manipulate the data warehouse with query and access tools purchased from third-party vendors. The metadata definitions inside the technical directory are used by these tools to interpret the organization of data inside the data warehouse.



## State of the Practice in Information Directories

The components described in figure 7.8 are supported to various degrees of detail by vendors of information directories. To date, vendor support for all aspects of these three components has been limited. The predominant area of vendor support is to provide technical directories. *Technical directories* are a natural extension of data dictionaries, repositories, or database catalogs because the information they manage also is contained in these systems. It is a natural progression for vendors of these systems to move into providing the technical directory component of the information directory. Technical directories are tied to the database technologies that they must support.

The business directory, however, is closely tied to the organization's business and to the terms and definitions used within that business. Therefore, it may be difficult to find vendor-supplied solutions that can be applied immediately. Often, the business terms and data definitions exist in data models and enterprise models that were built internally by organizations. These models are built by using Computer Aided Software Engineering (CASE) tools. Some vendors now offer interfaces to their information directory for popular CASE tools.

Some companies (such as IBM) are offering server-based business directory solutions that can be set up by administrators. The administrator stores metadata as objects on the server that is associated with specific object types (for example, Tables, Documents, Reports, and Queries). Administrators also can define custom object types or can use predefined types. Objects also are organized by administrator-defined subject areas. The business directory can be loaded with metadata from a variety of database sources, CASE tools, documents, spreadsheets, and word processors. End users can search or browse catalog information by either subject area or object type.

Data access tools that are currently available usually are desktop-based and manage their own metadata for access and query purposes. The metadata is tool-specific, and cannot be shared across users.

## Metadata Data Dictionaries and Repositories

In most organizations, metadata management has traditionally been assisted by the following systems:

- Data dictionary
- Data repository
- RDBMS system catalogs and separately maintained glossaries

Each of these systems has the following minimum components:

- **A flexible way of organizing metadata into a well-understood classification scheme**—This kind of scheme allows metadata administration personnel to define the classes and to associate them where necessary. The classification scheme is sometimes known as the information model of the repository, or data dictionary. The information model for a good repository or data dictionary must be extensible—it should be possible to define new classes of metadata as technology evolves and to relate the new metadata to the old.
- **A rich range of impact analysis and lookup capabilities**—These capabilities can retrieve metadata information as well as follow relationships between metadata elements. This range includes graphical tools for browsing metadata.
- **Compartmentalization capabilities to separate design and development metadata from operational metadata**—Typically, these capabilities are used to separate logical analysis models from physical database models. This facility is generally termed software development lifecycle partitioning or simply lifecycle partitioning.
- **Versioning of metadata to reflect change history**—Versioning also maintains dates and names of people responsible for making changes. Versioning and dates are crucial to the data warehouse because historical data

must be accompanied by the definitional metadata, indicating how it is organized and when.

- **Facilities to maintain definitions and descriptions of metadata**—This capability is important, in both technical terms and business terms.
- **Facilities for applying data naming and data standardization conventions to relate similar metadata**—How data elements are named is very important to understanding their significance. Organizations usually establish formal policies for creating names of data elements. Names must be created using lists of standard building blocks called prime words, class words, and modifiers. Organizations also maintain a list of approved prime words and class words that characterize the terms and definitions commonly used in their business.
- **Synchronization capabilities**—These capabilities are used to keep the metadata in the data dictionary/repository up-to-date and current with metadata inside operational database systems. These capabilities are either available instantaneously (the repository is always synchronized with the databases that it manages) or they are applied at periodic intervals (a specific request for metadata synchronization is made to the source databases at preset intervals).

### State of the Practice in Data Dictionaries/Repositories

Several commercial implementations of data dictionaries and repositories are available and are being used by organizations on a day-to-day basis. Client/server implementations are based on the use of a repository running on a UNIX-, Windows NT-, or OS/2-based server with Windows, UNIX, and OS/2 client workstations. Popular mainframe-based repositories usually run on DB2 on an IBM mainframe. Most commercially available repositories use a relational database for storing and managing metadata. Some new repository solutions based on Object-Oriented Database Management System (OODBMS) technology are emerging.

To date, the use of standards is limited. Most commercial repositories are built to vendor-defined standards. The information model also has seen very limited standardization. As a result, the classification of metadata has not followed broadly accepted standards which, therefore, makes the job of interchange difficult and complex.

## Metadata Standards

With the increasing interest in the role of metadata in the data warehouse, the realization has come that metadata standards are truly needed to allow vendors of metadata management products to exchange metadata information. Unfortunately, metadata standardization has been evolving slowly. The challenge in metadata standardization has been in the following areas:

- **Metadata administration**—The primary objective of data administration has been to standardize the definition of metadata within an enterprise.

Standardizing the definition of metadata involves setting up well-understood and well-communicated processes for naming metadata elements, standardizing datatypes and lengths, and maintaining expressive and descriptive glossaries.

- **Metadata representation and classification**—The primary objective of a representation and classification scheme is to categorize metadata into classes that are based on technology. Because of the number of storage technologies used by an enterprise, this classification can be quite diverse. Relational technology, for example, requires classifying the metadata into the following categories: `TABLE`, `COLUMN`, `VIEW`, `INDEX`, `DATABASE`, `QUERY`, and others. IMS technology requires that the metadata be classified into the following categories: `DBD`, `PSB`, `PCB`, `SENSITIVE_SEGMENT`, and others. Part of the classification scheme also is the need to express and manage relationships between these classes of metadata.

The primary efforts in data administration have resulted in data naming standards and procedures in large organizations. Notably, the U.S. Department of Defense has formulated the DoD 8320 data administration standard. Other large organizations have developed their own internal standards for naming and metadata definitions.

The primary efforts in metadata representation and classification resulted in the formulation of data dictionaries and repositories with information models. These information models represent various database technologies and either connect to operational databases directly (active) or derive their metadata through periodic extractions from operational database systems (passive). The information models provide the classification scheme for metadata. The standard in this area is the ANSI Information Resource Dictionary Standard (IRDS) and its 4-layer representation method. A number of repository vendors also provide custom information models to classify the metadata stored in their repositories. A significant attempt was made by IBM, through its AD/Cycle Information Model, to define an industry-standard information model for database and Computer Aided Software Engineering (CASE) technology, supplied or sponsored by IBM. The AD/Cycle Information Model encompassed relational (DB2) and non-relational technology (IMS, DL/I, and VSAM).

Efforts also are under way by a consortium of vendors, known as the Metadata Council, to standardize metadata interchange between diverse vendor products within the data warehouse arena. These efforts are directed toward specifying the format and structure of metadata so that vendor products can interchange metadata information. The Metadata Council is sponsored by Arbor Software Inc., Cognos Corporation, Business Objects Inc., Evolutionary Technology Inc., Platinum technology Inc., and Texas Instruments Inc.

# The Consumerization of Metadata

As more end users get more and more access to data inside the data warehouse, it becomes increasingly necessary to treat data (and by implication, metadata) as commodity items. The role of the IS organization is changing rapidly, from controlling the information to enabling access to information in a controlled manner.

To use a simple analogy from the consumer marketplace, think of the role of the sales person in an intensely service-oriented business. The customer is received by a salesperson, who receives a request for product information. The salesperson then satisfies the request for product and eventually takes the order. As the store reduces its service component (and as customers demand direct access to the product itself), the store displays the product in a manner designed to attract the customer into the store. The customer can handle and touch the product, and then determine whether he or she wants to buy the product. In a further evolution, customers are presented with printed and illustrated catalogs that describe and show off the product in great detail. The consumer then places an order. The store fulfills the order and provides a money-back guarantee if the product was not found satisfactory.

In the commodity view of information, the IS organization is responsible for collecting and organizing the information in much the same way as the storekeeper. Due to increasing budget pressures and the need for justifications, IS wants to purvey the information that they have collected to a broad audience of people who want to deploy the information usefully. The information catalog is one example of a vehicle that is used by IS to communicate the contents of the data warehouse to the business audience. Other vehicles include the use of the World Wide Web, electronic mail, and consumer-like catalogs targeted for functional departments. The data warehouse, in this kind of environment, truly becomes a resource for the entire organization.

# Summary

- Metadata is an important component of a data warehouse. Metadata is the roadmap into the data warehouse. Understanding the metadata is important for the various components of the data warehouse to function correctly. Data extractors must understand both the metadata of the data sources and the metadata of the target data warehouse. The metadata of the data warehouse must be understood by the end user's access tools so that these tools can retrieve data correctly and efficiently.
- The metadata of the data warehouse, and also all metadata captured during the extraction process from data sources, must be centrally managed in an information directory. This information directory has three components: a technical directory for supporting the development and operation of the data warehouse, a business directory to communicate the contents of the data warehouse to business users, and an information navigator to enable end users to access data warehouse information in many ways, including browsing through the warehouse.
- The state of the practice is evolving. Currently, vendors have demonstrated the maximum support for the technical directory component of the information directory. Support for the business directory and the information navigator has been more limited.

- Metadata standards are still evolving. Currently defined standards include the ANSI Information Resource Dictionary System (IRDS). A Metadata Council was established with a charter for defining a minimum standard to allow interchange of metadata between metadata management products provided by multiple vendors.
- The data warehouse represents a consumer challenge to supplying metadata information to end users. Unlike repositories and data dictionaries that cater to a knowledgeable and technical audience, the data warehouse metadata catalog must cater to a business audience that has limited technology familiarity.

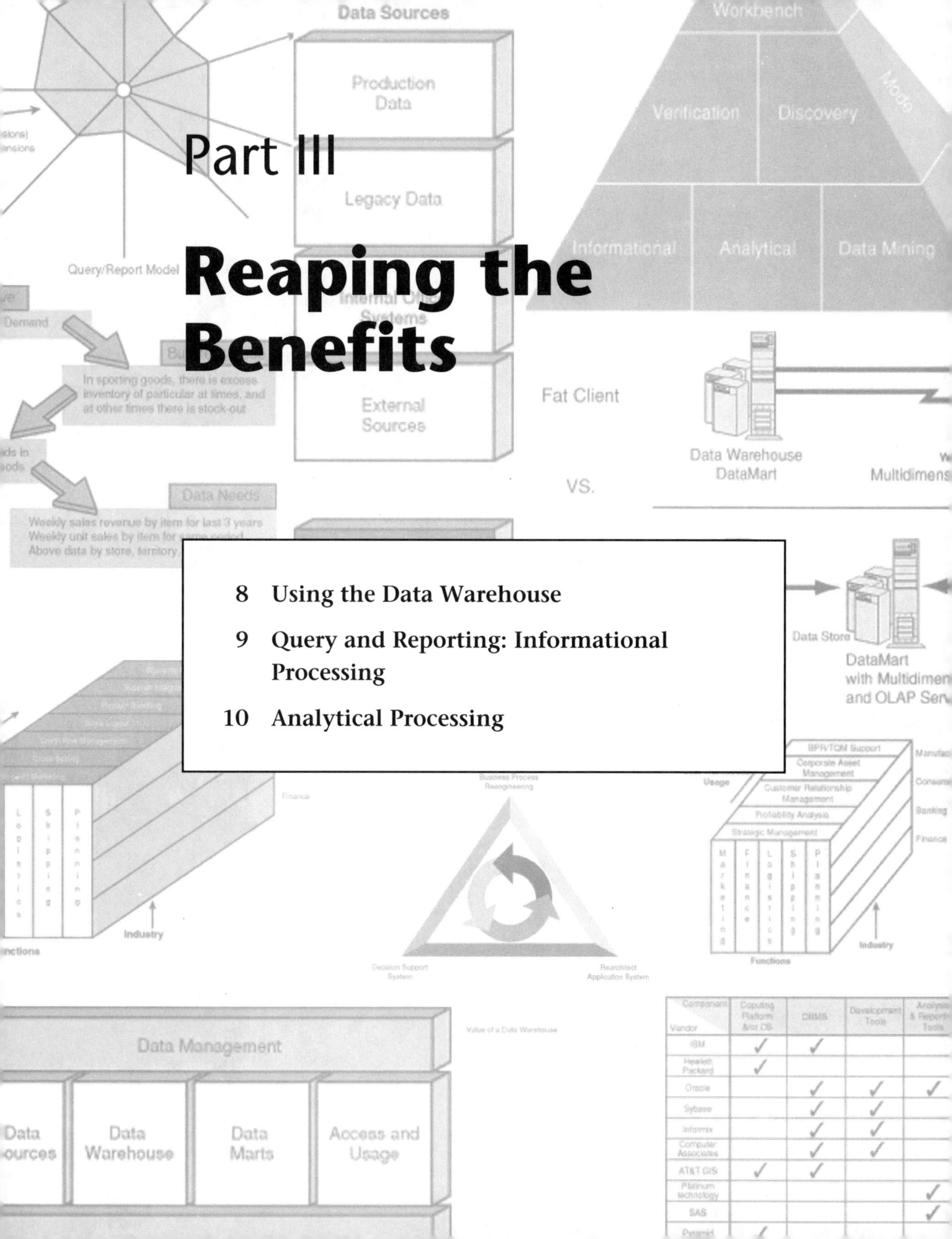


# Part III

# Reaping the Benefits

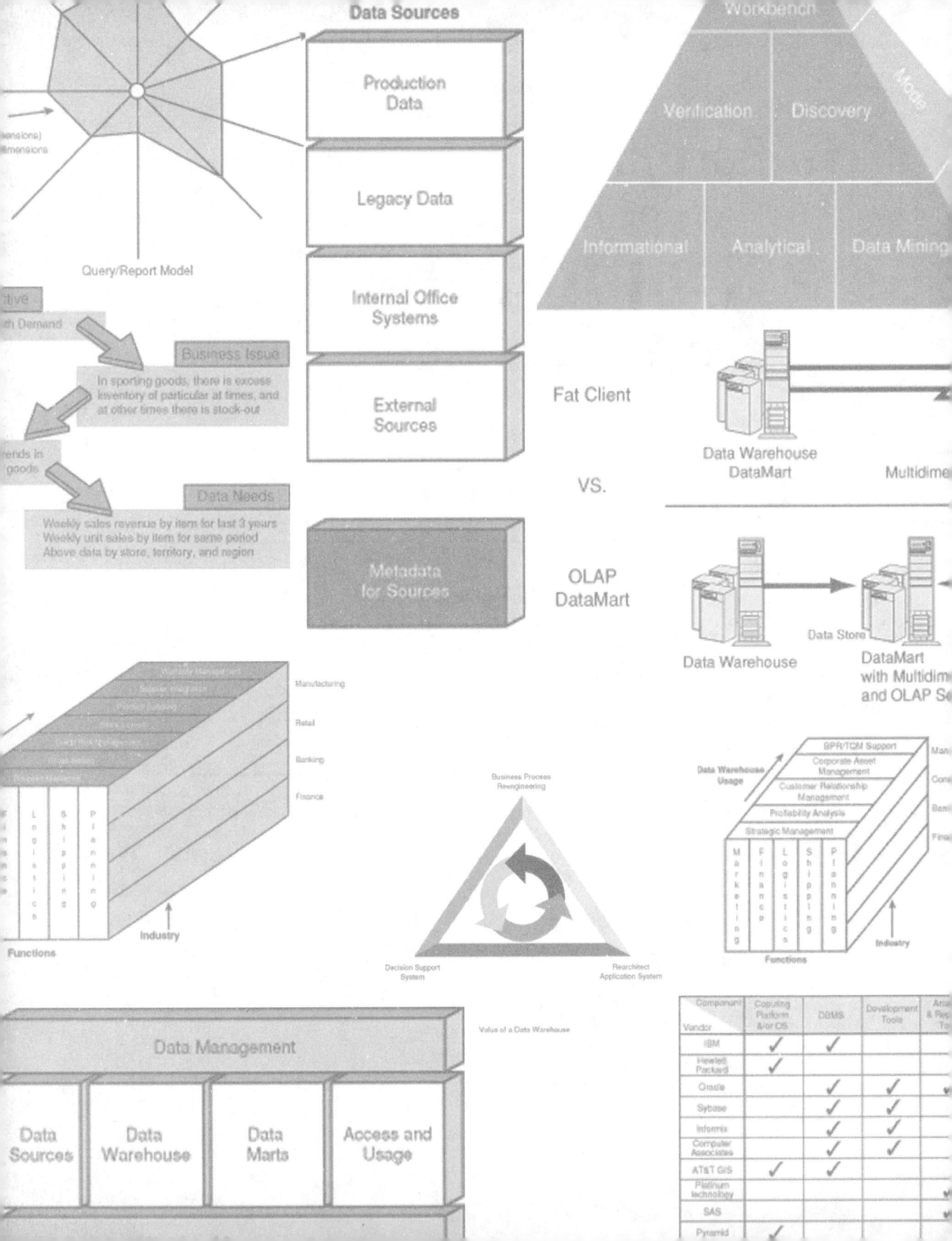
Data Sources
Production Data
Legacy Data
Internal Office Systems
External Sources
Metadata for Sources
Query/Report Model
Business Issue
In sporting goods, there is excess inventory of particular at times, and at other times there is stock-out
Data Needs
Weekly sales revenue by item for last 3 years
Weekly unit sales by item for same period
Above data by store, territory, and region
Workbench
Verification
Discovery
Informational
Analytical
Data Mining
Fat Client
VS.
OLAP DataMart
Data Warehouse DataMart
Data Warehouse
Data Store
Manufacturing
Retail
Banking
Finance
Functions
Industry
Business Process Reengineering
Decision Support System
Rearchitect Application System
Value of a Data Warehouse
Data Warehouse Usage
BPR/TQM Support
Corporate Asset Management
Customer Relationship Management
Profitability Analysis
Strategic Management
Functions
Industry
Data Management
Data Sources
Data Warehouse
Data Marts
Access and Usage
Component
Vendor
Computing Platform &/or OS
DBMS
Development Tools
IBM
Hewlett Packard
Oracle
Sybase
Informix
Computer Associates
AT&T GIS
Platinum technology
SAS
Pyramid

CHAPTER 8

# Using the Data Warehouse

Management's goal is to develop successful strategies and plans to grow profitably, maintain delighted customers, and increase market share. According to *Business Week*, "With competition mounting in every industry, data warehousing is the latest must-have marketing weapon—a way to learn more about customers' needs and how to hang on to them."

## Purpose of the Data Warehouse

The purpose of a data warehouse is to assist management in understanding the past and planning for the future. Management is seeking answers to questions like:

- What are our customers buying? What are they not buying? What incentives have worked previously with the same customers at this time of the year?
- How many of our sales people are calling on the same customer? What do our customers think of this?
- What are our competitors doing? How has it affected our relationship with our customers?
- How do our costs for each product line compare over the last three years? What factors caused increases? Did it affect our margins?

One question leads to another. Management wants to get answers to the crucial questions and make better decisions. The answers to many such questions were previously "locked up" in the operational systems.

### "Getting the Data Out"

The promise of data warehousing is to "get the data out" of the operational systems to help businesses make better decisions. Now, the right operational data is in the data warehouse. The challenge is to "get the data out" of the data warehouse and convert it to information that helps businesses make more informed choices, which will yield better decisions and create a sustainable business advantage.

The concept of data warehouse is not new. Over the years, data warehouses (the name is new, not the concept) have been used as reporting databases, query and analysis data stores, and so forth. The purpose then was to offload the operational systems and still meet basic operational decision support needs. In today's data warehouse (in this chapter, the term *data warehouse* includes both the data warehouse and the data mart), the contents are organized to derive strategic value from the historical operational data collected. One can "get the data out" in a myriad of ways, from simple reports to advanced data mining. One can write custom applications and queries, create crisp reports and charts, perform multidimensional analysis, and surf the data warehouse. The value derived from the data warehouse is limited by the creativity of its users, the capabilities of tools applied, and, of course, by what is stored and how it is structured for access.

Data warehouse usage evolves through multiple phases. In the first phase, the data warehouse is generally used for reports and predefined queries. Next, data warehouses may be used to analyze summary and detail data, with the results presented in the form of reports and charts. These early phases are also used to verify the quality and sufficiency of the data contents, and to train business users. As business users become increasingly more comfortable with the data quality and tools, they can start to use the data warehouse for strategic purposes with multidimensional analysis and sophisticated slice and dice operations—looking at the past now leads to planning for the future.

## Overall Value and Usage

A typical data warehouse is a repository of corporate knowledge. It contains detailed information (selected and stored as described in Chapter 5), such as:

- What customers and suppliers you know
- What you know about your customers, suppliers, and business
- How you are doing—your profitability and performance

Even though the data warehouse has crucial strategic information in it, deriving business value from the data warehouse is a complex endeavor. To get value requires an alchemy of business skills, technical know-how, intuition, and experience. Businesses want to use the data warehouse to not only report the past, but *help plan the future.* Getting there requires a strong partnership between business users and Information Technology (IT) professionals.

The data warehouse is an integral part of the enterprise management "closed-loop" feedback system. As shown in figure 8.1, the basic segments of the "closed-loop" feedback system are *plan, execute, and assess.*

The data warehouse can assist in planning the business and assess the effectiveness of the plan's execution. For example, a marketing strategy may be to define the right customer segments for micromarketing and promotional campaigns or to define a new services strategy to improve customer retention with an improved warranty program. The assessment activities—growth and profitability of the new micromarket customer segment and customer satisfaction with the warranty program—help fine tune the marketing strategy and plans.

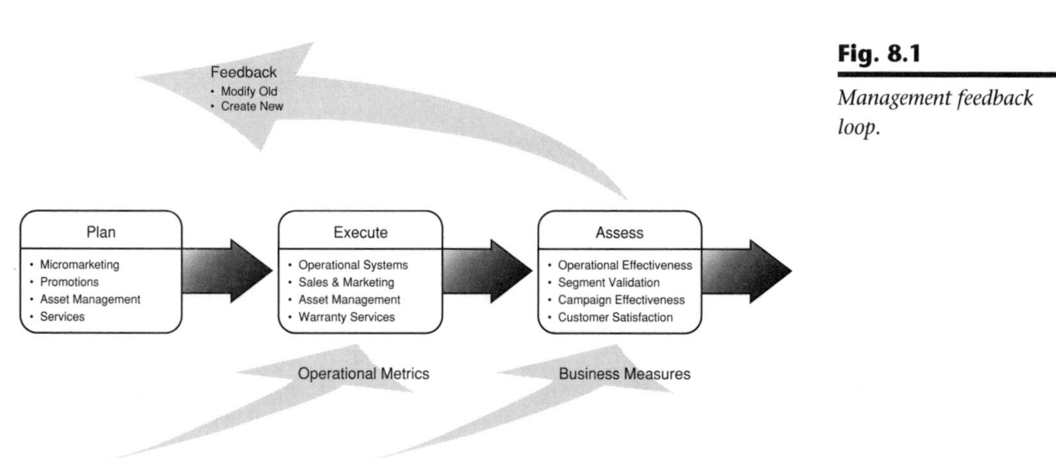


**Fig. 8.1**

*Management feedback loop.*

In figure 8.1, data analysis and mining tools are used to ferret out, from the data warehouse, the most promising micro customer segments and their buying preferences and patterns. This information is synthesized to develop marketing plans. Past performance, derived from the historical data in the data warehouse, is used to develop operational and business measures to assess the effectiveness of the new plans. After the initial execution of this plan, actual purchase transactions, coupled with operating costs and results, are extracted from the operational systems and fed into the data warehouse. Now data analysis tools are used to compute the resulting business measures and compare them to the plans. The overall effectiveness of the micromarketing plan is gauged. The resulting analysis is "fed-back" to the planning segment to fine tune the previous strategies and plans.

Just as a data warehouse helps to tame a data jungle, one must refrain from creating an information jungle. Data warehouse technology can run away and assume a life of its own. For example, pinpoint marketing ratchets up the risk/reward equation for a telemarketing campaign. Solicit the right customer at the right time and you hit the jackpot. Solicit the right customer at the wrong time and you increase the customer's annoyance, which could lead to the potential loss of a valuable customer.

## Information Harvesting

The data warehouse does not magically produce results. Business managers and analysts must access and retrieve the data from the data warehouse and convert it into information and facts. These facts form the foundation of a knowledge base which can be used to determine the health of the enterprise and the future direction of the business. As in farming, users will harvest only information that can be derived from the data that has been sown in the data warehouse, and only using the appropriate harvesting tools. Some of the harvesting tools needed are access and retrieval tools, database reporting tools, analysis tools, and data mining tools.

One of the challenges in harvesting a data warehouse is not to make molehills of information into mountains of data. It is easy to fall into the trap of "the more, the better." It not essential to know all the facts, just the crucial ones. As an example, a marketing campaign for children's clothes needs to pin-point and profitably harvest only those families that have children.

## Data Warehouse versus Operational Systems

If reporting and query databases already exist and are in use, how does the value and usage of a data warehouse differ from that of operational systems and operational databases?

Figure 8.2 shows usage and value derived from operational systems and data warehouses for business, financial, and sales and marketing analysis. Operational systems focus on the management and measure of business measures, such as capital, investments, and all enterprise assets; financial measures, such as gross and net margins, inventory turns, and delinquent accounts; sales measures, such as who are the repeat customers; pricing for maintenance contracts and spot orders; and order fulfillment response times.

**Fig. 8.2**

*Operational systems versus data warehouse.*

| | Operational Systems | Data Warehouse |
|---|---|---|
| **Business Analysis** | Operational Effectiveness<br>ROI and ROA<br>Capital Management | Revenue/Profitability Growth<br>Market and Customer Growth<br>Asset Management |
| **Financial Analysis** | Margins<br>Accounts Receivable/Payable<br>Operating Parameters | Revenue/Profitability<br>Assets Analysis<br>Product Cycle<br>TQM |
| **Sales and Marketing** | Customer-Orientation<br>• Response Time<br>• Repeat Business<br>• Maintenance vs. Spot Orders | Market-Orientation<br>• Market Share<br>• Distribution Channel Strategy<br>• Product Bundling |

A data warehouse is used to understand, measure, and manage strategic business parameters, such as growth of revenue and profitability, market share and customer segments, and enterprise-wide effectiveness of asset management. For example, to improve asset management and the return-on-assets (ROA), analysis of enterprise-wide purchasing may unearth opportunities for volume discounts, reduced shipping costs, and reduction in procurement personnel without significantly impacting service levels.

# Data Warehouse Potential

In today's competitive environment, slow is not an option. Figure 8.3 describes business needs to access data and information in the data warehouse in order to make better decisions.

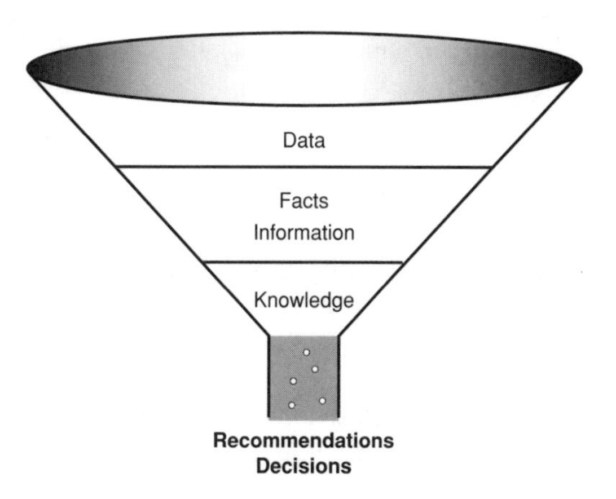


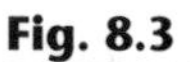

**Fig. 8.3**

*From data to decisions.*

With data warehouses, users can view the data in the right business context to yield information and facts. The user can then add business acumen and subject matter know-how to the facts to distill knowledge, and then apply this knowledge to make recommendations or decisions. Data warehouse users armed with the right complement of tools and training, as well as with the ability to access and retrieve the right information, can and do convert the corporate data assets in the data warehouse into a potent and competitive business tool.

A data warehouse can yield the right information to business executives, managers, and analysts. These users can leverage the data warehouse to build a range of strategies and plans, from managing customer relationships better to changing the basis of competition.

Tapping the potential of a data warehouse is limited only by the capacity, capability, and creativity of the business users. Early experiences point to a broad array of values, in many business sectors, derived from the data warehouse.

## Profitability Analysis and Growth

Profits can be enhanced by understanding, for example, the correlation of products and services, and margins and product lines. Analysis can guide decision as to, for example, which product lines provide larger service opportunities, especially if there was no obvious relationship between product sales and service revenue; only a historical trends analysis demonstrated such a relationship.

## Strategic Management

Business growth can be achieved by leveraging new revenue opportunities with existing customers, or by cross-selling or even up-selling. An enterprise's operational data is a unique source of information available only to the enterprise. Combining this data with demographic data provides a unique information base that can be mined to better understand its customers—buying patterns, product bundles, service experience. Armed with this know-how from the data warehouse, marketing programs can be tailored to create quantum increases in revenue and build a franchise of delighted customers.

## Change the Basis of Competition

A factual and complete knowledge of a customer, gleaned from the historical data in the data warehouse and augmented with a faster feedback loop of operational effectiveness, may make feasible newer and faster ways to more accurately and comprehensively meet customer requirements. For example, pin-point marketing of the right products, with the right feature sets, at the right time, increases customer satisfaction. Delighted customers form ever tighter and exclusive relationships with vendors. Such relationships lead to increased revenue, better margins, and are difficult for competitors to sever.

## Customer Relationship Management

Customer relationship management is data warehouse's solution to the age-old quest: know thy customer. Integrating disparate marketing functions/organizations does lead to better understanding of each customer. For example, when a customer who purchases different products from different marketing organizations is viewed as a single enterprise-wide customer, surprising new information could surface. The total revenue generated from the single customer by all organizations may very well put the customer in the enterprise "Top 20" list. A new customer relationship management strategy of providing enterprise-wide focus to such a customer may lead to increased management attention, higher-level selling, and opportunities for product bundling and brand extension. Improved appreciation of who the customer really is and what the full scope of needs are can guide marketing to send just the right communications—not any extra communication that is often so annoying. Customers appreciate that in today's mass mailing world.

## Corporate Asset Management

A data warehouse is capable of providing a "big picture" of enterprise-wide purchase patterns and suppliers. This knowledge can produce fresh insight into current practices and highlight opportunities for volume discounts through volume purchases (economies of scale). It can also offer feasible options for downsizing the purchase organization where the organization, instead of being overworked, is now empowered by the data warehouse capability available.

### Business Process Reengineering (BPR) and Total Quality Management (TQM)

Data warehouses generally offer a customer-oriented view of the organization. The process of defining and building the data warehouse, coupled with analysis of the data in the data warehouse, provides a sharper picture of the enterprise's current practices. This know-how is not only valuable but also essential for both BPR and TQM. The data warehouse can also be used to measure the results of the BPR process and ongoing progress of the TQM program. The availability of a data warehouse with powerful analysis tools empowers people.

## Data Warehouse Applications

Early experience in the banking and finance, consumer goods, and manufacturing sectors shows multiple applications of data warehouses for multiple functions of an enterprise (see fig. 8.4).

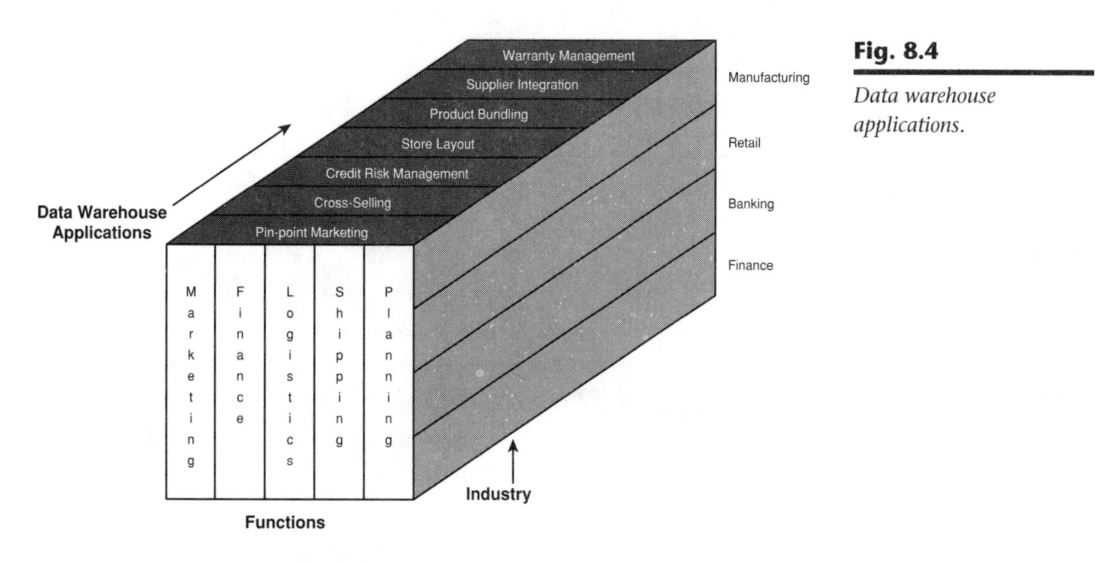


**Fig. 8.4**

*Data warehouse applications.*

### Banking and Finance Sector

In the finance and banking sector, some of the data warehouse applications are in the areas of relationship management and credit risk management. Data analysis has led to successful programs in pin-point marketing, cross-selling, and product bundling.

### Consumer Goods and Retail Distribution Sector

In this sector, data warehouse applications are playing a key role in store layout and product bundling—even product bundling of complementary products from different vendors. This was achieved through improved understanding of consumer buying patterns and habits.

Another area is logistics integration and value chain analysis. For example, an enhanced understanding of historical shipping patterns and practices has led to strategies of reduced numbers of vendors, lower costs, and guaranteed delivery dates. Some organizations have even outsourced their shipping or distribution functions.

Analysis of historical and recent data has led to the creation of micromarketing strategies, mentioned earlier. Integrating micromarketing strategies with logistics has improved the availability of "hot goods"—goods in vogue and in demand in many fast moving markets—resulting in much improved profitability in a notoriously low-margin sector.

### Manufacturing

The early applications in manufacturing are warranty and service management, order fulfillment and shipping, and supplier and logistics integration. In the logistics area, data warehouses have assisted in improving the performance of Just-in-Time (JIT) inventory of raw materials and components, smarter product packaging and bundling, and more accurate forecasting of demand-based production.

## Data Warehouse Users and Their Needs

Data warehouses address the decision support needs of a range of users who have different levels of comfort and experience with computing technology (see fig. 8.5).

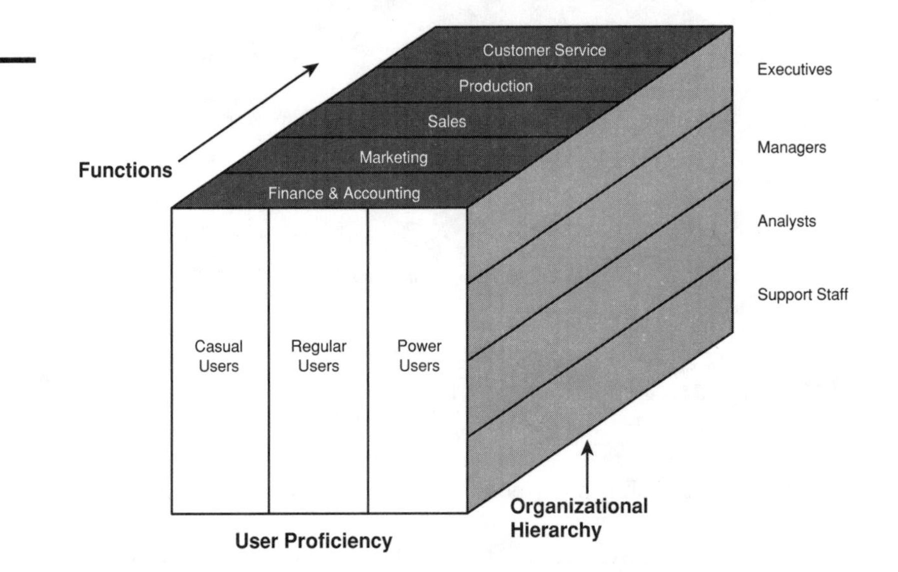


**Fig. 8.5**

*User profiles.*

From the data warehouse perspective, users can be categorized by organization hierarchy, function, or computing proficiency. The organizational hierarchical cut includes the CEO and COO; senior executives, such as the CFO and Controller; middle managers; business and IT analysts; and the administrative or support staff. A functional cut constitutes departments such as Finance and Accounting, Marketing and Sales, Production and Engineering, Customer Support Services, Information Technology, and Administration. A computing proficiency cut would divide users into three broad groups with increasing proficiency: casual users, regular users, and power users.

The basic assumptions about typical data warehouse users made by most data warehouse builders are the following:

- Users have knowledge of the area of business that the data warehouse supports
- Users understand the semantics of the data retrieved from the data warehouse
- Users will learn how to access and retrieve the data in the data warehouse
- Users have the capability and capacity to convert data (retrieved from the data warehouse) into facts and information, convert the facts into knowledge, and then use the knowledge to make decisions or offer recommendations and alternatives

## Basic Needs

The basic needs of all data warehouse users is to have the means to know what exists in the data warehouse, access the contents of the data warehouse, analyze the contents, and present the results extracted and derived from the data warehouse. This can be done by answering the following questions:

- What exactly does the data warehouse contain and how good is it (metadata)?

  The first need of any data warehouse user is to find out what exists, what it means, how much of it is there, and how it can be accessed and navigated. The second need is to understand the quality of the data warehouse contents to determine the confidence level of any usage, analysis, and recommendations.

- How can I access and retrieve the contents of the data warehouse (data)?

  All users need to access and retrieve the contents of the data warehouse, albeit at different levels of granularity, from detail records to lightly summarized records to heavily summarized records. A range of abilities is needed to access and retrieve charts, predefined reports, multidimensional data, summary data, as well as detailed data.

- What are the analysis tools?

  As users try to get value from the data warehouse, tools are needed to interpret and analyze the contents, create and verify different business hypotheses, and develop recommendations and alternatives. Basic tools needed include spreadsheets, statistical analyzers, and analytical processors that support multidimensional analysis.

- What are the reporting and presentation tools?

  To communicate the results of analysis, powerful tools are needed to clearly present recommendations and alternatives with information-rich reports, charts, and presentations.

## Business Needs

The business needs of some data warehouse users, senior executives, managers, and analysts are shown in figure 8.6.

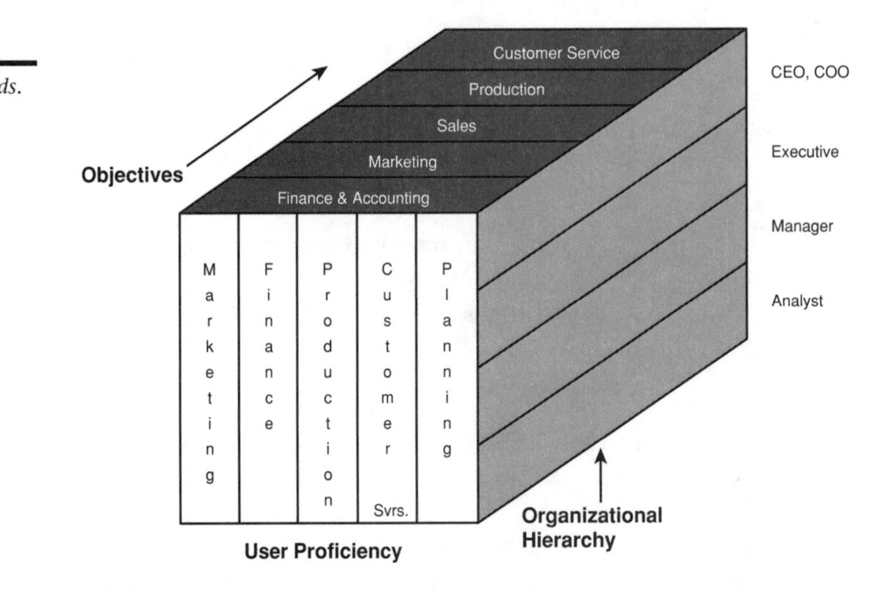


**Fig. 8.6**

*User objectives and needs.*

The CEO and COO want to use the data warehouse for developing strategies such as entering new markets, gaining market share, and managing risk. The CFO and Controller want to measure profitability and growth, analyze and forecast the budget, and develop programs to integrate suppliers and reduce the costs of logistics. Marketing managers would like to leverage the data warehouse for relationship management, product bundling and customer/market segmentation, as well as analyze the validity of existing market segments. And sales management desires to create programs for cross-selling and up-selling, and measure and increase the effectiveness of telemarketing plans. The business analyst wants to mine the data warehouse to unearth rich new markets and micromarkets, and discern their buying profile.

## Technology Needs

From a technology needs point-of-view, users can be classified into three broad categories: executives and senior managers, managers and business analysts, and business and Information Technology (IT) analysts (see fig. 8.7). Executives and managers are generally considered casual users, while analysts are usually considered power users.

**Executives and Senior Managers.** Executives and senior managers need the data warehouse contents analyzed, and recommendations and business measures presented in the form of charts and reports. For ease of interpretation, they want the information packaged in predefined enterprise business models. The information is, by and large, required in highly summarized form. They need to visually walk through the information, sometimes drilling down in well-defined paths. The information delivery can be enhanced with a multimedia presentation of, for example, new markets and opportunities. The sophisticated software necessary to deliver these capabilities is customarily developed by IT professionals.

| | Analysis Tools | Interaction | Information Packaging | Workstation Capability |
|---|---|---|---|---|
| • **Executive** • **Senior Manager** | • Reports • Charts • Predefined Business Models • Multimedia Presentation | • View Information • Predefined Drill-down | • Predefined Business Model • Planning & Forecasting Model | • Sophisticated Graphics • Visual Walkthrough |
| • **Manager** • **Business Analyst** | • Queries • Reports & Charts • Data Imported: Spreadsheets & MDDBMS Applications | • Create Information on demand • Drill-down • Verify Predefined hypotheses | • Predefined Business, Planning & Forecasting Models • "What if" of Models | • Graphical Point & Click • Visualization of Analysis Information |
| • **Business Analyst** • **IT Facilitator** | • Summary Data • Detailed Transaction data • Living Sample Database | • Verify New hypotheses • Data Surfing • Slice & Dice | • Spreadsheets & MDDBMS • Internal DBMS • External Data • Living Sample Database | • Data Surfing • Data Mining • Data Analysis • Data Visualization |

**Fig. 8.7**

*Technology needs of different users.*

**Managers and Business Analysts.** Business managers and analysts need access to information in two forms. They need summary data in the form of reports and charts, as well as direct access to data warehouse information that can be imported to tools such as spreadsheets and multidimensional databases for subsequent analysis. They are driven by two needs: to understand the data warehouse information already packaged in predefined business models and to personally perform "what if" analysis for planning, business and financial analysis, and budgeting. For these users, information visualization tools greatly aid the analysis activity and verification of business hypotheses. The software needed to support these users is generally developed by IT professionals and is supplemented by some development by the managers and analysts themselves.

**Business Analysts and IT Facilitators.** Business analysts and IT facilitators are the heaviest users of the data warehouse. They create the necessary reports, charts, and recommendations for management. They need the tools for data mining and analysis, data surfing, and data visualization. They need access to both summary and detailed data in the data warehouse. Sometimes they need access to "living sample databases" to create and verify new hypotheses. For data mining, they need access to detailed transactional data in the databases of the operational systems. The software required for these users is developed by the analysts themselves, with active support of IT analysts and facilitators.

# Using the Data Warehouse

From a business perspective, data warehouses are built to: deliver usable data and information in a usable form and format to the business user, and empower business users with a range of tools and capabilities to analyze the data and make decisions. In other words, they are built to provide a flexible access to the data from a wide variety of powerful and popular desktop tools.

Using the data warehouse in the everyday course of business consists of two broad activities: access and retrieval, and analysis and reporting. These activities are supported by the Access and Usage block of the reference architecture (described in Chapter 2). The Access and Usage block contain the same two components—Access and Retrieval, and Analysis and Reporting (see fig. 8.8).

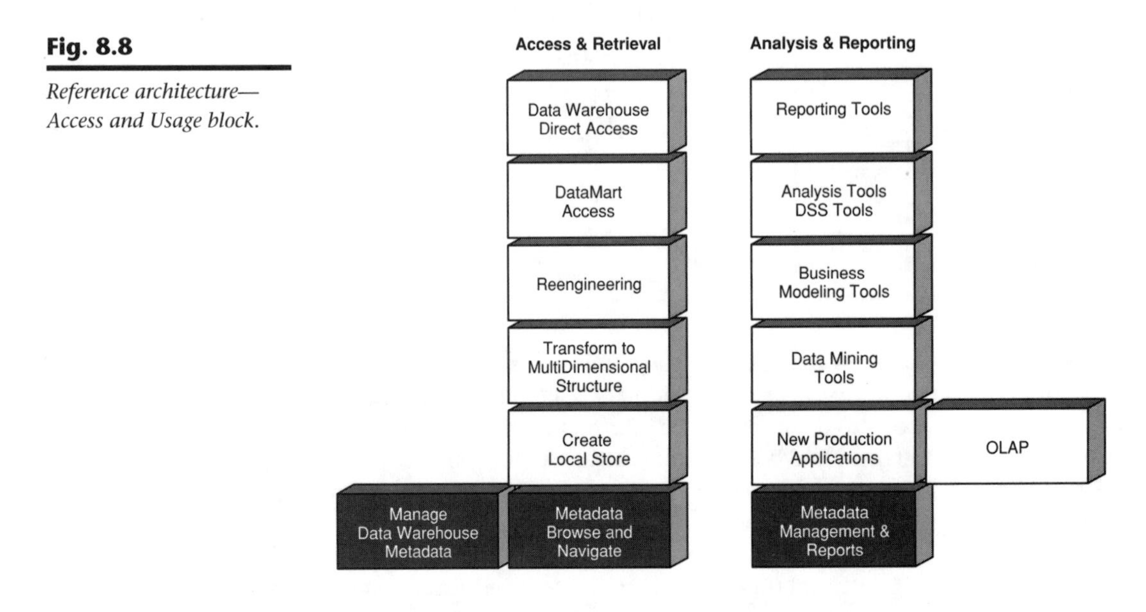


**Fig. 8.8**

*Reference architecture—Access and Usage block.*

The *Access and Retrieval* sub-block provides direct access to both the data warehouse and the data mart. This sub-block also offers services such as re-engineering the retrieved data for storage into multidimensional databases or providing multidimensional views for subsequent analysis, and transforming and "downloading" data into local stores for local analysis, reporting, and data mining. Considerations for managing the full range of potential queries with their incumbent issues, such as size and processing time, are supported in this sub-block. Support for accessing and browsing metadata is a key feature of this sub-block.

Business users tap the metadata browsing and navigation capabilities to do the following:

- Find and understand what exists in the data warehouse and data mart
- View the data in its proper context to convert data into information
- Learn the location of the data and how to access it
- Interpret the quality of the source of the data, the validity of the transformation actions that have been performed on the data from the time it was extracted to the time it was stored, and judge the reliability and quality of the data

The *Analysis and Reporting* sub-block provides a family of tools and applications to extract value from the data warehouse. Types of tools available include reporting tools, statistical and data analysis tools, business modeling tools, analytical processing tools, and data mining tools. Additional tools to navigate and report on the metadata provide the essential road map of the data warehouse and data mart. This road map guides the business user in understanding the data in the right context, with information on level of granularity, level of summarization, source of the data, date of origin, and business rules applied to the data.

Additionally, new business applications that leverage the structure of the data and data itself may be created and used as a competitive advantage. For example, if the data warehouse contents center around the customer, then applications like pin-point telesales and product bundling can be developed by the enterprise.

## Techniques for Using a Data Warehouse

*Decision support tools* is the generic term used to refer to data warehouse applications and tools that are used to retrieve, manipulate, and analyze the data, and then present the results. Figure 8.9 shows that these tools are used in two modes: *verification* and *discovery*. With the verification mode, the business user creates a hypothesis—a business question—and tries to confirm the hypothesis by accessing the data in the data warehouse. Tools that implement the verification mode include query tools, reporting systems, and multidimensional analysis tools. In the discovery mode, tools try to discover characteristics in the data such as patterns of purchasing or associations between the purchase of different items. In the discovery, or eureka, mode, the discovered patterns and associations are not previously known or suspected by the business user. The data mining tool is an example of the discovery mode.

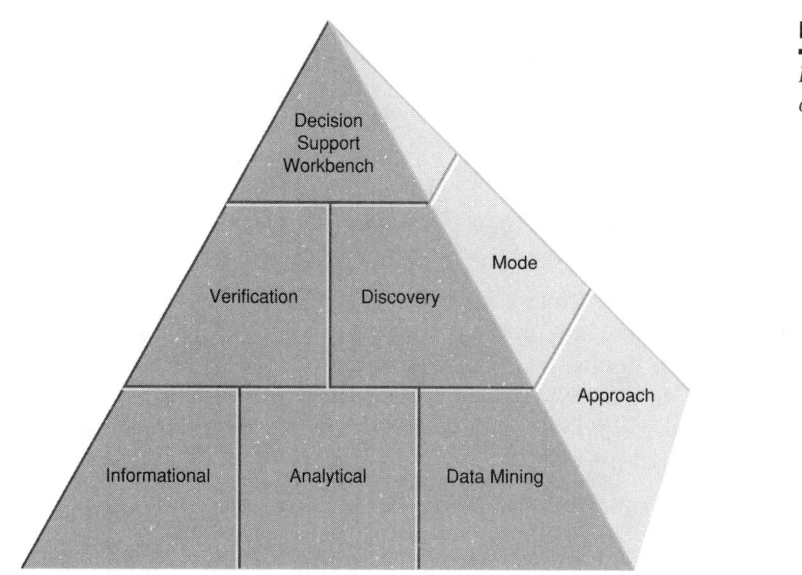


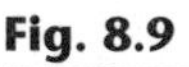

**Fig. 8.9**

*Decision support tools overview.*

From a tools availability perspective, the two modes of verification and discovery are generally classified into three approaches—informational processing, analytical processing, and data mining.

**Informational Processing.** Informational processing supports the verification mode of decision support. It includes techniques such as data and basic statistical analysis, query, and reporting. The data that is accessed and processed may be historical or fairly recent, and may be lightly or heavily summarized. The results are presented in the form of reports and charts.

**Analytical Processing.** Analytical processing also supports the verification mode of decision support. Its goal is to make the data available to the business user in the business users' perspective of business dimensions. Complex questions like, "how many cars did we sell in the United States in the first quarter of 1995 that had a CD audio system with a price of less than $25,000?," can be answered and interpreted. It supports capabilities such as "slice and dice," drill-down, and roll-ups. The data used in analytical processing is generally historical in both summary and detail form.

**Data Mining.** Data mining supports the discovery mode of decision support. Data mining tools scan through detailed transactional data to unearth hidden patterns and associations. Results are generally available in lengthy reports or can be analyzed with emerging data visualization tools.

Informational processing is excellent and cost-effective for mass deployment of query, analysis, and reporting of two- or three-dimensional data. Analytical processing tools allow multiple data views, such as sales by brand, store, season, and time periods to be defined, queried, and analyzed. Data mining tools are essential to understanding customer behavior.

The choice of the wrong tools leads to business user frustration, lower productivity, and a loss of competitive and strategic understanding of the business.

## Data Characteristics

The data available in the data warehouse has a range of characteristics: multiple granularity, many predefined queries and reports that can be processed on demand, and preprocessed and prepackaged results. The quality of the data may also vary. The objective is to meet the wide-range of needs of an array of users.

**Granularity of Data.** The data may be at multiple levels of detail—current detail, old detail, lightly summarized, highly summarized, and aggregated. The business question determines which data is needed and what granularity is required. Not all levels of detail are necessary. For example, it may be appropriate to create highly summarized information from lightly summarized information, such as annual values from quarterly values, depending on the need.

Enterprises with a combination of data warehouses and data marts may store different levels of granularity in the data warehouse and in the data mart, with detailed data in the data warehouse for queries and summarized data in the data mart for frequent and quick retrieval.

**Preprocessed Information.** Data warehouses can and do contain information that is preprocessed and stored for fast access and usage. Routine information, such as monthly or quarterly reports, marketing summary reports and charts, are available in this manner. Sometimes prepackaged multidimensional databases are also preloaded and readily available for interactive analysis.

**On-Demand Selection and Processing of Information.** For non-routine information, predefined queries or reports are available and the business user can select the appropriate query or report and process it when needed. This eases customization of the report, and processing occurs only when needed. Summary reports, charts, and multidimensional database loading can be made available on an on-demand basis.

**Ad-hoc Access and Processing.** Not every need of a business user can be reasonably preplanned. To meet new or unstated needs of business users, ad-hoc access and processing is required. Tools to support ad-hoc access and processing are generally available only for regular and power users. A newer generation of tools is attempting to bring ad-hoc access to casual users.

**Data Quality Information.** It is the quality and reliability of the data that builds confidence and trust in the data warehouse. The higher the quality of the data, the more the usage of the data warehouse for making business decisions, and the greater the value extracted from the data warehouse investment. The data warehouse must contain information on the quality of the data so decisions are made with complete knowledge and risks can be appropriately managed.

## Data Sources for Analysis

Data warehouse architecture allows access to multiple sources of data. Data sources accessed include not just the data warehouse and data mart, but also multidimensional servers—sometimes referred to as On-line Analytical Processors (OLAP)—shared local stores and a personal local store at the business user's personal workstation. What is accessed depends on who the user is, the granularity and type of data to be retrieved, and the decision support activity that is performed at a particular time.

Figure 8.10 describes a scenario where the data warehouse supports the diverse analysis and processing needs of a range of users, each requiring data with different granularity. In this scenario, the CEO/COO and executives are presented reports and charts on his/her personal workstation but can access a shared executive local store for additional summarized information or drill-down analysis.

Managers and business users access and use OLAP servers, data marts, and the data warehouses for informational and analytical processing. An extensive range of data is accessed and processed, all the way from highly summarized to old details. The business analysts, in partnership with IT facilitators, access not only the details in the data warehouse but also detailed transactional data and external sources for intensive informational processing and data mining.

Figure 8.10 can also be used as a design approach to construct a three-tier architecture data warehouse to meet informational and analytical processing requirements (see the next two chapters for detail discussions). The data warehouse or data mart are one tier, the OLAP server and shared local store are the second tier, and the personal workstation is the third. In a large data warehouse configuration or for performance purposes, the OLAP server and the shared local store can be separate tiers.

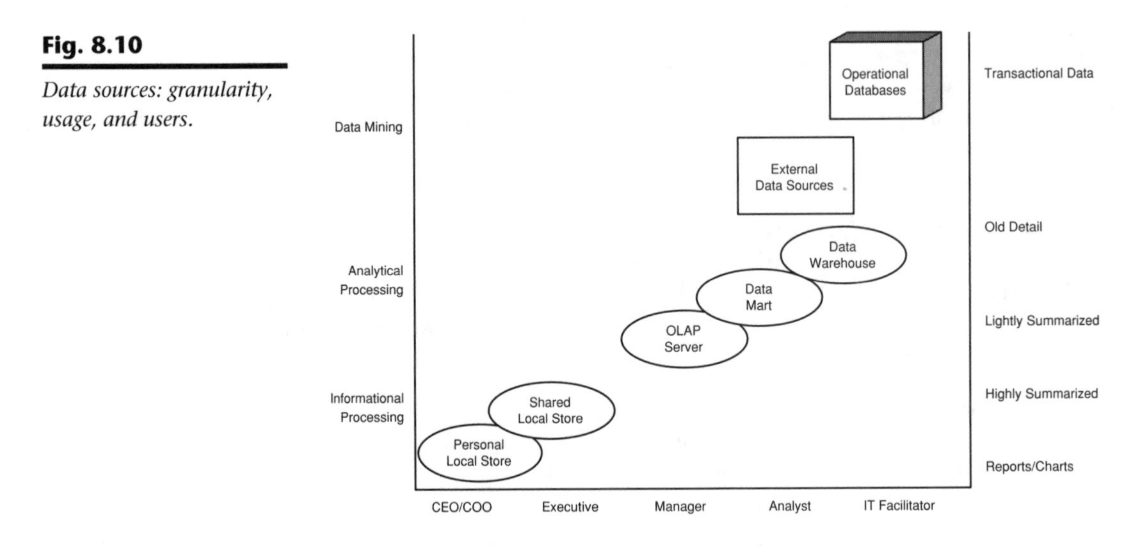


**Fig. 8.10**

*Data sources: granularity, usage, and users.*

## Steps to Addressing Business Issues

The data warehouse is a powerful decision support tool. The steps in using a data warehouse to address specific business problems are essentially the same steps an experienced manager uses to address other business problems (see fig. 8.11).

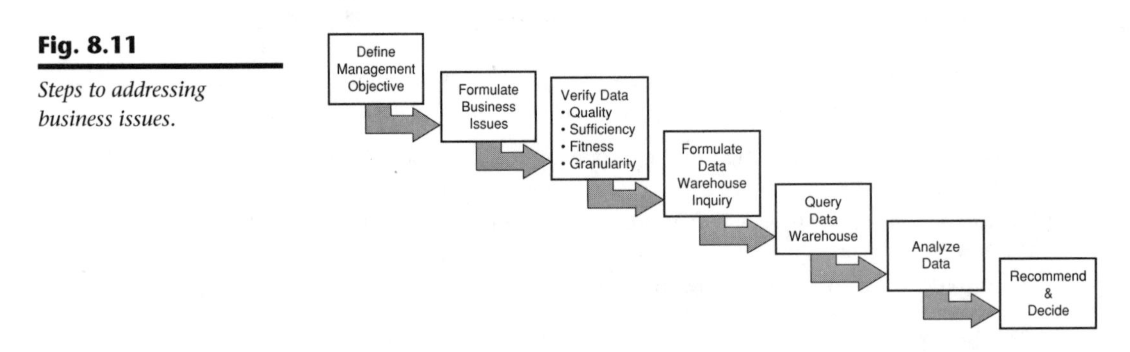


**Fig. 8.11**

*Steps to addressing business issues.*

There is, however, a major challenge: how to convert the management description of the problem or objective to a list of questions, inquiries, and results that can be extracted from the data warehouse. After successfully meeting this challenge, the rest of the steps in using the data warehouse are fairly obvious and straightforward.

**Management Objectives or Business Problems.** The first step is to capture the management objective or problem to be solved. Management objectives, shown in figure 8.12, are invariably stated in broad management terms such as "increase profits" or "need improved margins and reduced overhead." Some management objectives may be framed initially as issues or questions like "how can we be #1 or #2 in our business?" or "how can we increase market share?" Such objectives and issues must be clearly articulated with complete clarification of what the words in each statement mean. If management is asking "how can we be #1 or #2 in our business?," they must clarify whether their objective is to be number one or two in terms of revenue, profit, or both.

**Fig. 8.12**

*Management objectives and issues.*

**Business Analysis and Issues Formulation.** The second step is to decompose the management request into its business information components; i.e., what business information is needed to address the issues. In figure 8.13, data is needed on the organization's revenue, profits, sources of revenue, costs of generating that revenue, and so forth. In addition, data is needed on the competitors, as well as their historical and projected revenues, profits, and product costs.

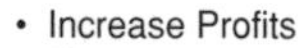


**Fig. 8.13**

*Conversion: management objectives to business analysis statements.*

Furthermore, the data needed is at a summary level and at a detail level. Data may be needed about demographics, industry trends, revenue and profit by geography, sales organization, product line, and, of course, by time intervals like monthly or quarterly.

To get full value from a data warehouse, a detailed map is generated showing the entire decomposition of the objective into a set of questions the data warehouse is capable of answering and what data is needed to answer the questions.

Figure 8.14 shows how the management objectives of wanting to be #1 or #2 in the business in terms of revenue is decomposed into business issues, such as current market share, market trends, quarterly and annual revenue, and profitability by organizational units, geography, products sold, and so forth.

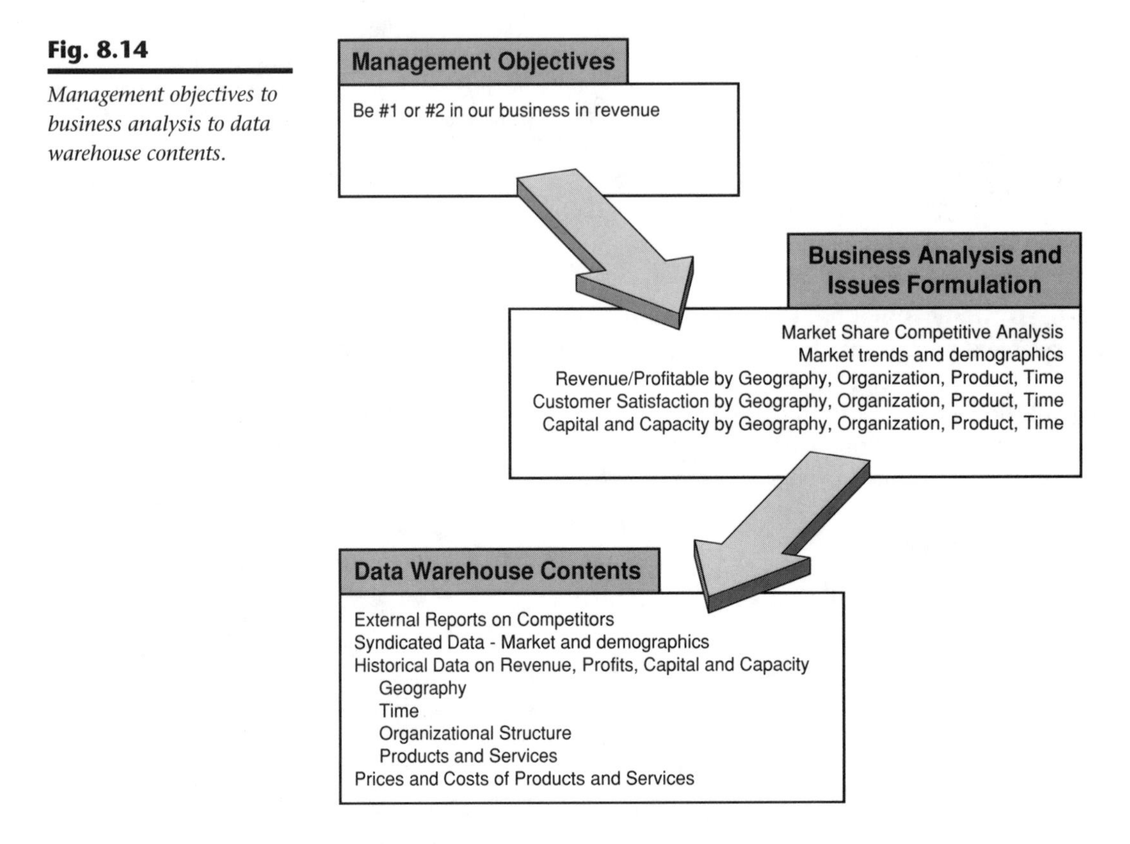


**Fig. 8.14**

*Management objectives to business analysis to data warehouse contents.*

To find the answers to these business issues, the data warehouse must contain information on competitors, syndicated data on the market, and historical data about the organization's revenues and profits by organizational unit, geography, products, and services over the time period of interest. Additionally, other information such as product pricing history, cost history, and capital and capacity are needed, either to develop the strategy to become #1 or #2, or to maintain the #1 or #2 standing in the industry. Note that the data warehouse cannot respond to the customer satisfaction business issue because desired information on customer satisfaction is not available in the form by organization or geography.

**Data Availability and Quality.** The next step is to verify the quality and sufficiency of the data. This is done by examining the data warehouse metadata. Assistance from the data warehouse Data Administrator (DA) and the Data Base Administrator (DBA) is, as a rule, necessary to interpret and understand the metadata. A metadata catalog, if available, is an excellent source to access the needed information. Some of the issues worth taking into account at the outset include the following:

- **Examining what data is available**—Does the data needed exist in the data warehouse? If not, can it be acquired and then stored in the data warehouse in the appropriate structure and format? Without the right data, the analysis may not be possible or the quality of the analysis may suffer. Important to ensure the data is accessible to the desired analysis tool, the data format is compatible with the analysis technique to be used, the size of the data, and on what media the data is stored. This information could have an impact on what analysis approach is feasible.
- **Understanding the granularity of the data**—Is the granularity right or can the detail or lightly summarized data be summarized to compute the right granularity?
- **Discerning the fitness of the data**—Is the data fit for the purpose at hand? Is the data from the desired time frame? Can comparisons be made between two fiscal years, i.e., do they cover the same time frames?
- **Validating the data quality**—Is the data accurate and complete? Data quality is of paramount importance since conclusions made from it may not just be suspect, but may lead to poor decisions with disastrous consequences. Data quality is influenced by the accuracy of the source, the validity of the transformations performed by the data warehouse construction process, and the ability of the access and retrieval process to fetch all the desired information. If the metadata of the data warehouse contains audit information on the source and transformations of the data, and description of the access and retrieval process, the challenge of validating the data quality is greatly reduced. The DA and DBA can provide invaluable assistance for this activity.

**Business Inquiry Conversion.** The next step is to convert the business questions and data needs to the data warehouse's computing language and semantics. This is the same as converting a business inquiry statement into a computing inquiry statement. The example in figure 8.15 demonstrates the conversion of the business query: "What are the top five colors of cars we sell in the $20,000 to $25,000 range?" The corresponding computing requirement may be to determine all cars sold in the $20,000 to $25,000 range, sort the results by color, summarize by color, and then rank the sorted results.

This activity requires domain or subject area knowledge, as well as some technical acumen. It is essential in extracting and deriving solid and reliable business value from the data warehouse.

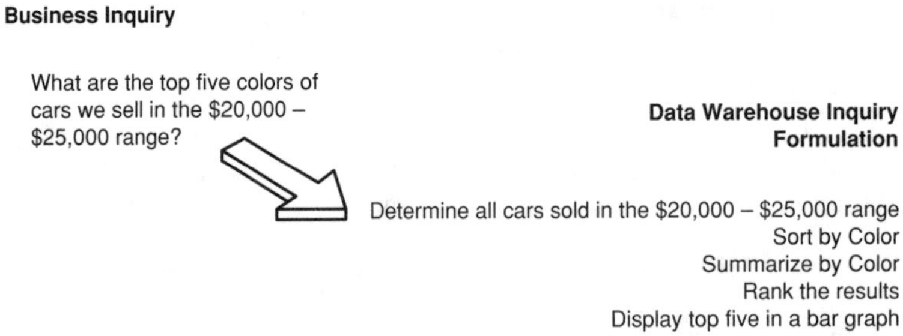

**Fig. 8.15**

*The conversion of a business inquiry to a data warehouse inquiry.*



**Data Warehouse Inquiry Formulation and Submission.** The next step is to decompose the computing inquiry statement into data warehouse queries, reports, or custom applications. This can be achieved with point-and-click graphical tools, report writers, or database system queries in computer languages, such as SQL. Many data warehouses have predefined queries and reports for many routine requests.

Queries and reports may access one or more data stores. Certain queries and reports may require an additional step of extracting data and downloading into spreadsheets, local store, or multidimensional databases before the actual query and analysis activity can start.

Depending on the capabilities of the data warehouse and the capabilities of the tool, the request may be ad hoc and submitted online; and the response may be instantaneous.

**Results Analysis and Interpretation.** Comprehensive knowledge of the subject matter and a thorough understanding of the data in the data warehouse is essential to interpretation. The quality of the data warehouse output can greatly ease the task of interpretation. If the data output is in the form of clear summaries or crisp charts and graphs, the analyst may quickly arrive at decisions or recommendations. Many a time, further analysis is required or additional data is necessary to proceed to a plan of action.

Techniques such as slice and dice, drill-down and roll-up, side-by-side comparison, trends analysis, and flip between numerical views and graphical views greatly assist the analyst in interpreting the extracted information.

**Recommendation.** The analyst may recommend a plan of action or offer alternatives. Presentation tools and capabilities of the data warehouse can greatly enhance the communications of the recommendations and influence their perceived value.

## Using Analysis Approaches

A wide range of approaches and techniques are available for analyzing the data in the data warehouse. Selection of the appropriate approach or a combination of approaches depends on the business issue, tools available, and the experience of the user. A sample list of general analysis approaches is as follows:

- Existence checking is used when the analyst is looking for occurrences of a particular piece of information, e.g., a query to determine if a particular product has been sold to a particular customer during the last five years.
- Standard or routine queries/reports are used when such information is already preprocessed and is made available for immediate access and analysis.
- Selected items comparison over single dimensions may be used to compare the purchases of two customers along the time dimension or along the geography dimension. The dimensions of interest are time, sales territory, and products.
- Trends analysis is used to find both meaningful and secular trends. For example, a product line manager wants to know the warranty service experience for a product or a product line. Finding a trend is one thing, interpreting it is another. Additional challenges arise when differences exist in the quality, definition, or minor differences in the transformation rules applied to the data.
- Ratios and rankings aid both the understanding and interpretation of the data. Ranking is used many times to determine if the 80-20 rule applies to an organization's customers, where 20 percent of the customers provide 80 percent of the revenue.
- Summarization and aggregation help to understand data in natural groups or capsules. It is a common management mechanism to interpret and then address larger issues with fewer actions. This is the prevalent mode of communication with management.
- Charting is used to capture the data in a visual mode to see potential patterns of affinity or other aggregations. The goal is to interpret data to gain insight or derive value if it exists.
- Browsing/surfing the lightly summarized or detail data looking for exceptions and unusual activities in the business. It always leads to further analysis using any of the other approaches described here.
- Iterative analysis is where interpreting one query or report can lead from one query to another until the root cause of a business fact is understood and appropriate action can be taken.
- Statistical techniques are used to detect unusual patterns of data. Some of the basic statistical techniques used include linear and non-linear modeling, regression analysis, and time-series analysis.
- Multidimensional or complex correlation is a sophisticated technique to deduce business behavior by trying to understand the impact of multiple dimensions and multiple business criteria on business. The dimensions of interest are usually, but not always, time, geography, organization, and product.
- Living sample databases are used when the amount of data to be analyzed is enormous, hypothesis or query formulation is challenging, and processing a query is costly. The analyst can use a subset of the data—a "statistically correct subset" which accurately reflects the actual total data—to verify the hypothesis and determine the metrics of the query. Once the hypothesis is verified, the

analyst can proceed to submit the query to the total relevant data, and extract the desired results.

- Slice and dice is used to look at multidimensional correlations to uncover business behavior and business rules. It is essentially surfing with multidimensional data.
- Drill-down and roll-up analysis is an attempt to "understand the news behind the news." If a report, chart, summary data, or the result of a complex analysis needs further exploration and understanding, then drill-down is used to explore the next level of detail, and successive levels of detail. For example, if the enterprise revenue has increased dramatically in the last quarter, it can be used to understand if this was due to an unusual purchase from a market segment, region, a single customer, or overall growth in the market. Drill-down analysis can assist in looking at market segments, sub-segments by market or territory, or customer-by-customer profiles (see fig. 8.16).

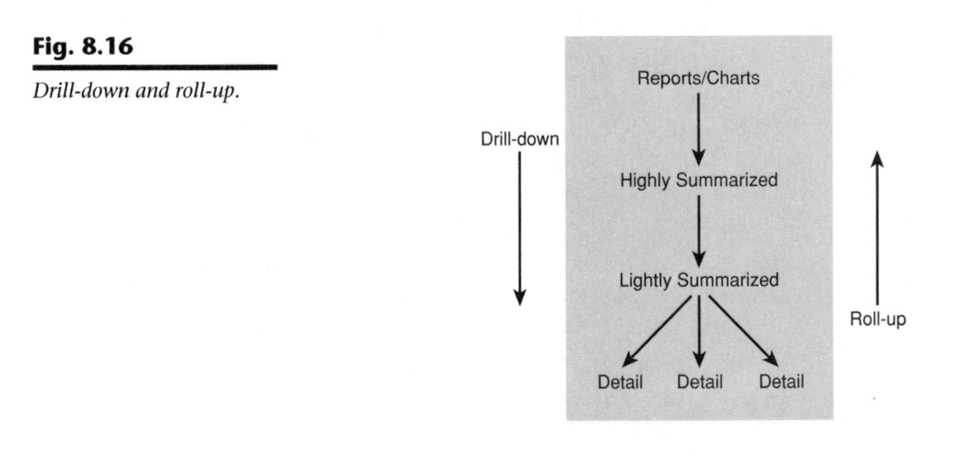


**Fig. 8.16**

*Drill-down and roll-up.*

- Roll-up, the opposite of drill-down, is exploring at a higher level of summarization to determine issues such as the health of the business or the veracity of a business issue. The goal is to ascertain what business actions are needed.
- Drill-down and roll-up can be along a single dimension such as geography, or along multiple dimensions such as a complex combination of customer, geography, and product-line (see fig. 8.17).

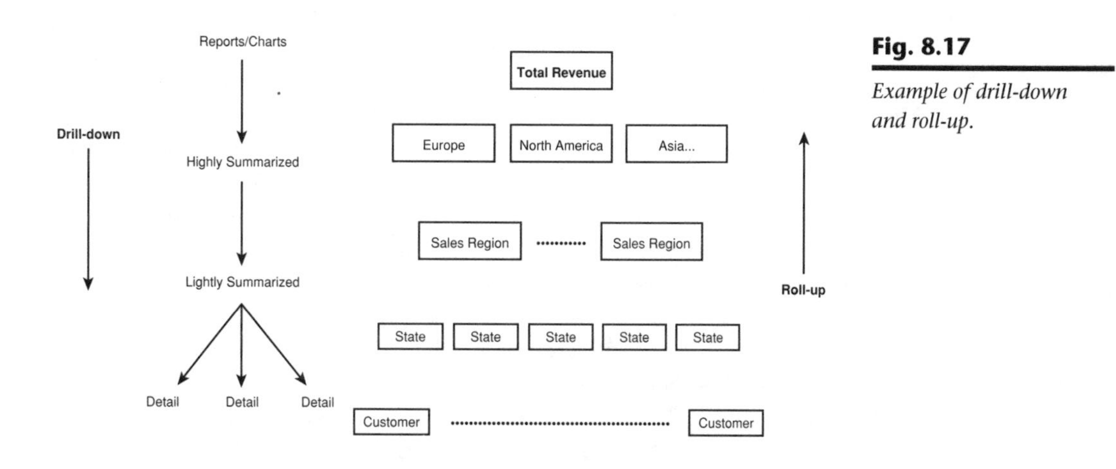


**Fig. 8.17**

*Example of drill-down and roll-up.*

## Communicating Results of the Analysis

Today's technology offers an overabundance of tools and an array of choices in how to convey the results of the analysis, i.e., the value extracted and gained by using the data warehouse. Choices include "soft-copy" queries, simple to colorful reports, simple to complex to sophisticated charts, and even multimedia presentations.

Other communication approaches consist of "downloading" the results into spreadsheets, executive information systems, multidimensional or OLAP processors, and custom application programs.

An emerging opportunity is to build application programs that leverage the data to create new business opportunities. For example, customer information in the data warehouse can be used to build a market segment strategy and a high potential promotion list of targeted customers.

Descriptions of the many tools and analysis techniques these tools provide are discussed in the following chapters.

# Summary

- The simple purpose of a data warehouse is to assist management in understanding the past and planning for the future. Even though the data warehouse has crucial strategic information in it, deriving business value from the data warehouse is a complex endeavor. To get value requires an alchemy of business skills, technical know-how, intuition, and experience.
- A data warehouse can yield the right information to business executives, managers, and analysts. Tapping the potential of a data warehouse is limited only by the capacity, capability, and creativity of the business users. Early experiences

point to a broad array of usage: profitability analysis and growth, strategic management, customer relationship management, corporate asset management, and BPR and TQM support. Data warehouses are being successfully applied in the manufacturing, consumer goods and distribution, and the finance and banking sector.

- Using the data warehouse in the day-to-day course of business consists of two broad activities: access and retrieval, and analysis and reporting. These activities are supported by the Access and Usage block of the reference architecture. Two models are available to extract value out of the data warehouse: verification model using informational and analytical processing techniques, and discovery model using data mining techniques.
- Data quality and reliability is what builds confidence and trust in the data warehouse. The higher the quality of the data, the more the usage of the data warehouse for making business decisions, and the greater the value extracted from the data warehouse investment.
- The steps in using a data warehouse to address specific business problems are essentially the same steps an experienced manager uses to address other business problems. There is a major challenge: how to convert the management description of the problem or objective to a list of questions, inquiries, and results that can be extracted from the data warehouse. The major steps in using a data warehouse are capturing management objectives, formulating the business issues, verifying the quality and availability of the right data, building the business inquiry and converting it into a data warehouse inquiry, analyzing and interpreting the results, and communicating the decisions and recommendations.
- Before long, enterprises will have multiple data warehouses, all focused on increasing revenue and profitability, and beating the competition. Syndicated data is available to everyone. However, the enterprise's own data is a unique asset. This data is a detailed history of the enterprise's business and its relationship with its customers. Enterprises that learn to leverage their data, i.e., their data warehouses, best are in a position to truly build plans and execute and fine tune them for competitive advantage.

CHAPTER 9

# Query and Reporting: Informational Processing

The return on investment of a data warehouse is based on the ability of business users to extract the right data from the data warehouse, convert it into information, and then use the information to make better decisions. Business users want to extract the right data with minimal investments in time and with the least amount of frustration. In other words, "get it right the first time" is the quality mantra. As was discussed in Chapter 8, there are multiple ways to extract and analyze information of value from the data warehouse (see fig. 9.1).

The data warehouse Decision Support Workbench (DSW) consists of tools and applications that are used to access, retrieve, manipulate, and analyze the data, and then to present the results in the form of recommendations and alternatives. DSW postulates two modes of use—verification mode and discovery mode. In the verification mode, the business user creates a hypothesis (a business question) and accesses the data warehouse information to verify and confirm the hypothesis. Informational processing, query, analysis, and reporting, and also analytical processing support the verification mode of usage. The verification mode—consisting of informational and analytical processing—is sometimes referred to as the *user-driven mode* as opposed to data mining, which is referred to as the *data-driven* mode.

Informational processing assists business users to seek answers to business questions, such as the following:

- Are sporting goods sales subject to seasonal trends? Which items are impacted, and how are they impacted?
- How many cars were sold last month? How does this number compare to the same month for the last five years?
- Who are the top ten salespersons or customers in the Midwest? What percentage of revenue do they generate?
- Which are the eight least-profitable items in the sales catalog?

As discussed in Chapter 8, data warehouses are initially used as reporting databases to generate reports and answer well-defined static business queries. Increasing confidence in the use of the data warehouse leads to additional use, from selected online queries to reports and analysis of summarized information; and to ad hoc queries of detail data. Informational processing—data warehouse query, reporting, and analysis—is sometimes referred to as *business intelligence querying.*

**Fig. 9.1**

*Decision Support Workbench.*

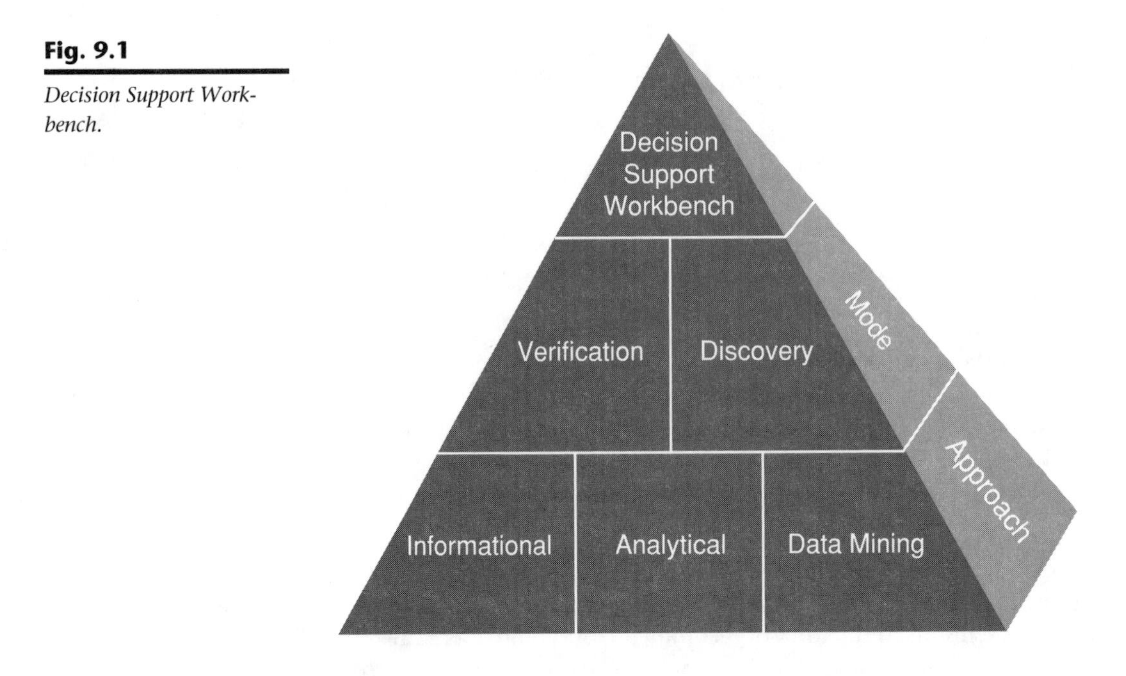

Informational processing consists of three distinct components: queries to access and retrieve the data from the data warehouse, analysis of the data, and presentation of the analysis in the form of reports, crosstabs and matrixes, tables, and simple-to-complex charts and graphs. The scope of informational processing is generally limited to two- or three-dimensional (2D or 3D) processing.

From the perspective of the reference architecture, informational processing is concerned with the Access and Usage block (see fig. 9.2).

The Access and Usage block contains two components—access and retrieval, and analysis and reporting. Informational processing features and functions are rendered by the sub-blocks (data warehouse and data mart access, create local store, reporting and analysis tools, and creating new production applications). Informational processing also impacts the metadata sub-blocks (metadata browse and navigate, manage data warehouse metadata, and metadata management and reports). These metadata sub-blocks provide the roadmap for the business user to extract maximum value from the informational processing capabilities of the data warehouse.

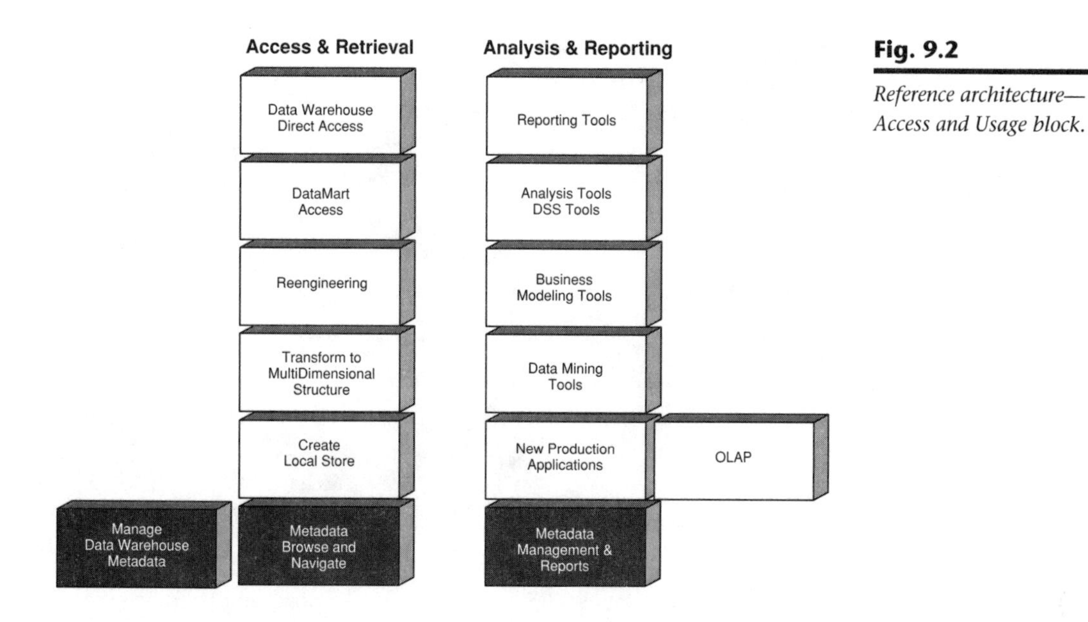


**Fig. 9.2**

*Reference architecture—Access and Usage block.*

This chapter focuses on informational processing. Analytical or multidimensional processing and data mining with their requisite query, reporting, and analysis are discussed in Chapters 10 and 11, respectively.

# Informational Processing

The steps involved in informational processing (query, reporting, and analysis) are essentially the same decision analysis steps that an experienced business user applies to addressing regular business issues (see fig. 9.3).

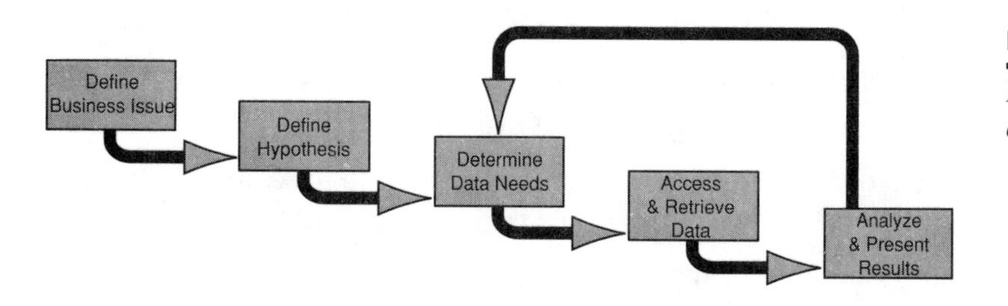


**Fig. 9.3**

*Data warehouse decision analysis steps.*

The business user first must define the business problem to address. Next, the hypothesis or questions that need answers must be defined. As discussed in Chapter 8, the transformation of a business problem into a hypothesis and into questions that a data warehouse can answer is a major challenge. This transformation requires business know-how, experience, and analysis acumen. For example, in figure 9.4, the business objective is "balance inventory with demand," which means the business issues of products, inventory status, sales, stores, time period, and so on must be selected and examined.

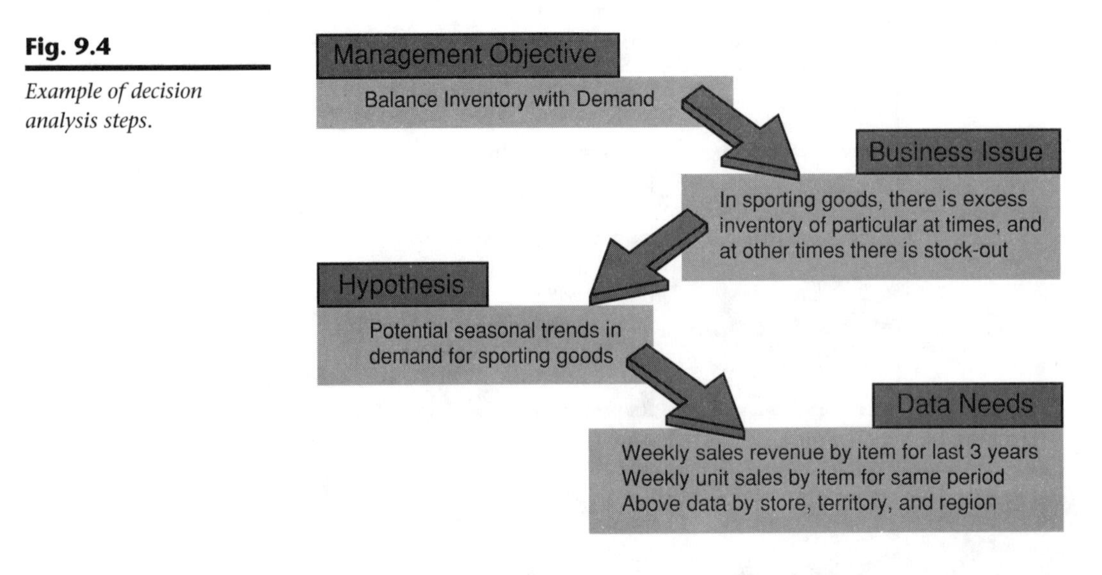


**Fig. 9.4**

*Example of decision analysis steps.*

This analysis leads to a business issue: "In sporting goods, suppose that there is excess inventory of skiboots at times and a stock-out of parkas." Corresponding to the business issue, the hypothesis of interest an experienced business analyst may define is, "There exists a seasonal trend in demand for these items—and what is it?" To verify this hypothesis, a variety of data must be accessed and analyzed. The approach may be to examine the seasonal trend first on a quarterly basis, and then later on a monthly basis.

Next, the business user determines if the appropriate data is available and if the data is sufficient to answer the questions. Now, the informational processing tools are used to access the data warehouse and retrieve the data. Finally, the data is analyzed, and the results are presented as actionable recommendations. Sometimes, iterative analysis is needed. For iterative analysis, the business user may redefine the original hypothesis or access additional data to verify the original hypothesis. Subsequently, a cycle of three decision analysis steps (determine data needs, access and retrieve data, and analyze results) is looped through, as many times as deemed necessary.

The usage of informational processing from query definition to disseminating results is shown in figure 9.5. Informational processing is a multiple-step activity.

The essential steps to a successful application of informational processing are explained in the following sections.

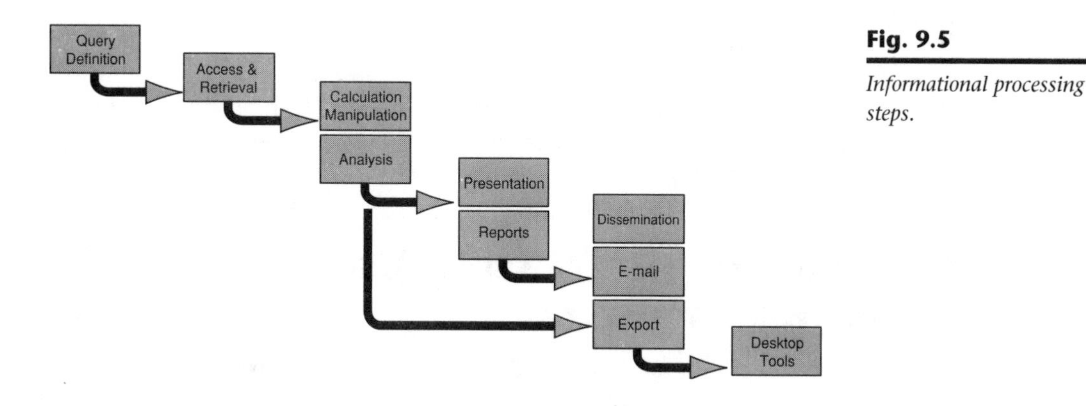


**Fig. 9.5**

*Informational processing steps.*

## Defining the Query

The business hypothesis or questions such as, "is there a seasonal trend in the quarterly sales of sporting goods?," must be translated into a computer query for submission to the data warehouse (refer to fig. 9.4). This translation is accomplished either by an IT professional or by a business user who is employing vendor tools or a custom application. The challenge is translating the business terms into terms that the computer understands (and therefore, terms that the data warehouse access and query tools understand).

## Accessing and Retrieving the Data

The access tools submit the computing query to the data warehouse and retrieve the appropriate data. The access and retrieval process may include the capability to perform calculations, such as sort the results or create subtotals of items. In our example, the daily sales figures from each store are summarized into both weekly sales and sales by item, for each store.

## Calculating, Manipulating, and Analyzing the Data

The business user may perform further calculations and manipulations on the results that the query fetches. Additional analysis may occur with the goal of converting the retrieved data into information or facts. A variety of analysis techniques, such as charts and graphs, are used to convert data into information to derive recommendations—for example, charts of monthly and quarterly sales by store for each item and sales by territory and region. The business users' experience, intuition, and domain expertise play a major role in successfully analyzing the data and formulating recommendations.

## Presenting the Information

The results of the analysis can be presented either as reports, charts, and graphs or as preprocessed data for further analysis. A range of options, such as simple break and crosstab reports, Pie, 2D and 3D Bar, Line, Histogram, and Scatterplot are available, and the choice depends on the nature of the information analyzed and the particular needs, communications style, and culture of the organization.

### Disseminating the Information

The recommendations may be disseminated as hard copy or soft copy or electronically mailed to the business user. With increasing frequency, the results of analysis now are exported to desktop applications such as spreadsheets for further analysis or to word processors for adding to reports and documents.

## Informational Processing Users and Environment

Data warehouses are built to meet the decision support needs of a wide range of business users, from executives to business analysts. These users are supported by information specialists or IT professionals to leverage the maximum value from the data warehouse.

### Informational Processing Users

Business users' needs can cover a wide spectrum: from charts and graphs to standard reports, predefined queries, and ad hoc analysis. Business users vary in their technical know-how. Some are comfortable accessing prepared reports and charts, while others can readily create complex ad hoc queries. To meet the informational processing needs of such users, the data warehouse's query, reporting, and analysis capabilities must run the gamut from accessing static (preprocessed) charts and summaries to accessing and querying detail data (see fig. 9.6).

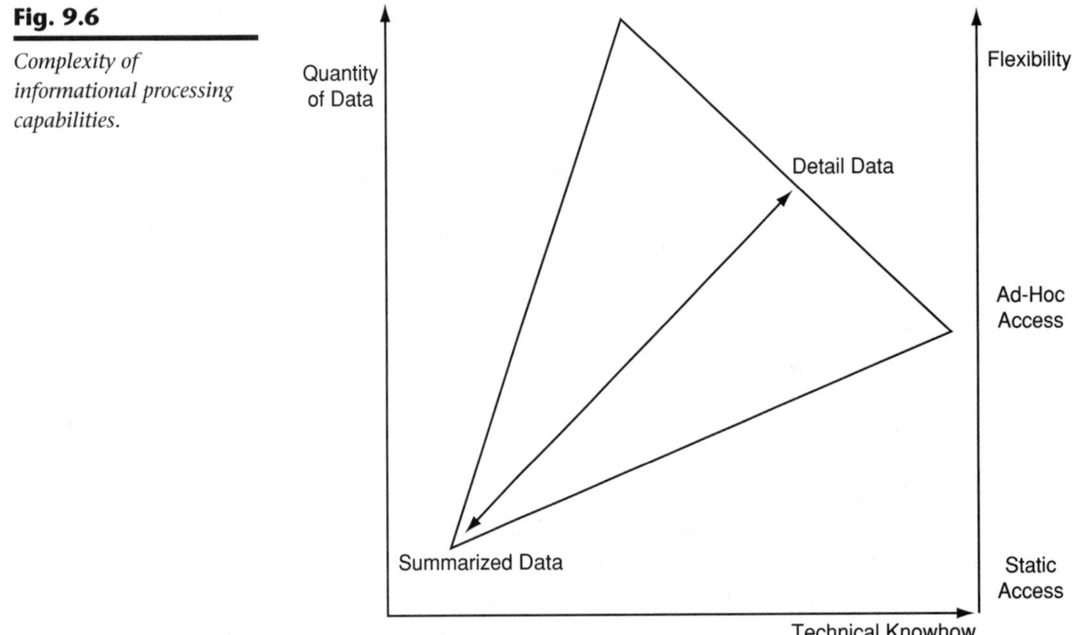


**Fig. 9.6**

*Complexity of informational processing capabilities.*

A well-designed data warehouse contains data with multiple levels of granularity, from coarse to fine. In response to the requirements of its business users, the data warehouse may contain the following data:

- **Preprocessed charts and reports**—This information is ready for access and presentation and may be created as a part of the data warehouse loading or populating process, or it may be created by information specialists or IT professionals. The quantity of data is comparatively small. The data is considered "static" because the business user retrieves the information as it is stored in the data warehouse—for example, a graph of quarterly sales revenue for multiple quarters for the last three years.
- **Precalculated summary and aggregated information**—This information, both highly summarized and lightly summarized, usually is created as a part of the data warehouse loading process or by a regularly scheduled "summarization application." This precalculation process may include creating rolling summaries and then an update of the data warehouse occurring on events such as month-end and quarter-end. This may include rolling summaries and updating occurs based on events such as month-end. The principal purpose of precalculating is to improve the response time of access and query, while offering flexibility in the information that is accessed and how it is analyzed—for example, weekly and monthly sales revenue totals by territory.
- **Detail data**—This data is available for maximum flexibility of ad hoc access and analysis. Ad hoc access to detail data is essential because the business user is looking for information that will give a competitive advantage by trying to test a variety of business hypotheses. But the quantity of data available is enormous, and defining the query is usually complex.

As the business user's informational processing needs increase—from summarized information to detail data—the informational processing technical complexity increases dramatically. On one hand, the quantity of data in the data warehouse increases multifold, and on the other hand, the technical know-how needed to intelligently define the query becomes daunting. The focus of many query and reporting tools is to address this challenge. The data warehouse implementation team's goal is to address this wide range of user needs with a minimal set of different informational processing tools.

The broad spectrum of business users have a continuum of informational processing needs, increasing in sophistication, as shown in figure 9.7.

Executives and senior managers usually are interested in viewing the results of an informational processing activity. For this class of business users, business analysts and information specialists use informational processing tools to extract, summarize, and convert the right information from the data warehouse into charts and graphs. They then save the results for later access by the executive. These results are represented as executive icons on the executives' personal workstations. Executives and senior managers use the executive icons to access the data, and then view the "canned" charts, graphs, and reports. As a rule, the information accessed is static and is periodically refreshed to keep the information current. The quality and richness of the presentation capabilities of the informational processing tools is fundamental to better understand the information and, therefore, to help make better decisions.

**Fig. 9.7**

*Continuum of informational processing needs.*

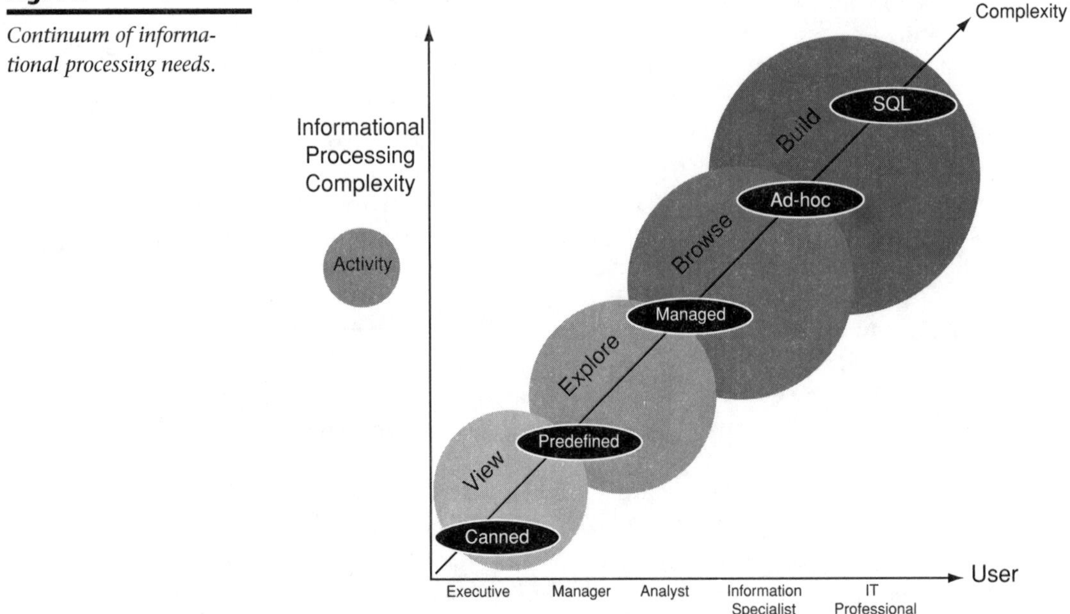


For executives, "less is more," but at times analysis of canned reports and charts may lead some executives to look for additional details in the data warehouse. They explore the data warehouse by invoking predefined queries—queries that require minimum input to select the correct data—to access lightly summarized data in the data warehouse and analyze the results. In this case, the informational processing tool or application usually converts the extracted data into charts, graphs, and reports. More complex needs are, in practice, fulfilled with the assistance of business analysts and informational specialists.

Managers usually know what they want to find. They want to verify predefined hypothesis—get answers to the same questions using standard or routine queries (predefined queries) from the data warehouse. Predefined queries meet most of their needs. Additional query or surfing generally is limited to accessing the data warehouse in a "managed query" environment. In a "managed query" environment, the business user can construct the query by using business terms and business rules. The technical complexity is hidden from the business user.

Also true for this class of users, the bottom line to successful analysis and decision making is the quality and richness of the presentation capabilities of the informational processing tools.

Business analysts are the important users of the informational processing capabilities of the data warehouse. They are the power users who define new business hypotheses as they seek strategic and competitive advantage. They understand business complexity. During analysis, one business question can lead to a second, and then to a third, and so on. One hypothesis may lead to another. The power to surf or browse the data warehouse, skim the data in the data warehouse, and create new ad hoc queries is essential for business analysts who must verify their hypotheses and get answers to the business issues. Raw informational processing power and ease of use in building complex queries is the name of the game for these users. Of course, business analysts also do support the informational processing needs of executives and managers.

Information specialists and IT professionals support the complex informational processing needs of the executives, managers, and business analysts. No matter how cleverly the data warehouse is organized, some queries are just too complex to define. These queries have complicated rules and predicates, and knowledge of the data structure of the data warehouse is essential to extract the right information within reasonable response times.

These specialists assist business analysts in surfing and searching the data warehouse. They also use the informational processing tools to create and build "canned" reports, charts, graphs, and predefined queries. Richness in functionality in building complex queries is the prime requirement of these users, who are the technical power users of informational processing tools.

## Informational Processing Environment

To meet the preceding described needs of the full range of informational processing users, the informational processing environment must support a range of query and report types, analysis capabilities, and data warehouse access and retrieval functions. Meeting these requirements may mean that the data warehouse must offer a range of (purchased) informational processing tools, as well as the development of custom applications.

The informational processing environment demands a range of performance capability, from instant response for executive and managerial requests to reasonable wait for ad hoc queries of analysts (see fig. 9.8). The triad of FAQs, FARs, and FADs must be architected into the data warehouse and the informational processing environment. Frequently Accessed Queries (FAQs) and Frequently Asked Reports (FARs) by executives and managers must be prepared in advance and stored in the data warehouse for instantaneous retrieval and presentation of tables, matrix reports, charts, and graphs. For managers and business analysts, FAQs and FARs—along with Frequently Accessed Data (FADs) for import into personal workstation analysis tools, such as spreadsheets—are required.

Data warehouses are challenged in two ways—at one extreme is business complexity and at the other is technical complexity. Meeting complex business needs (for example, of executives and managers) may require complex technology, but this usually is hidden from the business user. Executives and managers need "canned" charts and reports to manage business complexity. For these users, informational processing tools—query and reporting—must include a rich set of presentation functions.

**Fig. 9.8**

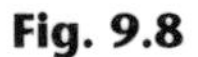

*Informational processing needs and environment.*

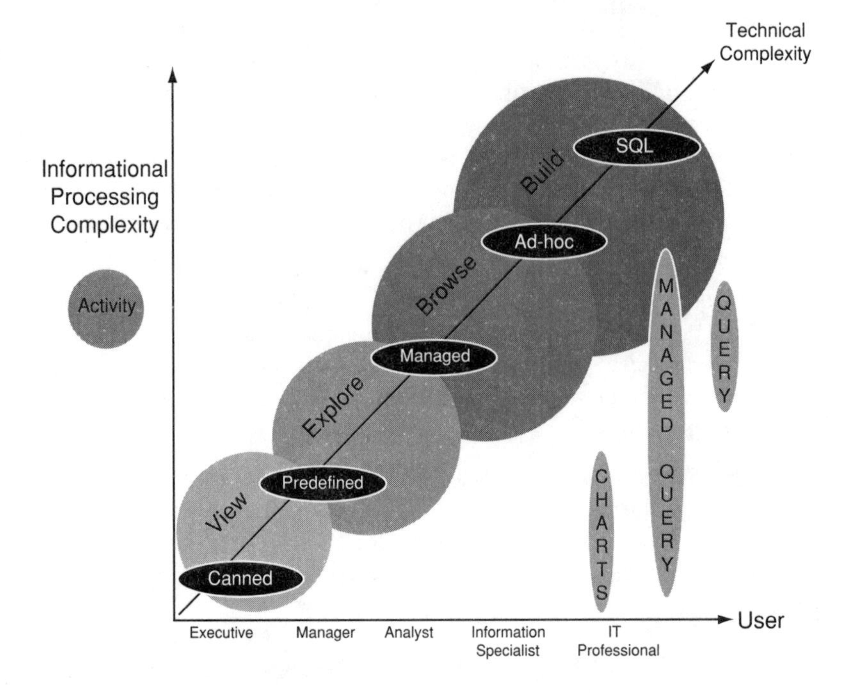


The needs of managers, business analysts, and many information specialists usually can be addressed in a *managed query* environment. In a managed query environment, informational processing tools hide the technical complexity of the data warehouse with a "thick semantic layer" of business terms and rules. This layer liberates the business user from the need to understand the intricacies of data warehouse's underlying data structures and from the daunting set theory relationships needed to join tables when formulating the query. Superior informational processing tools guide the user to define the access and query to the data warehouse in a "correct by construction" paradigm. These tools are also robust in analysis functions and rich in reporting and presentation capabilities.

Complex business hypothesis, which lead to complex business questions, require processing much detail data. Access and retrieval of detail data is usually tortuous and frustrating. In such cases, IT professionals need sophisticated informational processing tools with powerful technical functions. These functions support the creation of complex SQL queries that will precisely and completely access and retrieve the required detail data, and then make the results available to "managed query" tools for further analysis and reporting.

The secular trend in informational processing enables the business users to meet their own needs with a managed query environment with minimal assistance from information specialists or IT professionals. This capability enables the information specialists and IT professionals to focus on creating applications to meet complex business needs, and these applications deliver canned (or predefined) queries, reports, and charts for subsequent access by executives, managers, and business users.

# Informational Processing Functions and Features

As discussed previously in this chapter, the informational processing environment supports users with a diverse set of needs and skills. The features and functions required to meet these needs can be broadly classified into two major categories:

- User features to derive value from the data warehouse
- Administration features to manage the informational processing environment

## Business Users: Getting Value

Although "fast access and great response time" is important, the essence is data manipulation, analysis, and communicating the results with a crisp presentation. The informational processing environment must be enticing and inviting to the business user. The key criteria that keeps users coming back for more is *value* and *ease of use*.

Ease of use must be embedded in each aspect of the informational processing capability. Ease of use must encompass the activities building queries, analyzing and converting the data into information, generating reports, creating presentations, and exporting selected data to favorite desktop tools. Ease of use must also glue these activities with an intuitive work-flow methodology and a GUI that complements the user interface that the business user is familiar with, such as Microsoft Office.

To extract value, informational processing must support a strong suite of general functions and technical features. The general features are required by all the business users, and technical features are focused on increasing the productivity of experienced users and IT professionals. Additionally, access to a rich set of data warehouse metadata functions is needed to facilitate the extraction of full value from the data warehouse.

**General Functions.** General functions needed by a broad range of business users, include the following:

- Range of charts and graphs such as pie, 2D and 3D bar, scatter, line, and area
- Tabular, crosstab, and matrix reports
- Stockpile of summarized and aggregated data readily available via FAQs, FARs, and FADs functions
- Rich set of mathematical and logical functions for data manipulation and analysis
- Statistical analysis and trends analysis
- Ratios and rankings, comparisons, and existence checking
- Data browsing and visualization

- "Living sample database" access and retrieval
- Export to desktop analysis and presentation tools, and to other applications

**Technical Features.** Technical features are needed by experienced users and IT professionals to do the following:

- Access canned reports and charts by way of icons and buttons, which are enhanced by filter and match capabilities at time of use.
- Define complex queries by using business terms and rules, without a technical understanding of the underlying data structures.
- Enrich query—for example, edit the SQL of a query generated by the query tool to improve access and retrieval of the data (the query tool must verify if edit is correct or, at least, support error recovery).
- Use the results of one query as the input to another query.
- Add new formulas for analysis and new templates for reports and charts.
- Analyze by using multiple pivots, drill-down and roll-up techniques, and side-by-side comparisons.
- Preview reports and charts in WYSIWYG format before printing.
- Leverage reporting assistants such as report wizards, user-defined templates and layouts, and reusing one template to create a new one.
- Build reports with embedded tables, charts, and graphs.
- Enhance report templates by adding logos, styles, multiple fonts, borders, color highlights, page numbering, and page headers and footers.
- Create complex reports, such as to use the results of one query as the input to another query, and then consolidate the results from multiple queries into one report.
- Build complex reports and presentations—for example, retrieve data with multiple queries, perform post-retrieval calculations and analysis, present the results side-by-side for visual analysis, and subsequently create crisp reports, graphs, and charts.
- Construct parameterized queries, save ad hoc queries, and visually construct a query.
- Deliver executive quality reports which integrate corporate logos, charts, and matrixes and whose layout and format includes a choice of fonts, multiple fonts, borders, color highlights, annotated text, and master pages.
- Integrate to desktop tools by using ASCII, DDE, or OLE, with support for RTF (*rich text format*) for improved productivity.
- Export to custom applications, statistical analysis tools, and databases.

**Data Warehouse Metadata Catalog Functions.** Metadata catalog functions essential to assisting both business and technical users include the following:

- An organization-wide catalog of the tools available to extract value, where a particular tool is most appropriate, and how to gain access to the tool.
- At a minimum, a business user-friendly catalog or knowledge base of metadata that describes what is available in the data warehouse, what its meaning is (the context of the data), and how and where the data is useful.
- Informational processing FAQs, FARs, and FADs metadata to understand what is available for analysis: canned reports, charts, and graphs; predefined queries and reports; and lightly and highly summarized data.
- Easy-to-use browse and navigation functions: business user-friendly, and inviting and enticing to use.
- Ability to go directly from the metadata to the data it represents.
- Browse and navigation function to easily skim the data warehouse, especially for FAQs, FARs, FADs, and the high and light summaries.

## Data Warehouse Administrator: Delivering Value

To deliver value, the data warehouse administrator performs two key services: business user services and technical management services. The goal of business user services is to maximize the productivity of the business users and help them extract maximum value from the data warehouse. From a technical services perspective, the data warehouse administrator is charged to protect the organization's data assets and keep the data warehouse humming.

**Business User Services.** The data warehouse administrator should offer the following business user services:

- Create a stockpile of queries and reports with access via FAQs, FARs, and FADs (this improves reusability and standardization leading to productivity and profitability)
- Customize runtime environment with access icons, buttons, toolbars, and menus to enhance the ease of use for executives, managers, and business analysts
- Add prompts to predefined reports and queries so that business users can customize the queries and reports with runtime variables and filters
- Improve performance by using creative indexes, bitmap indexing, pattern indexes, and star schema indexes
- Keep data secure with responsible access
- Maintain security profile, up-to-date and synchronous with other security policies of the organization

**Technical Management Services.** The data warehouse administrator must minimally provide the following technical management services:

- Offer an informational processing metadata store, browse, and navigation facility by extending the Information Technology organization's technical repository, by purchasing a new one, or by building a custom one.
- Administer the metadata access, retrieval, and browse functions.
- Keep the informational processing metadata synchronized with data warehouse metadata. If the informational processing metadata is stored at the user workstation, then synchronize workstation metadata with the data warehouse metadata.
- Manage run-away queries through a variety of runtime limits such as: execution time, scope of the query, number of records retrieved.
- Improve performance by monitoring query speed and report speed because for joint query and report functions there could be a wide disparity between their performances.
- Enhance performance with batch scheduling of reports.
- Control performance by partitioning the workload between the client, the application server, and the data warehouse database server.
- Provide access control by user or user group; by database table, column, or row level (such as access to payroll information); or just the right portions. Reuse existing security profiles if available (the network security module).

# Informational Processing Economic Considerations

Selecting and using the right informational processing strategy is an essential ingredient of the successful roll-out of the data warehouse. As mentioned previously, informational processing is generally the first interaction of the business user with the data warehouse.

Careful analysis is needed to arrive at the optimum balance between business user needs, current investments in place, and the life cycle costs of buying or building the informational processing capability. A *pro forma* cost model is strongly recommended.

## Analysis Criteria

The customers of operational processing are the business users and the data warehouse administrator. The solution must be sensitive to current investments in the skills of business users (in other words, leverage the desktop tools currently used by business users). In this way, the business users can focus on their job, not become query and report experts. For the administrator, the solution must be quick to implement, easy to monitor and enhance performance, simple to administer access, and (as discussed previously) contain the detail features for experienced users.

From a technical perspective, the tools must smoothly integrate with the informational processing environment, including the data warehouse database management system, the data model, and the culture of the organization. If the buy option is exercised, the quality of the documentation and support is important.

From a cost perspective, the criteria is straightforward—the ideal solution has the smallest initial costs and the lowest ongoing operational costs.

**One-Time Costs.** One-time cost components include the following:

- The informational processing software tools that contain the requisite functions and features
- The metadata catalog or the cost of building one
- Initial semantic layer preparation costs for the managed query environment
- Initial costs of partitioning of processing components in a multi-tier architecture
- Access and security control setup
- Database access drivers, if provided, or the purchase of additional middleware
- Initial installation of middleware components (usually high)
- Price per seat (pertains to each business user)
- User and administrator training
- Initial startup and verification
- Predefined reports and queries creation

**Ongoing Costs.** These costs include both license and maintenance fees to vendors and ongoing operational expenditures, such as the following:

- Software and middleware maintenance fees
- Network communications costs (in a managed query environment, network costs can be substantial and business users are unaware of them)
- IT involvement and support
- Information Specialist involvement and support
- Administration support
- Performance monitoring and scheduling, tuning the multi-tier partitioning, and creation and maintenance of indexes (creative, pattern, bitmap, and others)
- If data access is through middleware, additional complexity and cost to the maintenance activity
- Help Desk to support business users

## The Balancing Act

During the initial economic analysis, and then the ongoing economic analysis, a delicate balance is needed between the needs of business users and the data warehouse IT administrator. Figure 9.9 provides an overview of the challenge.

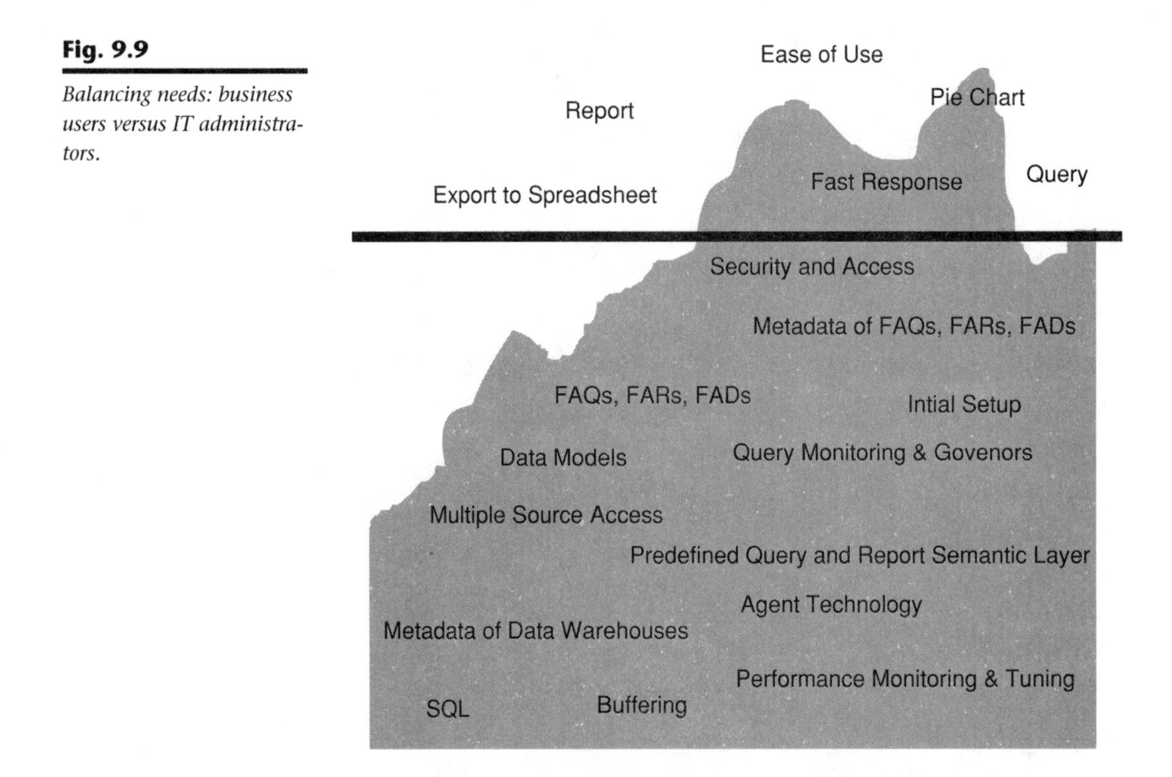


**Fig. 9.9**

*Balancing needs: business users versus IT administrators.*

While the business user sees the top of the "iceberg," the administrator sees what is below the surface. Examples of activities that require balancing are discussed in the following sections.

**Predefined versus Ad Hoc Query Access and Retrieval.** An excellent selection of predefined queries that are tuned for instantaneous responses make for happy users, but a substantial effort is involved from the administrator's point of view. Ad hoc queries are more challenging but necessary because not every need can be foreseen. This creates the need for sound security, governors for managing run-away queries, and a rich semantic layer to assist the user.

**Performance versus Administration Costs.** Performance and value is achieved with the help of the right summaries and aggregations. To meet this need, administrators must create and maintain the summaries and aggregations. Additionally, summary and aggregation navigation capability that is friendly to business users must be available.

**Standard Set Of Tools versus Custom Tools.** To leverage the existing skills of business users, an informational processing environment may need a large variety of tools. The more diverse the number of tools, the larger the costs of purchase (lower discounts), the greater the costs of maintenance, and more daunting the challenge of administrating them. A smart, well-balanced set of tools helps. For example, if a managed query tool allows for access to the data warehouse through the semantic layer as well as directly to the data, then it provides coverage for a larger range of users. Similarly, a tool with both ease of use and a scripting or macro language may address the needs of more users.

# Informational Processing Tools: Technical Considerations

Whether the informational processing environment consists of all vendor tools, all build in-house, or a mix, the technical issues in selecting or building the tools remain the same. The major issues are classified as each of the following sections.

## Architecture

The architecture challenge is how to offer performance, scalability, systems management, and administration. The two options are shown in figure 9.10.

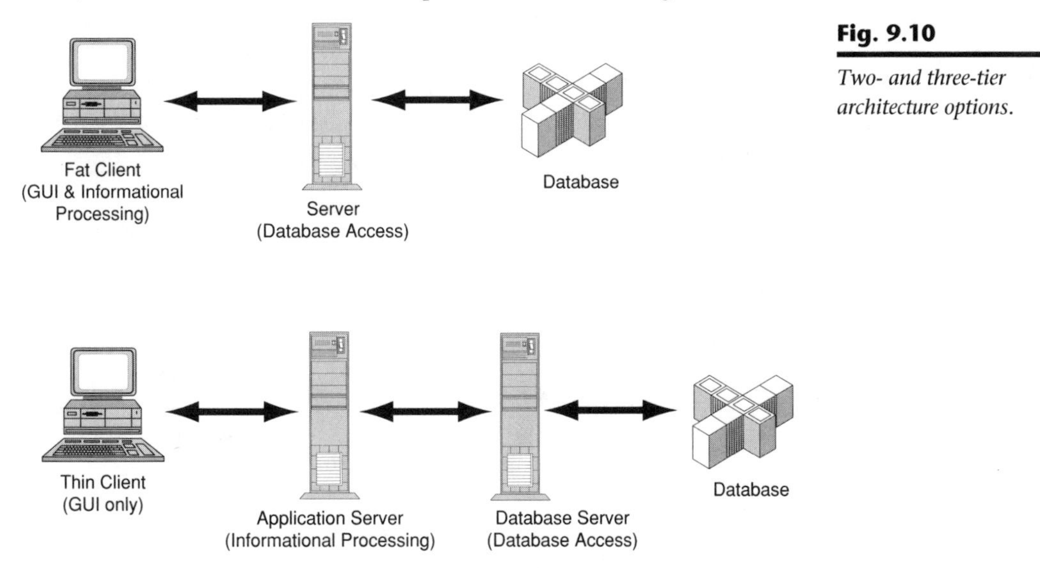


**Fig. 9.10**

*Two- and three-tier architecture options.*

In *two-tier architectures*, the client is "fat"—it has lots of processing power and memory, the scope is one department or function, the number of potential users is up to a hundred or so, and the usage is moderate. The data warehouse size is small to moderate. When small sets of data are retrieved and analyzed, the performance may be acceptable, but as the size of the data retrieved increases, the fat client can choke and the network can become an additional bottleneck. Therefore, scalability is limited, and the performance may be challenging but systems management and administration is simple.

In *three-tier architectures*, the client is "thin"—the scope is multiple departments or large functional areas of the organization, the potential users number in the hundreds or more, and the usage is moderate to high. The data warehouse size is moderate to large. The scalability is large and could incorporate a data warehouse architecture that consists of one or more data warehouses and multiple data marts. Performance can be managed by tuning where and when the processing takes place (more options). The systems management and administration, however, is complex with multiple servers, databases, middleware, and networks.

## Metadata Management

The metadata catalog is the "roadmap" of the data warehouse. It must contain information on the tools that are available to extract value, where a particular tool is most appropriate, and how to gain access to the tool. Minimally, a knowledge base of informational processing FAQs, FARs, and FADs metadata such as canned reports, charts, and graphs; predefined queries and reports; and lightly and highly summarized data is essential. The metadata management must support the following:

- Easy-to-use browse and navigation functions: business user-friendly, and inviting and enticing to use.
- Browse and navigation function to easily skim the data warehouse, especially for FAQs, FARs, and FADs, and the high and light summaries.
- Functions to synchronize the informational processing metadata with the data warehouse metadata. If the metadata is stored in the business users' workstations for performance, then an additional synchronizing of this metadata is essential.

## Performance

Performance is a critical success factor for user satisfaction. Functions to enhance performance include the following:

- Control and management of where the processing is done, in the client workstation or in the application server or the database server. (The administrator needs the ability to distribute the processing to gain maximum performance.)
- A range of index techniques.
- Large query support.
- No reissue and execution of query just for reformatting a report or analyzing from a different viewpoint.
- Retrieval of query results only as needed.
- Batch or background processing, as well as scheduling of requests to take advantage of low-usage hours and therefore minimize performance loads during busy hours.
- Extraction of subsets of data with its metadata for local/personal store for subsequent access and analysis and to reduce network costs and increase reliability.
- A range of query governors: scope of data warehouse that is accessible, length of time, number of records retrieved, and cancellation of a query in progress.

## Environment

The informational processing environment is dynamic and diverse. To minimize obsolescence and gain immediate flexibility, the environmental considerations include the following:

- Types of platforms supported: Windows, OS/2, UNIX, proprietary
- Types and number of DBMSes supported
- Types of interfaces to the data warehouse data store: DBMS Native, ODBC, or other open interfaces
- Programmatic interface available: build custom applications, disseminate results, and export results to desktop applications and custom applications
- Support of full SQL (at least) and vendor extensions (if possible)
- Smooth integration with the informational processing environment: the database management system selected, the data warehouse data model, and the culture of the business or function
- Support for access of multiple, heterogeneous databases and platforms to enable a full access to all the enterprise's data warehouses and data marts

## Security and Access control

Sound security and access control must balance the needs of the user for easy access and the need to protect the data assets of the organization. Some features that help include the following:

- Block user or user groups by day, date, or location or by report type or specific query
- Prevent access by RDBMS table or column or row (control access to sensitive business plans or payroll information or just the right portions of the plans)
- Reuse existing security profiles if available (network security module)

## Dissemination of Reports and Charts

After the hard work of creating the reports and charts is completed, communicating the results is important to extracting value from the data warehouse. A range of options are needed to meet the requirements of a range of recipients. The range of potential options includes printed reports, soft copy (particularly if the recipient wants to analyze it further), electronic mail, external or internal Internet, and private wide area networks (WANs).

In certain instances—for example, where sophisticated data visualization tools are important to understand the reports and charts—it may be essential to electronically mail the data visualizer with the report and charts. Emerging agent technology can assist by first creating and then disseminating the reports and charts.

### Agent Technology

This emerging technology has the potential not only to disseminate the reports and charts, but also to create them by detecting changes in data or when particular events occur, such as end of month or end of quarter. Agent technology has the promise of making today's passive decision support system into tomorrow's active decision support assistant. For example, by combining informational analyses with software agents, which monitor information exception conditions, a sophisticated exception management and information intelligence system can be constructed.

### Range of Users Supported

To manage costs, both one-time and on-going, the smallest number of tools must address the needs of the complete range of users. Additionally, requirements change over time and users gain experience and expertise grows, users want to do new things, and new data in the data warehouse necessitates new requirements and usage. There needs to be an ongoing delicate balance between the ease of use and richest set of features areas, and the acquisition, initial preparation, and ongoing operations costs.

### Scalability

The informational processing solution must grow at least in terms of the following:

- Number of users
- Size of the data warehouse
- Network capacity and costs
- Acceptable performance for retrieval and for subsequent analysis and reporting

## Informational Processing Technology Trends

The major technology trends impacting the informational processing environment are the following:

- **The Internet and the World Wide Web (Web)**—The Internet technology with the Web will impact how the results of informational processing are delivered to business users who need only the results of canned or predefined queries and reports. For business users who need simple access to reports and charts or the results of an analysis, the Web will be an attractive solution—low cost and easy access by using a Web browser.
- **Agent technology**—This technology has the potential to change a "passive" environment—the data warehouse is passive till a business user activates it—to an active environment. Software agents can be used for automatic scheduling of certain analyses, and then when exceptions are detected to automatically alert the business user. This technology has the potential to increase the productivity of experienced users and enhance the capability of the novice.

- **Convergence of tools**—Currently, there is a convergence of strong reporting tools that are adding GUI and business user tools, which add analytical power and reporting functions. The trend is to build a suite of "integrated" or "coupled" tools to meet the needs of business users, from managed queries to ad hoc queries, even On-Line Analytical Processing (OLAP).

# Summary

- Informational processing (data warehouse query, reporting, and analysis) is sometimes referred to as *business intelligence querying*. Informational processing consists of three distinct components: queries to access and retrieve the data from the data warehouse, analysis of the data, and presentation of the analysis in the form of reports, crosstabs and matrixes, tables, and simple-to-complex charts and graphs. The scope of informational processing is usually limited to 2D or 3D processing.
- Informational processing is a multiple step activity. The steps are: define the query on which data to extract from the data warehouse; access and retrieve the data; calculate, manipulate, and analyze the data; present the results in the form of reports and charts; and disseminate the information.
- Business users' needs cover a wide spectrum, from charts and graphs to standard reports to predefined queries to ad hoc analysis. Business users vary in their technical know-how; some are comfortable accessing prepared reports and charts. Others can readily create complex ad hoc queries. To meet the informational processing needs of such users, the data warehouse's query, reporting, and analysis capabilities must run the gamut from accessing static (preprocessed) charts and summaries to accessing and querying detail data.
- Executives and senior managers are interested in viewing the results of an informational processing activity in the form of reports, charts, and graphs. Managers want to access standard or routine queries. A "managed query" environment meets most of their needs.
- Business analysts are the predominant users of the informational processing capabilities of the data warehouse. They understand business complexity. They are the power users who define new business hypotheses as they seek strategic and competitive advantage. The name of the game for these users is raw informational processing power and ease of use in building complex queries. Business analysts also support the informational processing needs of executives and managers.
- Information specialists and IT professionals support the complex informational processing needs of the executives, managers, and business analysts. They also use the informational processing tools to create and build "canned" reports, charts and graphs, and predefined queries. The prime requirement of these users is richness in functionality in building complex queries. These people are the technical power users of informational processing tools.

- The secular trend in informational processing is to let the business users meet their own needs with a *managed query* environment, with minimal assistance from information specialists or IT professionals. This trend gives the information specialists and IT professionals the opportunity to focus on creating applications to meet complex business needs, and these applications deliver canned or predefined queries, reports, and charts for subsequent access by executives, managers, and business users.
- The informational processing environment demands a range of performance capability, from instant response for executive and managerial requests to reasonable wait for ad hoc queries of analysts. The triad of FAQs, FARs, and FADs must be architected into the data warehouse and the informational processing environment.
- Informational processing functions and features address the needs of both business users and data warehouse administrators. The business user needs an inviting, valuable, and easy-to-use environment. Data administrators, however, need a simple-to-prepare and maintained environment. These key criteria keep users coming back for more.
- Economic analysis of the informational processing environment is an ongoing, delicate balance between users and administrators, between performance and costs, and between initial installation and preparation costs and the ongoing operational costs.
- The major technical considerations of the informational processing environment are architecture, metadata catalog, performance, security and access control, dissemination and presentation sophistication, agent technology, and scalability.

CHAPTER 10

# Analytical Processing

On a daily basis, business managers are faced with two fundamental challenges: operate the business efficiently to maximize the return on investment, and plan for the future. Informational processing and analytical processing are two basic ways to extract value from the data warehouse to address these two challenges.

With informational processing, as discussed in Chapter 9, business managers and analysts seek answers to operations questions such as:

- What were the sales revenues for the Thanksgiving weekend (our biggest sales weekend) for all the midwest stores, broken down by department?
- Which were the top ten most profitable items during the post-Christmas sale? Which were the bottom ten items?
- How did the Thanksgiving sales this year compare to the same weekend for the last five years, by department and by store?

The same business managers and analysts need analytical processing functionality, when they need answers to complex questions like the following:

- How many down-hill skis, manufactured by SpeedSkiDown, Inc., were sold to men in the month of November, in our Midwest, Northwest, and Mountain region stores; how does it compare with the same month for the last year and the year before, actual versus projected?
- How many blue minivans did we have in inventory (at the end of a quarter) that had a CD player and a third seat, when the list price was less than $19,995? Need totals by country for each quarter for the last five years, compare actual to plan, and compare each quarter's inventory to the preceding and trailing quarters'.

Executive managers know "the future belongs to those who can see it and get there first." That is why business executives and managers want to not only understand "what is going on in the business," but also "what is going to happen next."

From an analysis perspective, business users want to extract the right data in an intuitive manner, with minimal investments in time and with the least amount of frustration. After extracting the right data from the data warehouse, they analyze, synthesize, and consolidate it into information and then use the information to make better decisions. As discussed in Chapter 8, there are multiple ways to extract information of value from the data warehouse and analyze it (see fig. 10.1).

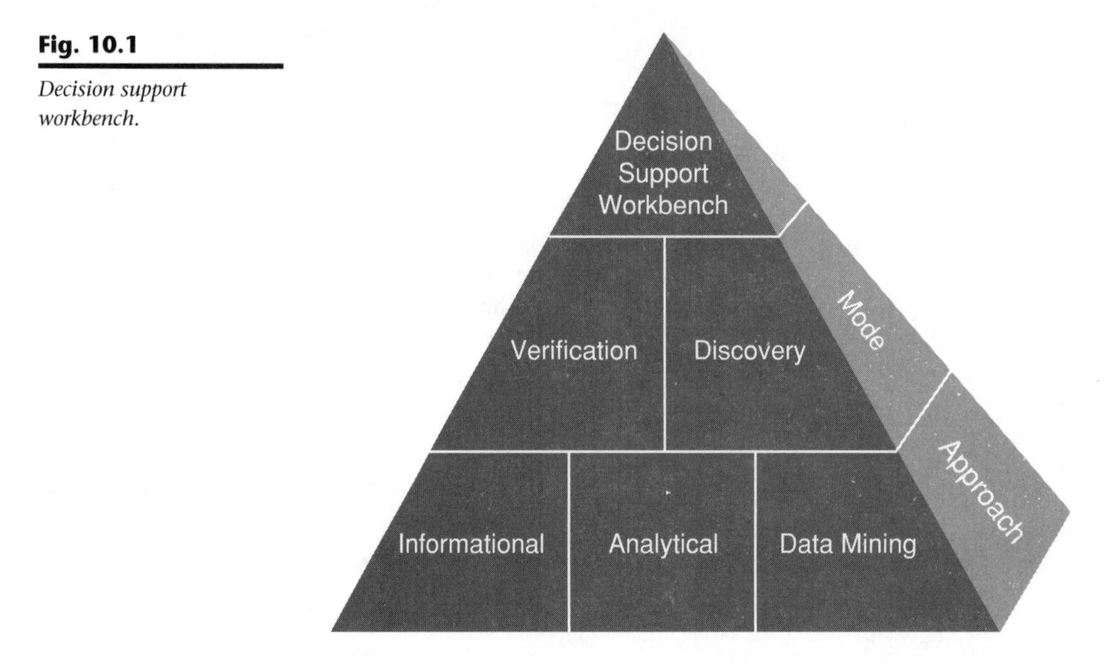


**Fig. 10.1**

*Decision support workbench.*

In the decision support workbench framework, analytical processing predominantly subscribes to the verification mode of usage. In the verification mode, the business user creates a hypothesis—in other words, a business question—and accesses data to verify or confirm the hypothesis. The analysis of the data is usually iterative, one business question leads to another, until a clear set of alternatives and potentially actionable recommendations is deduced. During the iterative analysis activity, experienced business users at times can "discover" unsuspecting relationships between business parameters, for example, the relationship of sales to age and gender of customers. Hence, analytical processing, though not generally thought of as subscribing to the discovery mode of decision support, does lend itself to discovery by serendipity and observation of the business user.

# Business User View of Data

Business data, as a matter of fact, is multidimensional. It is interrelated and usually hierarchical; e.g., sales data, inventory data, and budget forecasts are interrelated and interdependent. In practice, to forecast new specific product sales, analysis of the past purchasing patterns, adoption of new products, regional preferences, and other such business factors require analysis. The sales projection for our "skis from SpeedSkiDown, Inc." question requires understanding the sales patterns for the last few years.

Today's businesses, operating in a global economy with global competitors, need to seek markets where their products and services have clear competitive advantages and differentiators. Seeking new market opportunities and micro-market segments, and creating pinpoint marketing programs is a fundamental requirement. Multidimensional analysis is a requisite to achieve this.

Improving customer satisfaction while preserving a profitable competitive edge is a monumental challenge. Such a challenge requires understanding a whole set of interrelated business dimensions, establishing performance benchmarks, and tracking process metrics. Metrics provide a clue to "where the business is today" and analyzes the dimensions of the benchmark to seek clues on "why and how to improve" is needed. Analysis and interpretation of data from multiple perspectives is key.

# Multidimensional Analysis

For both operational efficiencies and forward planning, much interrelated business data must be analyzed. This business need is addressed by analytical processing. In analytical processing, the focus is on data analysis, specifically multidimensional analysis.

In multidimensional analysis, data is represented as dimensions such as product, territory, and customer (see fig. 10.2). Dimensions are usually related in hierarchies, for example, city, state, region, country, and continent, or state, territory, and region. Time dimension is a standard dimension with its own hierarchy, such as day, week, month, quarter, and year, or day and year-to-date.

To ease the task of complex analysis, analytical processing or multidimensional analysis presents a business friendly view of the data. A business user can access revenue by department and store for the last four quarters for a given set of products. The results can be pivoted or rotated to change the axes and perspective. Additionally, business users can navigate the dimensions by drill-down or roll-up along elements of a dimension, or drilling across dimensions to see other perspectives. A computational engine also offers capabilities like rankings of top or bottom of list; moving averages and growth rates; financial calculations of interest, internal rate of return, and depreciation; and currency conversions and statistical functions.

Analytical processing is used to "understand what's going on in the business" and has the promise of "what if" and "what now" analysis.

The scope of informational processing, described in Chapter 9, is usually a simpler (two- or three-dimensional) analysis of historical data for understanding the past—static data analysis. Analytical processing can be used for complex historical analysis, with extensive manipulation—dynamic data analysis, as well as for forward planning and forecasting—of the past as a prologue of the future. The choice of the wrong approach, informational processing or analytical processing, could lead to business user frustration, a negative impact on productivity, and loss of strategic competitive advantage.

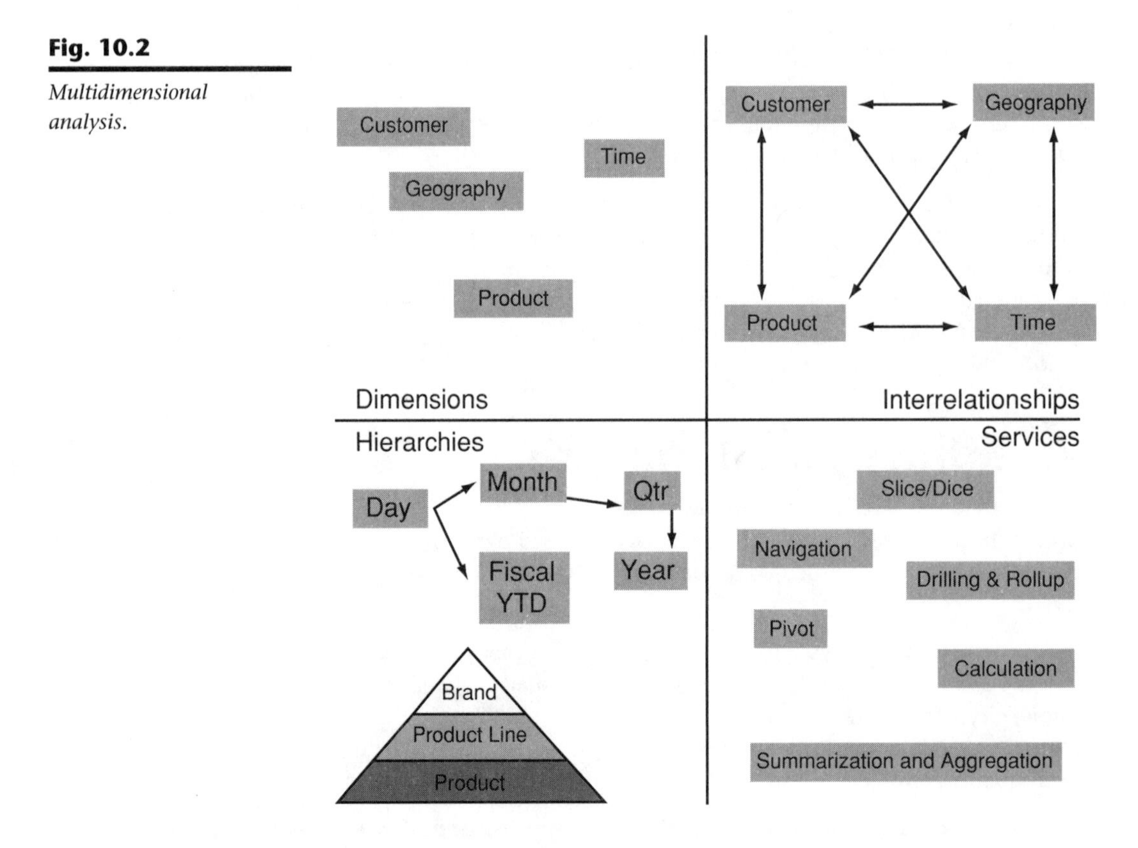


**Fig. 10.2**

*Multidimensional analysis.*

Analytical processing or multidimensional analysis is also referred to as On-Line Analytical Processing (OLAP).It is based on a multidimensional view of the business data in the data warehouse and, as we will discuss, it may have a multidimensional database store engine.

# On-Line Analytical Processing (OLAP)

In a data warehouse, data is stored for query, analysis, and dissemination purposes, as opposed to On-Line Transaction Processing (OLTP) where data is collected and stored for operations and control purposes. OLAP is an analytical processing technology which creates new business information from existing data, through a rich set of business transformations and numerical calculations.

## Defining OLAP

On-Line Analytical Processing is a data analysis technology which does the following:

- Presents a multidimensional, logical view of the data in the data warehouse. The view is independent of how the data is stored.
- Always involves interactive query and analysis of the data. The interaction is usually multiple passes, involving drilling down into successively lower levels of detail data or roll-ups to higher levels of summarization and aggregation.
- Offers analytical modeling capabilities, including a calculation engine for deriving ratios, variances, etc., involving measurements or numerical data across many dimensions.
- Creates summarization and aggregations (sometimes loosely referred to as consolidations), hierarchies, and interrogates all the aggregation and summarization levels at every dimensional intersection.
- Supports functional models for forecasting, trends analysis, and statistical analysis.
- Retrieves and displays data in 2D or 3D cross-tabs, charts, and graphs, with easy pivoting of the axes. Pivoting is key because business users need to analyze the data from different perspectives; and the analysis of one perspective leads to another business question to be examined from another perspective.
- Responds to queries quickly, so the analysis process is not interrupted and the information is not stale.
- Has a multidimensional data store engine, stores data in arrays. These arrays are a logical representation of the business dimensions.

OLAP technology can be applied in many functional areas of a business, such as product, sales, and marketing profitability analysis; manufacturing mix and logistics analysis; financial consolidations, budgeting and forecasting, tax planning, and cost accounting.

## OLAP Architecture

OLAP is a data analysis and reporting capability. It is an important component of the Access and Usage block of the data warehouse reference architecture (see fig. 10.3). OLAP technology components are captured in sub-blocks of the Access and Usage blocks.

The OLAP component of the analysis and reporting sub-block represents the analysis and reporting capabilities of the OLAP services required, while the transformation to multidimensional structure, as well as the access to the data warehouse and data mart components, are parts of the Access and Retrieval sub-block. The reference architecture offers the following options:

- Accessing the data directly from the data warehouse or data mart, then "morphing" it into a multidimensional structure and storing it in the workstation's local store.

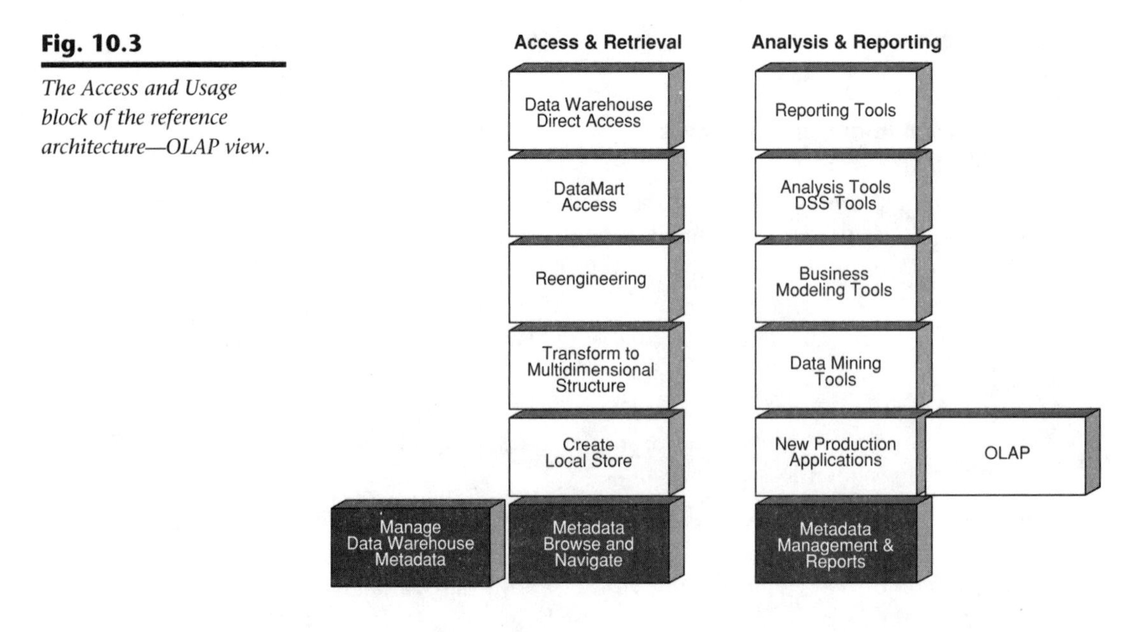


**Fig. 10.3**

*The Access and Usage block of the reference architecture—OLAP view.*

- Accessing the data directly from the data warehouse, then transforming it into a multidimensional structure and storing it in the data mart in a multidimensional data store, readily available for multidimensional retrieval and analysis at the workstation.
- Accessing the data directly from the data warehouse or data mart, then "morphing" it into a multidimensional view and presenting it as a multidimensional structure to the business user for analysis and reporting at the workstation.

These options illustrate the potential logical and physical components of the OLAP architecture itself.

**Logical Architecture.** The logical OLAP architecture, as shown in figure 10.4, consists of two parts:

- **OLAP View**—The multidimensional and logical presentation of the data in the data warehouse or data mart to the business user, regardless of how and where the data is stored.
- **Data Store Technology**—The technology options of how and where the data is actually stored. The two popular options are multidimensional data store and relational data store.

The business user is only interested in the multidimensional view of the data and an acceptable level of performance. The IT support person is interested in where and how the data is stored and accessed to ensure acceptable performance and effective management of the data.

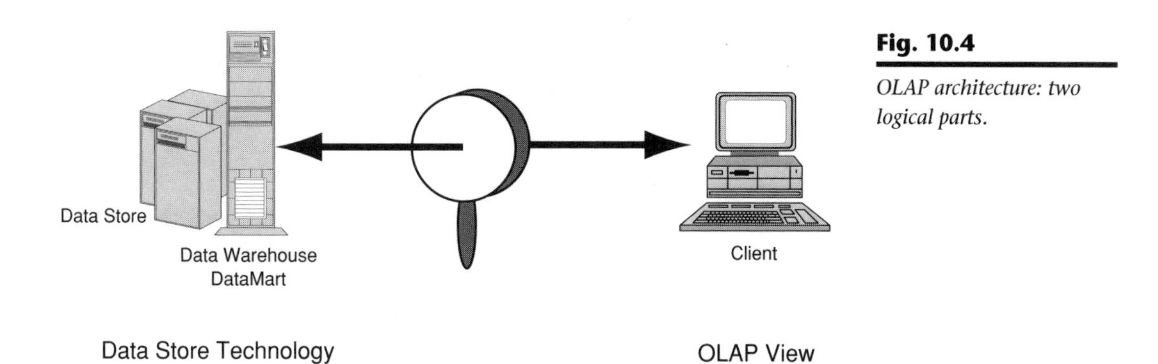


**Fig. 10.4**

*OLAP architecture: two logical parts.*

The OLAP functional architecture consists of three services components: data store services, OLAP services, and user presentation services. In this respect, the functional architecture is a three-tier client-server architecture (see fig. 10.5). The architecture offers multiple physical configuration options for the three functional services.

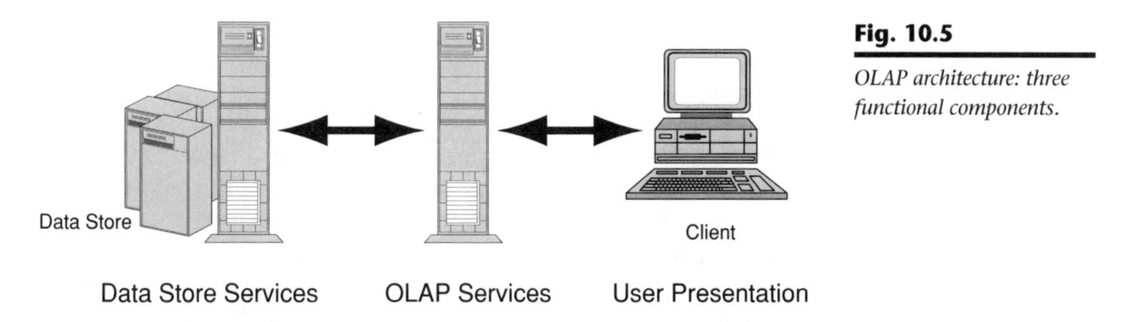


**Fig. 10.5**

*OLAP architecture: three functional components.*

**Physical Architecture.** The physical architecture consists of two broad categories based on data store technologies: multidimensional data store and relational data store (see fig. 10.6).

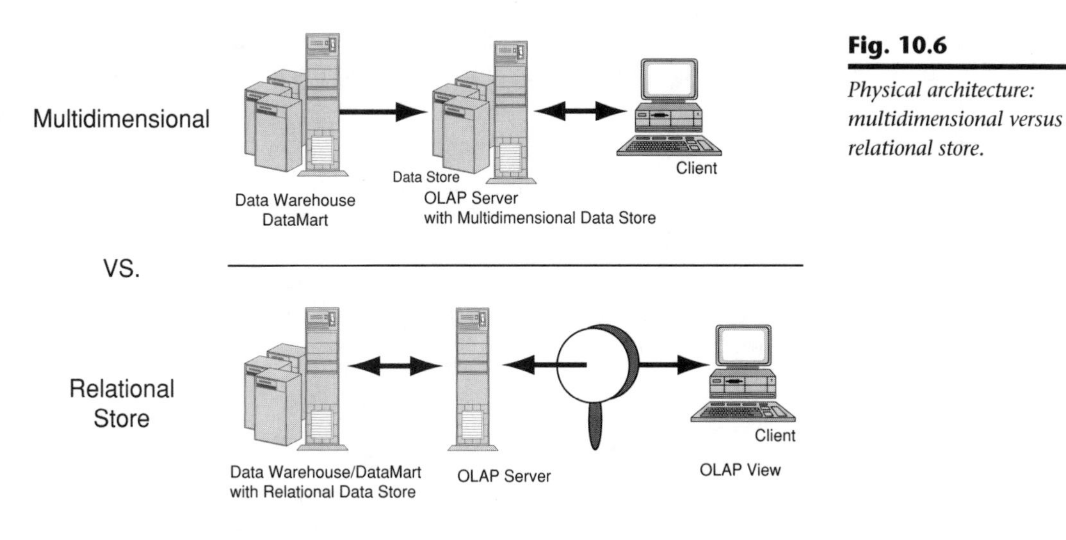


**Fig. 10.6**

*Physical architecture: multidimensional versus relational store.*

The major configuration option of a multidimensional data store offers two sub-options shown in figure 10.7. The multidimensional data is stored at the workstation client and/or at the OLAP server.

**Fig. 10.7**

*Physical architecture: Fat client versus OLAP data mart.*

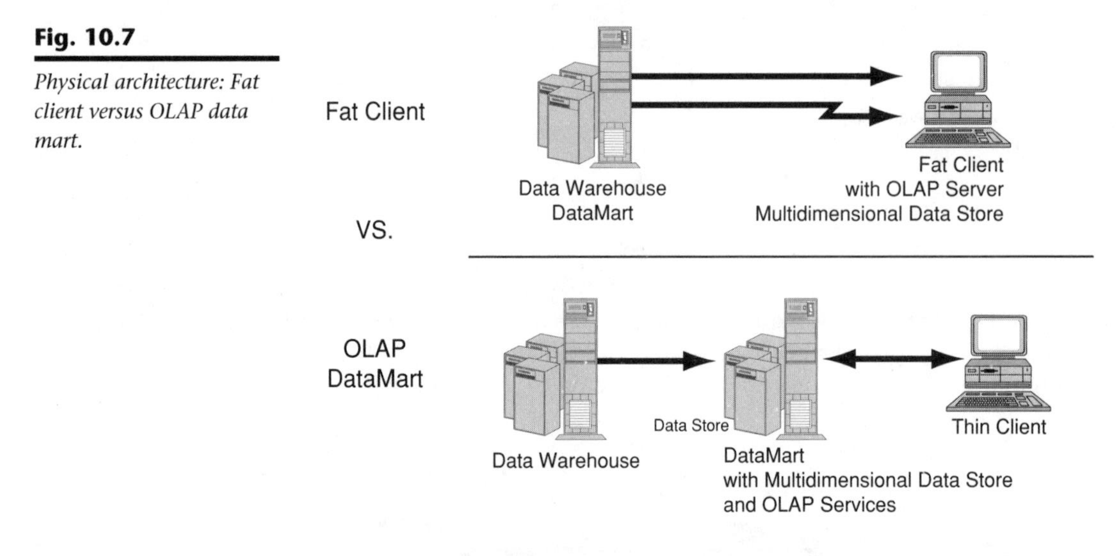


The first case, multidimensional data store at the client, results in a fat client with the business user capable of "analysis on the range"—the roaming option. The network bottleneck is only an issue when the data is loaded into the workstation. The potential negative impacts are performance and data security. A variation of this option has a multidimensional data store at the data mart level to distribute selected subsets of the multidimensional data to each workstation for local store and access.

In the second case, the multidimensional data store and OLAP services are combined. The workstation is "not so fat." Data from the data warehouse is extracted, then transformed into multidimensional data structures, which are stored at the data mart server. This is the classical data mart configuration where many data marts are loaded with previously refined and re-engineered data from an enterprise data warehouse. Additional refinement and re-engineering functions especially filter and match to create functional subsets, and are applied to the data from the data warehouse to create the functional data marts.

A variation of the second case, as shown in figure 10.8, separates the multidimensional data store at the data mart, from the OLAP services at an OLAP server. This option is needed when the multidimensional data store is large, the number of users are many, data sharing is a need, and the client workstations are "thin." In this option, the data mart may be loaded either from the data warehouse, as mentioned above, or directly from the data sources.

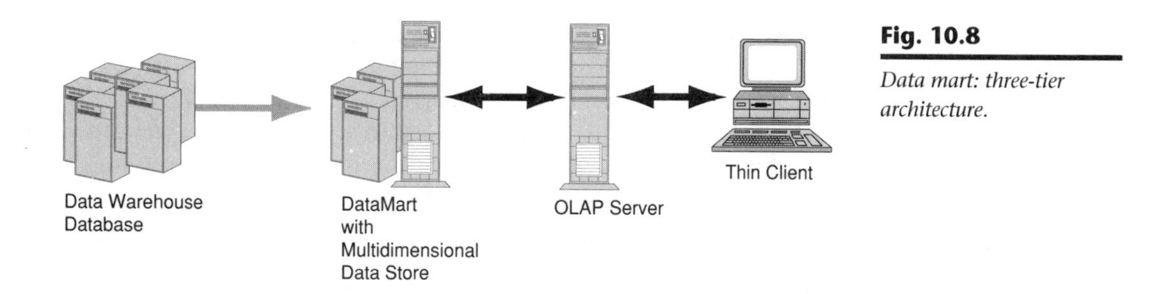


**Fig. 10.8**

*Data mart: three-tier architecture.*

# OLAP: Multidimensional versus Relational

The architecture options described previously raise two issues that need additional discussion: How is the data stored? How and where are the OLAP services provided?

## Multidimensional and Relational Data Store

The two options to store the data are multidimensional data store and relational store. Figure 10.9 summarizes the issues in selecting one or the other.

| | Relational Database | Multidimensional Database |
|---|---|---|
| Data Storage, Access, and View | • Relational<br>• Tables of Columns and Rows<br>• SQL languages with extensions<br>• 3rd-party tools using APIs | • Dimensional<br>• Arrays: Hypercube/Multicube<br>• Sparse matrix technology<br>• Proprietary of Spreadsheet |
| Usage and Packaging | • OLTP<br>• RDBMS Engine<br>• Drill-down to detail level<br>• Query performance: wide range | • OLAP<br>• Multidimensional engine<br>• Drill-down to summary/aggregate level<br>• Query performance: fast |
| Database Size and Update | • Gigabytes to Terabytes<br>• Storage of indexes and de-normalization increases size<br>• Parallel query and loading<br>• Update while in use | • Gigabytes<br>• Sparse data compression and aggregation<br>• Hard to update while in use; small changes may require reorganization |

**Fig. 10.9**

*Data store: multidimensional versus relational.*

Relational data stores conform to the relational data model. Relational databases store the data as keyed records in tables, and the data can be accessed by a common language, SQL. Multidimensional data stores, on the other hand, logically store the data in arrays. Since there is no common or agreed-upon multidimensional model, there is no standard or common data access method. Some products are available as an engine with APIs or with a spreadsheet front-end; but the majority have proprietary access methods and front-ends. Additionally, some products offer "turn-key" applications, such as sales forecasting and budgeting, with embedded multidimensional engines and substantial OLAP functionality.

With a relational data store, the data warehouse or data mart can be very large in size. The storage size is inflated by the use of indexes and denormalization techniques to achieve acceptable performance of multidimensional queries. The large size may indicate the need for parallel query and loading technology. With multidimensional store, the size of the data store is generally limited, but the data storage uses compression technology, such as *sparse matrix compression* to store more data in less space.

From the business user's perspective, the comparison issues are:

- How much business data is stored and available?
- Is the storage capacity adequate?
- Is the performance acceptable?
- Is the cost justified?

## Multidimensional Database Server versus Relational OLAP Server

When deciding how and where the OLAP services are provided, one must ask, "can multidimensional data store and OLAP services be combined or can relational data stores with OLAP servers meet the multidimensional needs of the business user?" The two options are illustrated in figure 10.10. Each of the approaches has its merits and challenges, with no simple answer.

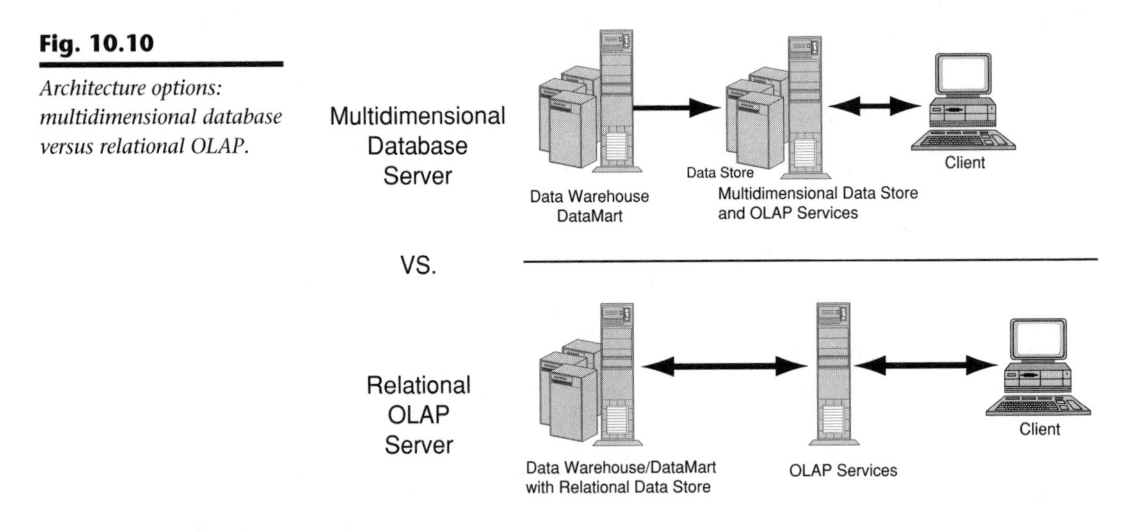


**Fig. 10.10**

*Architecture options: multidimensional database versus relational OLAP.*

## Multidimensional Data Store and OLAP Services

This approach consists of OLAP services and a proprietary multidimensional database (see fig 10.11). The data is logically stored in arrays, using one of two approaches: the hypercube or the multicube. In the hypercube approach, objects of greater than three dimensions are described with flat sides and with each dimension at right angles to all the other dimensions. Figure 10.11 shows that a single cell in a cube can store, for example, values of one dimension with reference to three dimensions. A cell could store sales revenues (dollars or yen) by store (MD-Store, Inc.), for a given time period (first quarter of 1996), for a selected product (skis by SpeedSkiDown, Inc.).

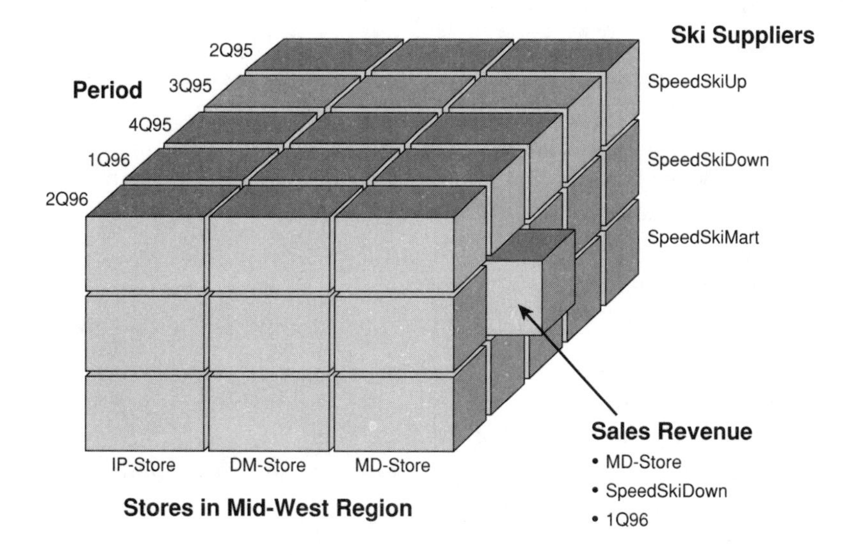


**Fig. 10.11**

*Example: multidimensionality storage and business view.*

The data is organized according to the business view of the data, and as a rule, stored in a summary or aggregated form, sometimes called consolidations. The index is smaller, resulting in very fast response to complex queries. Since the values are stored in arrays, updating the value does not impact the index. This feature leads to easy implementation of read-write or update applications such as forecasting and budgeting.

The initial design and setup activity is "logical design" or "information model" driven. The basic steps are as follows:

1. Select the business function, such as sales revenue analysis and financial reporting.
2. Identify the numerical values, i.e., measures to be stored like sales revenue and customers.
3. Determine the dimensions (time, geography, and product) and the granularity of each dimension, e.g., time by month and quarter, and geography by state or region.
4. Define the "logical model" and load the multidimensional data store, either directly from the data sources or by filtering and matching selected contents of the data warehouse or data mart.

The major functions offered to business users include the following:

- Fast response to compute intensive queries, such as what-if scenarios. The quick response does not disrupt the analysis and thinking process.

- Interactive update (read-write) of the multidimensional database to enable forecasting, forward planning, and budgeting applications.
- Exploitation of the rich relationships between elements or values of the dimensions to discover unsuspected relationships.
- Powerful calculation engine and comparative analysis: rankings, comparisons, percentage-to-class, maximum, minimum, averages, moving averages, period-to-period comparisons, and others.
- Cross-dimensional calculations, such as cost-allocations and inter-company eliminations, or row-level calculations for spreadsheet-oriented applications, such as Profit and Loss statements.
- Extension of the basic functions with user-defined functions or exploitation of the embedded modeling functions.
- Potent statistical and financial functions: currency conversions, depreciation, internal rate of return, trends, time-series analysis, etc.
- Time intelligence: year-to-date, current periods, fiscal and internal calendars.
- Drill-through to underlying detail data in the warehouse.
- Pivoting, cross-tabs, drill-down, and roll-ups along single or multiple dimensions, and other powerful navigation functions.

The administration and systems management of this approach requires the following:

- Initial data modeling where selection of the right dimensions and their granularity, anticipation of how the data will be accessed, and selection of the appropriate filters to load the data from the data warehouse are key considerations.
- Periodic transfers and bulk updates, because incremental updates are challenging and generally impossible during the time the database is in use.
- Aggregation, summarization, and precalculation during the loading process.
- Training in a different technology and use of new skills.
- Writing new applications in a proprietary language to extend and enhance the standard front-ends of the database.

Some of the issues presented by using this approach include the following:

- Size of the multidimensional database supported is smaller than a relational database. Sparse-matrix technology—seeking unused cells within the multidimensional matrix, eliminating them, and compressing the arrays—is used to save space. A by-product of this is improved performance. Generally, summary and aggregate information is stored, so the storage requirements are smaller.
- The side-effects of storing data at coarser levels of granularity (summary, aggregation, and precalculated and derived data), means drill-downs cannot reach the detail level.
- Access and security is available at high levels; there are no usage-based privileges or subset level access controls.

- Changes in dimensional structures require a reorganization of the multidimensional database; high-availability backup and restore facilities are limited.
- The need for specialized front-ends limits choices. Extensions to the front-end of one multidimensional database cannot be readily migrated to another multidimensional database.

A good-fit for the multidimensional database and OLAP services approach is when requirements call for the following:

- Computation of intensive applications with what-if scenarios and models
- Fairly static dimensions
- Read-write capability
- A relationship between the dimensions that is rich and complex
- Cross-dimensional and row-level calculations
- Powerful calculation, statistical, and financial functions
- Acceptable database size for the business function

## Relational OLAP

This approach consists of OLAP services and a commercial-off-the-shelf relational database (refer to fig. 10.6). The data is stored in relational tables and may be hundreds of gigabytes in size.

Although the data is stored in a relational form (columns and rows), the data is presented to the business user in the form of business dimensions. In order to "hide" the storage form, a semantic layer of metadata is created. This layer maps the dimensions to the relational tables. Additional metadata for any summarizations or aggregations, in order to improve response time, is also created. All this metadata is stored in the relational database—creating another metadata store in the overall data warehouse solution—to be maintained and managed.

The initial design and setup activity is "technical database design" driven. Follow these basic steps:

1. Build the "dimensional model" using techniques such as denormalization, star schema, snowflake, and mixed schema (balance between star and snowflake where only some dimensions are normalized).
2. Add appropriate aggregation and summarization data.
3. Partition the large datasets into smaller manageable partitions to improve performance. For example, time or organizational unit dimensions can be partitioned.
4. Add creative or bitmap indexes to enhance performance (note this increases the database size and the time to build the indexes).
5. Create and store the metadata. The metadata includes definitions of the dimensions, mapping of dimensions to relational tables, hierarchy relationships

between the dimensions, partition information, summarization and aggregation definitions and descriptions, formulae and calculations, usage monitoring, and many others.

From an operational perspective, the steps to execute a query are as follows:

1. Construct the client tool using a business or dimensional view of the data.
2. Query the OLAP server from the client tool, and examine the metadata in real-time.
3. Create multipass `SELECT` statements and/or correlated subqueries and submit to the relational database.
4. Perform multidimensional functions, such as calculations and formulae, translation from bits to business descriptions, etc., on the results of the database query.
5. Return results to the client tool for further processing and display, or immediate display.

The major functions offered to business users and administrators, include the following:

- Business view of the relational data
- Dimensional hierarchy support
- Calculation, statistical, and financial functions with user extensions
- Drill-down to the detail level
- Choice of front-end tools
- Database administration leveraging existing investments in backup and restore, and sub-setting the database for individual analysis
- Navigation using the metadata
- Multiple levels of security with usage privileges

The administration and systems management of this approach requires the following:

- No initial loading or periodic updates of the OLAP server.
- Use of the existing standard backup, restore, and security processes.
- Design of the "dimensional model" to provide the business view of the data. This requires training and expertise in modeling star, snowflakes, and mixed mode schemas; data partitioning; and aggregation and summarization levels.
- Management, synchronization, and maintenance of all the new metadata within the overall data warehouse solution.
- Monitoring usage to tune performance. Performance tuning may impact the database model, the partitions, or the levels of aggregation and summary. Tuning is complicated. Denormalization or indexing for performance could increase the scarcity and size of the database, thus requiring larger scans, more disk I=O, and more data buffer trashing.

Some of the issues presented by using this approach include the following:

- The use of star and snowflake schema, partitions, and denormalization. This improves the performance, but the trade-off is an adverse impact on flexibility and expandability of the relational database. This makes updating the database more of a challenge and bulk updates may be required.
- Star schema, with its variation and aggregations and summarizations, assume that the data is static except when bulk loaded.
- Row-level calculations, for example, when profit is equal to revenue minus cost, requires transposing rows and columns. There is a limit for such actions, even with multiple pass `SELECT` statements.
- Managing and maintaining the metadata is an ongoing challenge and cost.

A good-fit for relational database and OLAP services approach is when requirements call for the following:

- Data-intensive applications with significant data browse needs
- Fairly dynamic dimensionality and changing granularity
- Read-only capability with minimal write
- Minimal cross-dimensional and row-level calculations
- Large database size, simple relationships between the dimensions, and on-the-fly dimensional view

The previous discussion focused on business user functions, performance, data volume and scalability, administration, and fitness for purpose. Some of the other factors of interest include the following:

- Desired user interface
- Client tool features and functions
- Perception of "open versus proprietary" architectures
- Which approach best leverages the existing investments in client, server, database, and front-end technologies, and the skills of the data administrators, and of course business users

# OLAP: Technical Requirements and Considerations

The previous section described the two major architectural options for providing OLAP or multidimensional analysis services to business users. Since 1985, the relational database requirements have been strongly influenced by the 12 rules developed by Mr. E.F. Codd. In 1993, Mr. Codd, with S.B. Codd and C.T. Salley, devised 12 rules for evaluating analytical processing tools. Because the rules were originally the results of a client study, there is a fair amount of controversy about whether the rules are tainted or not.

## The 12 Rules of OLAP

These 12 rules provide a datapoint—not a benchmark—in evaluating and understanding OLAP needs and tools. The rules stated below are extracted from the Codd et. al. whitepaper.

**1. Multidimensional Conceptual View.** A business user's view of the enterprise is multidimensional in nature. So, OLAP models should be multidimensional in nature.

Business users are able to manipulate such multidimensional data models easily and intuitively. For instance, users can slice and dice, pivot, and rotate consolidation (summaries and aggregations) paths within a model.

**2. Transparency.** Where the analytical tool resides should be transparent to the business user.

OLAP should exist within an open systems architecture, enabling the analytical tool to be embedded anywhere the user desires without an adverse affect on host tool functionality.

**3. Accessibility.** The OLAP tool must map its own logical schema to heterogeneous physical data stores, access the data, and perform any conversions necessary to present a single, coherent, and consistent business user view.

The type of systems from which physical the data is coming should be transparent to the user and should be the concern of only the tool.

**4. Consistent Reporting Performance.** Reporting performance should not be degraded as the number of dimensions increases.

**5. Client/Server Architecture.** The server component of OLAP tools must be sufficiently intelligent so that various clients can be attached with minimum effort and integration programming.

The intelligent server must be capable of mapping and consolidating data between disparate logical and physical databases. This is necessary to maintain transparency and build a common conceptual, logical, and physical schema.

**6. Generic Dimensionality.** Every data dimension must be equivalent in both its structure and operational capabilities. There should exist only one logical structure for all dimensions. Any function applied to one dimension should also be able to apply to another dimension.

**7. Dynamic Sparse Matrix Handling.** The OLAP server's physical structure should adapt fully to the specific analytical model being created and loaded to provide optimal sparse matrix handling. When faced with a sparse matrix, the OLAP server must be able to deduce the distribution of the data and how to store it most efficiently.

The physical access methods must also be dynamically changeable and should provide different types of mechanisms, such as direct calculation, B-trees, and hashing, or the best combination of such techniques.

**8. Multi-user Support.** OLAP tools must provide concurrent access (retrieval and update), integrity, and security to support users who need to work concurrently with the same analytical model or create different models from the same data.

**9. Unrestricted Cross-Dimensional Operations.** In multidimensional data analysis, all dimensions are created and treated equally. The OLAP tools should handle associated calculations among dimensions, and not require the business user to define what the calculations should be.

If calculations require the definition of various formulas according to a language, then the language must allow calculation and data manipulation across any number of data dimensions, without restricting any relations between data cells, regardless of the number of common data attributes each cell contains.

**10. Intuitive Data Manipulation.** Manipulation, such as reorientation of the consolidation path, or drilling down across dimensions or rows, should be accomplished via direct action on the analytical model's cells, without requiring the use of menus or multiple trips across the user interface.

The dimensions defined in the analytical model should contain all the information the business user needs to perform any inherent actions.

**11. Flexible Reporting.** Using an OLAP server and its tools, a business user can manipulate, analyze, synthesize, and look at data in any way desired, including creating logical groupings or placing rows, columns, and cells next to each other.

Reporting facilities must also provide this flexibility and present synthesized information any way the user wants to display it.

**12. Unlimited Dimensions and Aggregations Levels.** An OLAP server should accommodate at least fifteen dimensions within a common analytical model. Each of these generic dimensions must allow an unlimited number of user-defined aggregation and summarization levels within any given consolidation path.

## Evaluating OLAP Servers and Tools

OLAP servers and tools can be evaluated using five sets of criteria: features and functions, access to the features and functions, OLAP services engine, administration, and the overall architecture view.

**Features and Functions.** OLAP is an analytical processing technology that creates and presents new information from existing data through calculation formulas and transformation rules. OLAP servers and tools must be able to do the following:

- Support multiple dimensions and hierarchies within a dimension.
- Aggregate, summarize, precalculate, and derive data along a single dimension or a set of selected dimensions.
- Apply calculation logic, formulas, and analytical routines against one or a set of selected dimensions.

- Support the concept of an analytical model—a set of selected dimensions and their elements, calculation logic, formulas, and analytical routines, and aggregated, summarized, and derived data. For example, a financial model for calculating an internal rate of return (IRR) on given financial data.
- Offer a rich library of functions, e.g., financial, marketing, logistics, algebraic, and statistical.
- Provide a powerful calculation and comparative analysis capability such as rankings, comparisons, percentage-to-class, maximum, minimum, averages, moving averages, period-to-period comparisons, and others.
- Perform cross-dimensional calculations, such as cost-allocations and inter-company eliminations or row-level calculations for spreadsheet-oriented applications, such as profit and loss statements.
- Offer time-intelligence such as year-to-date, calendar span of a given time-period, current periods, fiscal and internal calendars, moving averages, and moving totals.
- Transform one dimension to another dimension, particularly useful after a merger or acquisition.
- Navigate and analyze using pivot, cross-tabs, drill-down, and roll-up along a single or multiple dimensions.

The performance must meet the analytical needs of the business user so that the analysis process is smooth and nondisruptive.

**Access to Features and Functions.** The business users' interface and access to OLAP services must offer multiple choices and must leverage the existing know-how of the business user and the embedded knowledge in the OLAP analytical models. Potential choices include the following:

- **Spreadsheet**—Minimally, business users should be able to load OLAP data into their spreadsheet tools for additional analysis and reporting.
- **Proprietary client tools**—An application-specific offering, such as for budgeting, is desirable to quick-start analytical processing. The richness of the functionality and fitness to business needs is the key criteria.
- **Third-party tools**—These leverage the APIs of the OLAP server (if the APIs are proprietary, there is a potential of a lock-in to an OLAP server).
- **4GL environment**—This must support all the rich functions and features of the OLAP server.
- **Interfaces to "defacto standard"**—These are application environments such as Visual Basic and Powerbuilder, and interfaces such as OLE, DDE, CORBA, and others.
- **Client "cube navigators"**—These are tools from third parties which interface to OLAP services.

To leverage the embedded knowledge of the analytical model, the access interface must do the following:

- Access and extract data subsets based on hierarchies, models, time, and other selected dimensions
- Access multiple levels of hierarchy with a single extract request
- Be "aware" of aggregation and summarization data, partitions, and indexes, to create the right query
- Be optimized for the particular relational database, including its SQL extensions, when accessing a relational data store

**OLAP Services Engine.** The OLAP services engine in either configuration, with multidimensional store or relational store, must meet the capacity, scalability, and the technology features of the planned analytical model and application. The capacity and scalability issues were discussed earlier in this chapter. The technology features required are dependent on the analytical model and usage contemplated. Some of these features include the following:

- **Read-write capability**—This is for interactive forecasting and budgeting applications.
- **Multi-user write**—This is to support workgroup multidimensional analysis. OLAP multi-user write access is more challenging than a straight relational data write access. Instead of just being concerned with a row or table, an OLAP update or write request may require recalculation of derived and calculated values impacting many dimensions and hierarchies within the dimensions. The scope of the write-lock can be very wide and recalculations may be compute-intensive, resulting in long locks and perceived poor performance.
- **Multiple databases**—If there is one database for each OLAP application, then it may require a mechanism for interaction between the databases because values derived from one may be the input to the other. For example, values of revenue from a sales OLAP application are needed in a finance OLAP application to build a profit and loss report and comparison of actual versus forecast.
- **Range of Datatypes**—These are from numeric, to time/calendar period, to descriptions (for display and reporting purposes), to BLOBs. Further image datatypes can enhance the communications of complex analysis with improved and inviting displays and executive reports.

**Administration.** The administration functions needed for initial preparation, setup, and ongoing operational purposes (many of which were discussed earlier) include the following:

- Definition of the dimensional analytical model.
- Creation and maintenance of the metadata repository.
- Access control and usage-based privileges. The focus here must be on what the business users want to do and who can get access to the analytical model and its data.
- Loading the analytical model from the data warehouse or data mart.

- Tuning the performance to acceptable levels to permit nondisruptive analysis.
- Reorganization of the database to improve performance, change the dimensional model, or update the data.
- Management of all parts of the system, including middleware. The reference architecture provides an orderly way to understand the scope of the systems management task.
- Distribution of data to the client for additional and local analysis.

**Overall Architecture.** From an overall architecture perspective, there is no simple choice between the relational or multidimensional data store for OLAP. The business needs provide the criteria for making the right choice.

Fortunately, the industry trend is to offer OLAP services with a combination of an OLAP server front-end (with embedded multidimensional store for coarse data) and a relational store back-end (with fine-level detail data) (see fig. 10.12). This configuration addresses the relative weakness of the other two options, while leveraging their respective strengths. In practice, some enterprises start with a relational store and add multidimensional stores where needed.

**Fig. 10.12**

*Combined multidimensional store and relational store.*

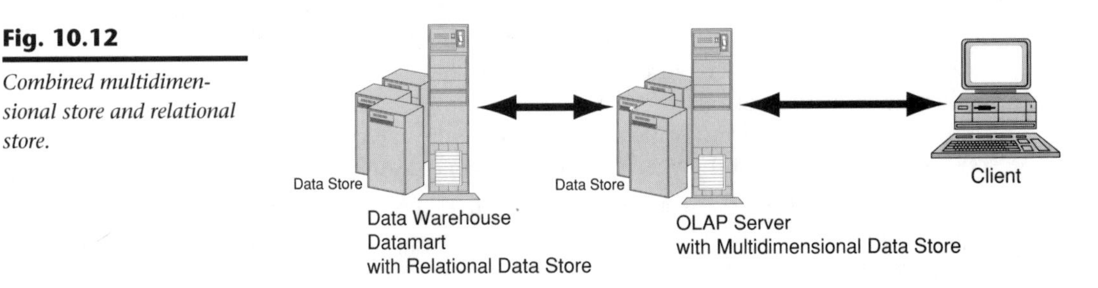


In this architectural configuration, frequently accessed information and queries are precalculated, summarized, aggregated, and then stored in the OLAP server's multidimensional data store. This can be done during the initial loading of the analytical model from the data warehouse or data mart relational data store. Complex or compute-intensive queries, or complex calculation-based data are also preprocessed and stored. This provides very fast performance.

Infrequently accessed data or values computed from a small number of dimensional elements are calculated only when a query is received. This infrequently accessed data may not even be stored in the multidimensional data store, and can be retrieved by the OLAP server from the relational data store only when the need arises.

The usage monitoring function can store the data (previously infrequently accessed) or the results of what was an infrequently accessed query in the multidimensional data store for subsequent requests. This improves the overall performance and increases the storage only on a demand basis.

This configuration also supports drill-down to detail data, detail data which is not available in the multidimensional data store, by creating a request and retrieving the detail data from the relational data store.

The important issue is to keep business goals and the business users' perspectives in mind. A good OLAP solution provides the correct business balance between the five sets of criteria discussed and the life-cycle costs (initial acquisition and installation, training, maintenance, and operations) of the solution.

# Summary

- Executive managers know "the future belongs to those who can see it and get there first." That is why business executives and managers want to not only understand "what is going on in the business," but also "what is going to happen next." Analytical processing can be used for both complex historical analysis, with extensive manipulation, as well as for forward planning and forecasting—the past as a prologue of the future.
- The logical OLAP architecture consists of two parts—OLAP view, the multidimensional and logical presentation of the data in the data warehouse or data mart to the business user, regardless of how and where the data is stored; and data store technology, the technology options of how and where the data is actually stored.
- The OLAP functional architecture consists of three services components: data store services, OLAP services, and user presentation services. In this respect, the functional architecture is a three-tier client-server architecture. The architecture offers multiple physical configuration options for the three functional services.
- In an OLAP configuration, there are two options to store the data: multidimensional data store and relational data store. From the business user's perspective, the comparison issues include: how much business data is stored and available?; is the storage capacity adequate?; is the performance acceptable?; is the cost justified?
- From an overall architecture perspective, there is no simple choice between the relational or multidimensional data store for OLAP. The business needs provide the criteria for making the right choice. Fortunately, the industry trend is to offer OLAP services with a combination of an OLAP server front-end (with embedded multidimensional store for coarse data) and a relational store back-end (with fine-level detail data). This configuration addresses the relative weakness of the other two options, while leveraging their respective strengths.
- OLAP is achieving wider usage in functional business areas such as customer profitability, product profitability, budgeting and forecasting, sales analysis, manufacturing mix and logistics analysis, and financial consolidations and analysis.

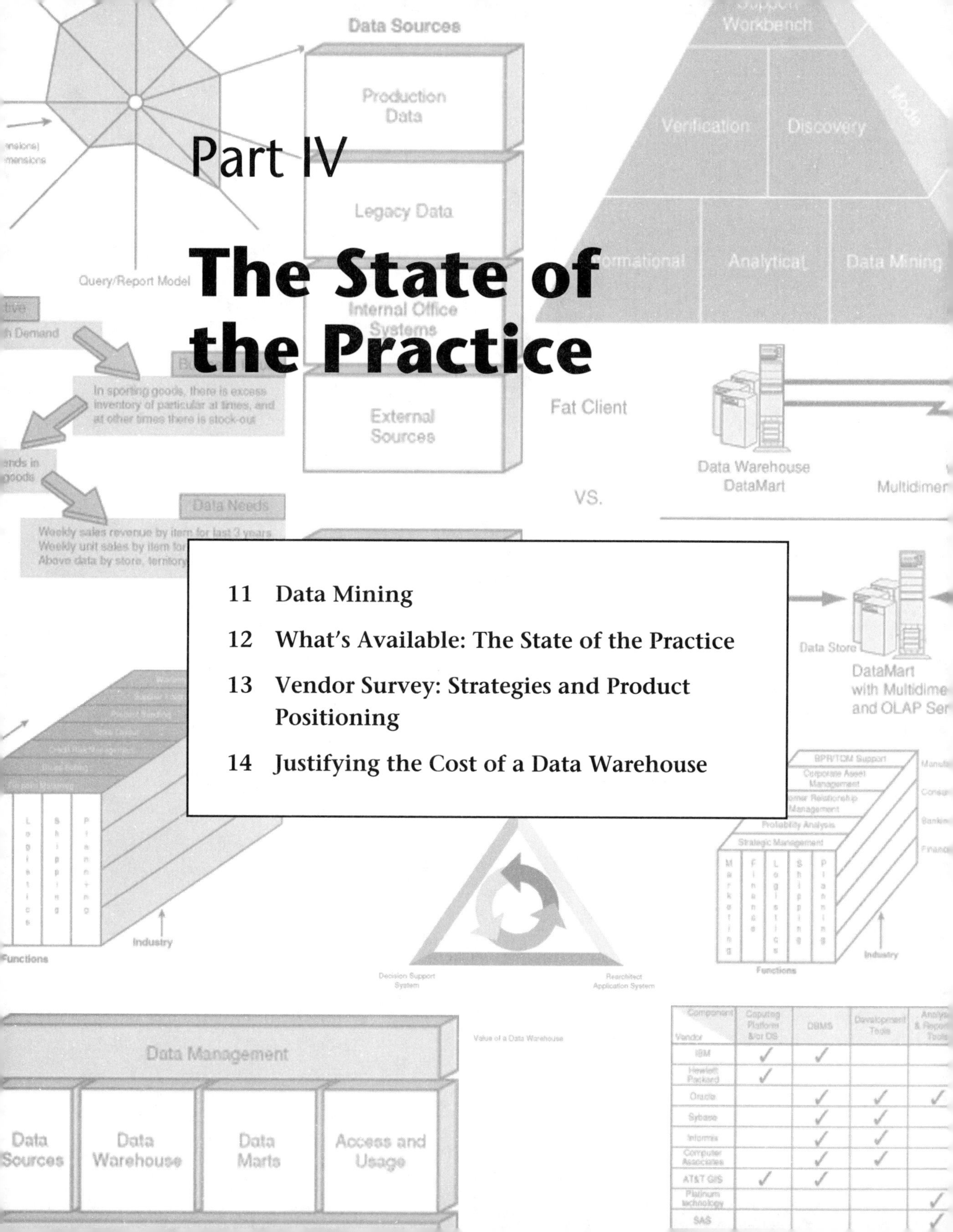


# Part IV

# The State of the Practice

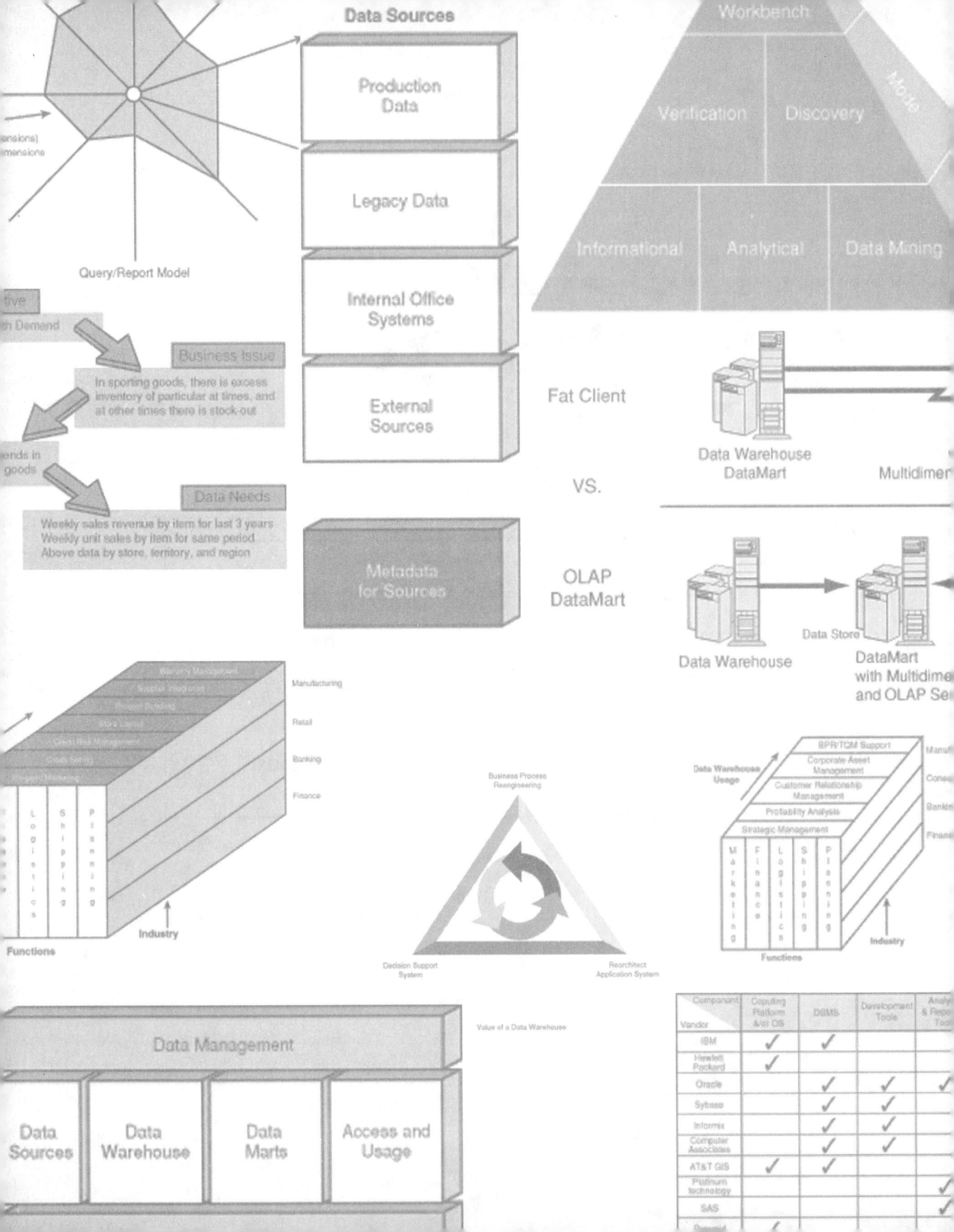

Data Sources
Production Data
Legacy Data
Internal Office Systems
External Sources
Metadata for Sources
Query/Report Model
Business Issue
In sporting goods, there is excess inventory of particular at times, and at other times there is stock-out
Data Needs
Weekly sales revenue by item for last 3 years
Weekly unit sales by item for same period
Above data by store, territory, and region
Workbench
Verification
Discovery
Informational
Analytical
Data Mining
Fat Client
VS.
OLAP DataMart
Data Warehouse DataMart
Data Warehouse
Data Store
DataMart
Manufacturing
Retail
Banking
Finance
Logistics
Shipping
Planning
Industry
Functions
Business Process Reengineering
Decision Support System
Rearchitect Application System
Value of a Data Warehouse
Data Warehouse Usage
BPR/TQM Support
Corporate Asset Management
Customer Relationship Management
Profitability Analysis
Strategic Management
Marketing
Finance
Data Management
Data Sources
Data Warehouse
Data Marts
Access and Usage
Component
Vendor
Computing Platform &/or OS
DBMS
Development Tools
IBM
Hewlett Packard
Oracle
Sybase
Informix
Computer Associates
AT&T GIS
Platinum technology
SAS

CHAPTER 11

# Data Mining

When business analysts use the data warehouse to seek what their customers are doing, an important question still nags them—why are they doing it? Understanding customer behavior or, for that matter, business behavior is key to improving the business bottom line and having delighted customers. Business managers and analysts seek answers to achieve objectives like the following:

- Find and reach better customers (customers with higher profit potential), not just any new customer
- Gain critical business insights that will help to drive market share and raise profits
- Understand the total relationship with each customer to develop the right pricing strategies and correct product bundling based not on intuition, but on actual product usage and customer experience
- Discern a customer's lifetime value
- Reduce promotional spending and at the same time increase net effectiveness of promotions overall (analyze buying behavior and promotion response)

## Data Mining Ingredients

To achieve these objectives, the data warehouse provides the business manager with two essential ingredients. The first ingredient is a large amount of clean and organized data on its customers, as well as the history between the customer and the organization. The second, far more important, is the uniqueness of this data—none of the competitors have this data. The business owns this haystack of data, this data mine, and can potentially find the needle and mine the nuggets of critical insights into the behavior of its customers, its own products, and even its suppliers. For this capability, the data warehouse solution must add data mining to its decision support workbench (see fig. 11.1). Data mining is an essential weapon in the business analyst's decision support arsenal.

**Fig. 11.1**

*The decision support workbench.*

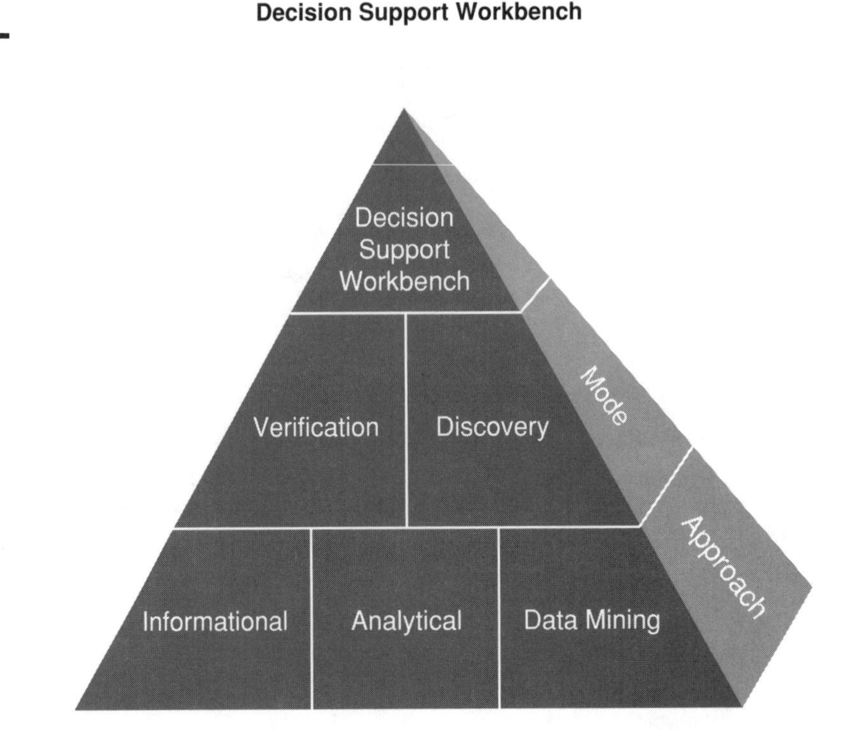


Data mining assists business users in processing vast reservoirs of data to discover "unsuspected relationships"—for example, between products and customers or customer buying patterns. The goal is to uncover "strategic competitive insight" to drive market share and profits. Human beings are keen detectors of exceptions and anomalies but do not have the stamina and capacity to infer relationships in large data stores. After the relationships are extracted and presented to business analysts, however, the analysts can sift through and select the most interesting and useful ones.

Business analysts have a range of needs (see fig. 11.2). The first need is to understand what is happening in the business. The next need is to understand why is it happening—what is the behavior of customers and markets? The final need is what can be done—what action can be taken? The value of an analysis to managers is highest when the analysis results in an actionable recommendation. Understanding customer and market behavior and forecasting, and what can be done, are challenges to traditional analysis techniques. Traditional query, reporting, and multidimensional analysis techniques focus mainly on what is happening and to a lesser degree on why. Data mining focuses on filling the need to discover the why, and then to predict and forecast possible actions with a certain confidence factor for each prediction.

Data mining tools are an important component of the Analysis and Reporting sub-block of the Access and Usage block of the reference architecture described in Chapter 2 (see fig. 11.3). Data mining tools use the Access and Retrieval sub-block to interface to the data warehouse and data mart. Many data mining tools also need the local

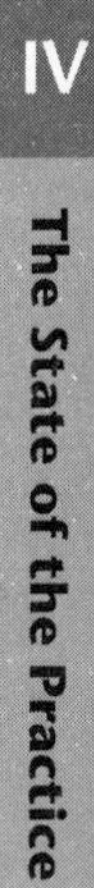


store component of the Access and Retrieval sub-block to store the data in proprietary data structures for subsequent analysis and presentation of the results.

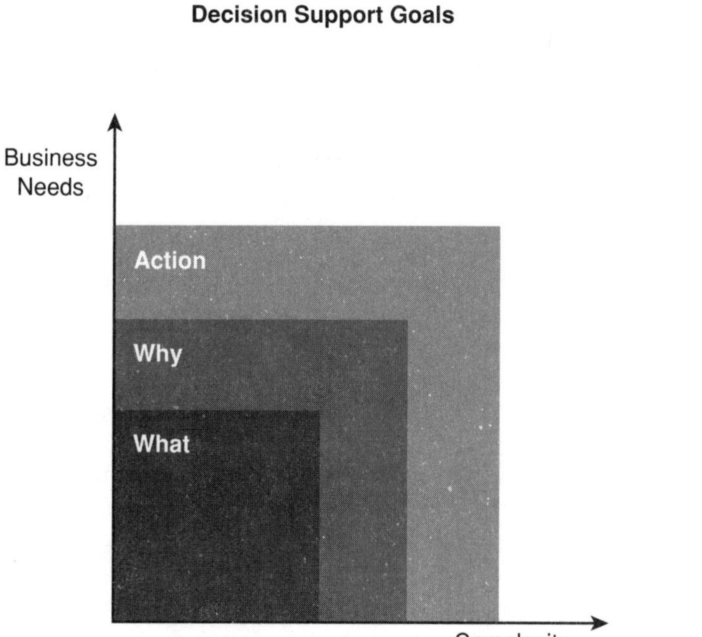


**Fig. 11.2**

*Decision support goals.*

Reference Architecture: Data Mining

Access & Retrieval

Data Warehouse Direct Access

DataMart Access

Reengineering

Transform to MultiDimensional Structure

Create Local Store

Manage Data Warehouse Metadata

Metadata Browse and Navigate

Analysis & Reporting

Reporting Tools

Analysis Tools DSS Tools

Business Modeling Tools

Data Mining Tools

New Production Applications

OLAP

Metadata Management & Reports

**Fig. 11.3**

*Access and Usage block of reference architecture.*

Most data mining tools can easily bypass the data warehouse or data mart and directly access the source of the data. Traditionally, data mining tools accessed the data at the source. However, data in the data warehouse or data mart is refined, integrated, and standardized. The standardization has removed issues such as multiple naming conventions, hidden encoding structures, and missing fields. The operational data at the source generally is inconsistent and scattered in a myriad of applications. Additionally, historical data is needed to discover temporal patterns of interest.

Data mining differs in a number of ways from informational and analytical processing. Figure 11.4 summarizes some of these major differences.

**Fig. 11.4**

*Informational/analytical processing vs. data mining.*

**Informational/Analytical Processing vs Data Mining**

| | Informational/ Analytical Processing | Data Mining |
|---|---|---|
| **Focus** | Summary Data | Transaction or Detail Data |
| **Dimensions** | Limited | Lots |
| **Number of Attributes** | Total in the tens | Hundreds for each dimensions |
| **Size of Datasets** | Small to medium for each dimension | Millions for each dimension |
| **Analysis Focus** | What is happening in the Business? | Why is it happening? Predict and Forecast Actions |
| **Analysis Technique** | Slice and Dice | Discover automatically |
| **Analysis Process** | Business Analyst Initiated and Controlled | Data and System Initiated Minimal Guidance from Business Analysts |
| **Confidence Factor** | Derived by Business Analyst | Derived from the Data |
| **State of Technology** | Mature | Mature in Statistical Analysis Emerging in Knowledge Discovery |

The data in the data warehouse must be at the correct level of detail. Due to the emerging nature of data mining technology, a close cooperation between business analysts and IT facilitators—especially in the beginning—is necessary.

Three ingredients are crucial to forming the right mixture for data mining activities: users, business applications, and technology and tools. These are discussed in the following sections.

## Data Mining Users

The key prospective users of data mining are business analysts, statisticians, and IT facilitators who assist the business users. Those who benefit from the results of data mining efforts are the business managers and executives who want to understand the crucial success factors of the business based on *full* customer data, and then use this knowledge to fine tune product, pricing, and marketing strategies; enhance the level of success of these strategies; and thus boost the bottom line.

To date, businesses have relied on informational and analytical processing to gauge and to understand the health of a business. Informational processing—query and reporting—is simpler to use but needs close analyst direction (see fig. 11.5). Analysts ask specific questions and verify the questions or hypotheses with the data. The data must be well-organized for this purpose. Analytical processing (OLAP) requires less analyst guidance, but the data must still be either organized in a special way (multidimensional database) or accessed in a special form (multidimensional view). Occasionally, a combination of query and OLAP techniques is used to understand customer behavior or to build market segment profiles; but the process in applying these techniques is essentially driven by the business analyst. In these cases, this process also is loosely called *data mining*. In Chapter 8, data mining was defined as the discovery mode of decision support, which is driven by the data and not by the business user.

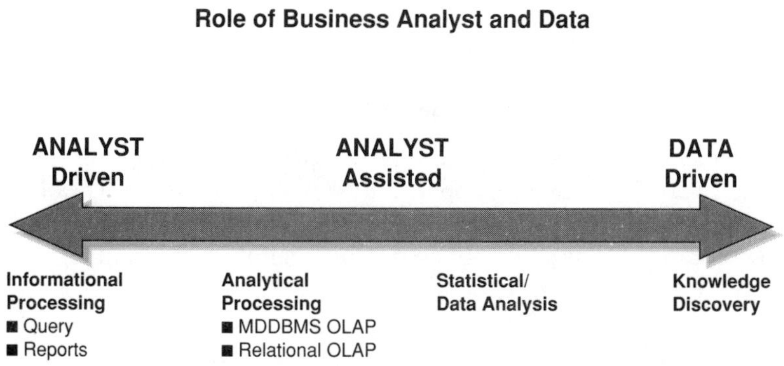

**Role of Business Analyst and Data**

ANALYST Driven | ANALYST Assisted | DATA Driven

Informational Processing
- Query
- Reports

Analytical Processing
- MDDBMS OLAP
- Relational OLAP

Statistical/ Data Analysis

Knowledge Discovery

**Fig. 11.5**

*Role of business analyst.*

## Emergence of Data Mining Applications

In business applications, data mining technology to date has been used principally in marketing, sales, and credit analysis applications. Data mining technology has been successfully applied in business areas with the highest potential, such as customer and market segmentation and consumer-behavior analysis, particularly in the retail, finance, and banking sectors. So far, the technology was generally expensive to apply and deploy, but this situation is rapidly changing. Today, a confluence of three key forces drives the growth in data mining:

- Data warehouse technology to provide a large pool of well-organized and quality historical data

- Parallel hardware and database products and tools at reasonable prices
- Increasing maturity of data mining technology and tools

The pace of growth in data mining usage is expected to accelerate. The number of data warehouse applications is mushrooming, and parallel hardware and supporting software product prices are sharply declining.

### Data Mining Technologies and Tools

A wide variety of data mining technology and tools are available, with even more coming to market. These data mining technologies and tools can be categorized into the following three broad types:

- Statistical or data analysis
- Knowledge discovery
- Others such as visualization systems, geographical information systems, fractal analysis, and proprietary tools

## Statistical Analysis

*Statistical analysis* (also referred to as *data analysis*) systems are used to detect unusual patterns of data. These patterns of data then are explained, using statistical and mathematical models. Some of the statistical and mathematical modeling techniques used are linear and nonlinear analysis, continuous and logistic regression analysis, univariate and multivariate analysis, and time series analysis.

Statistical analysis tools are used in a range of business applications: to increase market share and profits by zeroing in on best opportunities, to enhance customer satisfaction by improving the quality of products and services (Total Quality Management programs), and to boost margins by streamlining product manufacturing and logistics (Business Process Engineering). Statistical analysis tools have been available for some time and are the most mature of the data mining tools available. These tools have been successful in reducing the analysis time, which frees scarce resources for other analysis activities, which then leads to better decision-making.

Until recently, statistical analysis tools were aimed principally at statisticians and technical professionals for technical and engineering applications. Many businesses, however, are experiencing the twin pressures of downsizing—elimination of support personnel—and ever shorter time-to-market pressures. So, statistical analysis tools must evolve to the point where they can be successfully adopted and used by business analysts. These business analysts are experts in their field, but they aren't programmers or statisticians. They need to select the right data from the data warehouse, extract it, and then analyze it. Business analysts cannot dissipate their scarce resources to learn how to write computer programs, manipulate databases, and build formal statistical analysis approaches and strategies. The key skills expected of the business analyst are only the following:

- **Domain expertise**—This skill is knowledge of the subject matter.
- **Problem-solving**—These skills require knowing how to structure the analysis to address the business issues of the day.

As was shown in figure 11.5, statistical analysis tools lie in the middle ground between knowledge discovery tools at one end and the informational processing tools at the other. Limited but appropriate business analyst guidance can substantially speed up and enhance the quality of the statistical analysis activity.

## Using Statistical Analysis Tools

To use a statistical analysis tool, business users must select and extract the right data from the data warehouse or the data mart (see fig. 11.6).

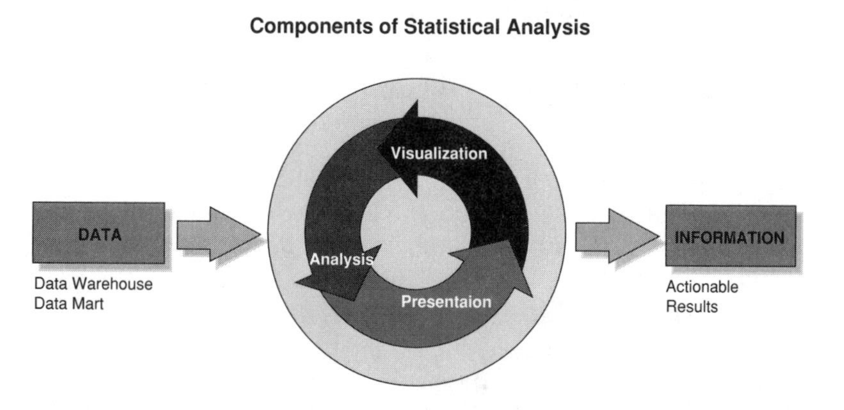


**Fig. 11.6**

*Statistical analysis components.*

Next business users must invoke visualization and analytic functions available in the statistical analysis tool to discover relationships in the data and construct statistical and mathematical models to interpret the data. An interactive and iterative process is used to refine the model; the goal is to develop the best-fit model to convert data into information. Business analysts problem-solving skills and domain expertise are key to selecting the best-fit model. The business analyst has a natural confidence in the model to develop actionable results.

## Features of Statistical Analysis Tools

Given the complexity of many statistical analysis tasks, statistical analysis tools must offer the following:

- **Visualization functions**—These functions assist in the discovery of relationships in the very large amounts of data. For example, functions must recognize patterns in time-series data and display line/logarithmic graphs, or perform curve fitting to find the "business rule or pattern" in the data, or manipulate the data by automatically grouping values of selected discrete variables or by altering the starting point and size of histogram bins.

- **Exploratory functions**—These functions help in the selection of the right statistical function and model that fits the data. Some of these functions are pivoting multidimensional tables; analysis-oriented help; slice, dice, sort, and subset the data; split files and take samples; and identify extreme values and outliers. The tool must dynamically produce and present to the business analyst appropriate charts, graphs, or tables automatically, as part of the exploration process.
- **Statistical functions and operations**—These functions and operations such as regression analysis, both continuous and logistic; time series analysis, including autocorrelation; Fast Fourier transforms and forecasting; multivariate analysis; ANOVA; CHAID; nonparametric tests; and multiple response analysis provide a rich set of tools.
- **Data management functions**—These functions drill-down into details, browse subsets of the data, drop outliers, compare subsets, and so on.
- **Recording and playback functions**—These functions record the analysis steps, transfer the records to another business analyst, and then playback the entire analysis task. The recording functions must include the analysis steps, data sets selection process, pallet or carousel of charts and graphs selected, and all other information to be communicated. This is key for communicating and sharing of both the results of the statistical analysis task and also the analytical techniques and process applied.
- **Presentation tools**—These tools graphically communicate the complex data and analysis in simpler business charts, graphs, and tables. The tool must quickly convert the data from one chart type and, when needed, display the data in a different chart type. The tool also should show the business user the variety of charts, graphs, and tables types that the data fits so that the best presentation options can be easily selected. A basic set of charts and graphs required consists of *xy* line and scatter plots, box plots, histogram, bar graph (pie and area), interval plot, 3D surface and contour plot, statistical charts (such as Pareto and X-bar), and reports such as crosstabulations.
- **Developers' Toolkit**—Use this kit to easily plug into desktop applications and complete components for statistical analysis, charting, graphing, and reporting. The availability of an object-oriented programming language with point-and-click interface, as well as data exchange through techniques such as Object Linking and Embedding (OLE), will empower the business analyst to incorporate statistical analysis right into desktop decision support applications.
- **Responsible response time**—This period, which may be measured in minutes or even hours, is acceptable for some business decisions. Of course exceptions exist, such as the securities industry; response time in days is unacceptable because the relevancy of the analysis declines as the data becomes stale, and the window of opportunity closes.

### Applications of Statistical Analysis

Statistical Analysis of data in the data warehouse can be used to address a wide range of business issues, including the following:

- **Marketing**—This area of analysis deals with understanding consumer buying habits and behavior and identifying market segments. Market basket analysis is one such technique used to analyze the purchase patterns of customers.
- **Sales**—This area of analysis deals with analyzing sales revenue and deviations from plans.
- **Telesales and marketing**—This area of analysis deals with conducting and analyzing responses to fine-tune the telesales strategy.
- **Business management**—This area of analysis deals with assessing loan applications and analyzing credit risks, measuring achievement tests, and assessing customer satisfaction.
- **Medical research**—This area of analysis deals with studying response to diagnosis and treatments.
- **Product warranty**—This area of analysis deals with monitoring product quality and analyzing warranty repair data.

### Challenges in Applying Statistical Analysis Techniques

Statistical analysis is a powerful technique to understand customers, markets, products, and other key business parameters. But there are some challenges, such as the following:

- It is labor-intensive.
- Success very much depends on the problem-solving skills of the business analyst.
- Many times, the business analyst doesn't know what to look for or is unable to select discrete variables to start the analysis process.
- It is difficult to integrate and analyze non-numeric data (such as geographical data) in a market segmentation effort.
- Achieving acceptable response time at reasonable costs is arduous.

## Knowledge Discovery

In statistical and data analysis, it is essential that the business analyst knows what the variables are before analysis can start. What if you don't know the variables, and what if the data is so large and has so many variables that you don't know where to begin? Maybe you aren't quite satisfied with your statistical analysis and suspect that the data is hiding something? In these situations, the business analyst needs knowledge discovery technology and tools.

Knowledge discovery has its roots in artificial intelligence and machine learning. Some of the definitions of knowledge discovery are described in the following list:

- Knowledge discovery may be a nontrivial extraction of implicit, previously unknown, and potentially useful information from data.
- Knowledge discovery may be the data search process, without stating in advance a hypothesis or question, and still finding either unexpected and interesting information in relationships and patterns among its data elements, or important business rules in the full data searched and analyzed.
- Knowledge discovery may mean to uncover previously unknown business facts in the gigabytes of data in the data warehouse or data mart.

Business managers and analysts are always seeking new and additional business insights so that crucial business decisions, which have significant impact on the health of a business, can be improved. Using the traditional techniques of business queries and data analysis requires asking the right questions. Knowledge discovery technology determines by itself the questions to ask, and then keeps on asking questions, digging deeper, to unearth the nuggets of knowledge the business seeks. Business analysts do not have the time, attention span, and stamina to ferret out all the implicit relationships and patterns that exist in the data warehouse.

Knowledge discovery is aimed at sifting through the vast amount of data in the data warehouse, searching for frequently recurring patterns, detecting trends, and unearthing facts. Knowledge discovery systems try to discover facts or knowledge with minimal, if any, guidance or direction from the analyst, all in the shortest amount of time. So, in knowledge discovery, large amounts of data warehouse or data mart data are inspected and facts/knowledge are discovered and presented to the business analyst. Now the business analyst exercises business know-how and domain expertise to discern useful facts from those that are not useful. This is the ideal combination of people and computers. The human brain possesses the best algorithms to analyze many variables at the same time, but it has limited data bandwidth. The computer, however, has enormous bandwidth, stamina, and patience but no understanding of multiple business variables. Data visualization and browse tools that aid in exploring and analyzing previously mined data further enhance the value of the knowledge discovery effort. A knowledge discovery activity is successful when an experienced business executive or manager staring at a newly discovered business fact says, "I didn't know that."

## General Structure of Knowledge Discovery Systems

A knowledge discovery system is a system that finds knowledge it previously did not have (i.e., it was not implicit in its algorithms or explicit in its representation of domain knowledge). A piece of knowledge is a relationship or pattern among data elements that is interesting and useful with respect to a specific domain and task. Implicit in the definition of discovery is a sense of autonomy—unsupervised learning. This autonomy is a real challenge. Most discovery systems have some analyst input or guidance. Consider the business analyst as part of the knowledge discovery system.

A knowledge discovery system consists of a federation of components that can identify and extract interesting and useful (to the business analyst) patterns and relationships from the data stored in the data warehouse or data mart (see fig. 11.7).

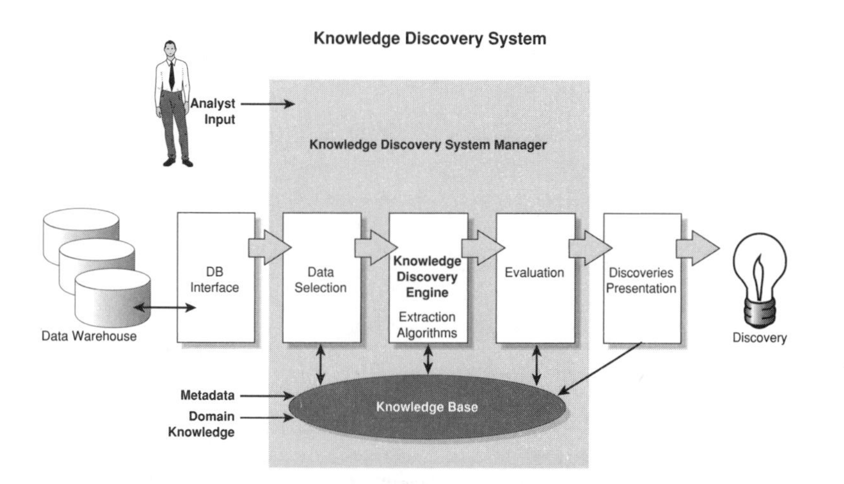


**Fig. 11.7**

*Knowledge discovery system: the logical view.*

In a knowledge discovery tool, the individual components may not be so cleanly separated. The major inputs to the knowledge discovery system are data from the data warehouse, business analyst's guidance, and the domain knowledge and expertise stored in the knowledge discovery system's knowledge base. Selected data from the data warehouse is processed in the knowledge discovery engine, where a variety of extraction algorithms are applied to produce candidate patterns and relationships. These candidate patterns and relationships are evaluated; some are identified as *interesting discoveries* and are presented to the business analyst. Some of these discoveries may be added to the knowledge base to enhance it for subsequent discovery extraction and evaluation.

**Knowledge Discovery System Manager.** The knowledge discovery system manager controls and manages the knowledge discovery process. Input from the business analyst and information in the knowledge base is used to drive the data selection process, the extraction algorithms selection and usage process, and the discovery evaluation process. The system manager also assists in the presentation of discoveries to the business analyst and the storage of desired discoveries in the knowledge base for subsequent discovery activities. The level of supervision of the knowledge discovery engine also is managed by the knowledge discovery system manager. A tradeoff is required between autonomy (level of guidance from the business analyst and the bias stored in the knowledge base), and versatility (types of discoveries attainable and domain types comprehended). Figure 11.8 describes the tradeoff for regulating the autonomy of the system and achieving the desired balance between autonomy and versatility.

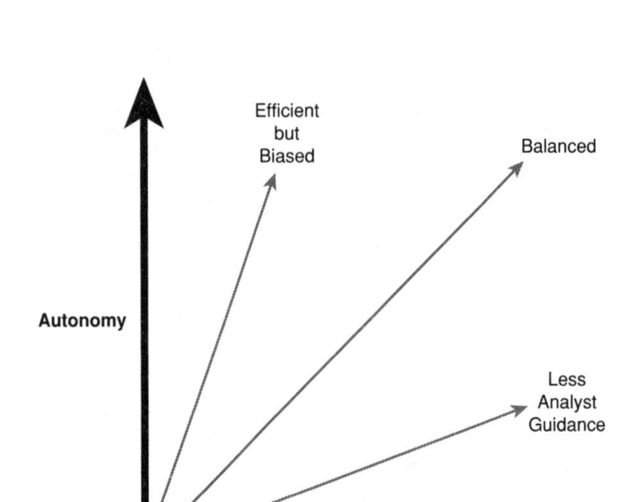


**Fig. 11.8**

*Balance between autonomy and versatility.*

**Knowledge Base and Business Analyst Input.** The knowledge base contains essential information from multiple sources. The metadata of the data warehouse is input to describe the data structures of the data in the data warehouse. Additional knowledge about the data, such as key data fields to focus on, business rules to derive data needed for analysis, any data hierarchies, and so on is also input in to the knowledge base by the business analyst. The goal is to bias the search for patterns of interest in an efficient manner. The risk of biasing is that potentially useful patterns and relationships may be missed. A balance must be selected by the business analyst. Knowledge discovery tools can be enhanced by storing new discoveries to drive and improve subsequent use.

The business analyst also can store information on the quantity of data that must be extracted for achieving a desired level of confidence in the discoveries. Occasionally, a sample of a certain amount may be sufficient while in other cases, the entire database must be processed. Also, information about the type and quantity of data needed for different pattern extraction algorithms is stored in the knowledge base.

**Data Warehouse Database Interface.** Knowledge discovery systems extract the data from the data warehouse database using the query facilities of the database. For relational databases, the SQL query language is used. The data warehouse's metadata in the knowledge base guides the database interface to correct organization of the data structures and how they are stored in the data warehouse (refer to fig. 11.7). For efficiency and performance, the knowledge discovery system's database interface must communicate directly with the data warehouse.

**Data Selection.** This component determines the data that needs to be extracted from the data warehouse and what the data structures of the data are. The knowledge base guides the data selection component about what and how to extract it. If only a sample of data is needed, the data selection component must have the capability to select and extract the correct random sample. Additionally, the type of data required by an algorithm is selected and input to the algorithm.

**Knowledge Discovery Engine.** The knowledge discovery engine applies the extraction algorithms in the knowledge base to the data extracted by the data selection component. The goal here is to extract patterns and relationships between the data elements. The bias built into the knowledge base has a critical effect on the discoveries extracted.

A wide range of algorithms can be incorporated into the knowledge discovery system, such as data dependencies, classification rules, clustering, summarization, deviation detection, induction, and fuzzy reasoning (many of these algorithms are discussed in following sections of this chapter).

**Discovery Evaluation.** Business analysts seek interesting patterns in the data that help in understanding what is happening to customers, products, market, and so on. A data warehouse has, potentially, a host of patterns. The evaluation or filtering component helps the business analyst sift through the patterns to select only the interesting ones. Techniques used to analyze interesting patterns include statistical significance, confidence factor of level of coverage, and visual analysis.

**Discoveries Presentation.** This component provides two essential capabilities—to assist the business analyst with discovery evaluation and storing of interesting discoveries in the knowledge base for future reference and usage, and to communicate the discovery to business managers and executives. Ineffective communications can seriously harm the value of the discovery. The aim here is to use the discovery in understanding the business, and then converting this understanding into actionable recommendations. Presentation techniques in a knowledge discovery system include visual navigation and browsing, natural-language text reports, and charts and graphs.

## Knowledge Discovery Technology

The key technology in knowledge discovery is the algorithms for pattern and relationship recognition. Many of these algorithms were derived from research activities in AI and machine learning. The technology is described from the perspective of four generic tasks or categories.

**Dependency Analysis.** Dependency analysis algorithms extract dependencies between items or objects in the data warehouse. A dependency is interesting because it reveals unknown dependencies among the data, and it possibly describes the causal relationship between data items of interest. Therefore, dependency analysis algorithms may be used to predict the value of one data object from the value of the other. Dependencies do not usually define an exact or certain relationship but rather, a probabilistic value—the confidence factor.

A collection of dependencies can be shown as a dependency graph that organizes all the dependencies in a single structure to communicate a complex set of relationships (see fig. 11.9). One use of dependency analysis is to explain and understand possible causes for discovered changes, where a change in some data can be traced through a dependency network graph to find changes in other data which may explain the observed change—for example, the effect of warranty services on product sales and follow-on services to a set of customers.

**Fig. 11.9**

*Dependency graph.*

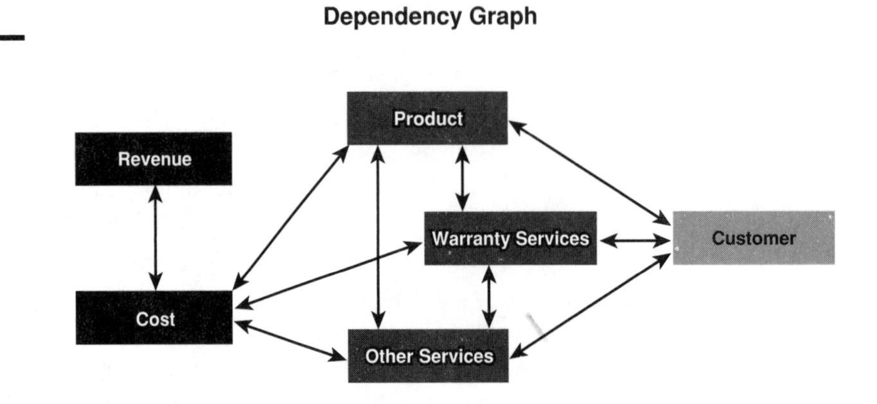


**Classification.** Classification algorithms group data into meaningful classes. You can use this algorithm to create a profile, for example, of preferred customers, or you can use it to generate a basis—a standard—for deviation detection. Clustering algorithms can be used to discover classes automatically. Some prevalent clustering algorithms are pattern recognition, profile generation, linear clustering, and conceptual clustering. Classification is enhanced if the knowledge discovery system uses the business analyst in the loop. In this scenario, the knowledge discovery system's computational power is combined with the business analysts domain knowledge and visual skills.

**Concept Description.** Concept description techniques crisply summarize the interesting rules or descriptions of the class. This category uses the following two types of descriptions:

- **Characteristic**—This describes what is common in the data items in the class.
- **Discriminating**—This describes how two or more classes differ.

Prevalent algorithms in concept description include decision trees, decision-tree inducers, neural networks, and genetic algorithms.

**Neural Networks.** *Neural networks* build models by learning the patterns in the data to be analyzed. Neural networks are classifiers of the implicit type. The implicit rules are created because no explicit rules are discernible. Image analysis is an excellent example of neural networks usage. Neural networks are useful for modeling nonlinear, complex, or noisy data (see fig. 11.10).

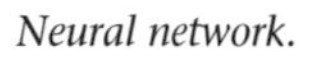

**Fig. 11.10**

*Neural network.*

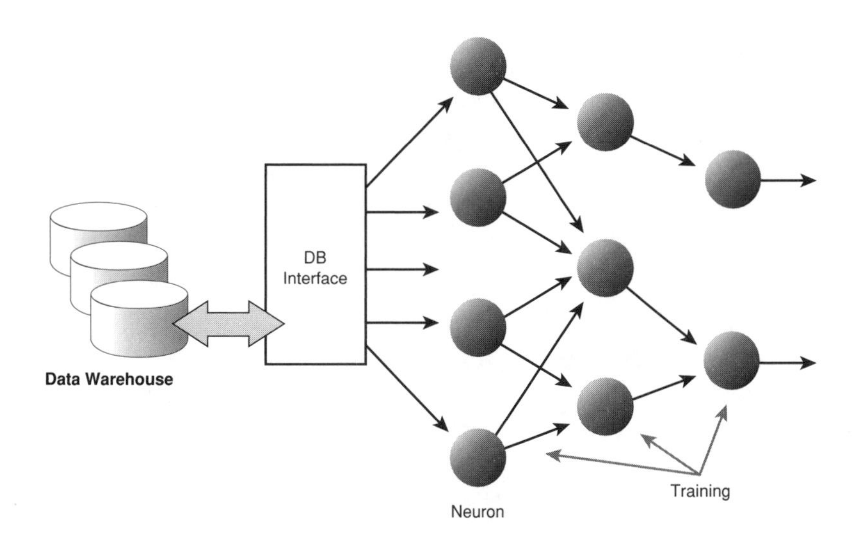


Neural networks consist of interconnected "neurons" or nodes organized in layers (refer to fig. 11.10). Usually, neural models consist of three layers: input, middle, and output. Each neuron evaluates the input values, calculates the total input value, compares the total with filtering mechanism (such as threshold values), and then determines its own output value. Complex behavior is modeled by connecting together a set of neurons. The learning, or "training," occurs by modifying the "connection strength," or parameters, that connect the layers. Neural networks are trained with appropriate samples of the database.

Neural networks learn in either a supervised or an unsupervised mode. In supervised mode, the neural network tries to predict outcomes for known examples. It compares its predictions to the target answer and learns from its mistakes. Supervised neural networks can be used for prediction, classification, and time-series models. Unsupervised learning is effective for describing the data, not for predicting outcomes. The unsupervised networks create their own class descriptions and validations and work exclusively from the data patterns. Neural networks can suffer from long learning times. Because they can act like a black box, they do not gain the confidence of some business analysts.

**Deviation Detection.** Deviation detection techniques extract deviation or anomalies in the data. Some of the deviations of interest are the following:

- Anomalies that do not fit the standard classes
- Classes that are significantly different from parent or sibling classes

- Changes in value from one time period to the next (change in sales revenue for a region from one quarter to another)
- Outliers that are on the fringe of a pattern

Deviation analysis aids in filtering out uninteresting extractions of the knowledge discovery engine or data that doesn't fit, for example, a class. At the same time, however, a deviation or anomaly may show a new fact of great interest—such as an "I didn't know that!" kind of anomaly. Statistical techniques such as ranking can be used to explore anomalies, but a business analyst's investigatory skills and domain knowledge are key in separating a "throw-away" anomaly from a key new business-behavior discovery. Additionally, the knowledge base of the knowledge discovery system can be augmented and enhanced over a period to perform some of these kinds of separations.

## Business Usage of Knowledge Discovery Technology

The different data mining algorithms and techniques described in the preceding section can be classified from the perspective of how and where business analyst use them to solve real-world data mining problems. They can be broadly classified into the usage types discussed in the following sections.

**Classification Usage.** The classification business problem involves finding business rules that partition the data records into disjoint groups. The partition is based on attributes of the data record. The class description may be explicit (characteristic and discriminating concept descriptions) or implicit (a mathematical function).

Examples of classification usage include credit approval and store location. In the store location, the process used is to first categorize current stores into successful, average, and unsuccessful stores. Then, the attribute profile of each of the three categories is developed. Next, a geographical database that contains location attributes is tapped. Then, the attributes of each prospective store location are analyzed to determine in which class—successful, average, and unsuccessful—the prospective store location belongs. Prospects that meet the successful category are selected as desired store locations.

*Profile Generation,* or *BestN,* is a variation of the classification method. Profile generation is used in target marketing, attached mailings, and treatment-appropriateness determination. In target marketing, the business would like to select the BestN candidates from a general mailing list. The business can analyze the previous experience of the business—the prospective customers on mailing list, their attributes, and their response. This information is used to build a profile of desired characteristics, such as largest revenue or highest profitability. The mailing list is filtered to include only customers who match the profile.

With a new product or service, the business has no previous experience base on which to generate a profile. In this case, a test mailing is sent to a selected sample of the prospective customers. The results of this test mailing is analyzed to generate the desired profile.

**Neural Network Usage.** Neural networks are being applied in many business areas, such as the following:

- **Marketing**—This area includes examining customer behavior to build micromarket segments and mailing lists, and to uncover customer preference groups.
- **Financial analysis**—This area includes cash flow analysis and fraud detection.
- **Business operations**—This area includes transportation planning and logistics analysis.

**Usage of Rule Discovery and Decision Trees.** Rule discovery algorithms are used where the data items have attributes or descriptors, and the aim is to explicitly describe the extracted rules. Explicit rules are sometimes modeled as decision trees or decision lists. Credit card analysis is a good example of rule discovery. In credit card analysis, it is imperative that the business analyst explicitly understand and state the rules for say a "good" or "poor" credit risk customer. The legal risk of "turning down a credit request" without appropriate explanation can be very high.

**Usage of Associations.** Associations describe the *affinity*, or relationships, between sets of data items. The relationship or rule is always described with some minimum confidence level. The confidence level is a measure of the strength of the association rule. A classical example of associations is Market Basket Analysis, where the association is a list of product affinities.

Association rules are derived by mining transactions data to understand the behavior of customers. Looking at individual customer orders for office supplies, for example, may generate a rule: 70 percent of customers who order pens and pencils also order writing tablets. "Pens and pencils" are the antecedents or left hand side (LHS) of the rule, and "writing tablets" is the consequent, or right hand side (RHS), of the rule. Any number of antecedents and consequents can be in an association rule. The knowledge discovery system tries to discover as many association rules or patterns as possible in a given set of data. The prevalence of the association rule is the number of order transactions the pattern appears in. Here, "70 percent" is the expression of the confidence factor, a measure of the predictive power of the discovered rule. The confidence factor is the ratio of the frequency or prevalence of the rule to the frequency or prevalence of the antecedents.

The business analyst usually is not interested in a single rule or association to understand business behavior, but rather in sets of associations. The following list shows some of these sets:

- Discover all associations that have "writing tablets" as a consequent to develop a strategy to increase sales of "writing tablets," a high margin item.
- If "pencils" are a low margin item, then discover all associations that have "pencils" in the antecedent to determine the impact of discontinuing the sale of pencils.

- If "writing tablets" are a high margin item, then discover all associations that have "pens" in the antecedent and "writing tablets" in the consequent to understand the required inventory to boost the orders for "writing tablets."

The transactions analyzed may not be ordered all at the same time. It may consist of all orders in a given time frame, such as monthly purchases of compact discs from a music club. Other examples of association rules is medical claim analysis to determine medical procedures that are either performed at one time or over a time period for a particular diagnosis.

**Usage of Sequential Patterns or Sequences.** In many cases, a customer transaction is relevant for a longer period of time—it is a piece of the total relationship with that customer. The business analyst is interested in what occurred before the order, such as mailing of a promotion catalog, the order itself, the customer service call, the order delivery (on time or not), warranty service, and subsequent orders and other ongoing customer interactions. A data warehouse could contain all this temporal data, spanning multiple periods.

Sequential pattern functions can analyze this kind of a collection of data in the data warehouse and discover frequently occurring patterns of customer orders purchased over time. As an example, customers ordering a laser printer today may order "printer paper" on an ongoing basis. The orders may have a pattern that is based on the life cycle of the printer: initial purchase, the warranty service, and maintenance service. There may be a large order at initial purchase, a given amount in between service calls, and again a large amount after each service call. Knowledge of these patterns is valuable in inventory management and revenue projection. Additionally, the business analyst may initiate a promotion program to change the pattern to a more profitable pattern congruent with improved customer satisfaction.

Sequential patterns or sequences could be viewed as a special case of association rules. Sequential patterns are used to discover sets of customers that engage in certain frequent buying patterns.

**Clustering.** When the data to analyze is relatively poor in description or it cannot be grouped into any classification scheme, clustering functions are used to automatically discover classes. The goal of a clustering function is to generate segments of the input data according to some criteria. Different clustering functions (algorithms) may generate different segments or classes of the same data. Clustering functions can be used in cash flow analysis for groups of customers who pay at a particular time of the month (for example, when the social security check is received or fortnightly paycheck is deposited in the account), market segmentation, and uncovering affinity groups. Many classification functions are applicable for clustering analysis.

## Systems Architecture of Knowledge Discovery Tools

Use of knowledge discovery tools comprises the following three phases:

- Data preparation
- Discovery of the patterns and relationships of interest

- Presentation of discoveries to the business analyst for evaluation and exploitation

The first phase, data preparation, is the standard population of the data warehouse. The major difference is that detail data, not summary, is needed. Selecting what data is needed is dependent on the domain expertise of the business analyst and the knowledge of the contents of the data warehouse of the data warehouse data administrator.

In the second phase, knowledge discovery is done by using the Knowledge Discovery System (see fig. 11.11). The knowledge discovery system is guided by the knowledge base to extract the right data from the data warehouse. The interface to the data warehouse generally is a SQL interface. Then the knowledge discovery algorithms, which are selected by the business analyst, are applied to detect patterns and relationships in the extracted data. (In the case of neural network, prior training is required.)

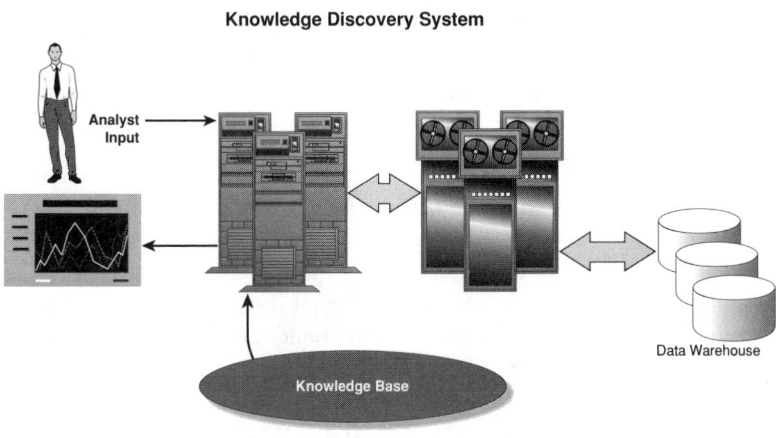


**Fig. 11.11**

*Systems architecture of Knowledge Discovery System.*

In the final phase, the discoveries are presented to the business analyst by using a workstation tool and an appropriate desktop tool.

The business analyst guides and controls the knowledge discovery system from a client workstation. The knowledge base may be stored either on the knowledge discovery system or on the data warehouse system.

The knowledge discovery system requires a robust computational server, which may be a parallel processor. The separation of the computational processor from the data storage platform helps in fine-tuning the system because now the performance and I/O bottlenecks can be addressed separately.

## Challenges in Applying Knowledge Discovery Tools

The base of much knowledge discovery technology is derived from the research done in AI and machine learning. The technology is slowly moving from the universities and research centers of vendors to business customers. Application-by-application, the technology is maturing from field experience. Besides the emerging nature of the technology, there are substantial challenges. Representative sets are described in the following sections.

**Data Quality.** Because knowledge discovery is data-driven and relatively unsupervised, knowledge discovery is susceptible to data quality problems. Many data warehouses tend to be dynamic, erroneous and incomplete, redundant, sparse, and, of course, large. Using the right knowledge discovery functions and techniques, with careful analysis of anomalies, is warranted.

**Visualization of Data.** Data warehouses contain enormous amounts of data, replete with data patterns. Visualizing such vast amounts of data means sophisticated data visualization tools are needed. Data visualization is a nascent technology but one which can assist the business analyst to leverage the power of human visualization—especially in cases where the dimensionality of the data is low. Knowledge discovery and data visualization can work well in tandem. By itself, data visualization can easily overwhelm the analyst by the sheer volume of data in the data warehouse. Knowledge discovery can help by suggesting a starting point for fruitful exploration and presenting the data in an appropriate metaphor.

**Very Large Data Base (VLDB) Issue.** Data warehouse designs try to keep the database to as small a size that will meet standard informational and analytical processing needs of its users. The data is summarized whenever possible for reducing storage space and improving the response time of queries and reports. But for knowledge discovery, transaction or detail data is essential to understanding customer behavior and buying patterns. Besides the systems management challenges of very large databases, the very large size of the data warehouse database presents challenges to many knowledge discovery tools and techniques. The size of data fetched may overwhelm certain techniques, such as neural network training. In many cases, additional data sampling techniques are required.

**Performance and Costs.** To meet the computational needs of many knowledge discovery systems, parallel technology for hardware, operating systems software, and RDBMS is needed. These resources add significantly to costs and puts a strain on the available IT resource pool of parallel technology experts.

**Business Analyst Skills.** Business analysts need extensive domain knowledge and very strong investigatory skills, and must at the same time be creative. Creativity allows the business analyst to try a variety of knowledge discovery techniques to potentially discover a wide range of patterns and relationships, then to analyze and understand them, and finally to create prediction models and communicate them in easily understood presentations.

## Value of Knowledge Discovery

In today's fiercely complex and competitive business environment, executives and managers—who set business or market strategy, plan sales campaigns, and determine the allocation of scarce resources—are very interested in understanding and gauging the health of their business within the context of their business data (their history), the industry and the economy, and ultimately in influencing future events for the benefit of their organization. They want to convert the raw data in the data warehouse into succinct business insights to steer their marketing, operations, investment strategies, and decisions. Knowledge discovery tools assist in business understanding, business discovery, and predictive modeling.

**Understanding the Business.** Knowledge discovery tools and technology assists businesses in understanding the details of the business and uncovering the critical (but as yet not visible and unknown) business facts. Customer behavior patterns can be analyzed in multiple ways: from affinity analysis to market segmentation, and from profile generation to sequential patterns of purchases. Both explicit and implicit rules can be generated and analyzed. Multiple knowledge discovery techniques are available that fit different types of data, from numeric, to descriptive, to images.

A combination of techniques or the sequential application of different techniques is helpful in understanding the business facts and developing actionable recommendations.

**Discovery of Business Anomalies.** Knowledge discovery tools can also assist in deviation or anomaly detection and analysis. Examination of some anomalies can lead to better decisions where the bias or skewing of the data by an anomaly is prevented. Examination of others may provide that critical business insight no one suspected.

**Predictive Modeling.** From understanding what is happening in the business and why, knowledge discovery techniques can lead to "now what to do"—you can predict and plan the future from the past. Predictable modeling systems, such as classification and dependency analysis systems, provide an understanding of their predictive actions, which combined with the business analysts domain know-how, forms a potent combination for sound decision-making.

Predictive models can be used in many crucial business areas, such as cross-marketing, affinity marketing, product bundling (single vendor or multiple vendors bundling their products), credit risk analysis, and store location analysis.

# Other Data Mining Techniques and Tools

Other data mining techniques and tools also are available. Some of these tools have just emerged from the research centers, while others have specific applications.

## Visualization Systems

Visualization systems enable business analysts to make discoveries by allowing them to graphically analyze data with many variables, and then to see patterns and relationships that would be extremely difficult to determine by machine algorithms, no matter what the computational capabilities of the system.

One visualization technique, visual representation of parallel coordinates, enables the business analyst to display relationships between many variables simultaneously, mapping coordinates as parallel axes rather than as the perpendicular axes of traditional visualization tools. This representation of multivariate datasets which preserves all the information and transforms multivariate relations into well-defined 2D patterns helps to manage large data sets and leverage visual analysis and query methods for complex analysis. Use of this visualization technique is emerging, from manufacturing defect analysis and medical research applications to marketing analysis, to help identify buyer preferences and buying trends.

### Geographical Information Systems

Geographical visualization systems relate warehouse data from different physical locations to geographical representations. The business analyst can visualize the data in the context of geography and compare territories for the same product, or for different products for the same territory. The temporal data in the data warehouse also can be analyzed by visualizing changes over time for sales, product inventory, and so on, within desired geographical areas.

### Fractal Analysis

Multidimensional databases provide a wealth of analytical information and have fast response time, but they suffer from size limitations if the entire data warehouse needs to be stored. Fractal analysis attempts to identify patterns by using *chaos* science, and then use fractals to store them in the warehouse. The goal is to offer OLAP-style responses for a very large data warehouse.

### Proprietary Discovery Engines

Most of the knowledge discovery technology discussed previously was published in technical journals and some were incorporated into products. Some vendors have developed proprietary or patented algorithms to build knowledge discovery tools. One of these tools generates expert system-like rules from historical data; and then these rules can be applied against new data for forecasting.

## Summary

- In today's fiercely complex and competitive business environment, executives and managers—who set business or market strategy, plan sales campaigns, and determine the allocation of scarce resources—are very interested in understanding and gauging the health of their business within the context of their own business data, the industry, and the economy, and then in influencing future events for the benefits of their organization. They want to convert the raw data in the data warehouse into succinct business insights to steer their marketing operations, and their investment strategies and decisions. Knowledge discovery tools assist in business understanding, business anomalies discovery, and predictive modeling.

- Data mining assists business users in processing vast reservoirs of data to discover "unsuspected relationships," for example, between products and customers or customer buying patterns. The goal is to uncover strategic competitive insight to drive market share and profits.

  The prospective users of data mining are business analysts, statisticians, and IT facilitators who assist business users. The beneficiaries of the results of data mining efforts are the business managers and executives.
- Data mining technologies and tools can be broadly categorized into three types: statistical or data analysis, knowledge discovery, and others such as visualization, geographical visualization systems, and fractal analysis.
- Statistical analysis, also referred to as data analysis, systems are used to detect unusual patterns of data. These patterns are then explained by using statistical and mathematical models. Some of the statistical and mathematical modeling techniques used are linear and nonlinear analysis, continuous and logistic regression analysis, univariate and multivariate analysis, and time series analysis. Statistical analysis tools are used in a range of business applications: increasing market share and profits by zeroing in on best opportunities, enhancing customer satisfaction by improving the quality of products and services (Total Quality Management programs), and boosting margins by streamlining product manufacturing and logistics (Business Process Engineering). Statistical analysis tools have been available for some time and are the most mature data mining tools available.
- A knowledge discovery system consists of a federation of components that can identify and extract interesting and useful patterns and relationships. The major inputs to the knowledge discovery system are: data from the data warehouse, business analyst's guidance, and the domain knowledge and expertise stored in the knowledge discovery system's knowledge base. Selected data from the data warehouse is processed in the knowledge discovery engine where a variety of extraction algorithms are applied to produce candidate patterns and relationships. These candidate patterns and relationships are evaluated; some are identified as interesting discoveries and are presented to the business analyst.
- A wide variety of knowledge discovery algorithms and techniques are available, such as classification, profile generation or BestN classification, neural networks, rule discovery and decision trees, associations, sequential patterns, and clustering.
- Few of the challenges in applying knowledge discovery technology include quality of the data, the ability to visualize the data, very large database size, adequate response time at reasonable costs, and the skills of the business analyst—the data miner.
- Finally, data mining is an essential component of an organizations' decision support toolkit. Because it is an emerging technology, ongoing technology and product evaluation is natural and vital. To assure a successful data mining project for a data warehouse, the business must select the right business

problem, recruit the most enthusiastic business analyst, conduct a requirements analysis, analyze the available technology and tools, and then creatively apply the selected tools to deliver the desired results, boosting revenue, market share, and profits.

CHAPTER 12

# What's Available: The State of the Practice

Once the decision to try to reap the benefits of a data warehouse (data mart) has been made, the enterprise's IT department is faced with the implementation challenge. The experience of pioneering data warehouse implementors is capsuled in sound bites (or should that be sound bytes) such as:

- "You can't buy a data warehouse, you have to build it."—*ComputerWorld*
- "Data warehousing is a process, not a place."—META Group

Since there is no off-the-shelf data warehouse at this juncture, IT must build it from the available components. The goal of most prudent IT organizations is to minimize the build and maximize the buy.

Figure 12.1 shows that after the business needs have been analyzed and a resultant architecture has been constructed, IT needs to examine the vendor frameworks and products that are available for purchase. As a part of this examination, IT must:

- Develop the list of what data warehouse components are currently available in the enterprise, what data warehouse relevant skills exist, and what enterprise computing standards and policies potentially apply to building and deploying the data warehouse.
- Map this list of potential data warehouse components, skills, and computing standards and policies to the reference architecture's blocks and layers described in Chapter 2, "A Framework for Understanding the Data Warehouse."
- Select the best-fit and applicable components and skills currently available in the enterprise via the approaches described in Chapter 3, "Applying the Data Warehouse Reference Architecture."
- Determine the optimum approach to vendor and product selection—in light of the technical architecture and the in-house available data warehouse components, skills, and computing standards.

The rest of this chapter focuses on vendor selection approaches, vendor analysis, and vendors' products.

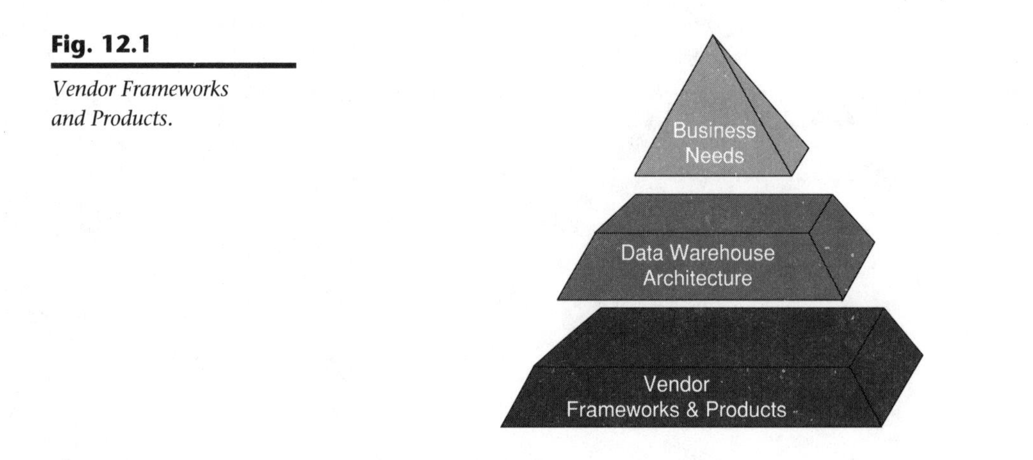


**Fig. 12.1**

*Vendor Frameworks and Products.*

# Data Warehouse Implementation Approaches

Data warehouses can be implemented using three broad approaches (see fig. 12.2). Selection of a particular approach is influenced by many factors:

- Existing investments in communications infrastructure—for example, IT skills, communications networks, network and systems administration.
- Capabilities and capacities of the IT organization.
- Corporate computing and technology standards and policies.
- Existing investments, selection of computing platforms, and database technology.
- Level of satisfaction with current suppliers.
- Corporate culture.

## Build Your Own

In the build-your-own approach, the IT organization builds the data warehouse using a custom architecture. Vendor products are selected and the IT team is responsible for the systems integration activity. The reference architecture is applied to define the technical architecture and the required functionality and products. The strategy is to select the best-of-breed products to meet the business needs and budget constraints. This approach is similar to building a custom home—product selection and systems integration are formidable hurdles.

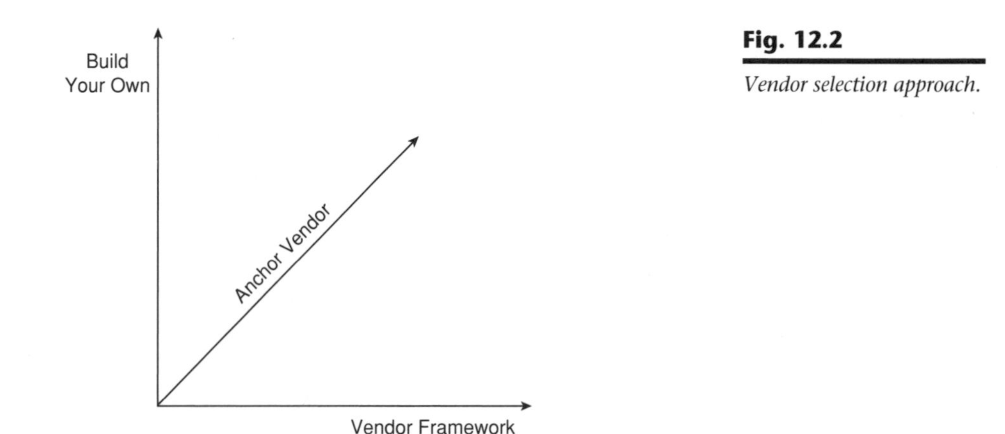


**Fig. 12.2**

*Vendor selection approach.*



## Vendor Framework

Major database and computing platform vendors offer data warehouse frameworks to influence and guide the data warehouse market. Most of the frameworks are similar in scope and substance, with differences greatly influenced by the core technology of the vendor. For example, relational database vendors' frameworks are centered around their RDBMS offerings. The selection of a particular framework limits the choice of products for certain functions and offers potential best-of-breed product options for other data warehouse functions. The stated goal of many frameworks is to offer a greater level of integration and hence, as a consequence, improved performance and systems administration. A representative list of framework vendors includes the following:

- IBM—Data Warehouse *Plus!*
- Oracle—Warehouse Technology Initiative (WTI)
- Hewlett Packard—OpenWarehouse
- Sybase—Warehouse WORKS
- Informix—Data Warehouse Framework
- Pyramid Technology—Smart Warehouse
- AT&T GIS—Enterprise Information Factory
- Prism Software—Data Warehouse Framework
- Platinum technology—Data warehousing as a part of POEMS framework
- SAS Institute—Data Warehousing Initiative

A pictorial description of some of these frameworks is included in Chapter 13, "Vendor Survey: Strategies and Positioning," in figures 13.1 through 13.10.

### Anchor Supplier (Product or Service Vendor)

In this implementation approach, the enterprise selects an existing supplier (product or service vendor) or a new supplier (product or service vendor) as its key or anchor vendor. The anchor supplier's products or services are then used to influence the selection of products and services to meet all the other functions required to build the desired data warehouse. As an example, the selection of IBM and its DB2 family as the database management system of choice means that the hardware and operating systems software platforms are now constrained to platforms supported by the DB2 family. (Note: Members of the DB2 family are now available on popular non-IBM UNIX platforms.) Other examples are database vendors such as Oracle, Sybase, Informix Software, and CA-Ingres, and computing platform vendors such as SUN Microsystems, Hewlett Packard, Pyramid Technology, and Sequent Computer Systems.

Key criteria for using this approach is generally the scope and size of the enterprise's existing investments in personnel skills and current usage of the anchor vendor's products. For analysis purposes, anchor vendors can be broadly divided into four groups:

- **Hardware and O/S Platform Vendors**—IBM, DEC, HP, Microsoft, SUN, Pyramid, Sequent
- **DBMS Vendors**—Oracle, Sybase, Informix, Computer Associates, Software AG, IBM, and Red Brick
- **Decision Support Tools Vendors**—SAS Institute, Sterling Software, and Information Builders
- **Systems Integration Services Suppliers**—Andersen Consulting, Price Waterhouse, Coopers Lybrand, Ernst & Young, Computer Sciences Corporation, ISSC, and EDS

## Overall Vendor Analysis

The reference architecture described in Chapter 2 clearly defines the big and the broad scope of technology and product components needed to implement the data warehouse. According to some industry observers, the data warehouse may be the killer application that will drive client/server technology solutions.

The data warehouse is an area where enterprises will invest significant resources. Hence, the data warehouse market has quickly drawn a very large number of vendors—from vendors with multi-billion dollar revenues to one million dollar revenues; from vendors with frameworks and multiple products to niche or single product suppliers; and from well-established companies to start-ups. At the same time, no single vendor has the complete breadth of products to meet the full complement of the enterprise's needs.

In such an environment, IT must conduct vendor and product selection by understanding both the data warehouse technology market and vendor dynamics. This assists in understanding and managing risks. So, vendor analysis must be conducted from different perspectives.

## Solution versus Component Suppliers

From the enterprise's perspective, data warehouse vendors can be sorted into two categories: full solution vendors and point product component suppliers.

**Full Solution Vendors.** Full solution vendors are defined as vendors who provide multiple components of the reference architecture, integrated in some manner for a customer to have a viable solution that delivers the features that the components promise. The integration of components is usually achieved through a strategic partnership or alliances between component vendors where one of the vendors acts as the lead. The goal of many partnerships or alliances is to broaden their solution offering or to assist the enterprise in leveraging existing investments in components that are not offered by the solution vendor, but rather by the component vendor. A representative list of solution vendors, determined by the authors' analysis, is contained in figure 12.3.

Solutions vendors can be further classified by the level of integration and scope of the solution offered (again, see fig. 12.3). From a data warehouse perspective, an integrated solution or integrated suite implies that the component products have been or are being designed, developed, tested, and deployed as a unified architectural solution. Integrated solutions inevitably yield better performance since they are optimized to work together. Another key advantage of integrated solutions is the potential that administration and monitoring tools are developed and tested, with the components of the solution, and all within the same architecture. The limitation, of course, is the reduction in choices of components in the solution. "The pundits may be scared of hegemony, but it's a good deal for users," is the opinion of David Greenberg, Chief Technical Officer of Visteon, Inc. in Florida (referring to the unity of DBMS vendors and operating systems—the tight integration of database management system engine and operating system means easier and simpler administration).

Integrated solutions are more easily achieved by IBM and Oracle by developing most of the components as part of a single architecture, or by acquisition of a few components to round out the solution. For some integrated solution suppliers, such as AT&T GIS, SAS Institute, and Pyramid Technology, data warehouse is a natural outgrowth of their core business. For other vendors such as Red Brick and Prism Software, data warehouse is the core business.

**Fig. 12.3**

*Data warehouse perspective: integrated and interconnected solution vendors.*

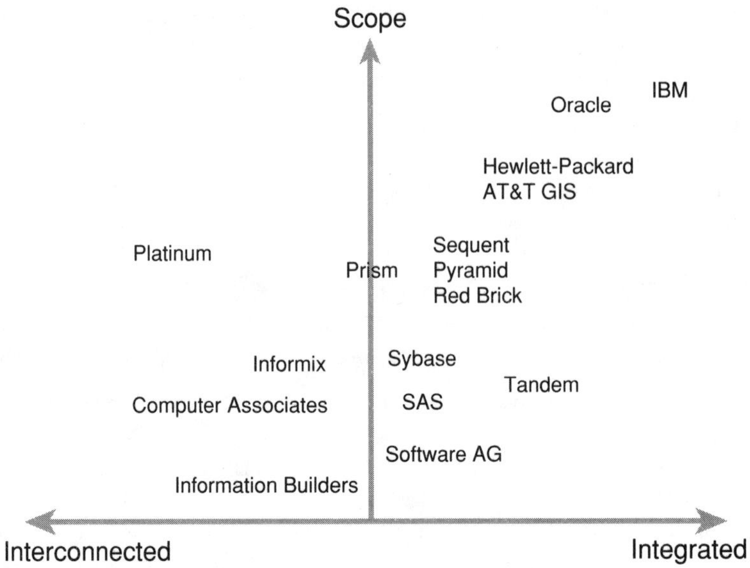

Interconnected solutions have the inherent advantage of choice—now and in the future. The main challenges of interconnected solutions are:

- **Isolation of points of failure**—Each product has points of failure and interconnected solutions have unknown points of failure as a result of interconnection. In some situations, there may be room for "finger-pointing" between suppliers in trying to isolate a point of failure.
- **Administration and performance monitoring**—The challenge of administering and monitoring performance of interconnected products has already been well-documented in the client/server environment. The data warehouse environment is equally challenging.
- **Continuing coordination and integration of software releases**—Even when all components are supplied by one vendor, integrating releases of components is a challenge. But when each component supplier has an independent release schedule, the interconnected solution vendor is challenged to keep up with the releases in a timely manner.

Readers are encouraged to discuss actual implementation experiences and challenges with vendors' customers.

**Component Suppliers.** Component suppliers are vendors who provide point products for specific blocks of the reference architecture. These point products must be integrated either by the IT organization or by systems integrators and consultants assisting IT. Most component suppliers are members of multiple partnerships or alliances formed by the solution providers.

**Data Warehouse Partnerships/Alliances.** Enterprises need a data warehouse solution that is comprehensive, customizable, enterprise-wide, and, if necessary, globally deployable. At this juncture, this is a vision. To achieve part of this vision, most framework providers have developed partnerships or alliance programs. From the enterprise perspective, the key issue is how well the partner programs offer and deliver "an integrated solution." Besides the initial challenge of which partnership program to select, there are other open issues, for example:

- Multiple component suppliers offer competing components in many partnerships/alliances—which is the appropriate or best component supplier?
- How and where are the components integrated? Is there joint development?
- How are the product releases synchronized? Who is responsible?
- What are the recommendations for resolving connectivity problems? Performance tuning?

Data warehouses are complex and intricate. IT can become, by default, the systems integrator. Regardless of the partnership/alliance, the key is how well do the vendors work together to meet customer needs. The best way to learn this is to discuss actual implementations and experiences with a partnership's customers. For example, on one major project, McKesson Corporation selected Oracle and Pyramid especially because of their close working relationship.

## Vendor Competitive Dynamics

The data warehouse product vendor market is very fluid. From the market's perspective, data warehouse vendors can be sifted into three groups: solution incumbents, challengers, and niche, or point product component, suppliers. Figure 12.4 provides, in the authors' opinion, representative members of each group. (The authors understand that in any such categorization, there is room for disagreement.)

**Solution Incumbents.** Solution incumbents are essentially the data warehouse framework providers described previously. A solution incumbent can be identified by three attributes to be a data warehouse solution provider: large market presence in the computer industry, provider of an essential data warehouse technology, and a current strategy.

The market presence of these vendors exerts a strong influence on product or vendor selection because of the existing investments by the enterprise in the vendor's technology and products. History is on the side of these solution incumbents.

As figure 12.4 shows, the solution incumbents are generally providers of the data warehouse computing platform or the database management system, or decision support tools, or all three. Representative solution incumbents include IBM, Oracle, Hewlett Packard, SAS Institute, Sybase, and AT&T GIS. In the three implementation approaches described earlier, solution incumbents can be selected as the framework provider or the anchor supplier.

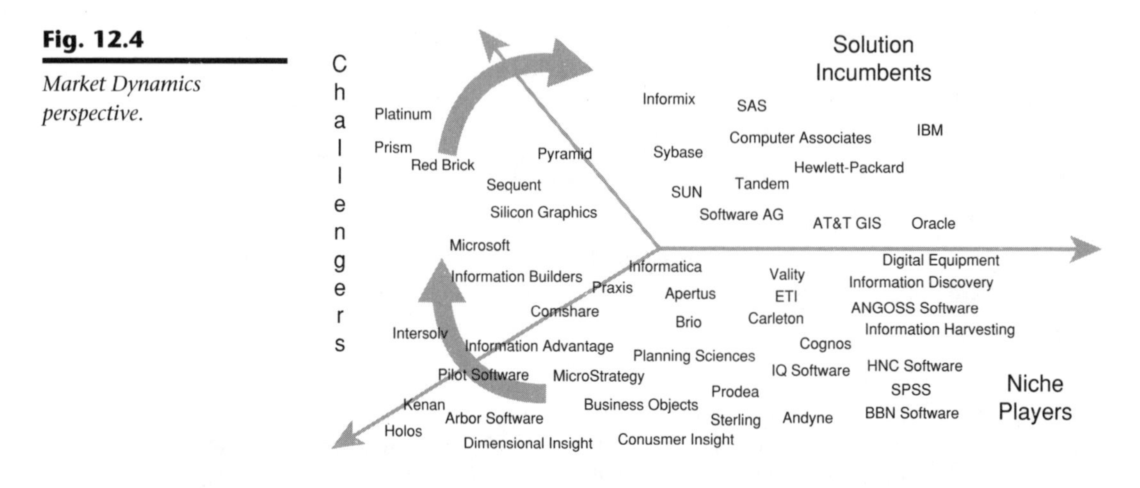


**Fig. 12.4**

*Market Dynamics perspective.*

**Challengers.** Vendors in the challengers group are characterized by market or technology presence, and the ambition to be a full solution provider. Some of these vendors provide a data warehouse solution framework much like the solution incumbents. Some are active in either partnerships with solution incumbents or are leaders of their own partnership or alliance program.

Challengers such as Platinum technology have an ambitious strategy to acquire many niche suppliers and then integrate them to offer integrated solutions much like the solution providers. Others like Pyramid Technology have a solution framework and an alliance program to move toward an integrated solution. Others, such as Red Brick and Prism Software, are major promoters of the data warehouse concepts and data warehouse is their core business. Microsoft is slowly adding products or features to its core products to mount a challenge in this market.

Challengers will continue to strengthen their product offerings through new product development, product integration, and acquisitions. In the three implementation approaches described earlier, some challengers have the potential to be the framework provider or the anchor supplier (refer to fig. 12.2).

**Niche Suppliers.** Niche, or component, suppliers provide point products for specific blocks of the reference architecture. Most niche suppliers are members of multiple partnerships or alliances formed by the solution incumbents or challengers. Niche suppliers can be further classified by which block of the reference architecture is supported. A representative list of niche suppliers is shown in figure 12.4.

Some niche suppliers, known as multidimensional functionality providers, have a strong potential to become challengers due to their ability to either extract data from the data warehouse data store or directly from the data sources, and then to offer a decision support solution—in other words, a mini- or micro-data warehouse. Some of these multidimensional functionality providers have their genesis in the Executive Information System (EIS) or Decision Support System (DSS) industry, one of the precursors of data warehouse. Examples of these vendors includes Pilot Software, Information Advantage, Comshare, Kenan, Planning Sciences, and Dimensional Insight.

**Technology Risk Assessment.** As the META Group said and others in the industry concur, "Data warehousing is a process, not a place," so finding and selecting the right partner and the right product/technology is important. To reduce risk, the vendor's technology must be mature and be continually updated and rejuvenated. This investment in technology is very expensive from the vendor's perspective. So the issue is, will the vendor invest in the technology the data warehouse needs, and how much will the vendor invest?

If the vendor's core business is data warehouse, the vendor must invest or perish. So the only issue is how much to invest? In this case, the ability to invest is influenced by its profitability or the ability to acquire investments from the outside. This investment information is necessary to assess the risks of the data warehouse vendors, for example, Prism Software, Informatica, and Planning Sciences.

If the vendor's core business is more than data warehouse, but the vendor's revenue is in the tens of millions, two issues need examination. One is what the other business areas of the vendor are. Many of the niche suppliers, shown in figure 12.4, are in other businesses, but their products are essentially the same for all their businesses. Second, the investment issues discussed in the previous paragraph are similar to those vendors who are only in the data warehouse business—the ability to invest is influenced by its profitability or the ability to acquire outside investments. This investment information is necessary to assess the risks of these vendors.

For solution incumbents and framework providers, it is important to understand their historical advantage and investments. Since these vendors have multiple businesses and multiple products for data warehouse, the issue is where will the technology investments be. The recommendation is to analyze their core businesses because this is where the major investments will be until the data warehouse business provides the level of revenues to match their core businesses' revenues. Figure 12.5 shows, in the authors' opinions, what the core businesses of some of these vendors are and where the vendors are likely to invest first.

For this technology investment analysis, the data warehouse components of interest have been derived from the reference architecture and include data warehouse computing platform and operating system, database management system, development tools, analysis and reporting tools, systems administration and management tools, middleware, and metadata management.

Figure 12.5 shows the influence of incumbency when selecting the framework and anchor vendor. It also shows where the historical investments have been and are likely to continue. The authors understand that there is bound to be some disagreement and also some incompleteness in such an analysis. You are encouraged to sit down with your vendors and gather the information you need to make the right choice. Figure 12.5 indicates the following potential vendor focus and on-going investments profile.

**Fig. 12.5**

*Technology investment analysis—solution incumbents and framework providers.*

| Component / Vendor | Coputing Platform &/or OS | DBMS | Development Tools | Analysis & Reporting Tools | Systems Admin. & Mgmt. | Middleware | Metadata Mgmt. |
|---|---|---|---|---|---|---|---|
| IBM | ✓ | ✓ | | | ✓ | ✓ | |
| Hewlett Packard | ✓ | | | | ✓ | | |
| Oracle | | ✓ | ✓ | ✓ | | | |
| Sybase | | ✓ | ✓ | | | ✓ | |
| Informix | | ✓ | ✓ | | | | |
| Computer Associates | | ✓ | ✓ | | ✓ | | |
| AT&T GIS | ✓ | ✓ | | | | | |
| Platinum technology | | | | ✓ | ✓ | | ✓ |
| SAS | | | | ✓ | | | |
| Pyramid | ✓ | | | | | | |
| Sequent | ✓ | | | | | | |
| Information Builders | | | | ✓ | | ✓ | |
| SUN Microsystems | ✓ | | | | ✓ | | |
| Microsoft | ✓ | ✓ | ✓ | ✓ | | | |

- **IBM**—MVS and AIX systems, DB2 family, Netview product line
- **Hewlett Packard** HP-UX systems, OpenView product line
- **Oracle**—RDBMS engine, Oracle Objects development tools, and relational and multidimensional reporting tools (and vertical market solutions)
- **Sybase**—RDBMS engine, Powerbuilder development tools, and middleware
- **Platinum technology**—Systems administration and management tools, followed by its acquisitions in analysis and reporting, as well as metadata management
- **SAS Institute**—Analysis and reporting tools
- **Pyramid Technology**—Parallel processor family
- **Information Builders**—Focus analysis and reporting tools, and EDA/SQL middleware
- **Microsoft**—NT family, SQL Server engine, and the Microsoft family of development tools

This type of analysis can be used to select the component products in the build-your-own approach, or to select the anchor vendor (product) while gauging the technology risks.

## Data Warehouse Reference Architecture

The third perspective in analyzing vendors is from the role the vendor plays in supplying components of the reference architecture. From this perspective, the vendors can be categorized into three groups: solution or multiple component suppliers, suppliers of a few components, and data warehouse services suppliers (including systems integration).

**Services Suppliers (Systems Integration Suppliers).** Most systems integration services suppliers are partners or alliance members of one or more framework provider. And for some of the larger organizations, data warehouse is generally an extension of one of their current practices; for example, Price Waterhouse's Data Warehouse Initiative is a part of its Knowledge Management Practice.

Services suppliers include very large organizations such as Anderson Consulting, ISSC, EDS, Coopers Lybrand, Price Waterhouse, CSC, and AMS—offering for all sizes of enterprises a full menu of services from strategic business needs analysis to technology selection to data warehouse construction and deployment—and medium-to-small consulting firms like Hadden, Tanning Associates, and Indica Group—offering, in some cases, only data warehouse consulting services.

**Solution or Multiple Component Suppliers.** The data warehouse reference architecture consists of four blocks and four layers. Solution or multiple component suppliers offer products for blocks and layers. Many of these suppliers also offer consulting services to offer a kind of one-stop data warehouse solution. A sample list of vendors and the blocks and layers of the reference architecture addressed by a particular supplier is mapped in figure 12.6.

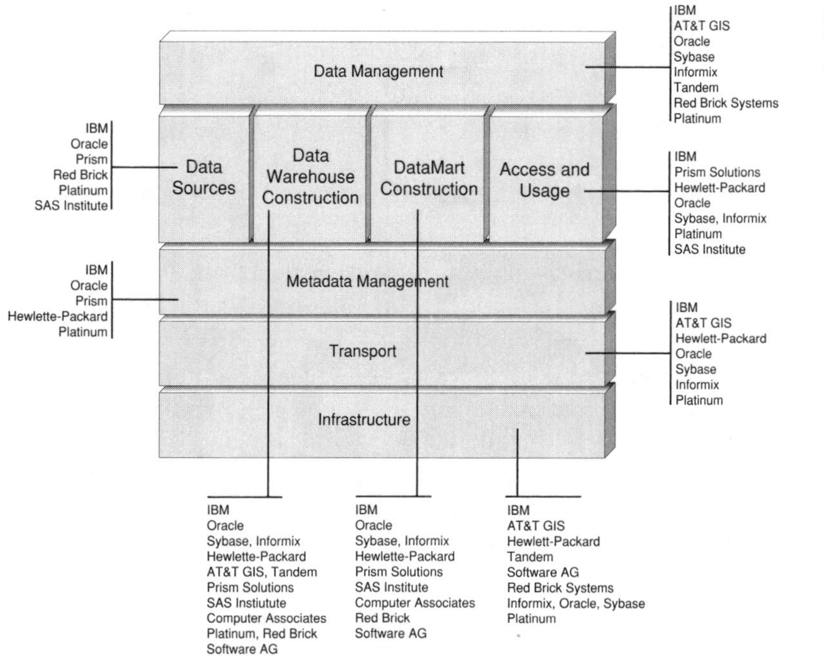


**Fig. 12.6**

*Solution suppliers.*

In figure 12.6, if a vendor is shown as addressing a particular block or layer, it does not imply that each sub-block or sub-layer is addressed. More detail analysis for the vendor's product is needed to understand what exact functionality the vendor product offers.

**Suppliers of Few Components.** Component suppliers address one or two or so of the blocks or layers of the reference architecture. A sample list of vendors and the blocks and layers of the reference architecture addressed by a particular supplier is mapped in figure 12.7.

**Fig. 12.7**

*Component suppliers.*

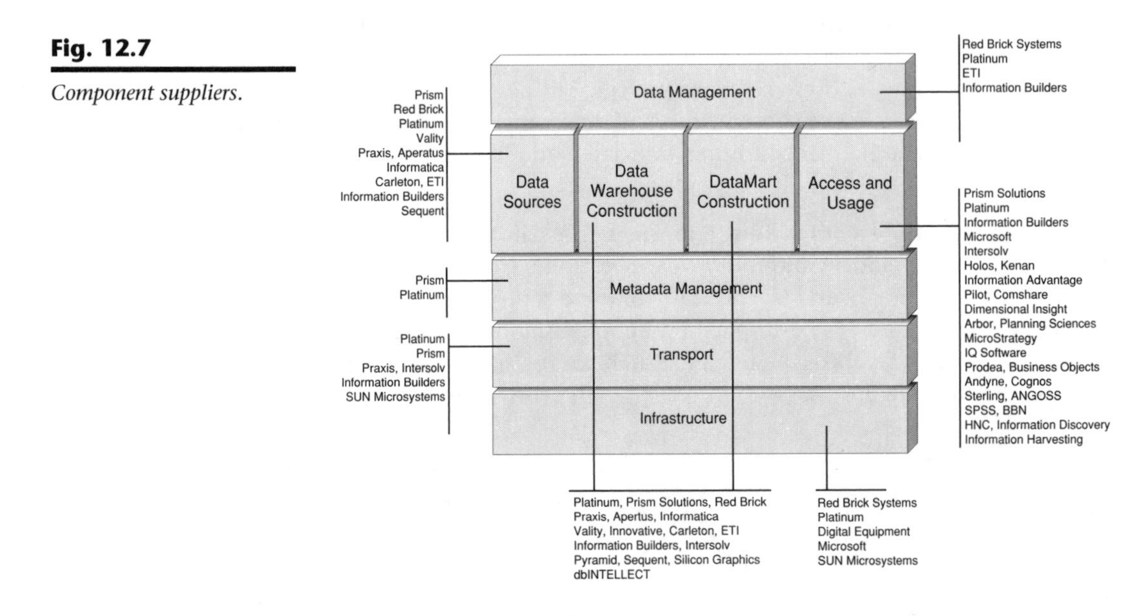


Figure 12.7 shows the following representative vendors for each block and layer of the reference architecture:

- **Data Sources (Extraction)**—Platinum technology, Red Brick, Prism Software, Praxis International, Apertus Technologies, Informatica, Carleton Corporation, ETI, Information Builders, and Sequent
- **Refinement and Reengineering**—Vality Technology, Platinum technology, Prism Software, Praxis International, Apertus Technologies, Informatica, Carleton Corporation, ETI, Information Builders, and Sequent
- **Data Warehouse and Data Mart**—Platinum technology, Red Brick, Prism Software, Praxis International, Apertus Technologies, Informatica, Carleton Corporation, ETI, Information Builders, Pyramid Technology, Sequent, Silicon Graphics, and dbINTELLECT Technologies
- **Access and Usage**—Platinum technology, Information Builders, Microsoft, Intersolv, Holos, Information Advantage, Pilot Software, Kenan Technologies, Comshare, Dimensional Insight, Arbor Software, Planning Sciences, MicroStrategy, Prodea, IQ Software, Business Objects, Andyne, Cognos, Sterling,

IBM Research, Information Discovery, ANGOSS Software, Information Harvesting, HNC Software, SPSS, BBN Software, and Customer Insight

- **Data Management**—Platinum Technology, Red Brick, ETI, and Information Builders
- **Metadata Management**—Prism Software, and Platinum technology
- **Transport**—Platinum technology, Prism Software, Intersolv, Information Builders, Praxis International, and SUN Microsystems
- **Infrastructure**—DEC, SUN Microsystems, Microsoft, and Platinum technology

Notice that in figure 12.7, if a vendor is shown as addressing a particular block or layer, it does not imply that each sub-block or sub-layer is addressed. More detail analysis for the vendor's product is required to understand what exact functionality the vendor product offers.

**Summary of Representative Suppliers.** The following is a summary list of representative solution and component suppliers categorized by reference architecture blocks and layers:

- **Data Sources (Extraction)**—IBM, Oracle, Platinum technology, Red Brick, Prism Software, Praxis International, Apertus Technologies, Informatica, Carleton Corporation, ETI, Information Builders, and Sequent
- **Refinement and Reengineering**—IBM, Oracle, Vality Technology, Platinum technology, Prism Software, Praxis International, Apertus Technologies, Informatica, Carleton Corporation, ETI, Information Builders, and Sequent
- **Data Warehouse and Data Mart**—IBM, Oracle, Sybase, Informix, Hewlett Packard, AT&T GIS, Tandem, SAS Institute, Software AG, Computer Associates, Platinum technology, Red Brick, Prism Software, Praxis International, Apertus Technologies, Informatica, Carleton Corporation, ETI, Information Builders, Pyramid Technology, Sequent, Silicon Graphics and dbINTELLECT Technologies
- **Access and Usage**—Platinum technology, Information Builders, Microsoft, Intersolv, Holos, Information Advantage, Pilot Software, Kenan Technologies, Comshare, Dimensional Insight, Arbor Software, Planning Sciences, MicroStrategy, Prodea, IQ Software, Business Objects, Andyne, Cognos, Sterling, IBM Research, Information Discovery, ANGOSS Software, Information Harvesting, HNC Software, SPSS, BBN Software, and Customer Insight
- **Data Management**—IBM, Oracle, Sybase, Informix, Computer Associates, Platinum technology, SAS Institute, Hewlett Packard, Red Brick, ETI, and Information Builders
- **Metadata Management**—IBM, Hewlett Packard, Prism Software, Oracle, and Platinum technology
- **Transport**—IBM, Hewlett Packard, Platinum technology, Prism Software, Oracle, Sybase, Intersolv, Information Builders, Praxis International, and SUN Microsystems

- **Infrastructure**—IBM, Hewlett Packard, DEC, SUN Microsystems, Microsoft, Computer Associates, Platinum technology, Oracle, Sybase, Informix, AT&T GIS, Tandem, Software AG, and SAS Institute

# Vendor Evaluation Guidelines

Given the range of architectures, frameworks, partnerships, and products, evaluating vendors is a challenging task. Enterprises must use the utmost care—data warehouse is a mission critical need, if not today, for sure tomorrow—in evaluating and selecting vendors and products. The reference architecture is an excellent tool to assist in understanding vendor offerings; see figures 12.8 and 12.9 as examples. The reference architecture provides a level field to compare the scope and functions of vendor products.

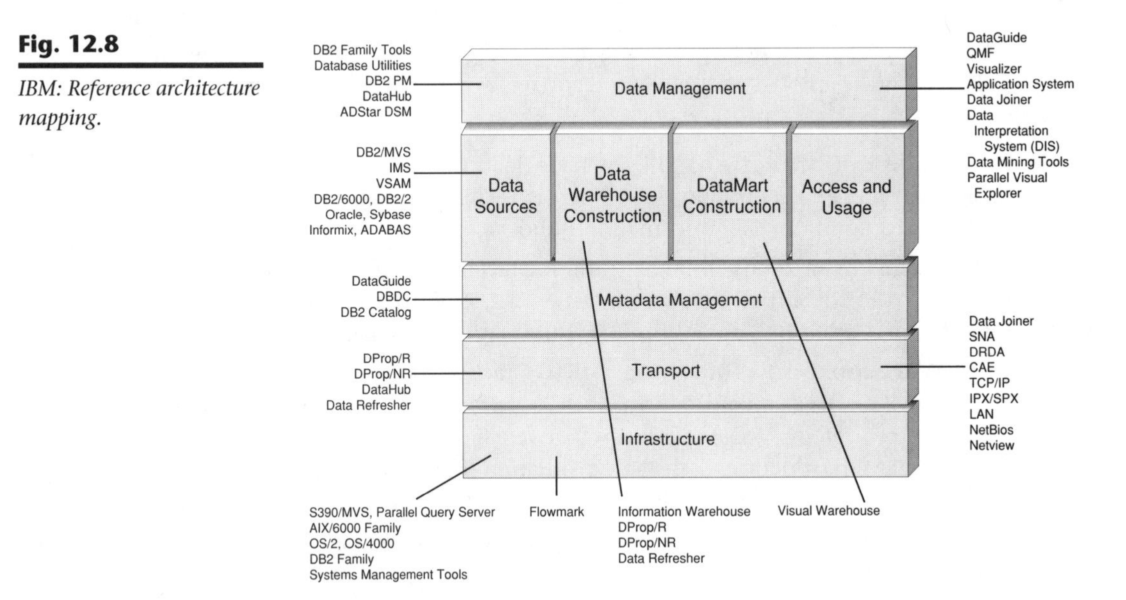


**Fig. 12.8**

*IBM: Reference architecture mapping.*

A set of general vendor evaluation guidelines follows.

## Vendor Reputation and Core Technology Competency

Readers are encouraged to discuss actual implementation experiences and challenges with vendors' customers. Check the data warehouse reference accounts in areas such as applicability to industry, data warehouse size, number of users, types of business users, and usage.

The vendor's core technology and competency is important, as shown earlier in figure 12.5.

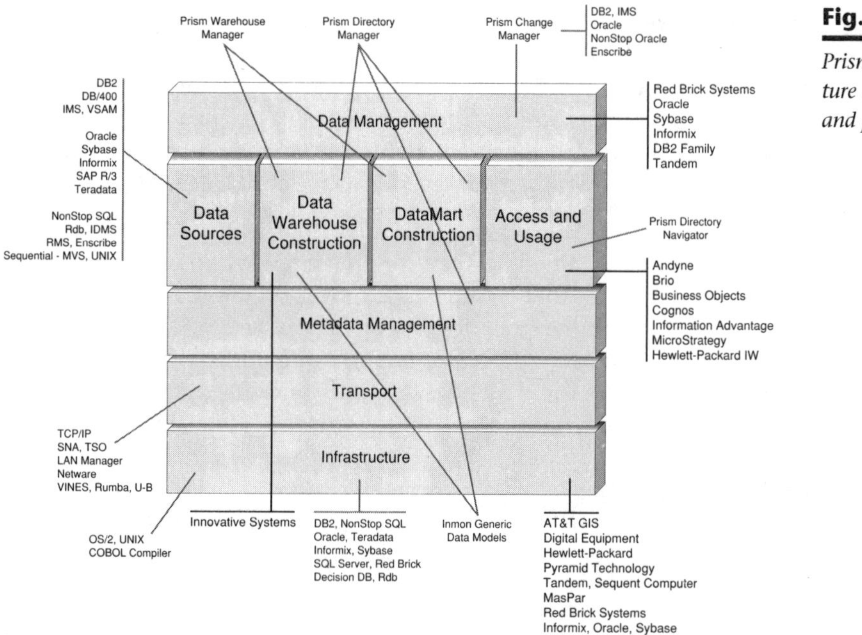


**Fig. 12.9**

*Prism: Reference architecture mapping of products and partners.*



## Product and Solution Competency

The data warehouse market has plenty of point products and very few solutions. Production grade installations for data warehousing beyond rudimentary decision support remain few and far between. Hence, the key challenge is in selecting vendors whose products today will meet the needs of tomorrow's solutions. The first focus must be on the vendor's architecture and its strategy to integrate the components, or pinpoint products—its own and its partners. The vendor's architecture must describe how products are integrated and/or interconnected, and what systems integration challenges the enterprise must prepare for. If the vendor has installed solutions, the references must be checked for applicability to the enterprise's industry, decision support needs, warehouse size, and so forth.

In addition, the solution must be examined in two important areas:

- **Data Management**—Data warehouse availability, data warehouse size scalability, data warehouse number of users scalability, interoperability and interconnection technology, replication, and systems administration and management (database tuning, network management, backup and recovery, diagnostics, automation of operations, etc.).
- **Metadata Management**—Extraction, storing, navigation, and access by technical and business users of all the metadata produced by each component of the solution, regardless of the fact that different vendors supplied different components.

## Ability to Walk the Talk and Recover from a Fall

In data warehouses, most vendors are more in the architecture and strategy phase and less in the delivery of solutions. At the same time, early experiences of data warehouse installations is that the data warehouse grows faster and is bigger than planned. You are encouraged to study the vendor's history in delivering on their strategies and technical competencies, specifically with regard to performance and scalability.

History shows that every vendor will at some time run into delivery and technology challenges. Additionally, there is an endless feature-driven horse race with vendors continuously leap-frogging each other. You are urged to examine the prospective vendor's history in either recovering from delivery or technology challenges, or from falling behind in the technology race. Also, it is important to understand how the vendor manages its customers in these adverse situations, and how forthcoming it is when adversity strikes.

## Quality of Partnerships

Since there is no market dominant one-stop solution from a vendor, partnerships or alliances are the order of the day. All partnerships are not equal, nor are all partners equal in a partnership. Again, you are encouraged to talk to partnership customers to better understand the quality of the partnership.

From a technical perspective, some of the issues requiring exploration include:

- Where, when, and how is the integration or interconnected accomplished and tested?
- How are product releases synchronized?
- How is metadata integrated and managed?
- How are customer identified problems analyzed and isolated?

## Scope of the Solution

Besides the issue of data warehouse and data mart, other scope issues include geographical coverage of the vendor and national languages supported. Enterprises contemplating world-wide roll-out of data warehouse installations must be aware of foreign language availability of all of the relevant products. For decentralized enterprises, it is essential to understand how the enterprise data warehouse is constructed and managed.

## On-going Technical Support and Service

Again, given that the data warehouse solution is constructed by integrating multiple products, as a rule from multiple vendors, on-going technical support and service is challenging. In this case, support and service is needed for lead vendor's products, partner products, problem isolation and resolution, performance tuning, and technology insertion.

## Professional Services

Integrating multiple products and multiple vendors is not for the faint-hearted. Vendors and partnerships need to be evaluated for planning and design methodologies, systems integration, growth management, and so forth. In cases such as Pyramid Technology, where the vendors offer some type of try-before-you-buy options, the quality of the professional services is easier to evaluate, or else talking to customers is suggested.

## Standards and Open Systems

Open systems is a baseline offering in data warehouse. Issues like computing platforms, and SQL for relational data store are mute. The areas for standard evaluation include:

- Match to corporate standards.
- Match to industry standards for infrastructure and transport layers of the reference architecture. This includes communications and networking standards, network management, and systems administration.

For the Metadata layer of the reference architecture, the formation of a Metadata Council to address data warehouse issues is important and needs to be tracked.

Overall vendors should be requested to indicate, by product and technology, which standards are supported and which standards are adhered to.

## Price

In addition to initial prices, key issues are: life cycle costs to administer and manage the solution, and level of systems integration required to build the initial warehouse and keep it refreshed both for data and technology.

# Summary

- Data warehouses can be implemented using three broad approaches: build your own data warehouse, which offers the ability to select best-of-breed products and services, but possesses the greatest systems integration risk; select a vendor framework, which decreases options available; and select an anchor vendor, which potentially decreases the options even more, but reduces the systems integration risk.
- From a data warehouse perspective, an integrated solution or integrated suite implies that the component products have been or are being designed, developed, tested, and deployed as a unified architectural solution. Integrated solutions inevitably yield better performance because they are optimized to work together. Another key advantage of integrated solutions is the potential that administration and monitoring tools are developed and tested with the components of the solution—and all within the same architecture. The limitation, of course, is the reduction in choices of components in the solution.

- Interconnected solutions have the inherent advantage of choice, now and in the future. The main challenges of interconnected solutions are: isolation of points of failure, administration and performance monitoring, continuing coordination, and integration of software releases.
- Readers are encouraged to discuss actual implementation experiences and challenges with vendors' customers.
- To assess technology risk when selecting a vendor, pay particular attention to the vendor's core business. This is where the vendor will invest and keep its technology competitive.
- Vendor evaluation must include vendor reputation; core technology and product competency; the vendor's past performance in delivering on its promises; the quality of the partnership; the scope of the solution; technical support and service; professional services availability; adherence to standards, price, and the data warehouse solution that will meet the business needs.

CHAPTER 13

# Vendor Survey: Strategies and Product Positioning

The focus of this chapter is to understand the data warehouse strategies of a large number of product vendors. Strategies are key to choosing vendor frameworks and architecture. Some representative frameworks and architectures are also illustrated, and salient or unique strategies or products are highlighted.

Vendor profiles were synthesized from corporate literature, customer discussions, and trade press comments. In addition, a detailed questionnaire was sent to many of the following vendors listed. The responses were analyzed to help classify the vendors and understand their strategies for data warehouse.

The vendors are listed in no particular order, except for the fact that the biggest vendors are earlier in the list.

## IBM

IBM's data warehouse solution is called A Data Warehouse Plus! IBM's focus is to deliver a full complement of products and services; its goal is to deliver an integrated solution based on a single architecture. R. Finkelstein of Performance Computing, Inc. stated, "It looks like IBM has the best overall, top-to-bottom, integrated data warehouse solution, based on a strong architecture." The DB2 family is the anchor of IBM's data warehouse strategy.

IBM has the advantage that a majority of the operational data to be extracted and stored in the data warehouse resides on IBM systems. Hence a tight integration is a natural outcome. The challenge at this time is that almost all IBM products are only for IBM platforms. Further, R. Finkelstein stated, "The only area of concern is the connectivity between third-party front-end tools and the DB2 family of relational databases." IBM's offerings in this area are rather weak. IBM currently has a partnership program to recruit more product and service partners.

IBM offers three data warehouse solutions:

- **Stand-alone data mart**—Focused on a department or business function organization, managed with minimal assistance from the IT organization.

- **Dependent data mart**—Similar to a stand-alone data mart, but connectivity to the data sources is controlled and managed by the IT organization.
- **Global warehouse**—Implemented and managed by IT, and supported by an enterprise architecture. This may imply both a centralized warehouse or a distributed one with data marts.

The major data warehousing functions supported by IBM are shown in figure 13.1.

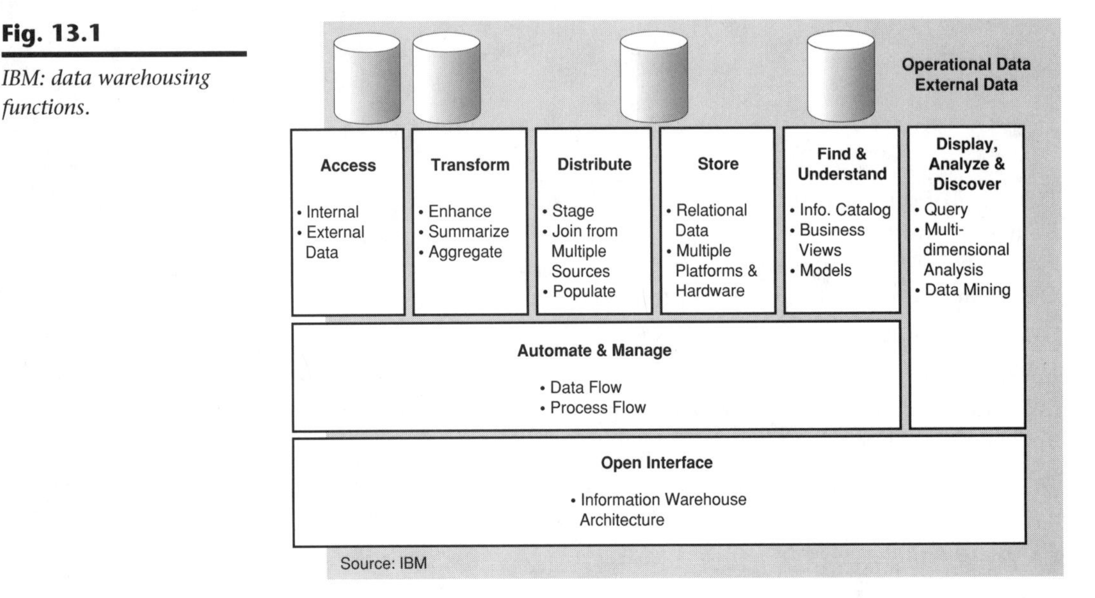


**Fig. 13.1**

*IBM: data warehousing functions.*

The major IBM products are shown in figure 13.2.

A global data warehouse solution can be based on DB2 for MVS, or DB2 for AIX Parallel Edition. The Visual Warehouse solution may be based on DB2 for OS/2, or DB2 for AIX, and is offered as the low cost-entry point. IBM addresses metadata management needs with the DataGuide family.

In data mining, IBM has an emerging family of knowledge discovery tools. The knowledge discovery techniques being applied by these tools are associations, sequential patterns, classifiers, and clustering. In addition, IBM Research offers the Parallel Visual Explorer—a powerful analysis technique for visualizing dimensional space with parallel coordinates, an alternate geometric representation of multidimensional data. The Parallel Visual Explorer is being applied in data mining applications in financial analysis, trading analysis, and manufacturing.

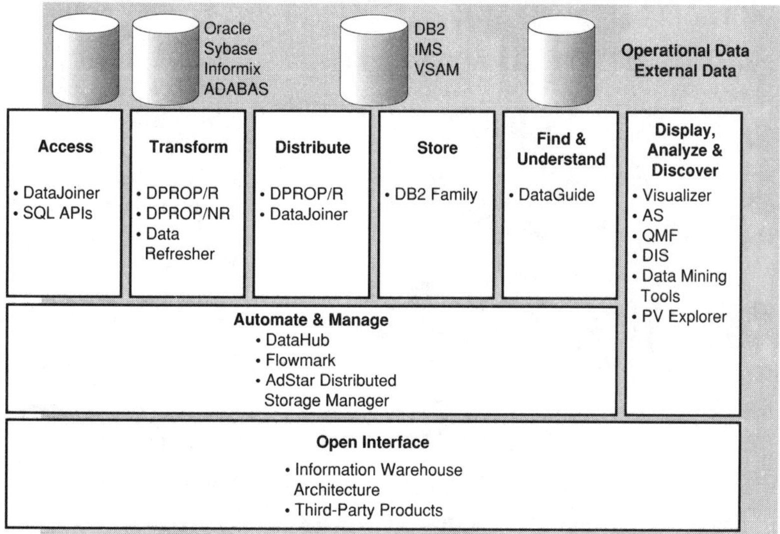


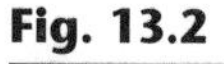

**Fig. 13.2**

*IBM: data warehouse architecture and products.*



# Oracle

Oracle offers a broad solution, with the focus on core competencies in data storage and management, vertical market applications, and data access and development tools. Its data warehouse solution can be characterized by two attributes—the breadth of Oracle's product line, and the number of partners in its Warehouse Technology Initiative (WTI) (see fig. 13.3). Oracle also is in a position to leverage its Systems Management Tools Initiative (SMTI) to meet systems administration and performance monitoring needs. The strength of Oracle's offering comes from its RDBMS engine, Oracle7, which is being continually enhanced to meet data warehouse functionality needs, its vertical market applications that offer the potential of pre-fab data warehouses, the breadth of its technology for development and data analysis, and the availability of third-party software products.

Figure 13.3 shows that Oracle is dependent on partners for data refinement and re-engineering, shown as Scrubbing Transform tools.

Oracle has grouped its WTI partners into three categories—design products (three partners), build products (15 partners), and analyze products (20 partners). From a data warehouse perspective, SMTI partners are grouped into five categories—administration products to administer databases and networks (ten partners); analysis products to improve performance and resource utilization (15 partners); monitoring and diagnostic products (20 partners); operations products to automate regular administrative tasks, for example, backup and scheduling of data warehouse extracts (24 partners); and interoperability components to enable communications between heterogeneous systems and networks (four partners). Please note that quite a few partners are in multiple categories, both for WTI and SMTI.

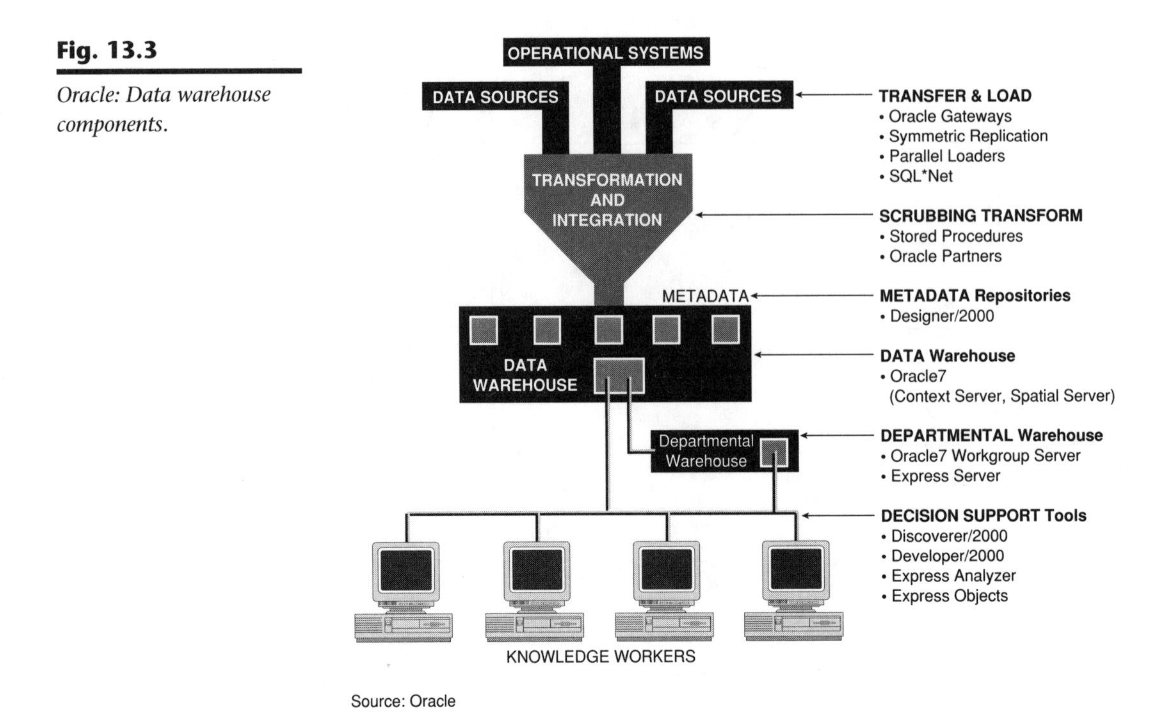


**Fig. 13.3**

*Oracle: Data warehouse components.*

# Hewlett Packard

Hewlett Packard's data warehouse offering is driven by its OpenWarehouse program. OpenWarehouse is characterized as a framework to build data warehouses based on best-of-class HP, and third-party hardware and software components. The anchors of HP's offerings are its UNIX platforms and its Intelligent Warehouse data warehouse management software product. The OpenWarehouse framework allows a choice of RDBMS, refinement and re-engineering tools, and data access and usage tools (see fig. 13.4). The OpenWarehouse partner program is specifically geared to recruit partners to offer the choices mentioned in the previous sentence.

The OpenWarehouse program also offers consulting methodologies and services for rapid deployment of data warehouses. The Intelligent Warehouse includes one of the few data warehouse usage monitoring tools.

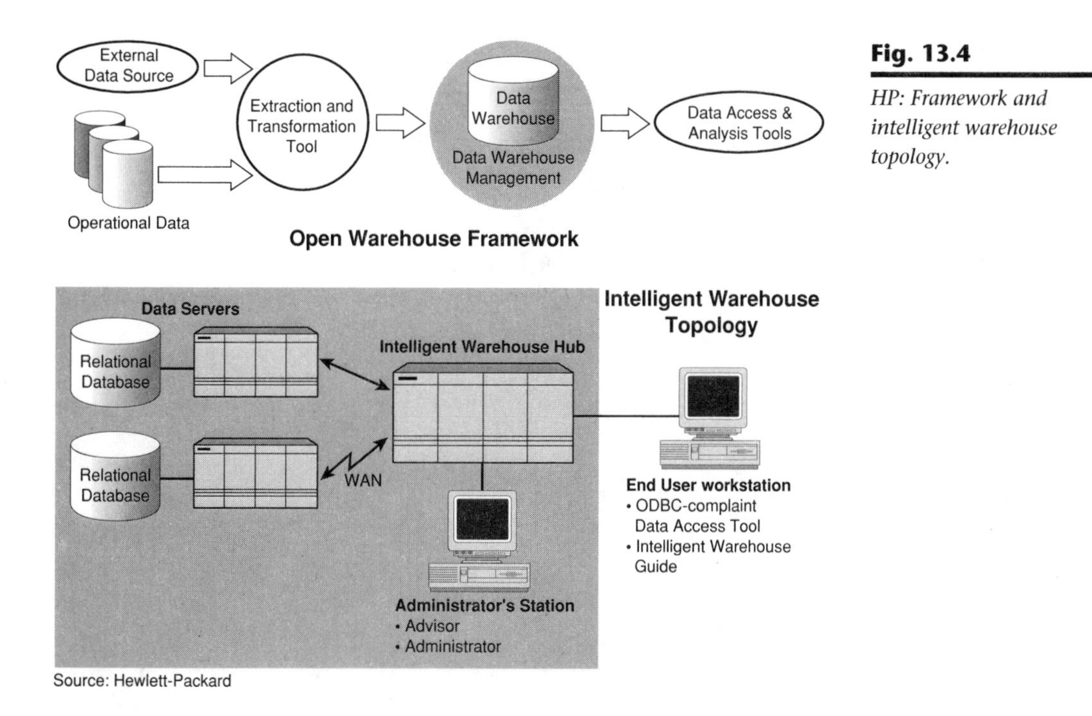


**Fig. 13.4**

*HP: Framework and intelligent warehouse topology.*

# Sybase

Sybase's corporate strategies focus on three markets: OLTP, data warehousing and decision support, and "mass deployment" of information throughout the enterprise. Its data warehouse strategy is embodied in its framework "Warehouse WORKS" (see fig. 13.5). Sybase's strength lies in its RDBMS engine (System 11), its data base connect and access capability (OmniCONNECT), and its development tools (Powerbuilder). Sybase continues to broaden its product line and product functionality through acquisitions. For example, the engine is being improved for data warehouse with features like bit-indexing acquired from Expressway Technology.

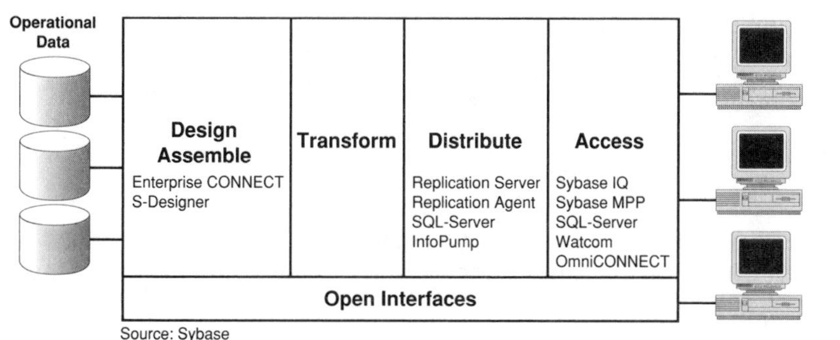

**Fig. 13.5**

*Sybase: Warehouse WORKS framework.*

Like its competitors, Sybase continues to build a stable of partners for its data warehouse solution.

# Informix Software

Informix Software's data warehouse strategy is aimed at growing the market for its RDBMS engine based on its Dynamic Scalable Architecture. Its data warehouse architecture, shown in figure 13.6, consists of four technologies—relational database, data warehouse management software, data access tools, and open systems platform.

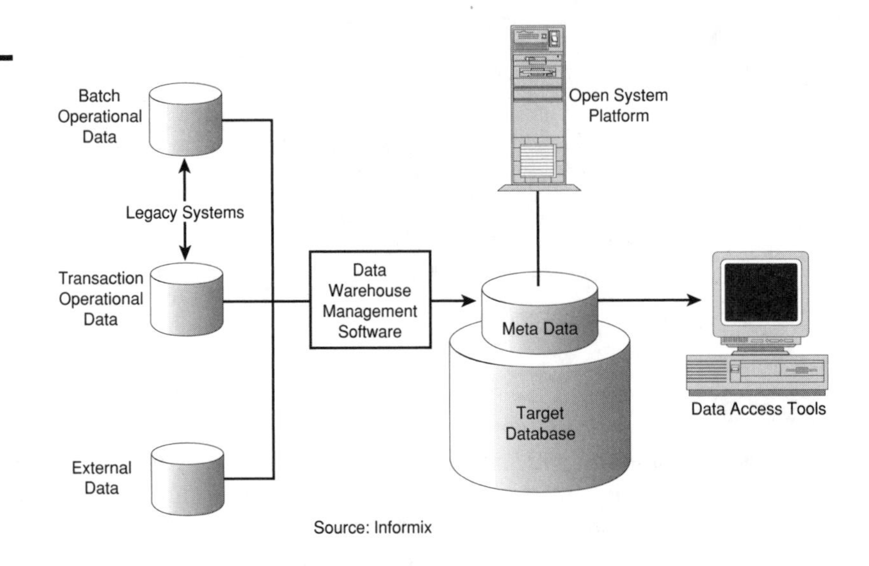


**Fig. 13.6**

*Informix: data warehouse architecture.*

Informix has established partnerships with multiple vendors for three technologies: data warehouse management software, data access tools, and open systems platform. To keep its database engine competitive, Informix first acquired Stanford Technology and its relational OLAP product line and then acquired Illustra Information Technologies for its nontraditional data management technology. The Illustra technology will be integrated into the relational engine to enhance support of spatial, video, text, and other nonnumeric data.

# AT&T GIS

The core of AT&T GIS' strategy is to address enterprise needs where the worlds of decision support systems and operational systems converge. It offers a sophisticated solution called the Enterprise Information Factory (EIF), leveraging its experience with its Teradata database management system and its parallel processing technologies.

From the EIF perspective, the data warehouse is a passive decision support system—ask questions, get answers, and then make decisions. The EIF is an active system where the decisions from a data warehouse are put into actions. The EIF is like an active operational data warehouse. The EIF framework envisions an evolution from currently separate operational/production systems and data warehouses, to a new extended environment consisting of data warehouse and operational environment communicating through active industry applications (see fig. 13.7). These active industry applications convert the decisions derived from the data warehouse into actions that impact the operational system.

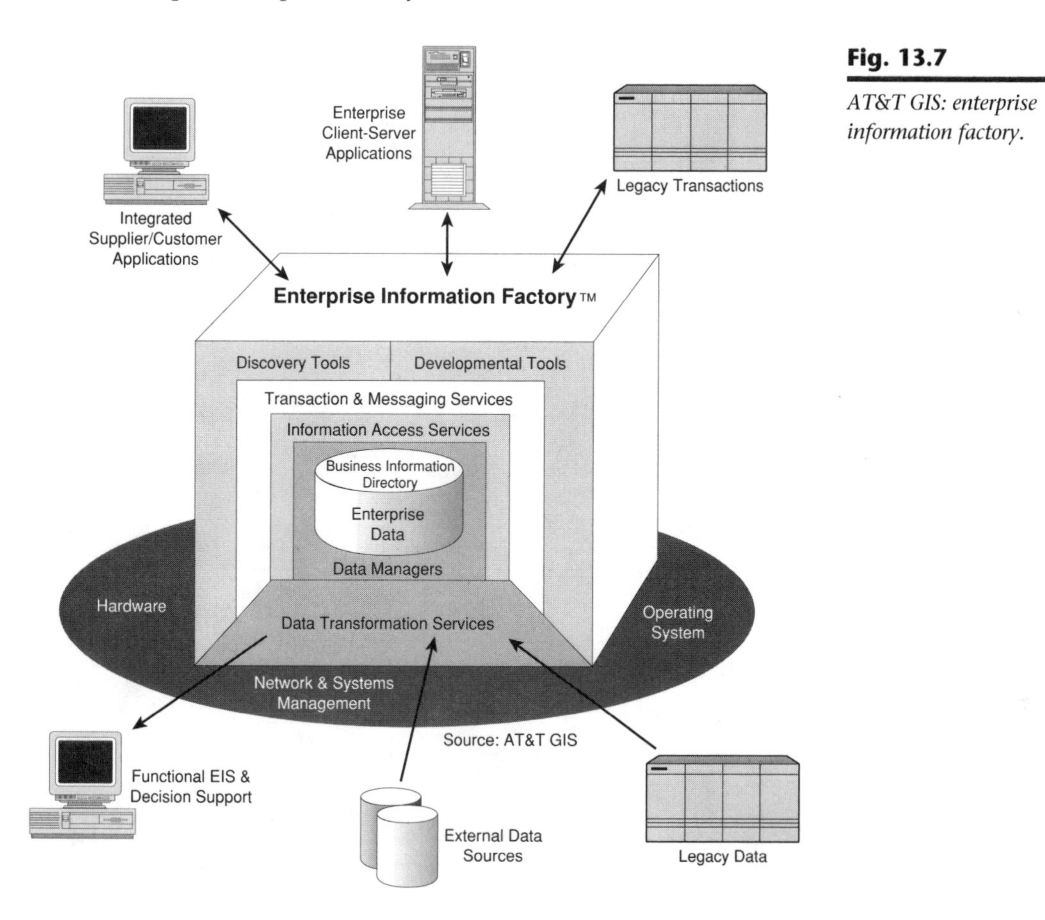


**Fig. 13.7**

*AT&T GIS: enterprise information factory.*

AT&T GIS' market focus is on industries where enterprises want to use data warehouse technology to change the basis of competition and to rationalize and leverage the enterprise's relationships to its customers. Targeted industry sectors include banking, insurance, retail, and telecommunications.

# SAS Institute

SAS Institute has provided strong data management, data analysis, and reporting functionality for 20 years. SAS expects to leverage its strength in powerful information management and data analysis across a broad range of platforms and database types. SAS is positioning itself to be a total data warehouse solution provider (see fig. 13.8). Its data warehouse solution is expected to leverage its competencies in the following:

- Data access with its extraction engine that supports a very large number of operational data stores—both relational and nonrelational
- Data transformation and manipulation using its 4GL
- Data storage engine with multidimensional functionality
- An impressive and broad set of analytical methods and tools for informational processing, analytical or multidimensional processing, and statistical analysis for data mining

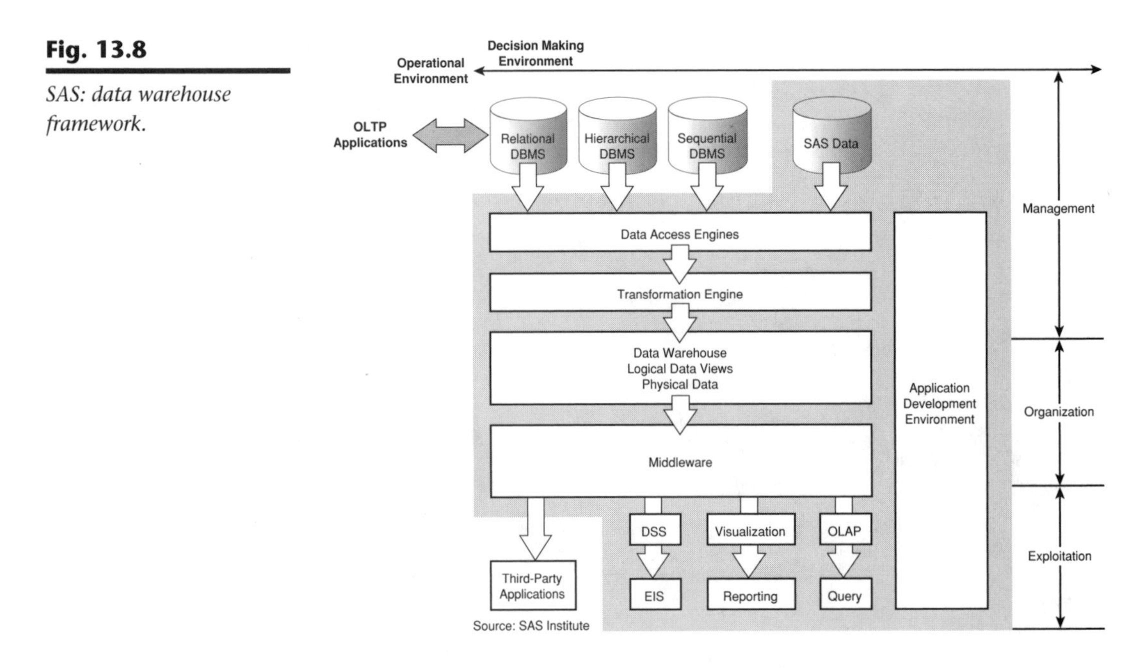


**Fig. 13.8**

*SAS: data warehouse framework.*

SAS is a premier supplier of statistical analysis tools for data mining. It is expanding its capabilities in metadata storage and management, and the management of the overall data warehouse environment from extraction to storage to access.

Historically, SAS is a technology company and is very loyal to its customers. It is developing partnerships with other vendors and service providers.

# Software AG

Software AG's strategy is to offer a full end-to-end solution through its Open Data Warehouse Initiative (ODWI). ODWI is based on the following:

- Its core products (ADABAS and Natural 4GL)

- Proprietary and third-party tools for data extraction and data analysis
- An automated Warehouse Manager

The Warehouse Manager, SourcePoint, is a UNIX-based warehouse administration tool to automate the process of data extraction, transport, and loading of data into a data warehouse.

Software AG is expected to continue to increase the efforts of its integration between its tools and third-party tools, including the integration of the metadata of each tool. At the same time, it offers a choice of database stores, including Oracle, Sybase, Informix, and CA-Ingres.

From a marketing perspective, Software AG has built close relationships with Carleton Corporation and Red Brick. It also participates in the partnership or alliance program of other vendors, such as Oracle.

# Platinum technology

Platinum technology's corporate strategy is to provide a comprehensive and integrated suite of software products to manage the open systems environment in each enterprise. It has developed the Platinum Open Enterprise Management Systems (POEMS) framework in which data warehousing is one of five solutions or categories offered. As a part of POEMS, Platinum has defined a data warehouse solution framework consisting of five functional groups: data replication and refinement, data movement/distribution, data access and analysis, repository, and warehouse database administration (see fig. 13.9).

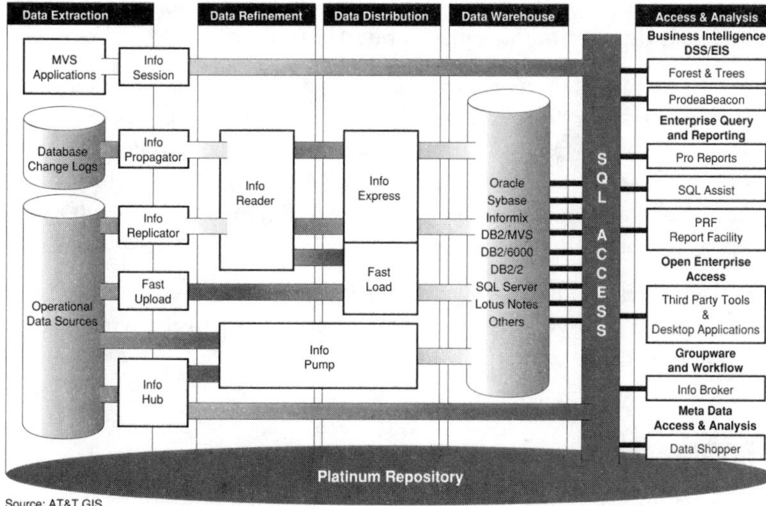


**Fig. 13.9**

*Platinum: data warehouse solution.*

Platinum's data warehouse solution is planned to deliver an enterprise-wide decision support system via the following:

- Metadata sharing and management with repository technology
- A comprehensive set of competitive point products to address specific IT needs
- Integrated systems management of the point products using the metadata in the repository and messaging technology

To quickly participate and achieve critical mass in the data warehouse arena, Platinum has acquired over a dozen small-to-medium companies. This has brought it technologies in non-DB2 database management—metadata management and repository, relational database access and reporting, software distribution, and help-desk management. Most of these are considered enabling technologies.

In data warehouse, Platinum expects to play to its strengths in systems management, with metadata management as a key differentiator. Platinum is now challenged with potentially overlapping products, multiple development centers, diverse cultures, and integrating all the acquired products within a single architecture. Platinum is an active member in many partnerships and alliances.

# Red Brick Systems

Red Brick is a pioneer in and is exclusively in the data warehouse market. Its goal is to become the next large database company. Its product strategy is focused on offering a market-leading data warehouse-tuned relational database for data warehouses only (not OLTP) and related software products. Red Brick also offers an architecture guideline, Universal Data Warehouse Blueprint, to assist enterprises in building and growing data warehouses from departmental to enterprise-wide in scope. It offers tools for data warehouse administration, query diagnostics, copy management, and metadata management. From the reference architecture perspective, it offers products for the data warehouse block and the data management and infrastructure layers.

In addition to products, Red Brick offers four fast start solution templates for retail, telecommunications, financial services, and health care decision support applications. This is projected to reduce the up-front planning and cost-justification phase of a data warehouse project from three to six months to a couple of months. Each solution template includes data warehouse data model and schema design, schema implemented in Red Brick warehouse, and a set of sample queries.

Red Brick has its own product and marketing partnership program. Its aim is to offer a Red Brick database anchored complete solution. It also participates in the partnership programs of other vendors.

# Silicon Graphics

Silicon Graphics data warehouse strategy is focused on its parallel processing computing platforms and its powerful data visualization technology. It is partnering with product vendors and systems integrators to leverage its data visualization technology to offer visual functions for analysis of very large databases and data mining applications.

## Pyramid Technology

Pyramid Technology's data warehouse strategy is focused on assisting customers in deploying operations critical data warehouses, which are data warehouses for the operational environment. Operational data warehouses need high levels of data availability, scalability, and data integrity (see the section on AT&T GIS earlier in this chapter). To meet its strategic goals, Pyramid is leveraging its core competency (parallel technology-based, high-end, open-enterprise database servers) to meet the needs of enterprises in customer service, marketing, and inventory management. Pyramid's market focus is on the telecommunications, retail, financial services, health care, and manufacturing sectors.

Pyramid offers a full data warehouse solution through its Smart Warehouse program. This program is aimed at integrating UNIX server technology with partner products for data extraction, data warehouse loading and storage, and data access and analysis. A unique aspect of its Smart Warehouse program is a try-before-you-buy SmartStart offering. SmartStart's goal is to allow the customer to test and validate ROI assumptions before making a costly and large investment in hardware and software. SmartStart is a three-phase program that includes a methodology: project definition, pilot project, and production system. Each phase has clear objectives, deliverables, and exit points. The customer can exit after the first two phases. Customers satisfied with the pilot can then invest in the solution that is already installed as part of the pilot—thus ensuring a smooth rollover into production.

The Smart Warehouse program has recruited a large number of partners for both products and services. Additionally, Pyramid participates in the partnership program of other vendors.

## Sequent Computer Systems

Sequent's data warehouse solution is focused by its experience on a multi-tiered architecture. In this architecture, a staging area named *distribution warehouse* is the common area from which data marts are populated. Operational data is sent to the data marts via the distribution warehouse. Data marts are subject-oriented data stores that are denormalized using star schemas and snowflake schemas to improve query responsiveness. The data warehouse is considered a virtual collection of both distribution warehouse and data marts.

In Sequent's experience, distribution warehouses are small not large, and data marts are large not small. The distribution warehouse only needs to hold as much data as is needed to supply the data marts; furthermore, the distribution warehouse can hold the data in normalized mode with minimal indexing—thus also easing data integrity issues. Data marts typically have two or three times the storage requirements due to denormalization and indexing.

In addition to its parallel technology based high-end UNIX servers, Sequent offers the following:

- **DecisionPoint for Financials**—A ready-to-finish corporate financial data warehouse for Oracle Financial's customers. This quick-start solution includes the data warehouse model, Oracle Financial's data extraction software, database and servers, and query and reporting tools.
- **DecisionPoint Method**—An end-to-end methodology for constructing a data warehouse using star-join schema, a prototype, and a reiterate approach.

Like other solution providers, Sequent has a partnership program and participates in the partnership/alliance programs of many other vendors.

# Information Builders

Information Builders, Inc (IBI) offers a data warehouse framework called Enterprise Data Access/Data Warehouse that leverages its strengths in EDA/SQL middleware, and its FOCUS database and 4GL. The framework additionally includes a methodology and a data warehouse analysis tool called SiteAnalyzer. SiteAnalyzer is a Windows-based data access and usage monitoring and analysis tool. It provides information as to what operational data is being currently accessed so that user needs and data demands can be understood before the data warehouse is designed and built. It is also a data warehouse planning and requirements gathering tool.

IBI is a member of numerous partnerships and alliances.

# Prism Software

Prism Software is exclusively in the data warehouse market. Its solution is based on the conceptual approach and development methodology advanced by W. H. Inmon, one of its founders. Its architectural framework envisions products that actively work together to offer a full solution (see fig. 13.10). The framework includes an active metadata-driven approach, which allows the capture, store, and management of information about changes to the data warehouse over time.

The Prism warehouse manager extracts, transforms, and integrates data from operational systems, and generates an information directory of metadata in the data warehouse. The Prism directory manager is designed to help business users understand and use the contents of the data warehouse.

Prism also offers pre-fab data models called Inmon Generic Data Models—an industry first. These models provide templates of data warehouse designs for a range of industry and business functions.

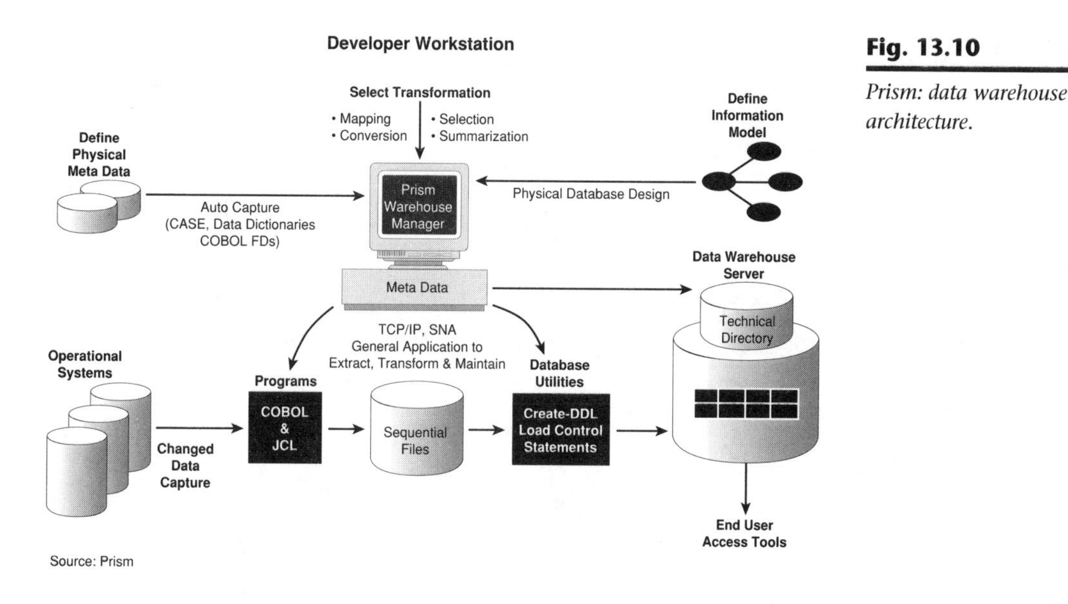


**Fig. 13.10**

*Prism: data warehouse architecture.*



Like other solution providers, Prism has a partnership program and participates in the partnership/alliance programs of many other solution providers.

# Informatica Corporation

Informatica's strategy is to develop single-subject data marts with a bottom-up and user-driven perspective. Its vision is a distributed warehouse consisting of interconnected data marts. Its product, OpenBridge, is a metadata-driven solution for data extraction and storage (see fig. 13.11). It maps to the data sources and the data warehouse block of the reference architecture.

OpenBridge consists of five components around a common metadata repository and data warehouse data store:

- **Designer**—Consists of a source analyzer, a warehouse schema designer, and a transformation designer. There is no 4GL for transformation, only the extraction and transformation rules are generated and stored in the repository for loading by the Load Server.
- **Server Manager**—Controls and manages the population of the data warehouse—initial load, full refresh, or changes only.
- **Repository Manager**—Creates and maintains the OpenBridge repository and its metadata. It also contains a metadata browser.
- **Load Server**—The key component that extracts the data from the selected operational data sources, transforms it according to the business rules generated by the Designer, and populates the data warehouse.

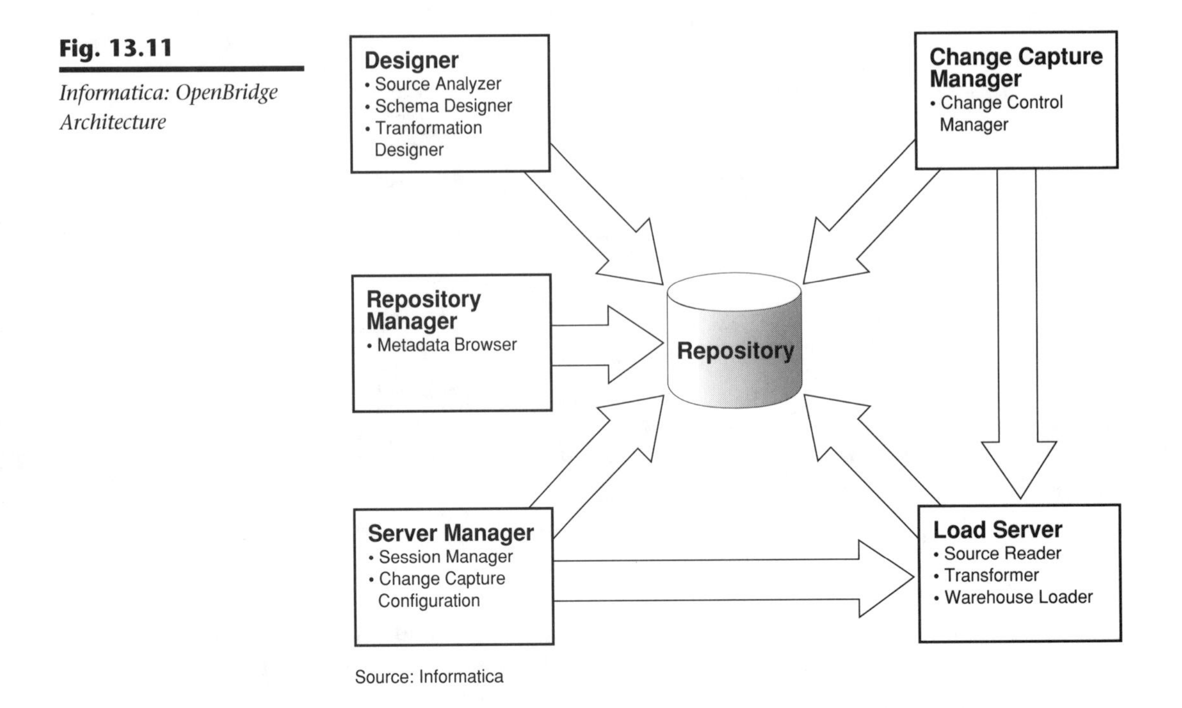


**Fig. 13.11**

*Informatica: OpenBridge Architecture*

- **Change Capture Manager**—Refreshes the data warehouse with changes in the operational data sources.

Informatica is a member of multiple solution provider partnership programs.

# Vality Technology

Vality focuses exclusively on helping IT organizations attain and maintain high quality data in the data warehouse. It offers a technology and methodology to investigate, standardize, condition, transform, and integrate the data from multiple operational databases, legacy data, and external sources. The aim is to recondition the data and raise the data quality before migrating it to the data warehouse. Data quality has been, and will continue to be, the Achilles' heel of many data warehouse projects.

The company's principal product, the Integrity Data Re-engineering Tool, is available for IBM MVS systems only—where most of the operational data exists anyway. A unique feature of the product is its ability to dig deep into actual operational or legacy data to surface essential business metadata missing from traditional data dictionaries and copybooks. This information, including obscure and undocumented business practices, is essential to build and validate the warehouse data model. One could call this metadata mining to discover hidden entities, entity relationships, and unknown or undocumented business rules.

Vality is a member of IBM's Information Warehouse partnership program.

## Evolutionary Technologies International (ETI)

ETI's strategy is to automate and expedite the migration of data between dissimilar storage environments, thus saving time and cost of manual data conversion. Its ETI EXTRACT Tool Suite is a component of a full data warehouse solution within many frameworks. The tool suite offers the following:

- Data collection, conversion, and migration to data warehouses
- Interfaces to specialized data refinement and reengineering tools
- Automatic generation and execution of programs in the appropriate language of the source and data warehouse platform, along with necessary JCL and scripts
- A metadata facility to track the schema definitions, source-to-target mapping, business rules, transformation rules, and interdatabase relationships
- A graphical user interface to define the data selection criteria, transformation conditions and rules, and movement

ETI's tool suite supports bidirectional interface between the operational data sources and the data warehouse. It also supports native database access. ETI has its own partnership program for both service and product partners, and participates in other industry partnership programs.

## Carleton

Carleton's primary focus is data warehousing. It offers a full solution—from planning to methodology to data warehouse construction. Carleton's flagship product CARLETON PASSPORT is aimed at automating the development and maintenance of data warehouse. Passport uses a metadata-driven environment to construct and populate the data warehouse. The Passport product line offers the following:

- A centralized metadata directory with global access and control. All required source and target database definitions are stored in the directory in a relational form.
- Direct access of legacy databases for extraction and transformation.
- Data formatting for target relational environment.
- Complex transformation logic for data refinement and re-engineering.
- Delta change propagation to data warehouse.
- A workbench to develop the Passport application for uploading to data warehouse platform.

The Carleton product line is available on all IBM and compatible mainframes as well as PCs, and is in cooperation with S/370, OS/400, and OS/2 operating environments.

Additionally, Carleton is the exclusive distributor of Earl Hadden's methodology for implementing a data warehouse.

# Praxis International

Praxis offers the OmniReplicator as a part of its OmniWarehouse data warehousing program. The OmniReplicator is used to support bidirectional replication between heterogeneous data stores. OmniReplicator assists data warehouse users in migrating data from operational databases to data warehouses or data marts. A companion product, OmniReplicator Administrator, allows the data warehouse database administrator to set up the replication schemes.

# Arbor Software

Arbor is focused on offering high performance, multidimensional database software for complex business planning and analysis applications. Its products include the following:

- **Essbase Analysis Server**—A multidimensional engine available on UNIX, NT, and OS/2 platforms.
- **Essbase Application Tools**—Software modules for currency conversion, SQL drill-through, SQL interface, and an extended spreadsheet toolkit.

Essbase is used by business managers and analysts for data access and reporting, planning, and multidimensional analysis. Arbor has cooperative development and marketing partnerships with numerous vendors. Arbor is a member of multiple partnership programs.

# Pilot Software

Pilot Software is focused on providing business users and IT professionals the tools and solutions to access and analyze mission critical business information. Its LightShip suite is a client/server software system for building and using OLAP technology based solutions. The LightShip Suite includes:

- **LightShip Server**—A multidimensional data server that is based on OLAP technology
- **LightShip Modeler**—A builder of models for applications such as financial models, budgets, forecasts, strategic plans, and operational analyses
- **LightShip Professional**—A graphical user interface client to access and analyze the data
- **LightShip Link**—A common access tool to relational data sources

Pilot also offers LightShip Sales and Marketing Intelligence System (SMIS)—a ready-to-use solution for sales and marketing professionals. In addition to the LightShip Suite, SMIS contains modules for 80/20 analysis, ranking, and ad hoc and standard reports. Pilot is partnering with numerous product vendors and service providers.

# Dimensional Insight

Dimensional Insight offers an integrated suite of analysis and reporting products called CrossTarget. CrossTarget consists of two components:

- **Builder**—A server-based multidimensional engine.
- **Diver**—A graphical user interface client. An interesting feature of Diver is its ability to join multiple-multidimensional models to create a new virtual model.

CrossTarget is available for Windows, NT, Macintosh, OS/2, UNIX, and VMS platforms.

# Information Advantage

Information Advantage (IA) is focused exclusively on business analysis applications that leverage strategic data warehouse investments. Its products are designed on a three-tier architecture: server-centric client/server. IA's product line, DecisionSuite, is an integrated solution architected to offer relational OLAP analysis against data warehouses and data marts. It includes functions such as the following:

- Delivery of information, reports, and alerts to business users using software agent technology
- What-if analysis, business charting, integration to GIS mapping systems, operational applications
- The power user capability to author reports, analyze scenarios, and command agents to navigate the data warehouse and deliver reports and alerts
- Resources and security management for DBAs and administrators
- Collaborative information sharing among business users

The three-tier architecture provides for scalability and performance by off-loading both the client and the database server. IA is a member of multiple partnership programs.

# Prodea Software

Prodea Software's strategy is to offer decision support tools that are integrated with workflow applications. The goal is to create decision-support lifecycles in which information yields action, not just reports. Prodea offers two companion products:

- **ProdeaBeacon**—A relational OLAP tool for multidimensional analysis available in a three-tier architecture, thus offering improved performance and scalability due to off-loading of both the client and the database server.
- **ProdeaSynergy**—A workflow tool used to integrate desktop applications in automated workflows.

In combination, ProdeaBeacon automates the retrieval of information from the data warehouse, and ProdeaSynergy automates the dissemination of that information to business users. Prodea is a member of multiple vendor partnerships.

Also note that Prodea Software has agreed to be acquired by Platinum technology (refer to fig. 13.9).

# MicroStrategy

MicroStrategy is focused on providing relational OLAP (ROLAP) products to assist business users and IT professionals to perform multidimensional analysis of information stored in relational data warehouses and data marts. Its architecture has a central ROLAP engine that provides business users with a multidimensional conceptual view of the data in the data warehouse and can dynamically transform data queries into SQL execution plans. The architecture offers one-tier, two-tier, or three-tier options with the goal of supporting very large data warehouses. Within this architecture, MicroStrategy offers the following four products:

- **DSS Agent**—An ad hoc ROLAP analysis, query and reporting, drill-down and pivoting, and workflow automation using software agents
- **DSS Server**—A ROLAP engine with a rule-based Query Governor, a warehouse administrator, and job scheduler
- **DSS Executive**—Used to build an Executive Information System (EIS) on top of existing decision support queries and reports
- **DSS Architect**—A design tool to define the multidimensional model for the relational data store

MicroStrategy is a member of many partnership programs.

# Brio Technology

Brio's strategy is to enable business users and IT professionals to get more value out of their data warehouses through easy and effective data access, and multidimensional analysis and reporting. Its BrioQuery tool is a visual informational processing tool with built-in multidimensional analysis. It is architected to leverage the performance capabilities inherent in star-schema designed data warehouses. It also has a repository for central management of shared queries and automatic distribution of them. It uses the metadata of the database. BrioQuery, available for both the Macintosh and PC environment, is offered in the following three modes:

- **Navigator**—Business users can query only using predefined data models
- **Explorer**—Power users can query with predefined data models and create new ones
- **Designer**—IT professionals can create predefined queries, reports, and data models

Brio is a member of numerous partnerships and alliances.

# IQ Software

IQ Software is primarily focused on delivering the access, query, reporting, and OLAP functions to seamlessly leverage the data in a warehouse into business intelligence. Its IQ/Objects product line has been architected to address the requirements of data warehousing environments—data size scalability, number of users scalability, and complex query management. IQ's products include the following:

- **IQ/Objects**—Object-based querying and reporting tools that can access heterogeneous data stores as well as correlate output from multiple queries.
- **IQ/SmartServer**—Three-tier architecture-based server for intelligently partitioning data access and reporting functions among clients, application servers, and database servers.
- **IQ/Vision**—A dynamic OLAP tool for multidimensional and drill-down data analysis. (IQ Software has a joint development agreement with Sinper Corporation to integrate Sinper's multidimensional engine with IQ products.)

IQ Software participates in multiple partnership programs.

# Business Objects

Business Objects' strategy is to offer graphical client/server tools that allow business users to manipulate and analyze data in relational databases. It provides query and reporting tools and additional multidimensional analysis functions. Business Objects is available for Windows, Macintosh, and UNIX environments.

# Information Harvesting

Information Harvesting focuses exclusively in the data mining area. Its International Harvester product is a hybrid knowledge discovery tool that combines decision tree/rule induction algorithms, statistics, and fuzzy reasoning. The tool engine is available on UNIX and Microsoft NT platforms, including some SMP and MPP platforms. Vertical market add-ons are available from third-party software suppliers for insurance, retail, banking, and health care sectors.

# Information Discovery

Information Discovery provides the knowledge discovery tool, IDIS (Information Discovery System), to mine hidden patterns, business rules, and anomalies in the data warehouse. IDIS uses statistics internally and applies a rule-discovery approach to generate and test hypotheses. The automatic hypotheses formation and testing cycle continues until interesting rules and patterns emerge. The discover rules can be utilized for predictive modeling and anomaly detection. A companion product, Neural IDIS, combines neural net technology and rules discovery.

IDIS is available on Windows and UNIX platforms and some SMP and MPP systems. It is a member of multiple partnership programs.

# HNC Software

HNC Software is focused on the application of neural network technology for knowledge discovery in order to use the knowledge for predictive modeling. HNC offers two products:

- **DataBase Mining Workstation (DMW)**—A general purpose tool to create and use neural-network models
- **DataBase Mining Marksman**—A neural-network tool focused on marketing applications

# SPSS

SPSS focuses on providing statistical solutions for survey research, marketing and sales, quality improvement, government reporting, and education. From the data warehouse perspective, SPSS products can be used in data mining applications using statistical analysis techniques. Its neural connection tool can be used for predictive modeling, classification, and data segmentation. SPSS offers a wide range of tools that support a comprehensive list of statistical analysis techniques.

# Summary

- The data warehouse market has quickly drawn a very large number of vendors: from vendors with multibillion dollar revenues to one million dollar revenues; from vendors with frameworks and multiple products to niche or single product suppliers; and from well-established companies to start-ups. At the same time, no single vendor has the complete breadth of products to meet the full complement of the enterprise's needs. In such an environment, IT must carefully select vendors and products by understanding both the data warehouse technology market, and a vendor's investments and commitment to data warehouse solutions. This will assist the enterprise in understanding and managing risks.
- Finally, data warehouse solutions are promising, but emerging, and there's much work to be done before data warehousing lives up to its potential. IT organizations must move cautiously and be ready for a demanding systems integration task. Even a data warehouse champion like Aaron Zornes of the META Group says that most of these products don't work together, and suggests that enterprises start with simple decision support solutions.

- While moving cautiously forward with small manageable projects, enterprises need to keep an eye out for four key events:
  - Increasing maturity of relational database technology with the addition of object extensions and data warehouse features
  - Integration of work flow tools to automate the data warehouse upkeep requirements
  - Industry standards so products can work together
  - Lessons learned from the pioneers

CHAPTER 14

# Justifying the Cost of a Data Warehouse

Today's businesses are experiencing intense global competition and the most accelerating pace of change ever. Competitors have sprung up that were not even on the business's radar. This situation impacts all decisions and strategies as businesses try to dominate their market or their industry merely to survive. This business state is affecting every aspect of the business—customer service, marketing, sales, product engineering, manufacturing, and every part of the organization—from the CEO to support personnel, from corporate headquarters to remote sales offices. As businesses develop new strategies, the IT community consensus is that the data warehouse and the direction in which it points is one of the critical survival factors.

To date, the justification for data warehouse usually was based on intuition and potential competitive pressures. Two example justifications are the following:

- "The business case for warehouses is simple: They help turn data into a competitive tool."—*ComputerWorld,* April 25, 1994
- "We have to roll up the information from cash registers in 1,000 stores across the nation every night. We take that information and make important business decisions every day about buying and marketing trends. It helps keep us competitive against Wal-Mart and Kmart."—J. Tucker, Senior VP and CIO, ShopKo Corporation (*InformationWeek,* December 11, 1995)

From a technical perspective, the IT industry view is the following:

- "Data warehousing is a process, not a place"—META Group
- "A data warehouse is an architecture, not a product!"—Gartner Group
- "You can't buy a data warehouse, you have to build it."—*ComputerWorld,* February 6, 1995

From a cost perspective, the IT industry consensus is that the initial price for a data warehouse project is U.S. $3 million and total costs can exceed U.S. $10 million.

Consequently, enterprises need a data warehouse plan (business and technical) and should examine the cost justification. A data warehouse plan and economic justification case are essential to balance the risks against the benefits, both tangible and intangible. (In this chapter, data warehouses includes data marts.)

# Why Build A Data Warehouse?

The complexity of today's businesses has changed the way in which enterprises are managed. Business managers not only need to know what is happening in the business, but also why (see fig. 14.1). In the data-processing automation phase of applying information technology, enterprises developed applications to quickly measure the "what is happening?" factor. Now in the information processing phase, enterprises need to know the "why is it happening?" factor; the competitive environment and the pace of change demands this. Enterprises want to quickly get to the next phase, "what should we do, and what are the risks?"

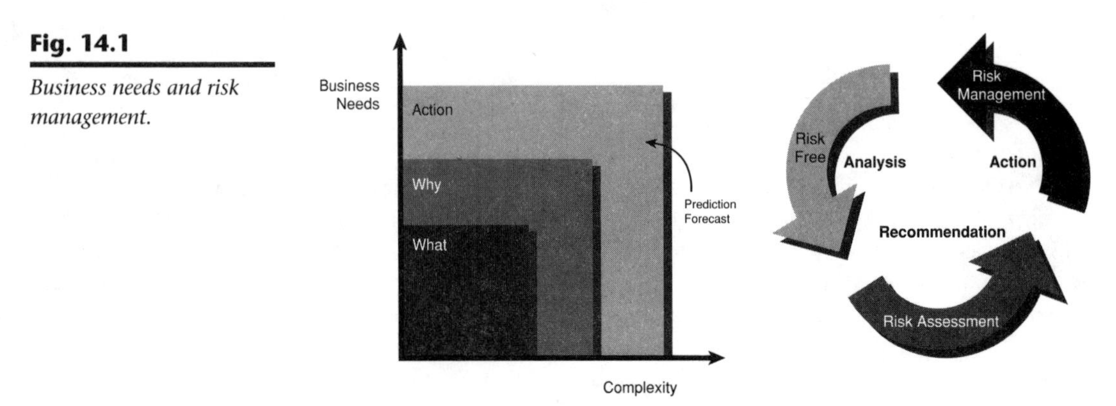


**Fig. 14.1**

*Business needs and risk management.*

Business managers need to analyze both their business performance and the state of the market to create actionable recommendations. Analysis is always risk-free because no action is taken or commitment made. Risk assessment is an essential ingredient of any recommendation to balance potential unforeseen costs against benefits. In the current fast-paced environment, besides every actionable recommendation, management also needs risk management guidance for the action taken. The consequences of a rash action can be suicidal if the reaction and counteraction is not timely. As discussed in Chapters 8 through 11, data warehouse technology can play a key role. Data warehouses can deliver actionable information—not just data, ad hoc query, and broadly summarized reports.

## The Management Challenge

In the business environment of the 1990s, executive management must examine the nature of their business because outside forces are intensifying competition and putting permanent pressure on prices. The enterprise must strive to continue either creating differentiation in the market place or supporting a commodity business. Data warehouse technology can assist in both endeavors.

The enterprise's historical data is a gold mine of information about its customers, its customer/product relationships, customer buying patterns, and so on. Because data warehouses have the potential to convert this information into knowledge, businesses with in-depth information about their customers have the potential to deliver value to them. Jonathan Berry states in *Business Week*, "Marketers increasingly are recognizing that past customer behavior, as recorded in actual transactions, is by far the best indicator of future buying patterns." This knowledge of its customers, mined from the historical transaction of its customers, is unique to the enterprise and therefore can be used to create differentiators, such as customized products for each micromarket segment, product or service bundling, and customer-specific service packages. Tracking customer relationships and their value over time (the customer life-cycle value) can assist a business in assessing overall marketing performance.

A commodity business is characterized by a passion for reducing or eliminating costs from the business system. Value chain analysis and logistics integration are two ways in which data warehouses can vaporize costs out of the business.

Usually, a well-architected data warehouse has the potential to dramatically lift sales, increase inventory turns, and be a positive factor on people productivity, which results in vastly improved operating margins.

## State of Current Systems

Possibly the biggest tactical driver to building a data warehouse is the inadequacy of current systems and the lack of business information, even when the enterprise is awash in data. Many production systems do not meet the needs of the business user. Usually, the data is inaccessible and inconsistent in both form and meaning. Due to inconsistent data, for example, the sales data in different reports does not match—the business lacks an accurate picture of its revenue. This lack of common metrics means managers cannot see a clear picture of the business' performance.

Marketing and sales managers need faster access to data, faster and more reports, quicker analysis, and nimbler reactions to manage the business and grow the revenue. Even with substantial IT costs in creating and generating reports, the reports are late and, therefore, the information is stale.

Different production systems keep different information about the same customer in different databases. This lack of a single and complete view of each customer means opportunities for cross-selling, target marketing, product bundling, and so on are challenging at best. Customers who want one-stop shopping, not sales by different people within the same company, cannot be serviced at all. So, rather than business growth, there is a loss of business.

## Data Warehouse Value

The value of data warehouses is potentially large and expansive. This value can be categorized into three parts (see fig. 14.2).

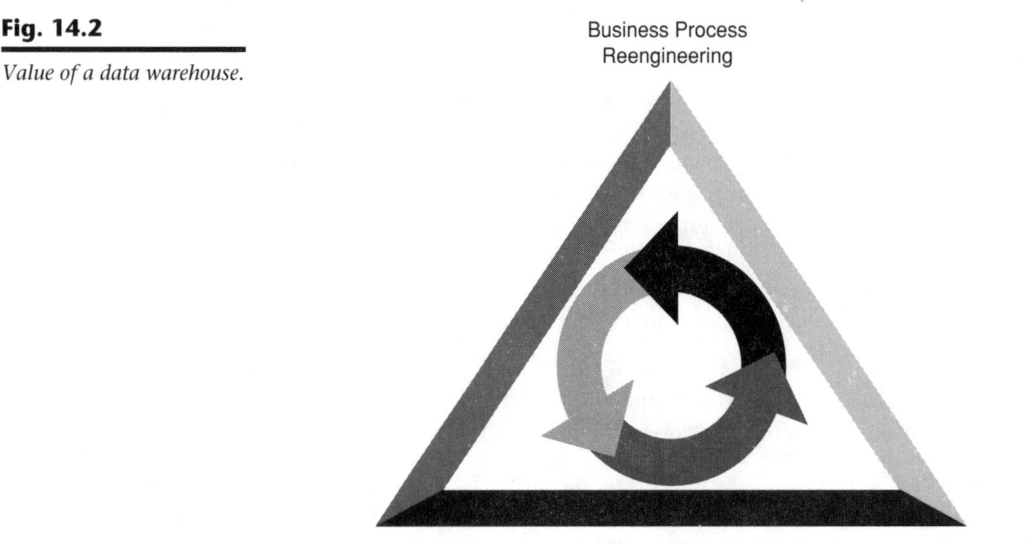


**Fig. 14.2**

*Value of a data warehouse.*

**Cost-Effective Decision Support.** Data warehouses off-load reporting and ad hoc queries from production systems. Additionally, IT professionals also are freed from supporting the business users. The availability of integrated, clean, and consistent data increases the quality and creditability of the reports and queries.

The decision support services—informational processing, analytical processing, and data mining—are used to develop actionable recommendations based on hard data, not just on intuition. A full understanding of the total customer relationship leads to improved customer service and consequently satisfied customers. Logistics integration assists financial managers to better manage assets, generally leading to reduced asset costs and improved return-on-assets (ROA). An improved understanding of customer-buying patterns helps in having the right inventory at the right place at the right time, which further improves the ROA and ROI.

**Re-Architect Application Systems.** The separation of the production systems from the decision-support data warehouse system offers IT a once-in-a-lifetime opportunity to clean up the legacy systems, while moving the enterprise system architecture forward. This cleanup can increase the life of the production systems or postpone or eliminate the need for an upgrade, which results in ROI and ROA improvements. The need to load the data warehouse with quality data—clean and consistent—provides feedback to improve the quality of the data in the production system. For some enterprises, data warehouse may be just the right first client/server architecture project for which they have been waiting.

**Business Process Engineering.** Data warehouses can also provide the business and organization measures required to gauge competitive standing. The integration of external data provides the appropriate benchmarks for competitive evaluations and analysis.

Because data warehouses are really focused on understanding the *why*, not just the *what* of the business, the design and subsequent use of the data warehouse help managers to understand the nature of their business. This dual focus leads to insights of what makes the business tick, which leads to business re-engineering actions that can change the rules of the game. At last, managers can achieve the strategic advantage that every business seeks!

The profit potential of re-engineering the business is far larger than cost-effective decision making. Re-architecting application systems not only improves asset utilization but may be essential to enable the other two categories. In reality, all three categories are closely integrated in a symbiotic relationship. Data warehouse pioneers have learned that the highest payoff for a business is when data warehouse use migrates from decision support to business process reengineering, because then the performance of people, the assets, and the whole enterprise rises.

# Early Data Warehouse Experiences

Data warehouse is a business-enabling technology. Pioneers in different industries already have tried a range of data warehouse applications, with diverse objectives.

## Data Warehouse Objectives

The objectives of some of these organizations are shown in figure 14.3.

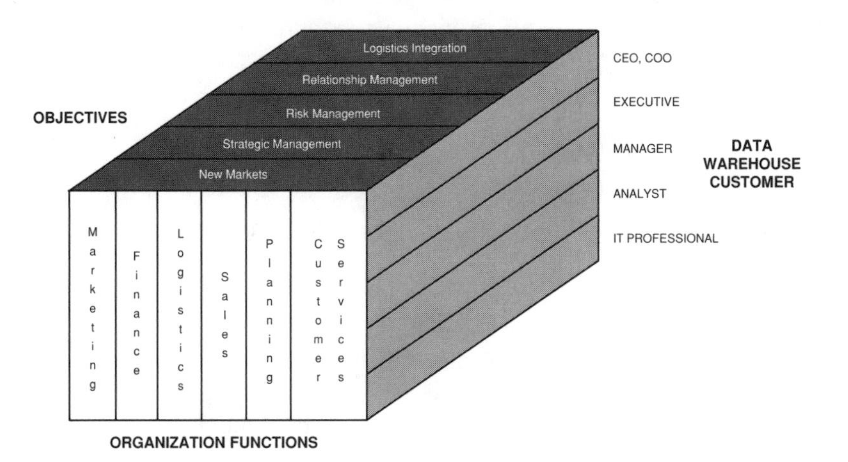


**Fig. 14.3**

*Data warehouse objectives.*

Data warehouse applications are addressing objectives in marketing, sales, customer service, finance, planning, and logistics. Data warehouse customers, such as the CEO and COO, are examining strategic alternatives and risk-assessment objectives. Executives in sales, marketing, and customer services are focusing on two objectives—new markets and relationship management—where the customer is the center of attention. Planning and finance managers and the analysts use the data warehouse to address cost-savings objectives such as vendor consolidation and volume purchase opportunities.

## Data Warehouse Early Usage

Data warehouse usage is widespread over a host of industries, with a range of specific applications (see fig. 14.4).

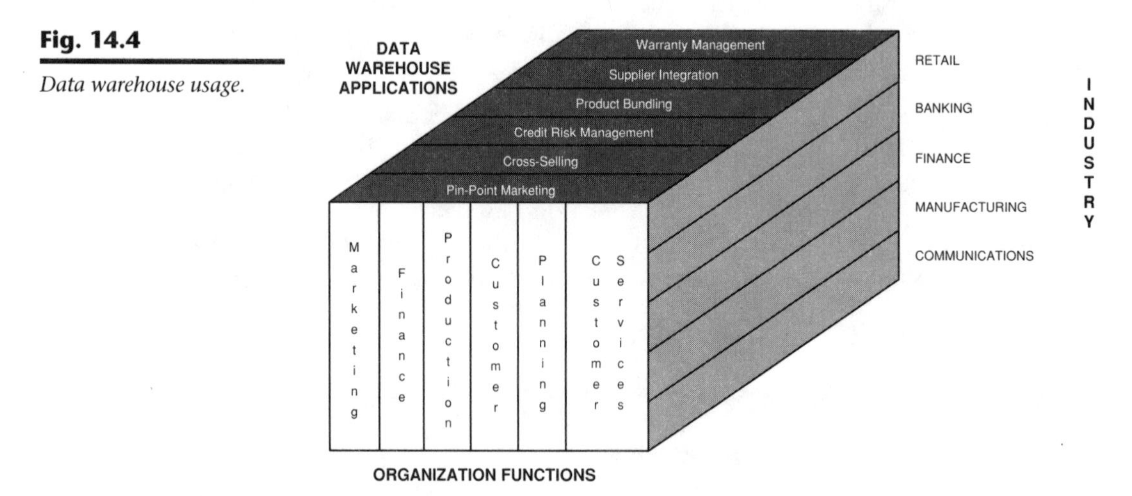


**Fig. 14.4**

*Data warehouse usage.*

The industries with the most activity are communications, retail (including consumer), banking, finance (including insurance), health, and manufacturing. The principal objective of most data warehouses is revenue generation, with cost savings as a secondary objective. The range of applications include the following:

- Pin-point marketing, especially into micromarkets to both add new customers and retain current ones
- Cross-selling or up-selling products, or bundling products to current customers
- Managing credit risk and warranty claims
- Integrating with suppliers to improve overall inventory management

## Economics

Early experiences in building a data warehouse indicate the need for a much larger investment than originally forecast. The average estimate for an initial data warehouse project is approximately U.S. $3 million. Of this U.S. $3 million estimate, approximately two-thirds is for hardware and one-third is for software. A more detailed breakout of this cost by the Gartner Group is shown in figure 14.5. The Gartner Group projects that data warehouse initiatives will cost in the U.S. $10 million range.

The Gartner Group's breakout of the data warehouse costs are the following:

- **Hardware**—31 percent
- **Data warehouse software, including RDBMS, Decision Support systems, and Extraction software**—24 percent
- **Data warehouse administration**—10 percent
- **Staff and system integrators**—35 percent

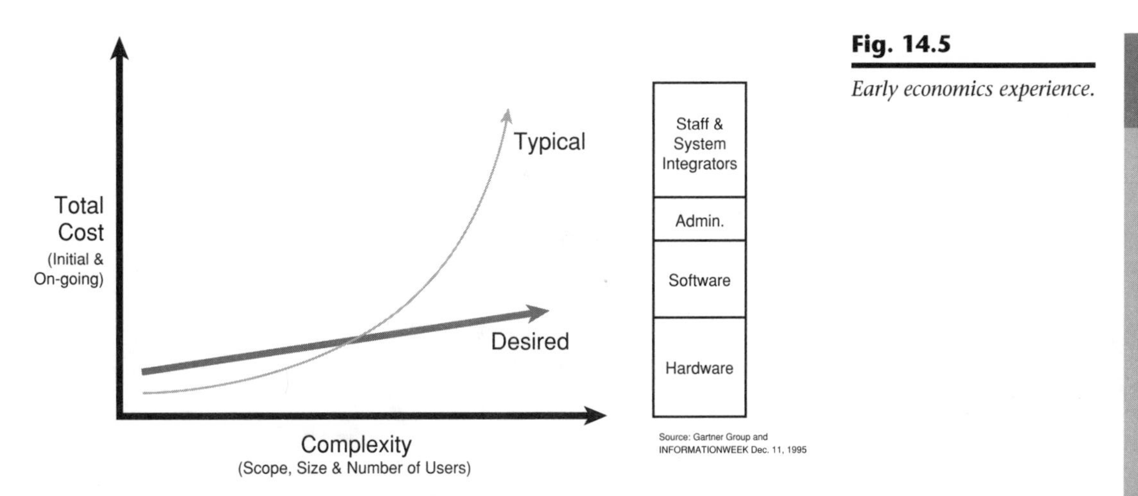


**Fig. 14.5**

*Early economics experience.*

When viewed from a life-cycle perspective, the total cost is at first increasing at a reasonable rate, and then seems to rise exponentially. The total cost is impacted adversely by the increased complexity of the data warehouse. This complexity is due to the increased scope of the data warehouse, the growth of the size of the database, and the addition of more users. So, issues such as parallel hardware, software, and RDBMS (and also administration of very large databases) are a mounting concern. Because the real "bang for the buck" is projected for data warehouses of multidepartmental scope and larger number of users, this cost curve needs to be addressed.

Seemingly, businesses are not averse to a reasonable higher initial cost, provided that the future growth is affordable, justifiable, and predictable. Figure 14.5 also shows the desired cost curve for increased complexity and growth.

## Challenges Encountered

The scope of early data warehouse projects has ranged from simple decision support—query and reporting—to business process reengineering. Generally, the number of projects is substantially more for decision support and fewest for business process reengineering (see fig. 14.6).

Initial success indicators are what one might expect—more success for decision support projects. Business process re-engineering projects have the potential of large positive impact on the enterprise, but the projects are essentially more complex and risky. The same thing can be said, but to a lesser extent, for the application system re-architecting effort; therefore the success rate is better.

It's no surprise that when decision support projects are further broken down into its own subprojects, the success rate is highest for reporting projects when compared to analytical/OLAP projects or data mining projects (see fig. 14.7).

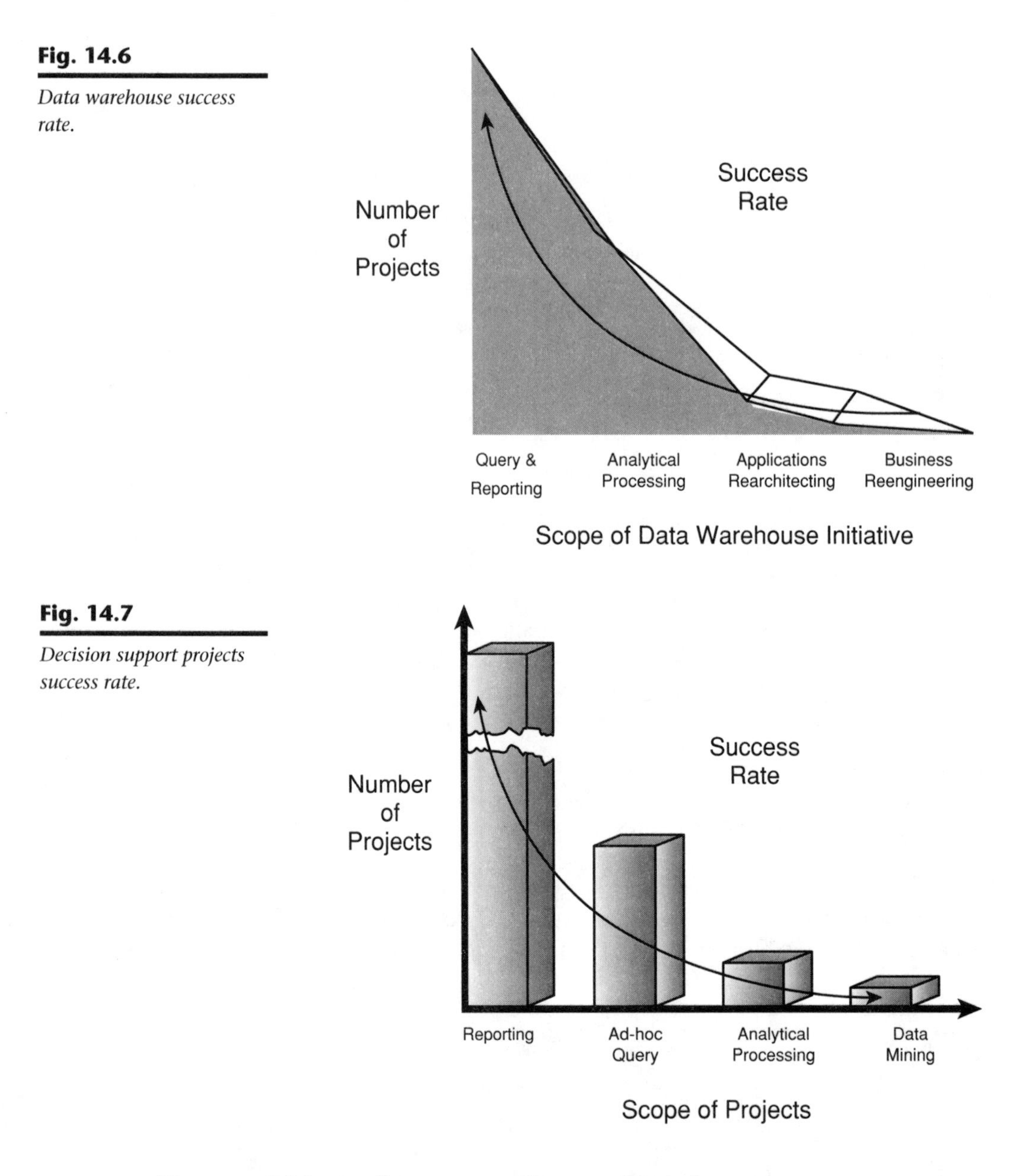


**Fig. 14.6**

*Data warehouse success rate.*

**Fig. 14.7**

*Decision support projects success rate.*

# Data Warehouse: Developing the Business Case

Data warehouse investments, so far based on intuition and competitive reactions, need to be based on a sound business foundation. For this foundation, an in-depth analysis of both business and technical considerations, shown in figure 14.8, is warranted.

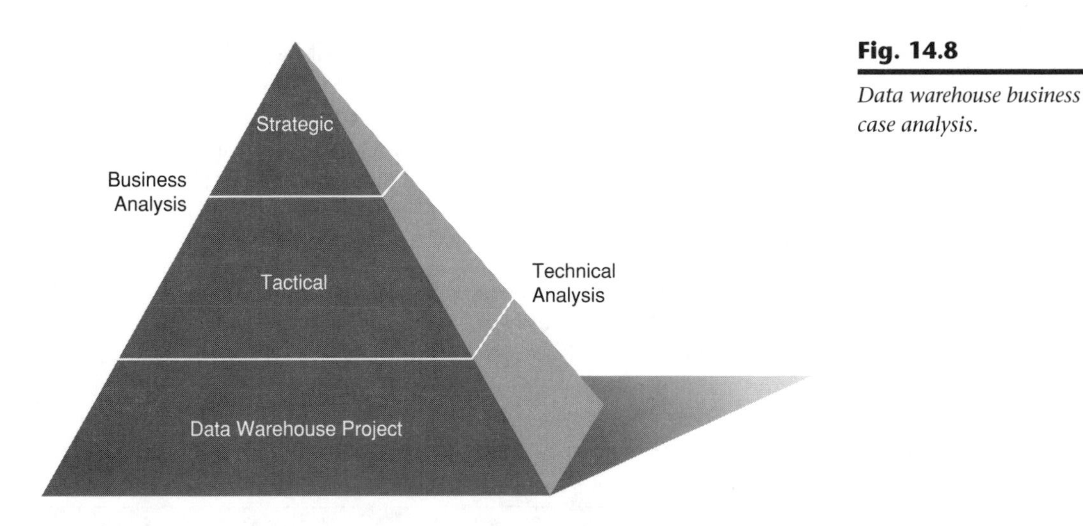


**Fig. 14.8**

*Data warehouse business case analysis.*

Business users must work hand-in-hand with IT professionals to develop the business justification of a data warehouse initiative. IT professionals need to move from a "yes we can, and we have the know-how and capability" position to "why do it, and what is the value of IT to this business endeavor called data warehouse?" Although no fool-proof technique exists to measure IT's value to the building of a data warehouse, it is essential in today's economic environment. Every measurement used better show a positive impact on the bottom line, and justifications that are not easy to quantify in monetary terms better be communicated in business language.

Wayne Spence, director of business and strategic services at Texas Instruments, in the July/August 1995 issue of *Beyond Computing,* said "Business is the only place you can measure value, so the value of technology (data warehouse) must be measured on a business level." Business value is expressed in language such as the following:

- Profits and dividends
- Earnings growth
- Revenue growth
- Return-on-investment, return-on-assets
- Marketing share growth and industry rank
- Operating margin growth and pricing pressures
- Contribution to revenue and profitability

Measuring the value of a data warehouse in business terms (ROA, ROI, and operating margins) helps bridge the communications gap between the CIO, the data warehouse idea initiator, and the CEO/CFO—the essential idea sponsors. For a project of U.S. \$3–\$10 million, the CEO/CFO sponsorship is necessary. An additional benefit of measuring the data warehouse value is that it can help IT establish priorities for applying its scarce resources.

The business analysis case for data warehouse initiatives must be led by business executives with the active involvement and support of IT executives. The analysis must include financial and organizational considerations. A successful data warehouse initiative will certainly impact the way in which business is conducted; and business processes will change. The technical considerations should include an in-depth analysis of current IT investments, with an eye for reuse. Reuse or additional use of existing investments certainly makes it easier to meet both ROI and ROA hurdles.

The initial business and technical analysis should result in a strategic vision of the data warehouse initiative, with focus areas well-articulated. Figure 14.9 illustrates the types of potential focus areas in a wide range of business sectors. Other business focus areas are mergers and acquisitions, vendor negotiation, BPR and TQM, market competitiveness through product development and product positioning, customer (not market) profitability, and customer frustration assessment.

**Fig. 14.9**

*Example business focus areas.*

| Industry / D/W Usage | Finance | Consumer | Communications | Transportation | Retail | Public Sector | Manufacturing | Health |
|---|---|---|---|---|---|---|---|---|
| Customer Life Cycle Mgmt. | Y | | | | | | | Y |
| Credit Risk Management | Y | | Y | | Y | | Y | |
| Target Marketing | Y | Y | Y | Y | Y | | Y | Y |
| Logistics | | Y | Y | Y | Y | Y | Y | Y |
| Financial Analysis | Y | Y | Y | Y | Y | Y | Y | |
| Promo. & Ad. Effectiveness | Y | Y | Y | Y | Y | | Y | |
| Merchandising Support | | Y | | | | | | |
| Customer Service Data | | Y | | | Y | | Y | Y |
| Market Segmentation | Y | Y | | | Y | | Y | |
| Customer Profitability | Y | Y | Y | | | | | |
| **Industry Specific** | Customer Relationship | Supplier Performance | Customer Profile Analysis | Yield Management | Fashion Merchandising | Claims Data | Warranty Analysis | Client Claims Analysis |

Beyond the common strategic vision, the business case must include the economic model, the architectural and construction model, and the operational model. The latter two models were addressed in the first part of the book, in Chapters 2 through 6. The economic, architectural, construction, and operational models form the tactical analysis portion of the business case and are the sources from which the data warehouse project is derived. (refer to fig. 14.8)

## Building the Business Economics (Cost Justification) Model

Building the economic model for a data warehouse means defining and quantifying the business objectives, and stating the strategies and tactics to be used. Next, the proforma revenue and cost models must be developed, leading to the proforma financial model (see fig. 14.10). Finally, business performance measures and an audit plan must be defined for the data warehouse. Essentially, the economic model consists of a three-part financial model, sandwiched between the objectives and the performance measures.

The initial step is to focus on a business area or issue, such as customer profitability or

|  |  |
|---|---|
|  | Quantified<br>Strategies and Tactics<br>Strategies and Tactics |
| Proforma Revenue Model | Revenue & Benefits<br>Tangible<br>Intangible |
| Proforma Cost Model | Data Warehouse Costs<br>Initial<br>Recurring |
| Proforma Financial Model | Financial Analysis<br>Risk Analysis |
|  | Audit Plan<br>Performance Measures |

**Fig. 14.10**

*Economic model.*

target marketing. The choice of area or issue results in different business objectives and strategies. A range of approaches, fitting different objectives, is available to analyze the value and benefits of both the stated objectives and the strategies.

For profitability analysis objectives, whether for a product or market or even a single customer, the analytical activities are to determine the true or apportioned costs and revenue (see fig. 14.11). The factors that impact the revenue and costs must be measured and analyzed, which implies that, for performance measures, the data warehouse must provide the relevant information. To determine, for example, the profitability of a product, the data warehouse must provide information on all revenues and also all costs (fixed, variable, promotion, sales, and so on) of the product. Without this type of information, a profitability objective cannot be selected in the cost-justification economic model.

When the data warehouse objective encompasses multiple functions of the organization, the value-added chain analysis approach is needed to supplement the profitability analysis approach (see fig. 14.12). The cost and revenue model can get fairly complex, but if each function is first analyzed as a revenue and cost center, a net revenue and cost model can be applied.

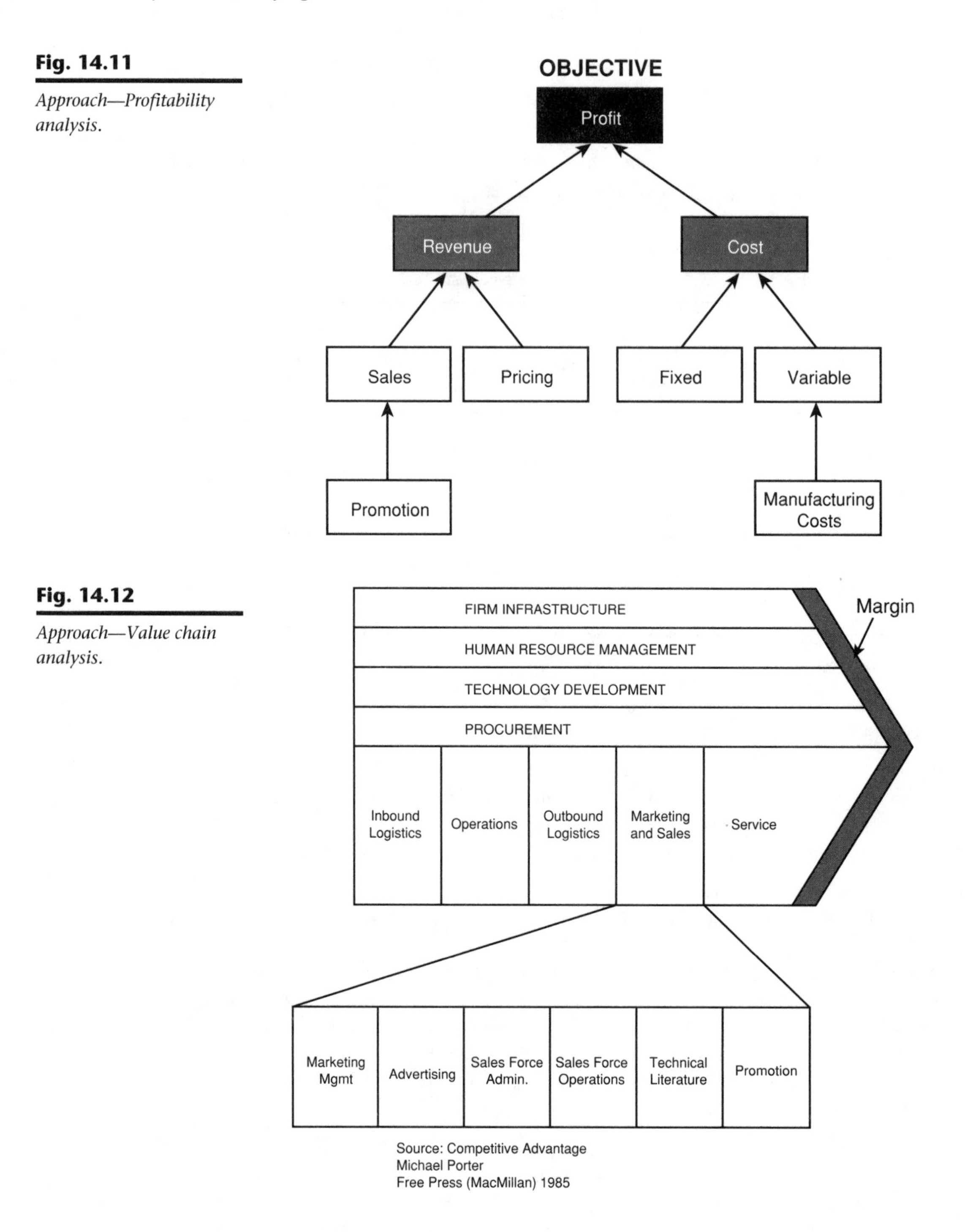


**Fig. 14.11**

*Approach—Profitability analysis.*

**Fig. 14.12**

*Approach—Value chain analysis.*

A customer satisfaction objective implies balancing the needs of customers with the capability of the enterprise to earn a profit and to add value (see fig. 14.13). Customer objectives usually are set for a market or product, not for an entire enterprise. This helps to significantly decrease the analytical effort needed to build a business model and develop performance measures.

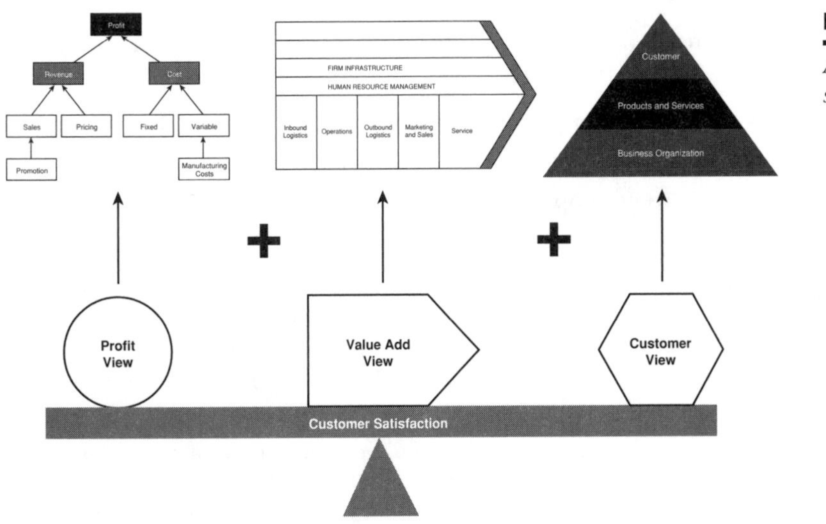


**Fig. 14.13**

*Approach—Customer satisfaction analysis.*

Usually, the data warehouse objectives must be such that each objective can be reduced to a revenue stream, a set of costs, and a profitability and benefits target stated as measurable objectives. A measurable objective may be, "increase the customer retention rate by five percent." Any non-quantifiable benefits, tangible or intangible, must be stated in business language so they are easily communicated and can be qualitatively measured.

**Proforma Revenue Model.** The revenue model can have both tangible and intangible measures (refer to fig. 14.10). The tangible measures are either monetary values or statements of objectives. In the revenue model, the challenge is to convert everything to a monetary value. For example, if the data warehouse objective is "product promotion will increase the number of customers by seven percent," this needs to be translated into an increase of revenue of *X* percent. Then the goals may be stated as both "increase revenue by *X* percent and customers by seven percent." Later, this can help in the performance measurement phase to tune the initial financial model. If the confidence level in converting "increase customers by seven percent" to revenue "increase revenue by *X* percent" is low, a pilot promotion may be a solid recommendation before the enterprise commits to a full promotion program.

Revenue objectives include the following four types:

- **Increase in revenue**, such as for a product or market or channel
- **New revenue**, such as for a new product or new market or new channel
- **Maintain revenue** along with cost reduction
- **Decrease in revenue**, (if a product or market or channel is being eliminated)

Some potential measures of revenue improvements include customer profitability, product profitability, channel profitability, and telemarketing productivity.

In today's business climate, the incremental or new revenue stream in the proforma revenue model should be limited to no more than three years.

**Proforma Cost Model.** To develop the cost model requires the following two cost sub-models:

- **Business costs**—There are of two types of business costs: new costs or increases in current costs. These costs are incurred to generate new revenue or to increase revenue. To quantify incremental costs, it is essential to first baseline current costs. The incremental costs should include all IT professional costs to support the data warehouse business user.
- **Data warehouse**—There are two types of data warehouse costs: initial and recurring (ongoing). Initial costs are either one-time expenses (design, build, and deploy the data warehouse) or capital costs (hardware, software, infrastructure, and so on). The recurring costs also can be divided into two classes—fixed and variable. An example of a fixed recurring cost is the ongoing refreshment of the data warehouse from the data sources. Variable ongoing costs are for items such as the growth of the data warehouse as the scope is increased, when more users are added, and so on.

The proforma cost model must include all costs—IT costs and costs of the business users' organization. Hardware and software costs, including maintenance fees, must be appropriately classified, allocated, and included in total costs.

IT's data warehouse cost mantra should be: lowest initial costs, lowest recurring costs, fastest implementation schedule (time is cost and investment), and maximum reuse of existing investments.

**Proforma Financial/Profit Model.** The proforma financial model is a measure of the profitability (tangible benefits) of the data warehouse initiative and the intangible benefits to achieve. From a quantitative perspective, the data warehouse initiative is profitable in any one of the four ways shown in figure 14.14.

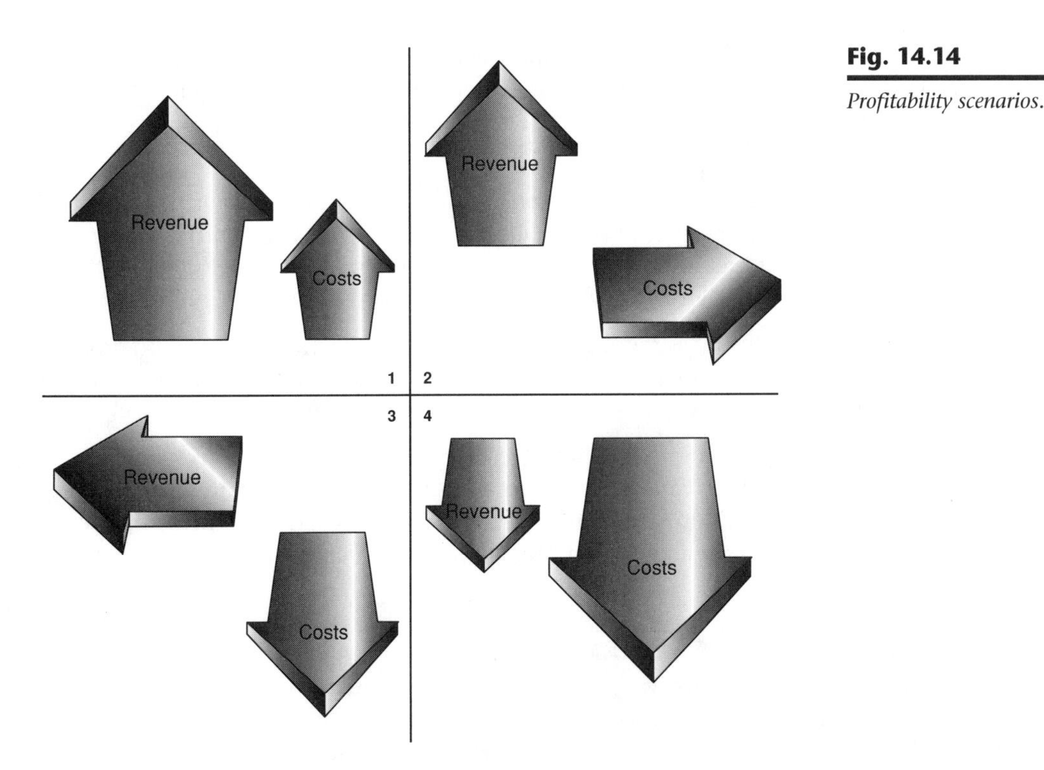


**Fig. 14.14**

*Profitability scenarios.*



The following are the four profitability scenarios for the data warehouse initiative:

- **Scenario 1**—Revenue and costs increase, but the increase in revenue is much larger relative to the cost increase. An example is the increased revenue, derived from a marketing promotion campaign.
- **Scenario 2**—Revenue increases, but costs remain the same. An example is target marketing project, with no increase in the current marketing budget.
- **Scenario 3**—Revenue is flat, but costs decrease. An example is the revenue is same for a product family, but ineffective marketing programs are identified and dropped.
- **Scenario 4**—Revenue decreases, but costs decrease even more relative to the revenue decrease. An example is the elimination of unprofitable products, unprofitable services, or the planned "shipping" of unprofitable customers to the competition.

Actually, a fifth scenario exists—revenues increase dramatically and costs decrease tremendously. It is every businessperson's dream project. The reader can supply the example.

The proforma financial model should include projections for no more than three years—the business environment is too dynamic and changeable. Only in certain circumstances, such as a major enterprise re-engineering effort, should a five-year projection be considered.

**Performance Measures and Audit Plan.** An audit plan to measure value is essential to fine-tuning the data warehouse. The audit plan should measure both the tangible and intangible performance measures. Audit plans are needed to fine-tune pilot programs before the enterprise commits to a major roll out of a strategy.

Tangible performance measures include monetary ones, such as revenue and profit growth and cost-management targets, and goals dictated in business language, such as increase number of customers by *N*, increase inventory turns to *M*, and so on.

Intangible performance measures include customer satisfaction improvement (it would be better if this intangible measure was translated into a tangible measure such as customer retention rates), enhanced customer perception of the company, or the productivity improvement of a business analyst (more time freed up and available for other activities).

## Technical Analysis and Risk Management

Foremost, the technical analysis should have a passionate focus on cost control. The lower the costs of the technology, the higher the ROI and ROA. The second challenge is not technical, but rather involves requirements and design—how to translate the business issues and objectives into technical requirements. This challenge was discussed in the first part of this book.

## Technical Risk Management

The technical risks to a data warehouse initiative can come from many sources—from scope, needs, or the complexity of the systems integration task.

**Scope Risk Management.** The scope of a data warehouse project can be from a reporting database, to query and analysis database, to analytical processing, and all the way to application re-architecting (see fig. 14.15). If the business objectives are not well-defined and not carefully translated into IT requirements, the scope may become much larger than planned. Increased scope means increased complexity and longer implementation cycle. All this results in increased risks and costs. It's crucial to grow the scope and capability, always building on success.

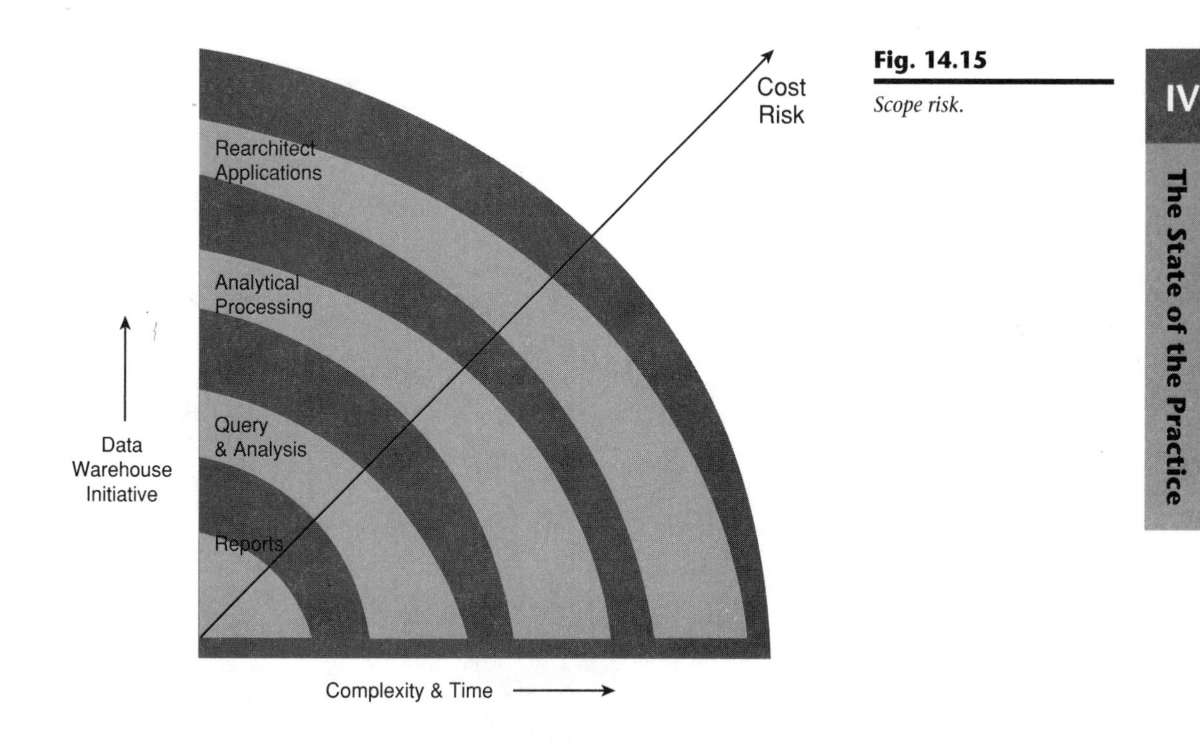


**Fig. 14.15**

*Scope risk.*

**User Needs Risk Management.** A second side to the scope issue is the user needs risk (see fig. 14.16). A data warehouse can be built to cover a wide-range of users with a complex set of needs. Complex business and technical needs translate into complex information processing requirements. The way to reduce scope is to either reduce the number and types of business users or to meet fewer needs of the prospective users. Fewer needs translate to a reduction in the number of subject areas in the data warehouse. Again increasing the scope based on success is prudent.

**System Integration Risk Management.** Data warehouses are built, not bought. Building a data warehouse, as was discussed previously, is a system integration task. So all the risks inherent in a systems integration project exist in any data warehouse project. Some of the unique risks for a data warehouse project are the following:

- **Vendor selection**—Data warehouse implementation is relatively new and a body of successful case studies is lacking.
- **Technology**—Many products and technologies are relatively new and not fully proven. Promising and important technologies, such as very large databases, parallel processing, and data mining are emerging technologies.

- **Performance and administration**—This risk can occur with very large data bases.
- **People/skill risks**—This risk can occur due to limited experience of people in data warehouse technology and the emerging nature of data warehouse technology.

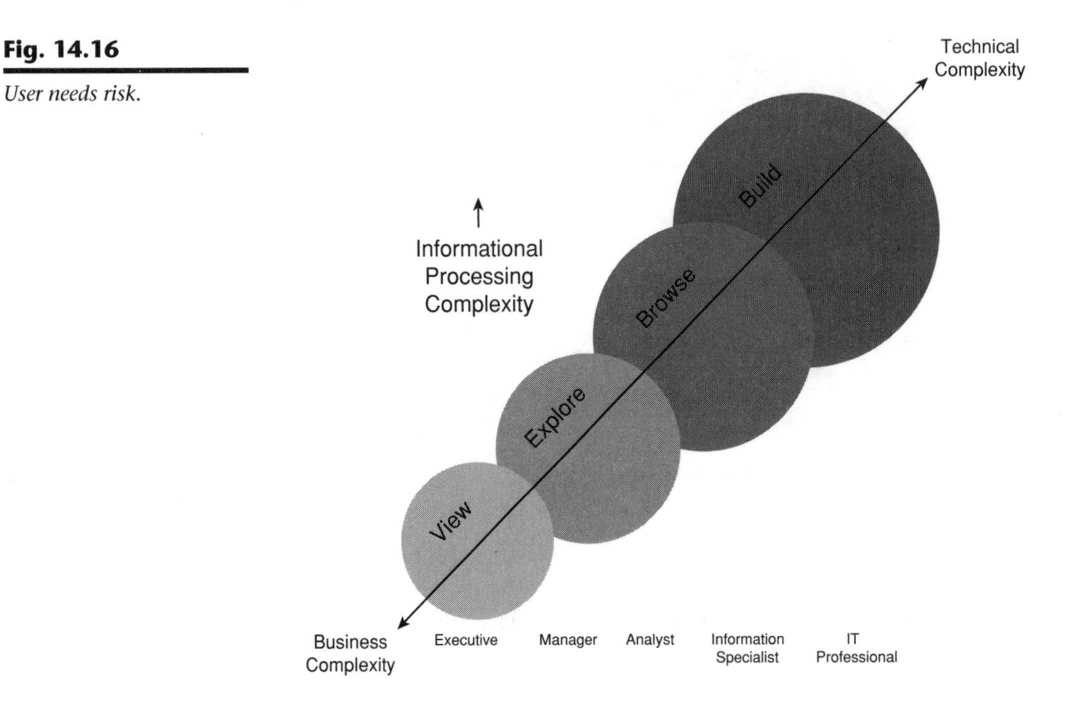


**Fig. 14.16**

*User needs risk.*

The reference architecture, described in Chapter 2, should be used to detail all the components necessary to build a data warehouse. The risks associated with each component, and the full solution as well, should be assessed. Many risks exist in the components included in the infrastructure and transport layers of the reference architecture. It is in these two layers, along with the data management layer, where investment cost creep can occur. Investment cost creep is noticeable in the areas of network bandwidth, support staff, and infrastructure upgrade.

# Examples: Business Analysis Cases

The following cases discuss only the business analysis portion of the data warehouse proforma financial model. The IT industry has a history of analyzing technical issues and developing the technology cost model.

## Increase Profitability (ROI Impact)

Figure 14.14 showed four potential scenarios to increase profitability. This example illustrates Scenario 1. The business objective here is to increase profitability by *X* percent, while holding cost increases to much less than *X* percent of revenue. Tactics to increase revenue include cross-selling, product bundling, and packaging services with certain products. These tactics use the data warehouse to determine the market segments and the predisposition of customer for particular products, product bundles, and packaging options. A proforma financial model is shown in the following table:

| Object | Current | Plan |
|---|---|---|
| **Revenue** | **100** | **115** |
| Cost of Revenue | 75 | 85 |
| **Gross Margin** | **25** | **30** |
| Product Development | 6 | 6 |
| Sales Costs | 10 | 11.5 |
| General & Administrative Expenses | 3.5 | 4 |
| **Profit (before taxes)** | **5.5** | **8.5** |
| **Profit Increase** | **155%** | |

Other similar scenarios, some of these have been mentioned earlier, include isolating unprofitable customers within profitable market segments or unprofitable micromarket segments within profitable market segments or unprofitable products within profitable product lines and product bands, and "selling them to the competition."

## Increase Asset Utilization (ROA Impact)

In this business analysis case, the business objective is to increase the productivity of existing assets—the ROA. As an example, in the telecommunications industry the capital assets deployed (as a business necessity) are enormous and the incremental costs of additional utilization is minimal. A proforma financial model is shown in the following table:

| Object | Current | Plan |
|---|---|---|
| **Revenue** | **100** | **115** |
| Cost of Revenue | 50 | 55 |
| **Gross Margin** | **50** | **60** |
| Product Development | 2 | 2 |
| Depreciation | 25 | 25 |

(continues)

(continued)

| Object | Current | Plan |
|---|---|---|
| Sales Costs | 10 | 10.5 |
| General & Administrative Expenses | 5 | 5.25 |
| **Profit (before taxes)** | **8** | **17.25** |
| **Profit Increase** | **215%** | |

Another example of improved asset use is the migration of query, reporting, and OLAP processing from the production systems to a data warehouse. This scenario is particularly feasible if the data is inconsistent between production applications and also is not easily accessible to the business analyst. Sharply decreased costs due to elimination of data search times, data reconciliation efforts, and data access times can provide the savings (translated as increased revenue) to balance the cost to build a data warehouse. This kind of a business case can be bolstered by postponing or entirely eliminating the cost of upgrading the production systems to meet the growth needs (revenue and customers) of the enterprise.

## Single Project: Marketing Campaign Return On Investment

The business objective in a marketing campaign is to meet a Return On Investment target of *X* percent. The strategy is to achieve a revenue level that meets the Return On Investment target for the budgeted campaign costs. The tactic is to use a customer-oriented data warehouse for targeted marketing within micromarkets to achieve a desired response rate—in terms of both number of customers and purchase per customer. An abbreviated proforma financial model is shown in the following table:

| Object... | Equals |
|---|---|
| Proforma Revenue | Average purchase per respondent × (Number of customers in targeted market × percent of respondents) |
| Proforma Costs | Fixed Costs allocated to campaign + Variables costs of campaign |
| Variable Costs | Number of customers in targeted market × Cost of reaching each target customer |
| Proforma Return On Investments | Proforma Revenue / Proforma Costs |

If the proforma Return On Investment is greater than *X* percent, the data warehouse is cost-justified.

## Summary

- You can categorize data warehouse value into three parts: decision support, re-architect existing applications, and business process re-engineering. The profit potential of re-engineering the business is much larger than cost-effective decision making. Re-architecting application systems not only improves asset utilization, but may be essential to enable the other two categories. In reality, all three categories are closely integrated in a symbiotic relationship. Data warehouse pioneers have learned that the highest payoff for a business is when data warehouse use migrates from decision support to business process re-engineering, because the performance of people, the assets, and the whole enterprise rises.
- "Anything not measured cannot be managed." Data warehouses can be measured and managed. The data warehouse cost justification economic model consists of a three-part proforma financial model, sandwiched between the business objectives and the performance measures. The three parts are a proforma revenue model, a proforma cost model, and a proforma financial or profit model.
- Management's key intention is growth in profits and dividends, earnings, market share, and operating margins. A business case can be made for data warehouses for profit improvement, ROI, and ROA improvement; market share growth (preserve prices and maintain a noncommodity business); and retaining competitiveness in a commodity business. IT executives who wrap a data warehouse proposal in bottom-line benefits will get a positive and enthusiastic response from top management.
- A well-architected data warehouse has the potential to dramatically lift sales, increase inventory turns, and be a positive factor on people productivity, which results in improved operating margins. Successful data warehouses can change the nature of the business and how work is done. People can use the information to reshape their jobs. The cultural change needs to be factored in. The data warehouse must evolve as its users do.
- Data warehouse is a powerful weapon in an enterprise's business management portfolio. Data warehouse investments can be measured and managed. Data warehouse project risks can be managed with executive sponsorship, business unit leadership and involvement, and business-needs-driven implementations.
- Data warehouse projects can be successfully implemented by a managed list of business needs, a sound technical architecture, a careful selection of vendor tools, and an established implementation methodology that incorporates a phased development approach that builds on success.

# Appendixes

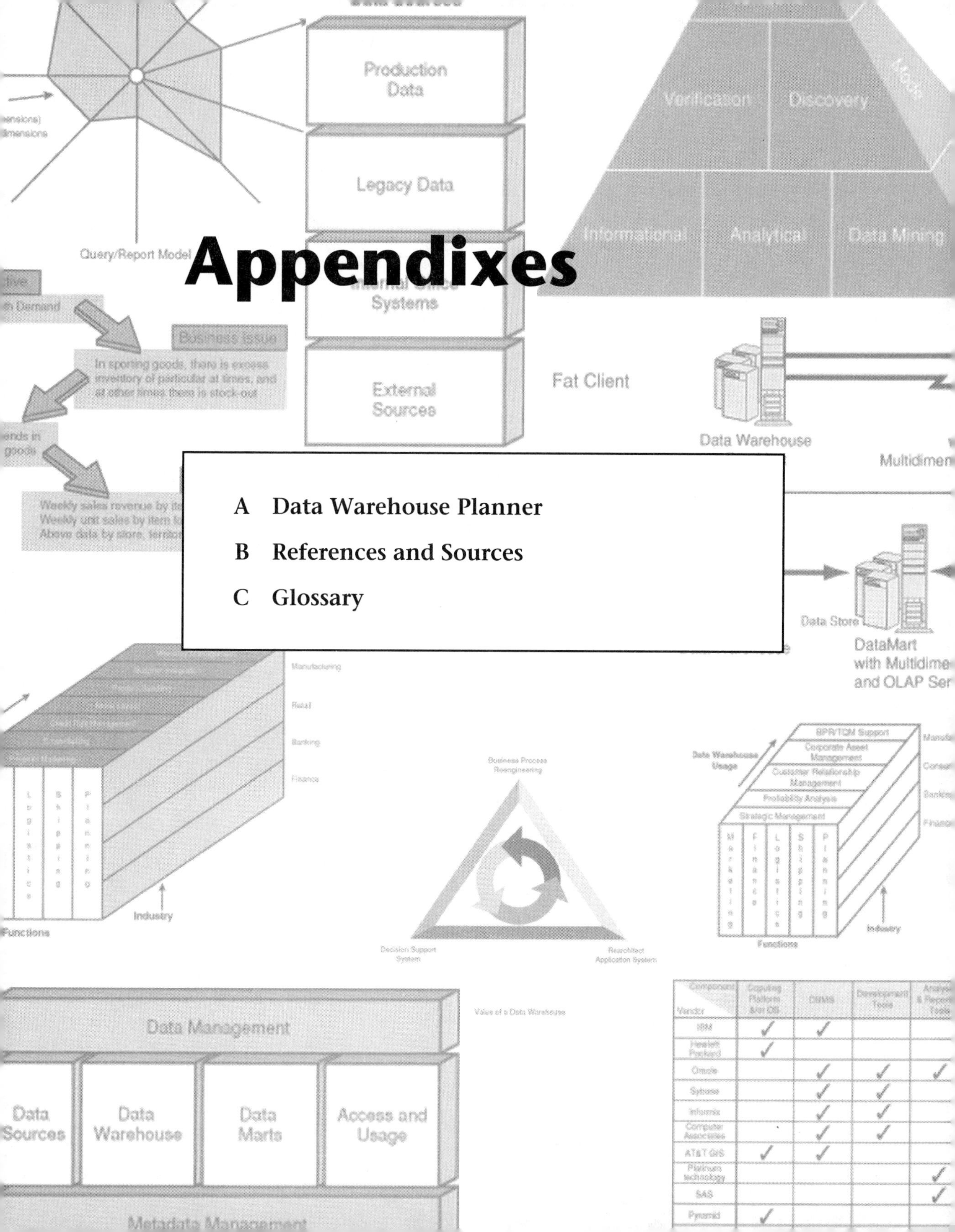


A Data Warehouse Planner

B References and Sources

C Glossary

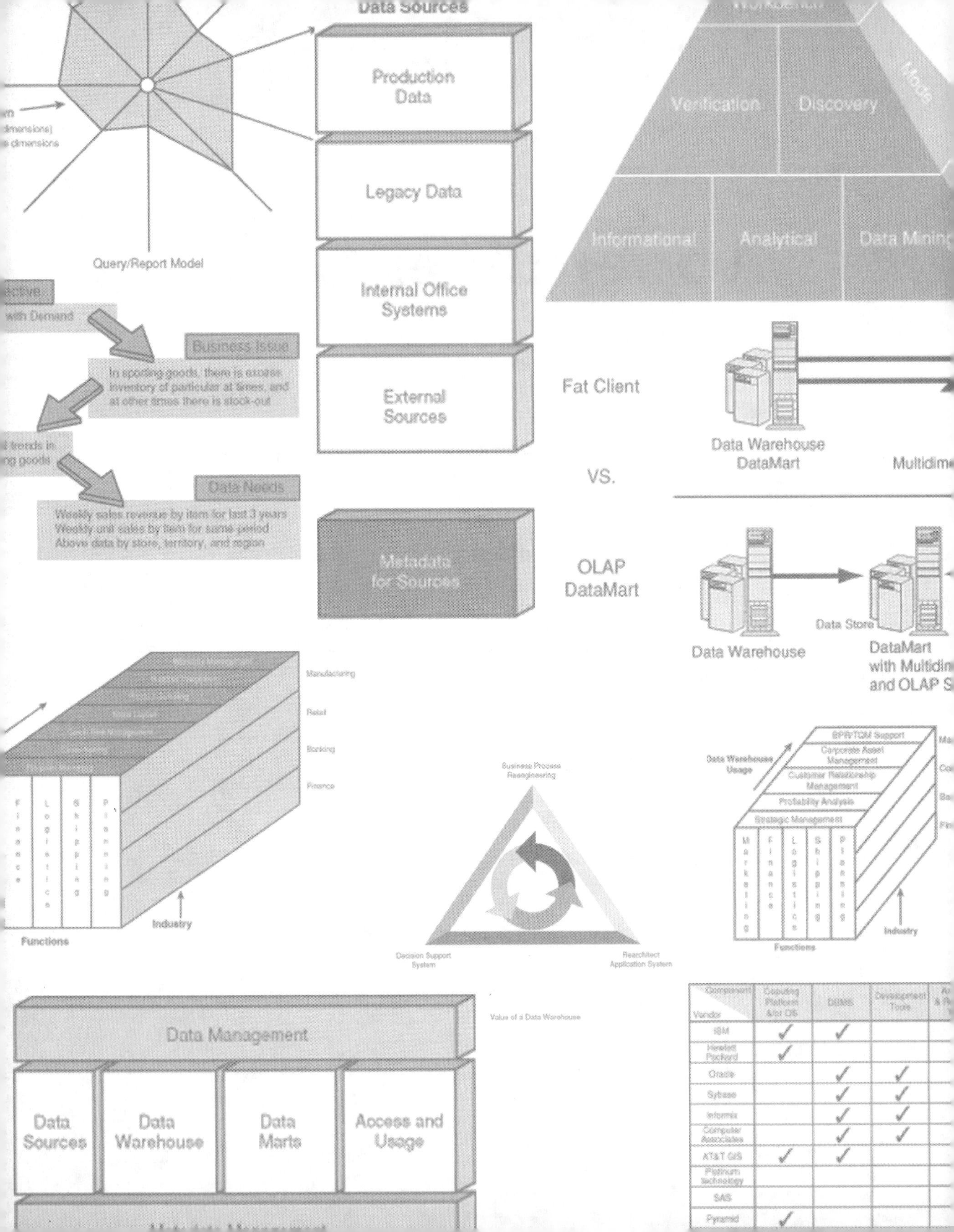


| Vendor | Computing Platform &/or OS | DBMS | Development Tools |
|---|---|---|---|
| IBM | ✓ | ✓ | |
| Hewlett Packard | ✓ | | |
| Oracle | | ✓ | ✓ |
| Sybase | | ✓ | ✓ |
| Informix | | ✓ | ✓ |
| Computer Associates | | ✓ | ✓ |
| AT&T GIS | ✓ | ✓ | |
| Platinum technology | | | |
| SAS | | | |
| Pyramid | ✓ | | |

APPENDIX A

# Data Warehouse Planner

The Indica Data Warehouse Planner (hereafter known as the Planner) is a computer based tool to assist you in planning your data warehouse. The Planner is a valuable tool for various users.

If you are a department within a larger corporation, for example, it allows you to start with a list of available planning options for data warehouse components supplied by your corporate IS department, and select items that match your needs and your specific environmental restrictions. This ability is important if you want to plan your warehouse starting with organizationally defined standards.

If you are a corporation starting off with the planning of your first data warehouse, it allows you to start with a list of options that are available from vendors and reference materials and select the items that match your needs. This ability allows you to get a "quick start" in the data warehouse implementation tasks and select from available product options.

If you are a corporate IS department trying to define standards for data warehouse component items, the Planner allows you to start from scratch and define a set of candidate components that can be distributed to departmental or business unit users who are planning their own data warehouse or data mart. This ability allows you to propagate standards in a manner that is easy to use for your customer departments and business units. By providing the standard architecture as a starting point for your customers to start their initial design, you are ensuring that their solutions incorporate organizational standards.

If you are responsible for the implementation of the data warehouse, it allows you to organize the various tasks and activities that must be performed in the various components of the data warehouse such as the Data Sources block, Data Warehouse construction block, Data Mart construction block, Access and Usage block, and the various layers such as Data Management, Metadata Management, Transport, and Infrastructure. The upper layers of the task breakdown structure are built into the Planner and you only need to spend time entering the detailed tasks. The Planner acts as a prompting tool for checklists of activities.

The Planner also allows you to plan your software architecture for the various blocks and layers of the data warehouse. It provides the upper layers for software categories. You can then enter the detailed vendor products or in-house developments that are necessary to tie the solution together. The Planner acts as a prompting tool for software components of the data warehouse architecture.

The Planner is also flexible enough to support entry of project resources and skills that are needed for various blocks and layers of the data warehouse reference architecture. This is an important feature for development managers who are trying to assess whether they have the skills in-house to undertake a data warehouse project.

The Planner organizes the information it manages along the exact blocks and layers of the data warehouse reference architecture. The main window of the Planner displays a replica of the data warehouse reference architecture (see fig. A.1).

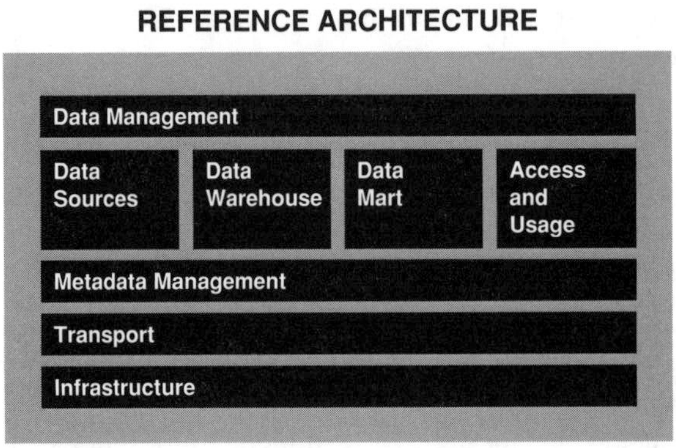

**Fig. A.1**

*Main window of the Data Warehouse Planner.*



The graphical screens that are displayed show the blocks and layers of the reference architecture. The activity of planning is simply that of providing instances for different blocks and layers of real world objects. To instantiate a block or layer, you are simply required to point-and-click on it inside the diagram of the reference architecture.

The Planner allows the specification of information at the following three levels of abstraction:

- High level
- Mid level
- Low level

The Planner also allows the specification of data warehouse plans in the following two dimensions:

- Functions
- Products

# Overall Concept of the Planner

Figure A.2 shows the overall organization of the Planner.

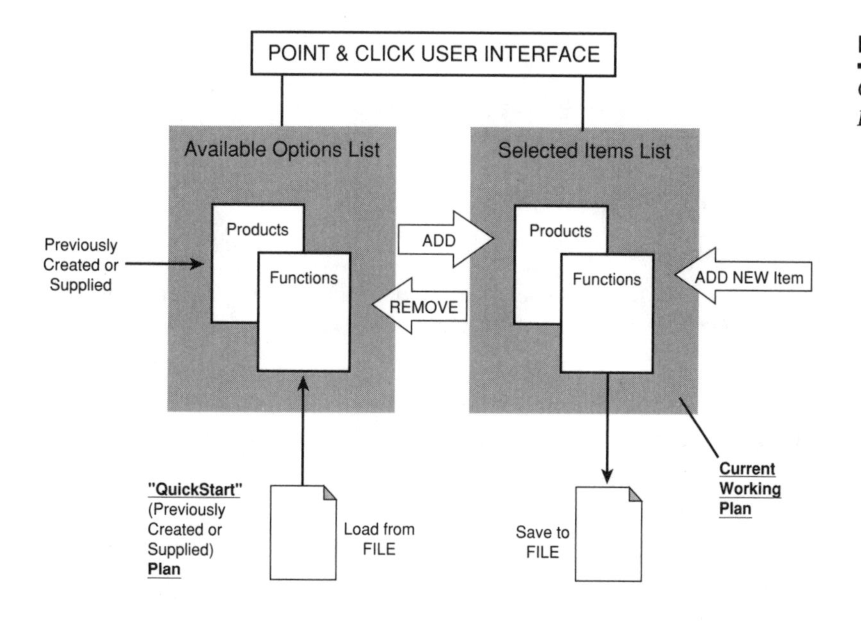


**Fig. A.2**

*Organization of the Indica Data Warehouse Planner.*

The Planner is always working with the following two sets of lists:

- The Available Options list set is loaded from a previously created Planner file (called a *Plan*). There are many ways to receive this previously created file, including the following:
  - A set of previously created files are supplied to you along with the Planner software. These have been created to illustrate the various components of typical data warehouse architectures.
  - Your corporate staff can create an organizational template for standard data warehouse component solutions and hand it to you. They need to use the Planner to create this organizational template file.
  - You can create your own template by entering every item for every component manually. The Planner supports the creation of a plan file starting from scratch. The upper layer categories are supplied to you as a checklist and a reminder of categories of information that are required to put together a data warehouse architecture.
- The Selected Items list is a list of items that was built up either by selecting items from the Available Options list above or by entering new items manually. The Selected Items list represents the user defined data warehouse architecture that is currently being worked on. This set of lists can be saved as your own data warehouse architecture plan file.

The user Interface displays these sets of lists diagramatically as blocks and layers just as in the reference architecture. You can expose increasing detail ("drilling-down") by clicking blocks in successive windows as you navigate through the data warehouse reference architecture.

# Features and Functions

The following is a summary of the features and functions of the Planner. A detailed Windows Help file is supplied with the Planner software to help you.

## Creating a New Plan

The Planner allows you to define a new data warehouse architecture plan starting from scratch. Information is organized within the Planner according to levels of abstraction and dimensions.

**Levels of Abstraction.** The data warehouse reference architecture is organized into three levels based on the depth of detail of information that must be managed. Each block or layer of the architecture is itself capable of supporting three levels of abstraction. These levels are as following:

- **High level**—The components at this level are at the highest level of abstraction.
- **Mid level**—Components at this level are defined using a predetermined first order classification scheme for the block or layer.
- **Low level**—Components are defined using a second order classification scheme for each block or layer.

The decomposition hierarchy based on the three levels for the various blocks and layers are discussed in the following sections.

***Data Source Block Hierarchy.*** The following table shows the various classification categories at the three levels of abstraction.

| High Level | Mid Level | Low Level |
|---|---|---|
| Data Sources | Data Sources | Production Sources<br>Legacy Data<br>Internal Office Systems<br>External Sources<br>Metadata Sources<br>Others (components not covered by the above) |

***Data Warehouse Block Hierarchy.*** The following table shows the various classification categories at the three levels of abstraction.

| High Level | Mid Level | Low Level |
|---|---|---|
| Data Warehouse | Refinement | Standardize<br>Filter and Match<br>Cleanup and Scrub<br>Stamp: Time/Data Source<br>Verify Data Quality<br>Metadata Extraction<br>Others (components not covered by the above) |
| | Reengineering | Integrate and Partition<br>Summarize and Aggregate<br>Precalculate and Derive<br>Translate and Format<br>Transform and Remap<br>Metadata Creation<br>Others (components not covered by the above) |
| | Data Warehouse | Modeling<br>Summarize<br>Aggregate<br>Reconcile and Validate<br>Build Architected Queries<br>Create Glossary<br>Metadata Browse<br>Others (components not covered by the above) |

***Data Mart Block Hierarchy.*** The following table shows the various classification categories at the three levels of abstraction.

| High Level | Mid Level | Low Level |
|---|---|---|
| Data Mart | Refinement/<br>Reengineering | Filter and Match<br>Integrate and Partition<br>Summarize and Aggregate<br>Precalculate and Derive<br>Stamp: Time and Date Source<br>Metadata Extraction and Creation<br>Others (components not covered by the above) |
| | Data Mart | Modeling<br>Summarize<br>Aggregate<br>Reconcile and Validate<br>Build Architected Queries<br>Create Glossary<br>Metadata Browse and Navigate<br>Others (components not covered by the above) |

***Access and Usage Block Hierarchy.*** The following table shows the various classification categories at the three levels of abstraction.

| High Level | Mid Level | Low Level |
|---|---|---|
| Access and Usage | Access and Retrieval | Data Warehouse Direct Access<br>Data Mart Access<br>Re-engineering<br>Transform to Multidimension<br>Create Local Store<br>Metadata Browse and Navigate<br>Warehouse Metadata Mgmt<br>Other (components not covered by the above) |
| | Analysis and Reporting | Reporting Tools<br>Analysis and DSS Tools<br>Business Modeling Tools<br>Data Mining Tools<br>OLAP Tools<br>New Production Applications<br>Metadata Mgmt and Reports<br>Other (components not covered by the above) |

***Data Management Layer Hierarchy.*** The following table shows the various classification categories at the three levels of abstraction.

| High Level | Mid Level | Low Level |
|---|---|---|
| Data Management | Data Management | Data/Query Request Management<br>Load, Store, Refresh, and Update Systems<br>Security and Authorization Systems<br>Archive, Restore, and Purge Systems<br>Others (components not covered by the above) |

***Metadata Management Layer Hierarchy.*** The following table shows the various classification categories at the three levels of abstraction.

| High Level | Mid Level | Low Level |
|---|---|---|
| Metadata Management | Metadata Management | Schema and Glossary Mgmt<br>Metadata Creation, Store, and Update Mgmt<br>Extraction/Creation<br>Predefined Query, Report, and Index Mgmt<br>Refresh and Replication Mgmt<br>Logging, Archive, Restore, and Purge Mgmt<br>Others (components not covered by the above) |

***Transport Layer Hierarchy.*** The following table shows the various classification categories at the three levels of abstraction.

| High Level | Mid Level | Low Level |
|---|---|---|
| Transport | Transport | Data Transfer and Delivery Systems<br>Client/Server Agents and Middleware Tools<br>Replication Systems<br>Security and Authentication Systems<br>Others (components not covered by the above) |

***Infrastructure Layer Hierarchy.*** The following table shows the various classification categories at the three levels of abstraction.

| High Level | Mid Level | Low Level |
|---|---|---|
| Infrastructure | Infrastructure | Systems Management<br>Workflow Management<br>Storage Systems<br>Processing Systems<br>Others (components not covered by the above) |

**Dimensions.** If the blocks and layers of the reference architecture are perceived as partitioning the data warehouse architecture vertically, the dimensions can be perceived to partition the data warehouse horizontally. Figure A.3 shows these dimensions graphically.

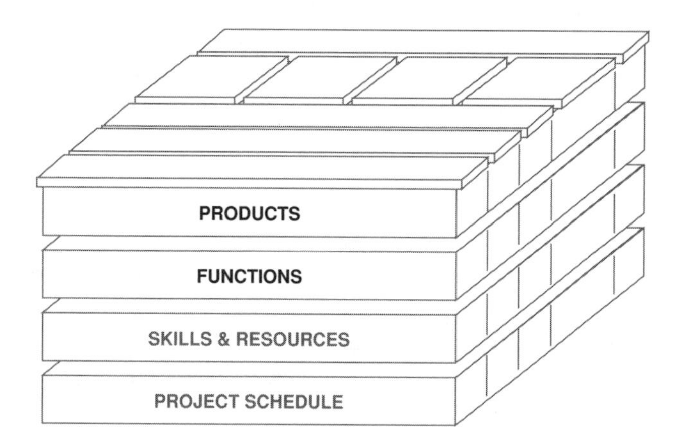


**Fig. A.3**

*Data warehouse architecture dimensions.*

The following dimensions are currently supported:

- Products
- Functions

In addition, it is possible to depict other dimensions by treating them as products or functions. You can only manage two dimensions at a time in a working plan. All dimensions are classified automatically into the three levels of abstraction. For some dimensions, this breakdown may be too detailed and only the high level of abstraction may need to be used.

## Customizing a Supplied Plan

The Planner allows you to start with a previously supplied plan and customize it for your operating environment and specific data warehouse needs. You can load the previously created plan into the Planner. The items are automatically loaded into the Available Options list and are available for selection. You can then start adding items from this list into the current working plan to create a customized set of selections. If there are items missing in the Available Options list, you can enter these items directly into the Selected Items list. You can save your customized plan with a new name inside a new file.

## Saving a Plan

The Planner saves its files as ASCII text files. This allows for easy distribution of plan information in text files. Saved plans can be opened for work at a later date.

## Merging Two or More Plans

An interesting and useful feature of the Planner is the ability to merge a previously saved plan with the current working plan. The merge operation results in the items of the previously saved plans being added as available options inside the current working plan. This feature allows an organization to consolidate data warehouse architectures from two or more departments.

## Generating Reports of Items in a Plan

The Planner also supports the generation of reports for architectures that are developed. These are text based reports and can be edited by any word processing utility.

## Sample Data Warehouse Architectures

The Planner software distribution also includes example data warehouse architectures. These can be used in one of the following scenarios:

- As a "quick start" for developing your own data warehouse architecture. You can load the example into the Available Options list and customize the items to create your own architecture.
- As a source for merging information into your current working architecture plan. You can open your working architecture and merge in one or more files. The loaded information is used to update the Available Options list. You can then select desired items and build your own custom architecture.

- As a reference for understanding how the Planner manages its information. The example files depict the Planner's storage level hierarchy for products and functions. The Help utility supplied with the software contains the interpretation of these levels.

### Windows Help

A Windows help file is supplied with the Planner software. The following table illustrates the organization of the Windows help.

| Subject | Description |
| --- | --- |
| About the Data Warehouse Planner | Briefly describes the layout and organization of the Planner. Links are also provided for definitions and terminology used by the Planner. |
| Menus | Describes the menu commands in the Planner software and their usage. |
| Screens | Describes the windows of the Planner and their significance and usage. |
| How To... | Briefly describes common Planner operations and links the operations to the corresponding menus and screens. |

In addition, the standard Windows help search capabilities based on topics, titles, and keywords is also supported.

## Installation

The Planner application is a Visual Basic 3.0 executable file that requires the Microsoft Visual Basic runtime interpreter `VBRUN300.DLL` inside your Windows directory. The Planner runs on Windows 3.1.

An automatic setup utility is provided to do the following:

- Install the software in a directory of your choice
- Install required Visual Basic files inside your Windows directories

To run the installation utility, select File, Run from Windows' Program Manager and type ***n*:\setup** (*n* being the drive letter where the installation media is inserted). The setup utility will guide you through the setup instructions.

APPENDIX B

# References and Sources

Appendix B consists of both references and sources. References are citations from either books and white papers or articles in industry publications. References are indicated by [ ] in the book, for example [ZACHMAN].

This appendix describes a number of publications that are available on various aspects of data warehousing. Sources include a few books, and many white papers, vendor literature, technical publications, articles in trade publications and newspapers, and other such sources. This is again a barometer of an evolving technology. These sources provide either additional avenues of information on data warehousing or more details on some topics discussed in the book.

Since data warehousing is an evolving and expanding technology, the list of publications mentioned here can be reasonably expected to provide you with ongoing articles and news on data warehousing. A number of these publications are focused on a single aspect of data warehouse technology, often providing in-depth narratives of experiences of actual implementors and users of this technology.

## References


- Inmon, W., *Building the Data Warehouse*, QED Technical Publishing Group, 1992.
- Inmon, W., Hackathorn, R., *Using the Data Warehouse*, John Wiley & Sons, 1994.
- Moriarty, T., "A Data Warehouse Primer." *Database Programming and Design*, July 1995.
- Kimball, R., "The Aggregate Navigator." DBMS November 1995.
- Kimball, R., "The Database Market Splits." DBMS September 1995.
- Raden, N., "Data, Data Everywhere." *INFORMATIONWEEK*. 30 Oct. 1995.
- McKie, S., "Software Agents: Application Intelligence Goes Undercover." *DBMS* Vol. 8, No. 4. April 1995.

- Matheus, C., Piatetsky-Shapiro, G., Chan, P. "Systems for Knowledge Discovery in Databases." *IEEE Transactions on Knowledge and Data Engineering*, December 1993, Volume 5 Number 6.
- Frawley, W., Piatetsky-Shapiro, G., Matheus, C. "Knowledge Discovery in Databases: An overview." in *Knowledge Discovery in Databases*. Cambridge, MA: AAAI/MIT, 1991, pp. 1-27. Reprinted in *AI Magazine*, 1992, Volume 13 Number 3.
- Zachman, J. "A Framework for Information Systems Architecture." *IBM Systems Journal* 1987.
- Spewak, S., "Enterprise Architecture Planning—Developing a Blueprint for Data, Applications, and Technology." *John Wiley* 1992.
- Demarest, M. "Building the DATAMART." *DBMS Magazine* July 1994.
- Indica Group, "Seminar: Data Warehouse. Training Materials 1995." *Indica Group*, 1995.
- Meredith, M., "Deliver Decisions, Not Data." *Information Week*, August 21 1995.
- Benson, S., "Integrating Processes for Software Excellence," *Software Development*, August 1995.
- Shelton, R., "Data Warehouse Infrastructure," *Data Management Review*, July/August 1995.
- O'Mahony, M., "Revolutionary Breakthrough in Client/Server Data Warehouse Development," *Data Management Review*, July/August 1995.
- Quinlan, T., "Building from Strength: Architecture and Design for Enterprise Client/Server," *Database Programming and Design*, September 1995.
- Informix Corporation., "Informix and Data Warehousing." *Informix Times*, Issue 3, 1995.
- Platinum Edge—A Database Survival Guide Summer 1995. "Replication in Data Warehousing."
- Platinum Technology Inc., "Build your Data Warehouse with Platinum," Product Tip Issue 3, 1995.
- Paper "Managing Your Universe of Data with Data Warehousing," Seminar, Prism Solutions Inc., September 1995.
- Technical Manual "Information Warehouse, Architecture 1," SC26-3244-00, IBM Corporation Department J58, P.O. Box 49023, San Jose CA 95161-9023, USA.
- Von Halle, B. "Life Beyond Data." *Database Programming and Design*, September 1995.
- Romberg, F., "Data Modeling: Answering Tough Questions." *Database Programming and Design*, September 1995.
- Dowgiallo, E., "Organizing Client/Server Security." *Database Programming and Design*, September 1995.
- "Data Warehousing: What works?" A compilation of case studies from The Data Warehousing Institute, 4610 Tournay Road, Bethesda MD 20816. Publication Number 295104.

- Inmon, W., "Growth in the Data Warehouse." *Data Management Review,* December 1995.
- Hackney, D., "Ensure a Good Beginning by Forcing a Bad Ending." *Data Management Review.* December 1995.
- Edelstein, H., "Faster Data Warehouses." *Information Week,* December 4 1995.
- Meador, C., "Planning for Data Replication." *Information Week,* December 18 1995.
- Kerwien, E. "The Cross-Platform Myth." *InfoWorld,* October 2 1995.
- Perera, P., "Synchronization Schizophrenia." *ComputerWorld Client/Server Journal,* October 1995.
- White Paper "Navigating around the Client/Server Iceberg." *Advertising Supplement to ComputerWorld,* August 7 1995.
- Baer, A., "The Dark Side of Data Warehousing." *ComputerWorld Client/Server Journal,* August 1995.
- Bischoff, J., "Achieving Warehouse Success." *Database Programming and Design.* July 1994.
- Rinaldi, D., "Metadata Management Separates Prism From Data Warehouse Pack," *Client/Server Computing* March 1995.
- Leinfuss, E., "Managing Data Diversity Poses Challenge in Corporate Data Warehouse," *Client/Server Computing* November 1994.
- Chasin, K., "Designing Data Warehouses Using CASE Technology," *Journal of Systems Management,* May 1994.
- Gleason, D. "Data Warehousing." *White Paper of Platinum Information Management Consulting,* Platinum Technology Oak Brook IL.
- "Shedding Light on Data Warehousing." Special Advertising supplement.
- Product Information. "Rochade Data Warehousing Support." R&O. The Repository Company. 39A Kingfisher Court, Hambridge Road, Newbury, Berkshire RG14 5SJ.
- Rennhackkamp, M. "Building a DBA Repository System." *DBMS,* January 1996.
- Product Literature "Metadata Management with the ETI EXTRACT Tool Suite." *Evolutionary Technologies International.* 4301 Westbank Drive, Bldg B., Austin TX 78746.
- Griffin, J. "Customer Information Architecture." *DBMS,* July 1995.
- Partee, S. "Data Administration in the '90s." *Data Management Review,* July 1993.
- White, C. "The Key to a Data Warehouse." *DATABASE PROGRAMMING & DESIGN,* February 1995.
- Mantha, R. "Data Architecture for Data Warehousing: Linking the Warehouse to the Enterprise." *DCI Data Warehousing Conference Presentation,* August 1995.

- English, L. "Why Data Modeling is Imperative." *Platinum Edge Summer* 1995 Volume 2.
- Ault, M. "Planning for a Multi-Gigabyte Oracle Data Warehouse." *Platinum Edge Summer* 1995 Volume 2.
- Moriarty, T. "Modeling Data Warehouses." *DATABASE PROGRAMMING & DESIGN* August 1995.
- Brooks, "Relational Databases and Multidimensional Modeling." *DBMS Magazine* August 1995.
- Kimball, R. "Is ER Modeling Hazardous to DSS?" *DBMS Magazine* October 1995.
- Porter, M. *Competitive Advantage,* Free Press (Macmillan) 1985.


# Sources


- "IRI Software." Aberdeen Group *Profile*. March 1994.
- Ricciuti, Mike. "Multidimensional Analysis: Winning the Competitive Game." *Datamation.* 15 Feb. 1994.
- Dutta, S., Shekhar, S. "Bond Rating: A Non-Conservative Application of Neural Networks." *Neural Networks in Finance and Investing,* Probus Publishing Co., Cambridge (UK), 1993.
- Glassey, K. "The Keys to the Data Warehouse: Access Tools for End Users." *Brio Technology, Inc.*
- Dickman, A. "Two-Tier Versus Three-Tier Apps." *INFORMATIONWEEK.* 13 Nov. 1995.
- Cole, B. "Avoiding the dark side of data access." *Network World.* 30 October, 1995.
- Mahoney, P. J. "Total Quality Methods in Information Systems Development." 17 March, 1995.
- Product Comparison: Report Writers. "Democratic data tools." *INFOWORLD* 23, Oct. 1995.
- Mann, C.; Mehta, R. "Selecting Data Warehouse End-User Access Tools." *DATA MANAGEMENT REVIEW.* July/August 1995.
- Mann, C.; Mehta, R. "Selecting Data Warehouse End-User Access Tools—Part II." *DATA MANAGEMENT REVIEW.* September 1995.
- Adhikari, R. "REPORT WRITERS: What Kind of Animal Are They?" *CLIENT/SERVER COMPUTING.* October 1995.
- Tyo, J. "Query Tools Help Users Dip Into Data." *INFORMATIONWEEK.* 10 Apr. 1995.
- Tyo, J. "Nailing Down More Query Tools." *INFORMATIONWEEK.* 17 Apr. 1995.
- PLATINUM Edge Magazine EXtrA, "Special Supplement on Data Warehousing." *PLATINUM technology, inc.* Summer 1995.

- Edelstein, H., Millenson, J. "How to Succeed with End-User Data Access." *A White Paper.*
- Frye, C. "Big Flap Over OLAP." *CLIENT/SERVER COMPUTING.* May 1995.
- Codd, E. F.; Codd, S. B.; Salley, C. T. "Beyond Decision Support." *ComputerWorld.* Vol. 27, No. 30. 26 July 1993.
- Bulos, D. "How to Evaluate OLAP Servers." *DBMS* August 1995.
- Frank, M. "The Truth About OLAP." *DBMS* August 1995.
- "Data Warehouse Query Tools: Evolving to Relational OLAP." Aberdeen*Group Market Viewpoint.* Volume 8 / No. 8. 7 July, 1995.
- Richman, D. "OLAP vendors at loggerheads." *ComputerWorld* 30 October, 1995.
- White Paper, "Designing the Data Warehouse on Relational Databases." *Stanford Technology Group* part number 7103-20-0195.
- Weldon, J. "Managing Multidimensional Data: Harnessing the Power." *DATABASE PROGRAMMING & DESIGN* August, 1995.
- Finkelstein, R. "Understanding the Need for ON-Line Analytical Servers."
- Finkelstein, R. "MDD: Database Reaches the Next Dimension." *DATABASE PROGRAMMING & DESIGN* April, 1995.
- Gill, P. "Sears' Big Budget Epic." *open computing* December 1995.
- Core, G. "Express Analysis." *open computing* December 1995.
- Stevens, L. "Polishing Sales with OLAP." *open computing* December 1995.
- Baer, T. "Do you really need... OLAP Databases?" *open computing,* September 1995.
- King, P. "The More Views, the Merrier." *CLIENT/SERVER COMPUTING,* May 1994.
- Callaway, E. "The Flavors of OLAP." *PC WEEK.* 17 July, 1995.
- Menninger, D. "OLAP: Turning Corporate Data Into Business Intelligence." *IRI Software* White Paper.
- IBM White Paper, "Data Mining: Extending The Information Warehouse Framework." First Edition (April 1995).
- Information Discovery, Inc. "Decision Support Solutions for Turning Data into Information." *Information Discovery, Inc.,* 1995.
- Fahey, M. "Mining for Data Gold." *RS/Magazine.* January 1995.
- Parsaye, K. "Large-Scale Data Mining in Parallel." *DBMS Parallel Database Special* pp. H-W.
- Reeves, L. "Data Mining." *DATA MANAGEMENT REVIEW.* July/August 1995.
- Ingalls, M., Wang, P. "Databases and decision makers: The need for an analytical system." *The Journal of Database Marketing* February 1994. Vol. 1 Number 4.
- Swami, A. " Data Mining with Silicon Graphics Technology." *Silicon Graphics White Paper* 1994.

- Hedberg, S. "The Data Gold Rush." *BYTE*. October 1995.
- Watterson, K. "A Data Miner's Tools." *BYTE*. October 1995.
- Krivda, C. "Data-Mining Dynamite." *BYTE*. October 1995.
- Information Harvester White Paper 1994.
- Agrawal, R., Imielinski, T., Swami, A. "Database Mining: A Performance Perspective." *IEEE Transactions on Knowledge and Data Engineering* December 1993, Volume 5 Number 6.
- Heller, J. "Advanced Data Mining." *DATA MANAGEMENT REVIEW*. September 1995.
- SPSS Inc. "Neural Connection." SPSS Inc., 9/95. SPSS order number, NEUBRO.
- Rymer, J. "Data Analysis: New Tools for Expanding Needs." Patricia Seybold Group White Paper prepared for BBN Software Products.
- Shapiro, S. *Encyclopedia of Artificial Intelligence*, John Wiley & Sons, 1990. Volumes 1 & 2.
- Swigor, J. "Database Marketing Is an Art Beyond Science." *DATA MANAGEMENT REVIEW*. November 1995.
- IBM White Paper, "Parallel Visual Explorer." 11/95.
- IBM White Paper, "Multidimensional Graphs—Visual data Mining." November 5/95.
- Strange, K., Varma, S. "The Data Warehouse Market—Setting the Record Straight." *SDM Research Notes*, Gartner Group. March 22, 1995.
- Zornes, A. "Transitioneering the Enterprise via Data Warehouse." *DCI Data Warehousing Conference Presentation,* August 1995.
- Morrison, D. "Value Judgments." *Beyond Computing* July/August 1995.
- Spence, W. quoted in "Value Judgments." *Beyond Computing* July/August 1995.
- Morrison, D. "Value Judgments." *Beyond Computing* July/August 1995.
- Pearce, S. "Quantifying the Value of Data Warehousing." *Pyramid Technology Presentation DCI Data Warehousing Conference,* August 1995.
- Goldberg, M. "Servers give new shape to Pyramid line." *ComputerWorld*, December 18, 1995.
- D. H. Brown Associates, Inc. "Pyramid Stakes Growth on Smart Warehouse." *Technology Trends*, September 20, 1995.
- Babcock, C. "Slice, dice & deliver." *ComputerWorld*, November 13, 1995.
- Barth, P. "Advanced Data Mining in Very Large Databases." *Tessera Enterprise Systems Presentation DCI Data Warehousing Conference*, August 1995.
- Bowen, B. "IT and Business Analysts Cooperate in Effective Data Warehouse Endeavors." *Client/Server Computing*, December 1995.
- Miller, G. "Turning Life-Cycle Costs into Company Profits." *Client/Server Computing*, November 1995.

- Baum, D. "Warehouse Mania." *LAN TIMES*, November 20, 1995.
- Lisle, R. "The Right Tool for the Job." *LAN TIMES*, January 8, 1996.
- Finkelstein, R. "Building a Fast and Reliable Data Warehousing Architecture Using the DB2 Family of Products." *White Paper*, Performance Computing, May 1995.
- IBM White Paper, "Data Management: IBM Strategies and Solutions."
- IBM White Paper, "Data Mining: Extending the Information Warehouse Framework."
- IBM White Paper, "Data Replication: the IBM Story."
- IBM White Paper, "IBM Information Warehouse Solution: A Data Warehouse—*Plus!*"
- IBM White Paper, "DataJoiner—A Multidatabase Server."
- IBM Corporation, "Information Warehouse: An Introduction." *IBM Document* Order number, GC26-4876.
- IBM Corporation, "Information Warehouse: Architecture I." *IBM Document* Order number, SC26-3244.
- Oracle Corporation, "Systems Management Tools Initiative." *Oracle* Brochure Part # A20736.
- Oracle Corporation, "Warehouse Technology Initiative." *Oracle* Brochure Part # A33661.
- Mendelson, N. "Oracle: Data Warehousing." *Oracle Corporation Briefing* 1995.
- White Paper "Oracle Test-to-Scale Program: Data Warehousing." *Oracle Corporation*, Part Number C10240.
- White Paper "Oracle7 Server: Scalable Parallel Architecture for Open Data Warehousing." *Oracle Corporation*, Part Number C10271.
- Technology Audit "Discoverer/2000." *Butler Group*, June 1995.
- Smalley Bowen, T. "Oracle building Warehouse." *PC WEEK*, July 3, 1995.
- Dorshkind, B. "Oracle Gives Legacy App Access." *LAN TIMES*, October 9, 1995.
- Richman, D. "Oracle7.3 focuses on data warehousing." *ComputerWorld*, September 25, 1995.
- Richman, D. "Oracle calls database detente on OLAP." *ComputerWorld*, November 27, 1995.
- Gates, L. "Oracle Now Manages Spatial Data." *Client/Server Computing*, May 1995.
- White Paper "ORACLE Parallel Server for Challenge Systems." *Silicon Graphics, Inc.* 1995.
- Bull, K., Richman, D. "Oracle's Single-Vendor Solution." *INFORMATIONWEEK*, July 10, 1995.
- Patricia Seybold Group, "Data Warehousing: Turning Data into Decisions." *ComputerWorld and CIO* Special Advertising Supplement 1995.

- Info Sheet, "Informix in Data Warehousing." *Informix Software, Inc. Document* Identification Number 000-20846-74.
- White Paper, "Data Warehousing for Enterprisewide Decision Making." *Informix Software, Inc. Document* Identification Number 000-20716-70.
- Press Release, "Informix to Acquire Stanford Technology Group." *Informix Software, Inc.* October 25, 1995.
- Press Release, "Informix Software Teams with Pyramid Technology and SNI to Support the Smart Warehouse." *Informix Software, Inc.* September 18, 1995.
- Press Release, "Informix, Digital and KPMG Form Data Warehouse Initiative." *Informix Software, Inc.*, September 19, 1995.
- Product Briefing, "Prism Directory Manager." *Prism Solutions, Inc. Form* no.: DOTTPB13.
- Product Briefing, "Prism Warehouse Manager." *Prism Solutions, Inc. 1995.*
- Indica Group Survey Response "The Official Client/Server Guide to Data Warehousing." *Prism Solutions*, January 1996.
- Kalman, D., Rigney, T. "System 11 Strategy." *DBMS* October 1995.
- Bull, K. "Will Rivals Leap Over Sybase?" *INFORMATIONWEEK*, November 13, 1995.
- Product Brief, "SYBASE IQ." *Sybase*, Inc. 1995.
- Product Brief, "SYBASE Replication Server." *Sybase*, Inc. 1993.
- Bull, K. "Sybase's Higher IQ Software." *INFORMATIONWEEK*, August 21, 1995.
- Atre, S., Storer, P. "Data Distribution and Warehousing." *DBMS*, October 1995.
- Briefing, "Warehouse WORKS." *Sybase* 1995.
- Bull, K., Wagner, M. "Sybase's Database Agent." *INFORMATIONWEEK*, July 17, 1995.
- Product Brief, "SYBASE Enterprise CONNECT." *Sybase*, Inc. 1995.
- Technical Paper Series, "SYBASE Interactive Query Accelerator." *Sybase*, Inc. 1994.
- Briefing, "KNOWLEDGE MANAGEMENT: A Total Approach to Data Warehousing." *Price Waterhouse LLP* 1995.
- Baer, A. "IBM Discloses Warehouse Plans." *Software Magazine*, July 1995.
- Phillips, B. "IBM to add data dimensions." *PC WEEK*, October 9, 1995.
- Stedman, C. "IBM seeks to take control of database administration." *ComputerWorld*, September 25, 1995.
- Ballard, C. "The IBM Visual Warehouse." *Data Management Review*, July/August 1995.
- DeVoe, D. "IBM to bolster data warehousing." *INFOWORLD* August 21, 1995.
- Product Brief "Visual Warehouse." *IBM Corporation* Order Number GC26-8468-00.

- Product Brief "DataJoiner" *IBM Corporation* Order Number GC26-8339-00.
- Product Brief "DataJoiner: Client/Server Database Middleware." *IBM Corporation* Order Number GC26-8241-00.
- Product Brief "From Datamarts to Enterprise-Wide Data Warehouses." *IBM Corporation* May 1995.
- LaMonica, M. "IBM lines up tool vendors for its Visual Warehouse." *INFOWORLD* October 30, 1995.
- Indica Group Survey Response "The Official Client/Server Guide to Data Warehousing." *Information Advantage*, December 12, 1996.
- Indica Group Survey Response "The Official Client/Server Guide to Data Warehousing." *Platinum technology*, December 1996.
- White Paper "The PLATINUM Open Enterprise Management System: Our Evolving Vision and Strategy for the Future of Open Enterprise Systems Management." *Platinum technology*, June 1, 1995.
- Tannenbaum, A. "MAINTAINING The Data Warehouse." *Platinum Edge Magazine Extra*, Summer 1995.
- Phillips, B. "AT&T grows Teradata; Platinum ships repository." *PC WEEK*, October 16, 1995.
- Smalley Bowen, T "Platinum polishes ProReports update." *PC WEEK*, August 14, 1995.
- Grygo, E. "McKesson Finds the Right Prescription—An Information Warehouse on SMP." *Client/Server Computing*, July 1995.
- Indica Group Survey Response "The Official Client/Server Guide to Data Warehousing." *SAS Institute*, December 8, 1996.
- Product Demonstration "The SAS System for Information Delivery." *SAS Institute*, 1995.
- Gates, L. "The SAS System for Data Warehousing: Puts Data in a People Format." *Client/Server Computing*, December 1995.
- Norton, A. "SAS System for Application Development." *Data Management Review*, November 1995.
- Brown, B. "Building a Data Warehouse for User Data Access and Reporting." *SAS Institute White Paper*, April 1995.
- Smalley Bowen, T "SAS polishes suite's data warehousing." *PC WEEK*, September 11, 1995.
- Bucken, M. "SAS Emphasizes R&D To Gain MIS edge." *Software Magazine*, May 1994.
- Fryer, R. "Relational Data Base Management Systems—Critical Success Factors for Data Warehouses." *AT&T GIS White Paper*, October 3, 1995.
- Vozel, K. "Beyond Data Warehouse™: Evolving Information Infrastructures." *AT&T GIS Technical Evolution White Paper*, 1994.

- Product Brief "AT&T Server Family." *AT&T*, September 1995.
- Product Brief "HP OpenWarehouse—HP Intelligent WareHouse." *Hewlett Packard Part Number* 5964-4021E.
- Product Brief "HP Intelligent WareHouse." *Hewlett Packard Part Number* 5963-6799E.
- Product Brief "HP OpenWarehouse." *Hewlett Packard Part Number* 5963-3521E.
- Product Brief "HP OpenWarehouse: Intelligent Warehouse Solution." *Hewlett Packard Part Number* 5962-08496E.
- NEWSFRONT "HP Announces Data Warehouse Lite." *Software Magazine*, April 1995.
- Sachdeva, S. "METADATA: Guiding Users Through Disparate Data Layers." *Application Development Trends*, December 1995.
- Hartlen, B. "Detect and Alert: A Revolution in EIS/DSS." Comshare White Paper.
- Frank, M. "Database and the Internet." *DBMS*, December 1995.
- Rauen, C. "Mining for Data." *Beyond Computing*, October 1995.
- Radding, A. "Support DECISION Makers with a DATA Warehouse." *Datamation*, March 15, 1995.
- Gill, H. "Data Warehouse: State of the Practice." Indica Group Draft Internal Paper, April 1995.
- Technical Overview "OpenBridge." Informatica Corporation, December 1995.
- Indica Group Survey Response "The Official Client/Server Guide to Data Warehousing." *Evolutionary Technologies International*, December 1995.
- Product Briefs "ETI·EXTRACT Tool Suite." *Evolutionary Technologies International*, 1995.
- Briefing "The ETI·EXTRACT Tool Suite Solution for Data Warehouses." *Evolutionary Technologies International*, 1995.
- White Paper "The Importance of Metadata in Reducing the Cost of Change." *Evolutionary Technologies International*, May 1995.
- Indica Group Survey Response "The Official Client/Server Guide to Data Warehousing." *Vality Technology*, December 4, 1995.
- White Paper "The Five Legacy Data Contaminants that you will encounter in your Data Migrations." *Vality Technology*, February 1995.
- White Paper "The Five Common Excuses for Not Re-engineering Legacy Data." *Vality Technology*, February 1995.
- White Paper "Specialized Requirements for Relational Data Warehouse Servers." *Red Brick Systems*, 1995.
- White Paper "Star Schemas and STARjoin™ Technology." *Red Brick Systems*, September 1, 1995.
- Petersen, S. "Praxis breaks ground with OmniRelicator." *PC WEEK*, September 25, 1995.

- Cole, B. "Praxis readies tool for data warehousing." *Network World*, October 16, 1995.
- Client/Server Connection "Praxis Acquires Power Thinking." *DBMS*, May 1995.
- Phillips, B. "Red Brick props up flagship foundation." *PC WEEK*, November 27, 1995.
- Phillips, B. "Bit-mapped warehouse index on tap." *PC WEEK*, October 16, 1995.
- NEWS BRIEFS "Dimensional Insight issues API for CrossTarget." *PC WEEK*, October 16, 1995.
- Nash, K. "Red Brick offers small warehouse data marts." *ComputerWorld*, July 31, 1995.
- White Paper "The Keys to the Data warehouse." *Software AG Document* Number KDW-WP01-0495.
- Black, G. "PUTTING STOCK in WAREHOUSING." *Software Magazine*, January 1996.
- Stodder, D., Pucky, A. "Software AG's Data Warehouse Push." *DATABASE PROGRAMMING & DESIGN*, July 1995.
- White Paper "DATA WAREHOUSING: A WHITE PAPER." *Software AG.*
- Mitchell, L. "Query and ye shall receive." PC WEEK, September 18, 1995.
- Busse, T. "Software AG eases data warehouse construction." *INFOWORLD*, July 17, 1995.
- Product Brief "EDA/SQL: Enterprise Copy Manager." *Information Builders* DN7501696.0495.
- White Paper "Data Warehouse Technology." *Information Builders* DN7501615.0395.
- White Paper "Building a Data Warehouse Using EDA/SQL." *Information Builders* 1995.
- Leinweber, M., Small, C. "EDA/SQL Copy Manager." *Information Builders White Paper*, March 22, 1995.
- Phillips, B. "IBI builds on middleware strategy." *PC WEEK*, November 6, 1995.
- White Paper "Relational OLAP: Expectations and Reality." *Arbor Software* Document Number MK0305-1095.
- White Paper "Multidimensional Analysis: Converting Corporate Data into Strategic Information." *Arbor Software* Document Number 0301-0894.
- Indica Group Survey Response "The Official Client/Server Guide to Data Warehousing." *MicroStrategy*, December 1995.
- White Paper "The Case for Relational OLAP." MicroStrategy, Inc.
- Eckerson, W. "MicroStrategy Enhances Relational Query/Analysis Tool." *OPEN INFORMATION SYSTEMS: Patricia Seybold Group*, Vol. 10, No. 8, August 1995.
- White Paper "An Enterprise-Wide Data Delivery Architecture." *MicroStrategy, Inc.* 1994.

- Eckerson, W. "Prodea Offers Next-Generation Decision-Support Tool." *OPEN INFORMATION SYSTEMS: Patricia Seybold Group*, Vol. 10, No. 7, July 1995.
- Nash, K. "PC tool agents ease database access." *ComputerWorld*, July 3, 1995.
- Taschek, J. "DataDirect Explorer: Jack of all trades." *PC WEEK*, October 23, 1995.
- Ricciuti, M. "Virtual data warehouses in the works." *INFOWORLD*, September 4, 1995.
- Product Briefings "VISION:Manage™; VISION: Journey™; VISION: Data™." *Sterling Software* 1995.
- Indica Group Survey Response "The Official Client/Server Guide to Data Warehousing." *Sequent Computer Systems*, December 27, 1995.
- Product Brief "Carleton PASSPORT™." *Carleton Corporation* 1995.
- Profile "Carleton Corporation." *Aberdeen Group*, August 1995.
- Product Brief "The Power to Predict: DataBase Mining Technology." *HNC Software*, Document Part Number: DMW0007-A.
- Cole, B. "Business Objects, Prism ready revised data warehouse tools." *Network World*, September 25, 1995.
- Ricciuti, M. "Business Objects blends OLAP, Data query." *INFOWORLD*, September 25, 1995.
- Mitchell, L. "BrioQuery Designer: Single solution for both Mac and Windows enterprises." *PC WEEK*, June 19, 1995.
- Glassey, K. "The Keys to the Data Warehouse: Access Tools for End Users." *Brio Technology White Paper.*
- Cole, B. "Red Brick builds new data warehouse." *Network World*, November 27, 1995.
- Profile "IQ Software Corporation." *Aberdeen Group*, September 11, 1995.
- Rymer, J. "IQ Software Introduces Object-Oriented Reporting into Mainstream Business Intelligence." *Patricia Seybold Group's SnapShots*, October 1995.
- Indica Group Survey Response "The Official Client/Server Guide to Data Warehousing." *IQ Software Corporation*, December 1995.
- Mitchell, L. "Where has all the information gone?" *PC WEEK*, November 20, 1995.
- Cole, B. "Database vendors flesh out their OLAP plans." *Network World*, November 20, 1995.
- DeJesus, E. "Data to the Nth Dimension." *BYTE*, December 1995.
- White Paper "An Introduction to Multidimensional Database Technology." *Kenan Technologies.*
- White Paper "Understanding Multidimensional Analysis: The Fifteen Keys." *Information Advantage.*
- Ricciuti, M. "OLAP tools ease access to data warehouses." *INFOWORLD*, November 20, 1995.

- White Paper "Decision Support Solutions for Turning Data into Information." *Information Discovery, Inc.* 1995.
- Bucken, M. "Data Warehousing Deserves Better." *Software Magazine Editorial*, December 1995.
- Dataquest White Paper "The Distributed Enterprise." *ComputerWorld Client/Server Journal Special Advertising Supplement* 1995.
- Baer, T. "Data Quality." *ComputerWorld Client/Server Journal*, November 1995.
- Mimno, P. "3 DECISIONS Critical to Make For Warehouse Development." *Applications Development Trends*, December 1995.
- Bartholomew, D., Gallagher, S. "Oracle's New 'House'." *INFORMATIONWEEK*, December 18, 1995.
- Bort, J. "Getting data Squeaky Clean." *INFOWORLD*, December 18, 1995.
- Brandel, M. "AT&T GIS dives into vertical markets." *ComputerWorld*, October 31, 1995.
- McWilliams, B. "Putting management back into INFORMATION SYSTEMS." *Enterprise*, February 1995.
- Phillips, B. "While the Web waits, data warehousing comes of age." *PC WEEK*, January 8, 1996.
- Black, G. "Wellcome Prescribes OLAP for Decision Support." *Software Magazine*, December 1995.
- Richman, D. "Database daring: Microsoft begins bold bid to make SQL Server an enterprisewide player." *ComputerWorld*, November 13, 1995.
- Bull, K. "Warehousing Isn't Enough." *INFORMATIONWEEK*, June 26, 1995.
- Cafasso, R. "Sears mines data with multidimensional tools." *ComputerWorld*, June 26, 1995.
- Girishankar, S. "NABISCO Net Brings Sweet Success." *CommunicationsWeek*, May 22, 1995.
- Harding, E. "Purina Mills Warehouses A Legacy of Success." *Software Magazine*, November 1995.
- Demarest, M. "LeadingEdge Retail." *DBMS*, December 1994.
- Janah, M. "Data lessons learned." INFOWORLD July 31, 1995.
- Bradway, W. "Using a Data Warehouse to Measure Customer, Product and Organizational Profitability." *DCI Data Warehouse Conference Proceedings*, August 10, 1995.
- Bank of America Presentation "Data Warehousing As a Corporate Asset." *DCI Data Warehouse Conference Proceedings*, August 10, 1995.
- Bull, K. "The Ideal File Cabinet." *INFORMATIONWEEK*, January 16, 1995.
- Crane, E. "The Data Conversion Gamble." *open computing*, November 1994.
- Danca, R. "DSS Built Around DEC's Alpha Delivers True Benefits." *Client/Server Computing*, May 1994.

- News Brief "Decision Systems: Sara Lee Upgrades Sales Analysis with Object-oriented Tool." *Retail Systems Alert*, Vol. 8, Number 1, January 1995.
- Alur, N. "Missing Links in Data Warehousing." *DATABASE PROGRAMMING & DESIGN*, September 1995.
- Radding, A. "Warehouse wake-up call." *INFOWORLD*, November 20, 1995.

APPENDIX C

# Glossary

Data warehousing is an emerging and evolving technology. In a rapidly growing technology such as this, terminology and definitions can be confusing and may bear no relationship to existing terms and definitions in related technologies. At the same time, the implementation of warehouse technology has been driven primarily by vendors who coin or invent terminology that is sometimes marketing oriented in their literature.

To lay down a common base of understanding for our readers, we present some terms and definitions as they relate to the reference architecture discussed in Chapter 2, "A Framework for Understanding the Data Warehouse," and other terms and definitions used in this book. Additionally, this glossary provides definitions of those data warehouse technology terms that may not be readily known to all our readers.

Although a universally accepted and used glossary of terms is not readily available, some early attempts are underway by consulting houses and product vendors. As standards evolve, some of the terms and definitions in this appendix will become standardized, too.

## Common Terms and Definitions

**Access and Usage Block**—The component of the data warehouse that deals with the facilities for accessing and using the information stored inside the data warehouse. Such facilities include query, reporting, and browsing tools.

**Agent Technology**—Software code that is event-driven and structurally invisible to the business user; it is always "alive" and ready for action.

**Aggregate**—Add multiple data sources or dimensions to create new dimension, such as sum of checking account and savings account balances to determine net cash on hand.

**Aggregation**—The activity of combining data from multiple tables to form a more complex unit of information frequently needed to answer data warehouse queries more easily and speedily. Most operational databases store data at the simplest unit where possible (normalization) to prevent update and delete anomalies.

**Analytical processing**—Verification mode of data analysis, usually multidimensional analysis of the data.

**ANOVA**—Acronym for Analysis of Variance, to test whether a value or set of values, in a data set, is within a normally expected range.

**Artificial Intelligence (AI)**—This is the science of programming a computer to perform functions that mimic human intelligence.

**Bitmap Indexing**—An efficient method for data indexing where almost all of the operations on database records can be performed on the indices without resorting to looking at the actual data underneath. By performing operations primarily on indices, the number of database reads is reduced significantly.

**Business Directory**—A component of the warehouse information directory. The business directory primarily supports business users who do not have a technical background and therefore cannot use the technical directory to find out what information is stored inside the data warehouse.

**Business intelligence querying**—Two- or three-dimensional data warehouse query, analysis, and reporting (see also *informational processing*).

**Business Re-engineering**—A term used for the activities related to modeling existing business processes to identify areas of improvement.

**CASE**—Acronym for Computer Aided Software Engineering. A software development methodology that is supported by computer-based tools for assisting the analysis, design, and development tasks.

**CHAID**—Acronym for CHi-squared Automatic Interaction Detection, which is an algorithm that iteratively segments data sets into mutually exclusive subsets based on their effect on nominal or ordinal variables.

**Characteristic description**—Describes what is common in the data items in the class discovered by a knowledge discovery algorithm.

**Classification**—Knowledge discovery technique involving finding rules that partition the given data into disjoint groups, called classes.

**Clean and Scrub**—Add missing fields and replace secret encoding with business rules and data structures.

**Client/Server System**—A software application system where the processing of the application is provided jointly by two architecture components that are distinctly separated: the client and the server.

**Clustering**—Clustering tables is the act of requiring physical database tables to reside physically next to each other on the storage media. Sequential pre-fetch can produce dramatic performance gains when accessing a large number of rows.

**Clusters**—Spreads work across multiple SMP machines.

**Data Cleanup and Refinement**—The activity of removing errors in source data before attempting to load it into the data warehouse or data mart.

**Data Consolidation**—The process of synthesizing pieces of information into single blocks of essential knowledge.

**Data Consolidation Path**—A series of consolidation levels or steps defined in terms of multilevel parameters. Consolidation paths determine the details visible to the business user when drilling-down or rolling-up.

**Data Dictionary**—A compendium of definitions and specifications for data categories and their relationships.

**Data Dimension**—A conceptual qualifier that provides the context or meaning for a metric, e.g., geography, product time. It is also the highest level in a data consolidation path.

**Data Integration**—The activity of combining data from multiple data sources inside the data warehouse to present a single collection of data to the data warehouse user.

**Data Management Layer**—The component of the data warehouse reference architecture that deals with data management facilities.

**Data Mart**—An implementation of a data warehouse with a small and more tightly restricted scope of data and data warehouse functions serving a single department or part of an organization. An organization generally has several data marts.

**Data Mining**—Discovery mode of data analysis, or analyzing detail data to unearth unsuspected or unknown relationships, patterns, and associations.

**Data Modeling**—The activity of representing the categories of data and relationships between them as an abstraction in diagram form.

**Data Propagation/Replication**—The ability to transmit a copy of the data inside specified tables in a database to another remotely connected database and, often, keeping the two databases synchronized for data changes.

**Data Refinement**—A term applied to the collective activities applied to data from sources to prepare the data for loading into the data warehouse.

**Data Refresh**—The activity of continuously updating the data warehouse's data contents from the data sources after the initial loading is completed. This is an ongoing process where today's operational data becomes tomorrow's historical data.

**Data Sources Block**—The component of the data warehouse reference architecture that represents activities that deal with the operational databases and external sources that provide data for loading into the data warehouse.

**Data Synchronization**—The activity of keeping the data warehouse data up-to-date with the data stored in the operational databases that loaded it in the first place.

**Data Transformation & Remapping**—Transformation and remapping is the process of converting the data source information into rows suitable for populating the fact tables of the data warehouse.

**Data Visualization**—Presentation of data in a graphical form to ease the analysis of complex and voluminous data.

**Data Warehouse Block**—The component of the data warehouse reference architecture that represents activities that deal directly with data warehouse operations.

**Database Schema**—The specification for how a database is organized.

**Decision Support System (DSS)**—An automated application systems that assists the organization in making business related decisions.

**Decision Support Workbench**—Tools and applications used to access, retrieve, manipulate, and analyze the data, and then present the results in the form of recommendations.

**Derived Data**—Data that results from calculations or processing applied by the data warehouse to incoming source data. Derived data resides only in the data warehouse and is used by the warehouse to precalculate a number of values that are required to answer queries frequently. The alternative to storing derived data is to compute the value when the query actually executes, causing significant performance penalties.

**Development Lifecycle**—The flow of activities that represent a data warehouse implementation and deployment project from conception to deployment and usage.

**Dimension**—Data warehouses organize a large store of operational and historical data using multiple dimensions of categorization. One important one is TIME.

**Dimension Table**—A component of the star schema (see also *Star Schema).*

**Discovery mode**—Data analysis technique where tools try to discover relationships in the data and relationships not suspected or known to the business user (in the context of decision support techniques).

**Discriminating description**—Describes how two or more classes differ from each other.

**Drill-down**—Expose progressively more detail (inside a report or query) by making progressive selections of items in the report or query.

**Dynamic data analysis**—Comparing data values from disparate data sources and a number of diverse dimensions.

**EAP**—Acronym for Enterprise Architecture Planning. A structured methodology for the architecture and design of information systems. The key architecture design steps are the formulation of a data architecture, an applications architecture, and a technology architecture.

**Enterprise Model**—A data model of the items important to the overall organization (enterprise) that hinges on the nature of the business itself rather than the categories of data managed by the current information systems.

**Executive Information Systems (EIS)**—A term commonly used for query and reporting systems that perform aggregations and summarizations against operational data directly, sometimes storing summarized and aggregated data privately, and providing query and reporting capabilities for decision makers (executives).

**Extraction**—The activity related to transferring data from operational databases (data sources) into the data warehouse.

**Fact Table**—A component of the star schema (see also *Star Schema).*

**FAD**—Acronym for Frequently Accessed Data.

**FAQ**—Acronym for Frequently Accessed Query.

**FAR**—Acronym for Frequently Asked Reports.

**Fat client**—Is in a client/server architecture where the client workstation manages the informational processing (business logic) as well as the graphical user interface.

**Filter and Match**—Remove operational only data and select operational data that data warehouse data design model calls for, i.e., match it to desired subject area or partition.

**Framework**—A framework is a way of looking at something complex and making it understandable by using a set of simplifying analogies to help break down a complex solution into smaller components.

**Granularity**—A term used in data warehouses to express the level of detail. The higher the granularity, the lower the level of detail (the higher the level of abstraction).

**Historical information**—Information that was collected in the past and usually archived and removed from operational databases. Because of the volumes of data collected by operational systems on a daily basis, historical information is generally moved to slower and less frequently used media such as magnetic tape.

**Homonyms**—Two data elements that outwardly have the same name but contain different types of data.

**Horizontal Architecture Cuts**—Horizontal cuts are representations of the reference architecture along different dimensions. These dimensions range from what personnel and skills are needed to implement the data warehouse to making vendor and product selections for various data warehouse components to making build versus buy decisions.

**Indexing**—A frequently used technique for improving database performance by improving the access method for finding and retrieving database records.

**Indica Data Warehouse Planner**—The Indica Data Warehouse Planner is a software tool supplied with this book that allows the user to graphically navigate through the various blocks of the data warehouse reference architecture and "drill" down hierarchically to expose finer levels of architectural detail. At the same time, the user can use the reference architecture as a classification schema and enter elements of his/her real world to map them against the reference architecture. The Data Warehouse Planner is, therefore, a graphical tool that provides a list of categories under which users can collect information about their specific implementation of the data warehouse. The Planner can therefore be used as a data collection and data organization tool that allows data warehouse implementors and other stakeholders to perform various forms of analysis.

**Information Directory**—A lookup system for data warehouse metadata management. An information directory generally consists of a technical directory, a business directory, and an information navigator.

**Information Navigator**—A component of the warehouse information directory. The information navigator is a facility that allows users to browse through the business directory as well as the data inside the data warehouse. The information navigator primarily supports business users who are not knowledgeable in formulating complex database queries but are instead served with a graphical point-and-click tool that allows them to navigate through the data warehouse.

**Informational processing**—Verification mode of data analysis—accessing and analyzing the data in 2D or 3D form, and then presenting the results in the form of reports or query results (also referred to as query and reporting).

**Infrastructure Layer**—The component of the data warehouse that deals with the platforms and computer support and the commercially purchased environmental hardware and software needed to support the data warehouse.

**Integrate and Partition**—Integrate is to combine multiple sources to create desired subject areas/dimensions. Partition is the breakup data into multiple physical units of the data on the basis of time, for example data breakup into year-by-year partitions. Integrate and partition is to combine multiple dimensions and partitions on a time basis, for example product by region on quarterly basis.

**Interesting discoveries**—Discoveries, by a knowledge discovery system, that are non-obvious, new, most important, and useful to the business analyst or manager.

**Internal Office Systems**—Sources of data that are not stored in databases. Such sources of data include word processing documents, spreadsheets, and presentations.

**IS or IT**—Acronym for Information Systems or Information Technology. A term used for the functional department responsible for development and deployment of information systems in an organization.

**Legacy Data**—Sources of historical data for the data warehouse, often stored in offline media.

**Living Sample Database**—A database that is a small subset of operational and historical data but provides a representative sample that is valid for query, decision support, forecasting, and simulation purposes. The database is refreshed periodically to ensure that changes in the real data are transferred to the sample database.

**Living Sample database**—A statistically correct sample of a set of data.

**Logical Data Model**—An abstract formal representation of the categories of data and relationships between them, in the form of a diagram. The representation is independent of the manner in which the classes and their relationships are implemented physically in a database.

**Managed query environment**—Informational processing capability where the tools hide the complexity of the data structures with a "semantic layer" of business terms and rules.

**Massively parallel processor**—Spreads that work over large numbers of processors.

**Measures of Association**—Statistical operations that assist in determining the nature and type of relationship between variables.

**Metadata Management Layer**—The component of the data warehouse that deals with the definitional aspects of the data that is captured and stored inside the data warehouse. The definitional aspects are used by all tools and processes that must interact with the data warehouse.

**Middleware**—The common term applied to software that makes interchange of information between applications and databases transparent. Middleware provides an abstract connection mechanism between the application software and the database and hides the specific implementation dependent items from the applications programmer.

**Mission Critical System**—A term commonly used to describe a software application that is essential to the continued operation of an enterprise. The failure of such a system can affect the very viability of the enterprise.

**Mixed Schema**—The mixed schema is a compromise between the star schema based on fact tables and unnormalized dimension tables, and the snowflake schema where all the dimension tables are normalized. In the mixed schema, only the largest dimension tables are normalized. These tables generally contain large volumes of columns of highly denormalized (duplicated) data.

**Modeling**—Developing the data warehouse data model and defining the physical data warehouse database.

**Multidimensional data analysis**—Simultaneous analysis of multiple data dimensions.

**Multidimensional database**—A database designed around a set of dimensions; used in multidimensional analysis.

**Navigation path**—A term used in browsing to describe a path taken by the browser through the data items that are progressively exposed to the user as he/she browses through the data warehouse contents.

**New Production Applications**—Newer operational applications that leverage the metadata and the data in the warehouse such as Post-analysis, derive a list of customers that meet a marketing promotion criteria, and use the list with all the customer (data warehouse subject area) information as input to a form letter and mailing list.

**OLTP**—Acronym for On-Line Transaction Processing. A term used to define any software system that gathers data using transactions between the source of data and the database at the time that the transaction occurs.

**On-line Analytical Processing (OLAP)**—Multidimensional data analysis technology and reporting capability.

**Operational Database**—A database that supports software systems that are currently supporting an organization's business operations. Also called an OLTP database.

**Operational Store**—The use of the operational databases that currently support an organization to also support the data warehouse applications instead of using a separate storage mechanism for the data warehouse.

**Outliers**—Anomalies or values that fall outside region of the statistical function; can be irrelevant values that may skew the results.

**Parallel Query Execution**—In this method for improving database performance, a database query is split up into components and all components that can be simultaneously executed will be executed in parallel through concurrent processes. The performance of the query is therefore at the highest speed given the natural data dependencies within the query.

**Partition**—This is the activity of splitting one data item into two or more smaller items. Partitioning is used to break up a single table from the source into two or more tables inside the data warehouse. Partitioning is also applied to break up the rows of a table into two or more tables with the same structure but each holding a subset of the rows, such as, for example, partitioning data into time phased series for analysis.

**POEMS**—Acronym for Platinum technology, Inc.'s Platinum Open Enterprise Management Systems framework.

**Precalculate and Derive**—Precalculate or derive data from single or multiple dimensions to build results for access by query or reporting tools (done to speed access on retrieval), such as quarter-to-quarter comparisons of revenue, product sales, operating costs, and so on.

**Production Data Sources**—Operational databases that act as sources of data for the data warehouse. The data they provide is online and stored in the database.

**Query**—A formal and clearly specified request for information from the data warehouse or data mart posed by a user or tool operated by a user.

**Query Footprint Model**—An abstract representation of a query showing the dimensions that it utilizes.

**RDBMS**—Acronym for Relational Database Management System. A data storage system built around the relational model based on tables, columns, and views.

**Reconcile and Validate**—Validate data prior to storage according to predefined validation rules. Reconcile data based on business rules, such as data source to denormalized data store.

**Reference architecture (data warehouse)**—A term used in this book to define a common model around which all data warehouses are built. The reference architecture is thus a general classification of the data warehouse's architectural components.

**Regression Analysis**—Statistical operations that help to predict the value of the dependent variable from the values of one or more independent variables.

**Report**—A document that is produced as a response to a query.

**Repository**—A compendium of all technology related definitions and specifications for items that are important to currently deployed software applications and databases.

**ROA**—Acronym for Return on Assets. A commonly used ratio of the measure of payback for assets deployed to produce the payback.

**ROI**—Acronym for Return on Investment. A commonly used financial ratio for a measure of the payback of any investment.

**Roll-up**—Looking at higher levels of summarization or aggregation.

**Rollout**—A common term that represents the activity of distributing the same data warehouse solution to a larger audience than the one served by the initial implementation. Rollout involves issues of scaling and standardization.

**Slice and dice**—A commonly used term by analysts for the activity of data analysis along many dimensions and across many subsets; also an analysis of a data warehouse from the perspective of fact-tables and related dimensions (see also *Star Schema*).

**Snowflake Schema**—The snowflake schema is an extension of the star schema where each of the points of the star further radiates out into more points. In this form of schema, the star schema dimension tables are more normalized. The advantages provided by the snowflake schema are improvements in query performance due to minimizing disk storage for the data and improving performance by joining smaller normalized tables rather than large de-normalized ones. The snowflake schema also increases flexibility of applications because of the normalization and therefore the lower granularity of the dimensions.

**Sparse matrix**—A matrix in which not every block in the grid is filled with data; a condition that applies to contents of multidimensional data bases.

**Spiral Development Method**—An iterative software development method where software functionality is delivered in stages and improvements are identified by actually successively deploying software with tightly controlled but increasing functionality.

**Stamp**—Time stamp the date of creation or date of origin; mark the source of origin of the data.

**Stamp Data Source**—Data from data sources must be marked with the identity of the data source. This allows the data warehouse to tell which data came from which source even after the data from all the sources is integrated inside the data warehouse.

**Stamp Time Dimension**—When data is extracted from its source and loaded into the data warehouse, it must be marked with the time stamp when it was originally generated. The time dimension is often not stored by operational databases as an explicit stamp of the data. Time stamps are used to drive aggregations and summarizations because data is frequently accumulated and totaled over a summary time period.

**Standardize**—The data names, definitions, and descriptions of the data; standard data scope (range or coverage); and units of measurement.

**Star Schema**—As the name suggests, the star schema is a modeling paradigm that has a single object in the middle connected to a number of objects around it radially. The star schema mirrors the end user's view of a business query: a fact such as sales, compensation, payment, or invoices qualified by one or more dimensions (by month, by product, by geographical region). The object in the center of the star is called the fact table and the objects that are connected to it in the periphery are called the dimension tables.

**Static data analysis**—Comparing one static data value with another.

**Subject Area**—The data in the data warehouse is subject-oriented to the major subject areas of the corporation, such as customer and product.

**Subject Oriented**—Classified by subjects or topics of business interest.

**Summarization**—The activity of increasing the granularity of information in a database. Summarization reduces the level of detail and is very useful to present data for decision support purposes.

**Summarize**—To add the same data or dimension such as annual summary of revenue or rolling summary of inventory of a product of the last three months.

**Symmetric multiprocessors (SMP)**—Breaks up work among multiple processors on one CPU.

**Syndicated Data Sources**—Commercially available databases for specific vertical markets that contain representative data. This is used for market assessment and simulation of proposed business strategies. Syndicated data sources are available either as one time database samples or as subscription services for more accurately tracking changes in the marketing environment.

**Synonyms**—Two data elements containing the same data but having different names.

**Technical Directory**—A component of the warehouse information directory. The technical directory primarily supports technical staff that must implement and deploy the data warehouse. The information contained within the technical directory is compatible with such an audience and contains the terms and definition of metadata exactly as they appear in operational databases.

**Technology Maturity Curve**—The curve that represents the insertion of technology from its early inception into prototypes to its ultimate embrace in mission critical systems.

**Thin client**—In a client/server architecture where the client workstation principally manages the graphical user interface.

**Time-intelligence**—Tool understands time concept such as year-to-date and current period.

**Transform and Remap**—Convert according to predefined transformational mapping rules. Map the data from the normalized input to the denormalized data warehouse store.

**Translate and Format**—From one datatype to another or from one storage encoding to another, such as EBCDIC to ASCII.

**Transport Layer**—The component of the data warehouse that deals with the conveyance of data between components of the data warehouse solution. Transport deals with communications capabilities at all levels to provide conveyance to data.

**Verification mode**—Data analysis technique where a hypothesis is created and then the contents of the data warehouse is used to verify it (in the context of decision support techniques).

**Verify**—Data quality checks defined per business rules, data warehouse model, and so on; consistency and integrity rules verification.

**Vertical Architecture Cuts**—Vertical cuts represent slices of the architecture that correspond to block boundaries. Each of the cuts separates the blocks and also segments the layers. All blocks that lie within the same cut therefore share the same layers (environment). In other words, if the Data Sources block and the Data Warehouse construction block are in the same cut, they must reside on the same platforms and share the same mechanisms for transport and infrastructure.

**Waterfall Development Method**—The classic development lifecycle used traditionally in software development projects. The name comes from the fact that the direction of water flow in a waterfall is always in one direction. In this method, the flow is from requirements gathering and analysis to system development and delivery.

**Zachman Framework**—A framework for analyzing and understanding the architecture of information systems first postulated by John Zachman of IBM.

**Zachman Framework Perspective**—A row of the Zachman framework.

**Zachman Framework View**—A column of the Zachman framework.

# Index

## Symbols



## A

# B

# C

## E



## F

## G



## H

# I

## J-K

## N



## O



## P

# Q

# R

## S

## T



## U

## V



## W

## X-Y-Z

# Complete and Return this Card for a *FREE* Computer Book Catalog

Thank you for purchasing this book! You have purchased a superior computer book written expressly for your needs. To continue to provide the kind of up-to-date, pertinent coverage you've come to expect from us, we need to hear from you. Please take a minute to complete and return this self-addressed, postage-paid form. In return, we'll send you a free catalog of all our computer books on topics ranging from word processing to programming and the internet.

Mr. ☐ Mrs. ☐ Ms. ☐ Dr. ☐

Name (first) ☐☐☐☐☐☐☐☐☐☐☐ (M.I.) ☐ (last) ☐☐☐☐☐☐☐☐☐☐☐☐☐☐☐

Address ☐☐☐☐☐☐☐☐☐☐☐☐☐☐☐☐☐☐☐☐☐☐☐☐☐☐☐☐☐☐☐☐☐☐☐

☐☐☐☐☐☐☐☐☐☐☐☐☐☐☐☐☐☐☐☐☐☐☐☐☐☐☐☐☐☐☐☐☐☐☐

City ☐☐☐☐☐☐☐☐☐☐☐☐☐☐☐ State ☐☐ Zip ☐☐☐☐☐ ☐☐☐☐

Phone ☐☐☐ ☐☐☐ ☐☐☐☐ Fax ☐☐☐ ☐☐☐ ☐☐☐☐

Company Name ☐☐☐☐☐☐☐☐☐☐☐☐☐☐☐☐☐☐☐☐☐☐☐☐☐☐☐☐☐☐☐☐☐

E-mail address ☐☐☐☐☐☐☐☐☐☐☐☐☐☐☐☐☐☐☐☐☐☐☐☐☐☐☐☐☐☐☐☐☐

**1. Please check at least (3) influencing factors for purchasing this book.**

- Front or back cover information on book ☐
- Special approach to the content ☐
- Completeness of content ☐
- Author's reputation ☐
- Publisher's reputation ☐
- Book cover design or layout ☐
- Index or table of contents of book ☐
- Price of book ☐
- Special effects, graphics, illustrations ☐
- Other (Please specify): ______________ ☐

**2. How did you first learn about this book?**

- Saw in Macmillan Computer Publishing catalog ☐
- Recommended by store personnel ☐
- Saw the book on bookshelf at store ☐
- Recommended by a friend ☐
- Received advertisement in the mail ☐
- Saw an advertisement in: ______________ ☐
- Read book review in: ______________ ☐
- Other (Please specify): ______________ ☐

**3. How many computer books have you purchased in the last six months?**

- This book only ☐
- 2 books ☐
- 3 to 5 books ☐
- More than 5 ☐

**4. Where did you purchase this book?**

- Bookstore ☐
- Computer Store ☐
- Consumer Electronics Store ☐
- Department Store ☐
- Office Club ☐
- Warehouse Club ☐
- Mail Order ☐
- Direct from Publisher ☐
- Internet site ☐
- Other (Please specify): ______________ ☐

**5. How long have you been using a computer?**

- ☐ Less than 6 months
- ☐ 6 months to a year
- ☐ 1 to 3 years
- ☐ More than 3 years

**6. What is your level of experience with personal computers and with the subject of this book?**

| | With PCs | With subject of book |
|---|---|---|
| New | ☐ | ☐ |
| Casual | ☐ | ☐ |
| Accomplished | ☐ | ☐ |
| Expert | ☐ | ☐ |

Source Code ISBN: 0-7897-0714-4

**7. Which of the following best describes your job title?**

- Administrative Assistant ☐
- Coordinator ☐
- Manager/Supervisor ☐
- Director ☐
- Vice President ☐
- President/CEO/COO ☐
- Lawyer/Doctor/Medical Professional ☐
- Teacher/Educator/Trainer ☐
- Engineer/Technician ☐
- Consultant ☐
- Not employed/Student/Retired ☐
- Other (Please specify): ____________ ☐

**8. Which of the following best describes the area of the company your job title falls under?**

- Accounting ☐
- Engineering ☐
- Manufacturing ☐
- Operations ☐
- Marketing ☐
- Sales ☐
- Other (Please specify): ____________ ☐

**9. What is your age?**

- Under 20 ☐
- 21-29 ☐
- 30-39 ☐
- 40-49 ☐
- 50-59 ☐
- 60-over ☐

**10. Are you:**

- Male ☐
- Female ☐

**11. Which computer publications do you read regularly? (Please list)**

____________

*Comments*: ____________

Fold here and scotch-tape to mail.

NO POSTAGE NECESSARY IF MAILED IN THE UNITED STATES

**BUSINESS REPLY MAIL**

FIRST-CLASS MAIL PERMIT NO. 9918 INDIANAPOLIS IN

POSTAGE WILL BE PAID BY THE ADDRESSEE

ATTN MARKETING
MACMILLAN COMPUTER PUBLISHING
MACMILLAN PUBLISHING USA
201 W 103RD ST
INDIANAPOLIS IN 46209-9042

## Licensing Agreement

By opening this package, you are agreeing to be bound by the following: